Participatory Politics and Citizen Journalism in a Networked Africa

A Connected Continent

Edited by

Bruce Mutsvairo
Northumbria University, UK

palgrave
macmillan

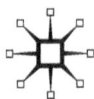

First published 2016 by
PALGRAVE MACMILLAN

Palgrave Macmillan in the UK is an imprint of Macmillan Publishers Limited,
registered in England, company number 785998, of Houndmills, Basingstoke,
Hampshire RG21 6XS.

Palgrave Macmillan in the US is a division of St Martin's Press LLC,
175 Fifth Avenue, New York, NY 10010.

Palgrave Macmillan is the global academic imprint of the above companies
and has companies and representatives throughout the world.

Palgrave® and Macmillan® are registered trademarks in the United States,
the United Kingdom, Europe and other countries.

ISBN 978–1–137–55449–9

This book is printed on paper suitable for recycling and made from fully
managed and sustained forest sources. Logging, pulping and manufacturing
processes are expected to conform to the environmental regulations of the
country of origin.

A catalogue record for this book is available from the British Library.

Library of Congress Cataloging-in-Publication Data
Names: Mutsvairo, Bruce, 1979–
Title: Participatory politics and citizen journalism in a
    networked Africa : a connected continent / edited by Bruce
    Mutsvairo, Northumbria University, UK.
Description: Houndmills, Basingstoke, Hampshire ; New York : Palgrave
    Macmillan, 2016. | Includes bibliographical references.
Identifiers: LCCN 2015025770 | ISBN 9781137554499
Subjects: LCSH: Citizen journalism—Political aspects—Africa. | Online
    journalism—Political aspects—Africa. | Social media—Political
    aspects—Africa. | Political participation—Africa.
Classification: LCC PN4784.C615 P37 2016 | DDC 079/.6—dc23
LC record available at http://lccn.loc.gov/2015025770

Contents

Part III Perceptions and Critiques

Tables and Figures

Foreword

Tracing the twists and turns in the evolution of citizen journalism in our digital age is a formidable challenge, not least because of the dazzling speed technological imperatives seem to unfold across the globe. Still, when reflecting on various enquiries delving into how such innovations have helped to recast what counts as journalism – and who can lay claim to the role of journalist – over the last decade, it is worth recalling contrary instances when the limits of technology-centred thinking were thrown into sharp relief.

Back in 2006 I came across one such example when reading a *New York Times* news story about Alfred Sirleaf and his plywood shed, The Daily Talk, in civil war-torn Liberia at the time. "In a country where wheelbarrows fill in for pickup trucks, water is carried on little girls' heads instead of in pipes and gallon-size jars replace gas pumps," *Times* reporter Lydia Polgreen (2006) wrote, "it is perhaps no wonder that a battered blackboard serves as newspaper and newsreel all in one." The story detailed how Sirleaf posted news and editorials on the blackboard positioned on the street outside his "newsroom" every day, thereby providing passers-by with important insights into what was happening in Monrovia. Equipped with his "nose for a good scoop", this "self-taught newshound" scours newspapers – and calls on an informal network of friends acting as correspondents – for the information necessary to keep everyone "in the know". News stories are concisely written in a style relying on street words that people used themselves ("big stealing" rather than "embezzlement", for example). "I like to write the way people talk so they can understand it well," he said. "You got to reach the common man" and woman. Sirleaf's dedication to citizen reporting has met resistance from those in power over the years; he was arrested and spent a brief spell in prison, then went into exile while his news-stand was torn down. Having rebuilt it by the time he met Polgreen, he remained as steadfast as ever in his belief that what he was doing mattered for the country's emergent democracy.

It is precisely this commitment to an alternative ethos of citizen-led reportage that shines brightly through the celebratory hype that so often accompanies discussions of prodigious "technological revolutions" transforming the digital mediascape. In 2014, I visited the Kenyan Red Cross and Red Crescent operations compound on the outskirts of Nairobi, where I heard how significant the first-hand reportage of health-care workers was proving to be for those tracking the Ebola crisis in West Africa. Their personal, impromptu accounts, photographs and video clips, shared across blogs and social media sites, were vital sources of news, bearing witness to what was actually transpiring on the ground, often with heart-rending poignancy. Meanwhile, criticisms of the African media's coverage of the crisis were growing ever sharper. Eric Chinje (2014), writing in Nairobi's *The Star*, pointed out that "coverage of the pandemic has brought to the fore some of the fundamental challenges facing media in Africa and, possibly, around the world". More specifically, he argued:

> Reports on the Ebola pandemic are replete with images of death and the violence of the disease, giving media consumers a real life equivalent of a Hollywood horror movie of alien invaders. [...] Media has not been complicit in some macabre plot to return Africa to the disease narrative. Certainly not media in Africa. If anything, media professionals on the continent have, in their cut-and-paste approach to coverage, demonstrated a debilitating ignorance of the issues and of their role in assisting society deal with the impact of the disease.
>
> (Chinje, 2014)

For Chinje, the crucial issue revolved around what he regarded as the failure of journalists and editors to ask the right questions. Coming to terms with the crisis meant pursuing robust lines of enquiry, such as looking "beyond the frightening body count" to examine coping mechanisms; addressing larger, structural problems of governance, leadership and trust; identifying breakdowns in the use of foreign aid; recognizing "the havoc on fragile societies brought about by the unregulated international market for guns and bombs"; and unravelling for scrutiny how the pharmaceutical industry operates in Africa, amongst other exigent issues. As Chinje reminded us, "until the real questions are asked, the real story will never be told".

It is in striving to inspire African journalism to move swiftly beyond "cut-and-paste approaches to coverage" that Bruce Mutsvairo's edited collection *Participatory Politics and Citizen Journalism in a Networked Africa: A Connected Continent* makes its intervention. Gathered on these pages is a remarkably impressive range of studies exploring how, when and why ordinary individuals are engaging in news-making, and what it means for re-visioning journalism's future prospects. It opens with Mutsvairo's introduction, "Recapturing Citizen Journalism: Processes and Patterns", which sets the terms for the ensuing discussion and debate. From there, in Part I, we turn to Farooq A. Kperogi's examination of the role of the "guerrilla press" in articulating dissent in Nigeria since the 1990s. Last Moyo's chapter focuses on certain "moral panics" engendered by perceived lapses in citizen journalism ethics and their implications for African journalism. Short Wave Radio Africa is centred for attention in Everette Ndlovu's study, which considers how this UK-based diasporic radio station encourages political activism in Zimbabwe. Terje Skjerdal investigates "why the Arab Spring never came to Ethiopia", offering an effective contrast to triumphant treatments of social media. Next, Mirjam de Bruijn draws upon her personal experience in Chad when sharing findings from a research project dedicated to illuminating how citizen media have influenced political and social changes.

Part II begins with Glenda Daniels' chapter proffering an analysis of South African journalists' engagement with their publics through Twitter, thereby highlighting news professionals' perspectives on citizen journalism's democratic potential. Erika Rodrigues and Anya Schiffrin's co-written study assesses citizen journalism initiatives such as SaharaReporters (Nigeria) and @Verdade (Mozambique), and their relative success involving citizens in the coverage of economic news, particularly with regard to the extractive sector, where corruption is underreported by the mainstream media. In Kristin Skare Orgeret's chapter, three different crowdfunding models for journalism are considered, with a view to evaluating their potential for realizing citizen journalism's possibilities in Africa. Turning to Zimbabwe, Bruce Mutsvairo critiques articles drawn from *The Herald*'s print and online editions, in order to investigate its role in contributing to the political endurance of President Mugabe's ZANU-PF Party. Still in Zimbabwe, Cleophas T. Muneri's chapter aims to explain the reasons why, in his view, the advent of new communication technologies has not led to the wider participation in public life promised by citizen journalism.

Part III's first chapter is by Susana Salgado: she identifies the factors shaping the development of citizen journalism in four Portuguese-speaking African countries, namely Angola, Cape Verde, Mozambique, and São Tomé and Príncipe. Wallace Chuma's chapter discusses the trend of "bottom-up" storytelling in South Africa by examining GroundUp (a non-profit online news portal generating news from professionals and citizens alike). Joseph Mujere and Wesley Mwatwara's study compares the role played by citizen journalism – via Facebook, WhatsApp and Twitter – in Zimbabwe's 2008 and 2013 elections, devoting particular attention to the emergence of counter-publics resistant to state power. Citizen journalism, George Ogola and Mike Owuor argue in their chapter, has enjoyed considerable success in enhancing the quality of professional media in Kenya, yet, as they proceed to show, it is now under threat of appropriation by state actors intent on controlling media spaces. And finally, rounding out Part III, two chapters address the Ebola crisis. Winston Mano and viola c. milton share their insights into how the politics of othering engendered by so much of the Western news coverage of the crisis was counteracted, to varying degrees, by citizen media reporting in South Africa and Zimbabwe. Ibrahim Seaga Shaw, adopting a conceptually focused position, proposes a refashioning of citizen journalism in more critical, human-rights-sensitive terms in order to improve tomorrow's crisis reporting.

Taken together, the chapters making up *Participatory Politics and Citizen Journalism in a Networked Africa* afford us a fascinating array of vantage points to rethink familiar assumptions about the rise of citizen journalism, as well as its strengths and its limitations. At the same time, it is a useful check on any tendency to make sweeping claims about the power of new media technologies, recognizing that it is in the tough, fearless grind of democratizing journalism that positive improvements will be made in ordinary people's communicative resources and opportunities. Here we turn once again to Alfred Sirleaf, who showed us what can be achieved by this kind of commitment. "Daily Talk's objective is that everybody should absorb the news," he explained. "Because when a few people out there make decisions on behalf of the masses that do not go down with them, we are all going to be victims."

Stuart Allan
Cardiff University, UK

References

Chinje, E. (2014). Kenya: African media has failed in Ebola crisis coverage, *The Star* (Nairobi), 3 November.

Polgreen, L. (2006). All the news that fits: Liberia's blackboard headlines, *New York Times*, 4 August.

Notes on Contributors

Wallace Chuma is Senior Lecturer in the Centre for Film and Media Studies, University of Cape Town. He holds a PhD (Journalism & Media Studies) from the University of the Witwatersrand, and degrees in English and Communication from the University of Zimbabwe. He was a former journalist and editor in Zimbabwe, and spent time at the Pittsburgh Post-Gazette (Pennsylvania, USA) as Alfred Friendly Press Fellow. He has co-edited the book *Media Policy in a Changing Southern Africa* (2010). He is also former vice chairperson for the Media Institute of Southern Africa (MISA) Zimbabwe Chapter.

Glenda Daniels is Senior Lecturer in Media Studies at the University of the Witwatersrand. She was previously (2013 and 2014) the project coordinator and lead researcher on the State of the Newsroom project at Wits Journalism. She holds a PhD in Political Studies (Wits) and is author of the book, *Fight for Democracy: The ANC and the Media in South Africa*. She is also a freedom of expression activist and serves as chairperson of the South African National Editors' Forum's (Sanef) Ethics and Diversity subcommittee. She has been a journalist in South Africa for over 20 years, having started her career as a trainee at the then *Weekly Mail* in 1990. She has since worked for most of the major newspaper companies in the country, with her last stint in the newsroom as advocacy coordinator at amaBhungane at the *Mail & Guardian* (2011 and 2012).

Mirjam de Bruijn is Professor of Contemporary History and Anthropology of West and Central Africa at Leiden University's Faculty of Arts. She is also an honorary fellow of the Department of Social Anthropology at the University of Cape Town, South Africa. An anthropologist whose work has a clearly interdisciplinary character, she has done fieldwork in Cameroon, Chad and Mali, and an important theme throughout is how people manage risk (drought, war, etc.) in both rural and urban areas. In Mali she worked in the Mopti area with the Fulbe (Peul) and in Menaka with the Tamacheck (Tuareg). While in Chad she worked in N'Djamena (the capital) and in Central Chad with Hadjerai and Arab groups. In Cameroon, she worked in the Grassfields and the north. Her programme 'Mobile Africa Revisited', which began in 2008, is a comparative study of the role of information and communication technologies (ICT) and ICT's interrelationship with agency, marginality and mobility patterns in Central and West Africa.

Farooq A. Kperogi is Assistant Professor of Journalism and Emerging Media in the School of Communication & Media at Kennesaw State University, USA. A former newspaper reporter and editor, he holds a PhD in Communication from Georgia State University, USA. His research broadly explores the intersection between communication in a global context and the singularities of the communicative practices of marginal groups within this context. He is particularly interested in the transnational, mass-mediated, online discourses of marginalized diasporas in the West. His scholarly articles have been published in *New Media & Society, Review of Communication, Asia Pacific Media Educator, Journal of Global Mass Communication, Journal of Communications Media Studies* and in many book chapters. His most recent book is *Glocal English: The Changing Face and Forms of Nigerian English in a Global World* (2015).

Winston Mano is Reader and Course Leader of the MA in Media and Development and Director of the Africa Media Centre at the University of Westminster. He is also the principal editor of the *Journal of African Media Studies*. He joined the University of Westminster's Communication and Media Research Institute (CAMRI) from the University of Zimbabwe in 2000. He holds a PhD from the University of Westminster.

viola c. milton is Associate Professor of Communication Science, University of South Africa, Pretoria. She is an executive editor for the oldest South African journal in Communication Studies, entitled *Communicatio: South African Journal for Communication Theory and Research*.

Last Moyo is an experienced researcher, academic and consultant in the fields of media and communication studies in Sub-Saharan Africa. He is a visiting professor at Midlands State University in Zimbabwe. He holds a PhD from the University of Wales, UK.

Joseph Mujere is a Senior Lecturer in the History Department at the University of Zimbabwe. He is also Research Associate in the Society, Work and Development Institute (SWOP), University of the Witwatersrand. He holds a PhD (History) from the University of Edinburgh. His research interests include migration, belonging, citizenship as well as media and society. Some of his articles appear in journals such as *South African Historical Journal, Journal of Southern African Studies, Africa and Journal of Peasant Studies*.

Cleophas T. Muneri is a lecturer at the University of New Mexico, USA, where he gained his PhD in Communication in 2012. His current scholarly work focuses on the intersection of identities and culture and on the role of media, both formal and social, in the democratization process – and how both impact political change. He is interested in the role of citizen journalism in the democratization process and how communication plays an important role in sustaining democratic struggles.

Bruce Mutsvairo is a Senior Lecturer in Journalism at Northumbria University, Newcastle. He was formerly a journalist with the Amsterdam Bureau of the Associated Press, where he reported from several African countries, including Angola, Zimbabwe, South Africa and Ghana. His research focuses on the nexus of citizen media, digital activism and democratization in sub-Saharan Africa.

Wesley Mwatwara is a Senior Lecturer in the War and Strategic Studies Unit, and Chairperson (History Department) at the University of Zimbabwe. He holds B.A, B.A (Special Honours) and MA Degrees from the University of Zimbabwe, and a PhD in History from Stellenbosch University. His areas of research interest are socio-environmental history, governance, conflict resolution, conflict management, peacebuilding, politics, mobile telephony, and social movements.

Everette Ndlovu is an academic with a broadcasting background. A holder of a PhD in Media from the University of Salford, UK, he worked for Zimbabwe Broadcasting Corporation as a TV producer/director for over ten years. His research interests are around the emancipatory role of digital communication technologies. He is passionate about how the public spheres created with the help of these technologies impact on the democratization of restrictive political environments. He has published journal articles and delivered conference papers on media and democracy. He lectures in New Media and Digital Culture, Alternative Media, Media Texts and Audiences, Film and TV History and Theory, and Media Institutions and Ecologies.

George Ogola is Senior Lecturer in Journalism at the University of Central Lancashire, UK. He is an alumnus of the University of the Witwatersrand, where he pursued his MA and PhD. He previously worked as a journalist at *The Standard* newspaper in Nairobi and as a news and features correspondent for newspapers and magazines based in Kenya, South Africa and the UK. His research interests include understanding the impact of new media technologies on the broader media ecology in the developing world and how these address questions of power and democratization, and the interface between popular culture, politics and the news media. He is co-editor of *The Future of Quality Journalism: A Cross-Continental Study* (2013).

Kristin Skare Orgeret is Professor in Journalism and Media Studies at Oslo and Akershus University College in Norway. The main focus of most of her research is the role of media and journalism in democratization and nation-building processes. She wrote her MA thesis in Zimbabwe, her PhD in South Africa, and has lived and worked as a researcher and lecturer in several countries on the African continent and in Asia. She is currently heading the Norwegian side of the five-year research project "Post-Conflict Journalism", which involves South Sudan, Uganda and Nepal.

Mike Owuor is an associate editor at the Nation Media Group in Nairobi, Kenya. He is a journalist with vast newsroom experience who has previously worked as a reporter, sub-editor and senior editor at *The Standard* newspaper and the *Nairobi Law Monthly* journal. He holds an MA in International Journalism from the University of Leeds, UK.

Erika Rodrigues, from Mozambique, is a stakeholder engagement specialist, working in the country with UX, Information Technologies Ltd. with a focus on boosting the competencies and employability of the Mozambican youth; she represents Ulula, a company that has developed a platform for mobile communication between mining, oil and gas companies and communities. She has worked in Mozambique, Uganda and the USA, assessing the opportunities and challenges of the extractive sector. She holds a Master's degree in Social Anthropology from Columbia University in New York, where she studied ICT4Development and Natural Resources Management. She was a Fulbright Scholar to Mozambique in 2011.

Susana Salgado is currently Foundation for Science and Technology Research Fellow and Professor of Political Communication at the Institute of Social Sciences, University of Lisbon. Her main research interests are political communication, comparative media studies, media and democratization, media and elections, and Internet and politics. Her most recent publications include the book *The Internet and Democracy Building in Lusophone African Countries* (2014) and two books on Portuguese media and politics (*Presidential Candidates: Construction of Images and Discourses in the Media*, 2010; and *The Vehicles of Political Communication: Studying an Electoral Campaign in the Media*, 2007, both in Portuguese).

Anya Schiffrin is Director of Media Specialization at Columbia University's School of International and Public Affairs. She serves on the sub-board of the Open Society Foundation's media programme and, among other topics, she writes on media in Africa and the extractives. Her latest book is *Global Muckraking: 100 Years of Investigative Journalism from Around the World* (2014).

Ibrahim Seaga Shaw is Senior Lecturer in Media and Politics, and Programme Leader for MSc Mass Communication Management at Northumbria

University in Newcastle upon Tyne, UK. He is also the Secretary General of the International Peace Research Association (IPRA), following his election at the organization's biennial conference in Japan on 24–28 November 2012. A PhD holder from Sorbonne, he has published several articles in leading academic journals, including the *Journal of Global Ethics* and *International Communication Gazette*. He is also the author of *Human Rights Journalism* (2012) and co-editor of *Expanding Peace Journalism* (2012).

Terje Skjerdal is Associate Professor of Journalism at NLA University College, Kristiansand, Norway. He has a particular interest in African media issues, and has researched and taught journalism in Ethiopia and Uganda. He serves on the editorial/advisory boards of *Journal of African Media Studies*, *African Journalism Studies* and *African Communication Research*. His PhD dissertation discussed the phenomenon of competing loyalties among journalists in the Ethiopian state media. His current research includes the role of China in African journalism and the history of African media studies.

1

Recapturing Citizen Journalism: Processes and Patterns

Bruce Mutsvairo

In today's increasingly innovative and globalized world, it is impossible to ignore the dominance of an emerging new form of journalism characterized by rapid reporting, interminable interactivity and ubiquitous multimedia content sharing and customization. Indeed, digital technologies have had a profound effect on the way news content is perceived, produced, shared and analysed. It therefore is by no surprise that the emergence of citizen journalism has not escaped scientific scrutiny (see Allan and Thorsen, 2009; Benkler, 2006). Produced in a matter of seconds, news can be shared instantly across the world, with the supremacy of citizen-inspired content becoming an overriding feature of contemporary news production. The etymology of "citizen journalism" barely needs to be studied anymore as the term is widely used and commonly accepted. But in a world where any computer or mobile phone owner is potentially a news publisher, concerns will be raised about the long-term reliability and expediency of news and content produced by non-professional actors in a technologically deterministic and fast transforming world of journalism. It is against this background that this book uses a case-to-case analysis of citizen journalism practices, based on specific studies from sub-Saharan Africa, with a view of scrutinizing this palpable emerging force – which, thanks to the ubiquity of new media technologies, continues to gather significant momentum in Africa and beyond – and investigating positivistic claims linking technological revolution to democratic changes.

A study by Gulvady (2009) concluded that mainstream media was no longer the only viable source of information available to citizens. While, globally, there is plenty of scientific literature analysing the threats and opportunities citizen journalism pose to the newspaper industry as well as society at large (Deuze *et al.*, 2007; Domingo *et al.*, 2008), very few empirical accounts have focused on the impact of and challenges faced by activists, participants and recipients of alternative media in sub-Sahara Africa (for examples, see Mudhai, 2013; Wasserman, 2010; 2011; Wasserman and

Garman 2012) – a central objective of this book. Is citizen journalism offering Africans a first-rate opportunity to tell their stories the way they like? If that is the case, does this help empower citizens and lead them to embrace democratic changes? How have Africans embraced new technologies as a potential tool for participatory political participation?

As the conceptualization of citizen participation has largely been determined by case studies in Western settings, this book provides a geographic counter-narrative, offering African-based perspectives, experiences and responses, potentially demystifying the Western reliance on the cognization of citizen journalism. Not only is the literature analysis based on reflections from studies published between 2000 and 2008, but the leading discipline examinations are, in most cases, dominated by thoughts from the same authors, including Axel Bruns, Stuart Allan and several others. The reliance on these scholars isn't a problem. However, Africa is a richly varied continent with several differences among its vast cultures. By proposing a wider analysis from different parts of the continent, the book hopes to make a major contribution towards challenging not only Western but also dominant, Anglo-centric notions of citizen journalism in Africa. By zooming in on "alternative" analysis of citizen participation from the continent's Francophone and Lusophone countries, and building upon scientific interpretations from other case studies, the book, through case-by-case empirical accounts, provides a wider understanding, capturing debates surrounding citizen journalism, which, from the little that is available, has arguably been dominated by scientific reports from "English-speaking Africa".

It must be noted that, while scholarship on citizen journalism in African settings has been limited, in recent times, attempts have been made to bring the subject to the core (see Mutsvairo *et al.*, 2014; Tufte *et al.*, 2014). Several scholarly accounts have tended to take a broader approach, preferring the thematization of "online" instead of just "citizen" journalism (Mabweazara, 2015; Mabweazara *et al.*, 2013; Mudhai 2013). The broader conceptualization is not just limited to the field of journalism. Most recently, attempts to parade struggles faced by civic participants in online and offline African settings have been examined by Obadare and Willems (2014). Furthermore, research looking into the everyday use of media instruments such as television, radio and the press in African communities is also being developed (Willems and Mano, forthcoming). In another broader approach, Tettey (forthcoming) stresses the significance of media and information literacy, arguing lack of it could severely undermine democratic participation and engagement in African countries. A broader approach is therefore not only key to understanding the immediate role, purpose and problems associated with citizen journalism in sub-Saharan Africa, but helps explain how and why, even with abundant access to technology, political and social reforms have been impeded in the digitally connected continent.

The consequences of the online environment's ability to instantaneously disseminate news have been widely examined by several scholars (see Deuze, 2003; Matheson, 2004; Osborn, 2001; Thurman, 2007; Volkmer, 2005). Citizen journalism can best be defined by two scene-setting scenarios. First, when a group of people "formerly known as the audience" (Rosen, 2008, p. 163) are involved in producing and sharing content, then citizen journalism is likely at work. Again, when citizens are engaged in an active "process of collecting, reporting, analysing and (distributing) news and information" (Bowman and Willis, 2003, p. 9), they are practising citizen journalism, whose history Schudson (2003) associates with the distribution of political pamphlets in major American cities in the 1700s. For Bruns (2005), citizen journalism occurs when "users of news websites who engage with such sites interchangeably in consumptive and productive modes and often both at the same time" (p. 23).

While it has been referred to as "community journalism", "networked journalism" (Kelly, 2009, p. 17) or "open-source journalism" (Bentley *et al.*, 2005), it is the "citizen journalism" concordance that has been widely used in scholarly citations. But with the rapid rise of social media, the proliferation of social networks has overshadowed the use of the term "citizen journalism". As argued in some chapters in this book, it would certainly be misleading to suggest citizen journalism has not only lost its appeal, but also the conceptual relevance that made it attractive to scholars from around the year 2000 onwards. This is because, far from facilitating its societal oblivion, the global social media explosion has actually provided the market for citizen journalism by providing an indispensable platform for technology-savvy citizen journalists to report eyewitness accounts and share stories at remarkable speed. Therefore, the assumption that citizen journalism is "losing out" to social media is somewhat invalid considering citizens have, regardless of their location, benefited through the use of hashtags, retweets and image shares in a powerful citizenry collaboration and engagement that intriguingly rivals reports provided by mainstream media outlets.

While commonly referred to as citizen "journalists", it is not clear whether such people are indeed journalists. Due to the opinionated nature of content produced by citizens (Nah and Chung, 2009), citizen journalism cannot be considered "journalism". Keen (2007) propounds that citizen and professional journalists cannot work hand in hand because the former does not leverage ethical issues such as neutrality and objectivity, which form the foundation of the latter's reporting. Since they do not adhere to accuracy, independence or autonomy, fairness, transparency, professional responsibility and objectivity (Kovach and Rosenstiel, 2001), citizen journalists cannot be classified as "journalists". Interestingly, a research by Bruns and Highfield (2012) showed concern among traditional journalists that citizen journalism was on course to replace the conventional journalism industry.

Needless to say, the power of citizen journalism in terms of participation cannot be underrated. Time will tell whether its presence will or could ignite political revolutions in sub-Saharan Africa, a recurring question in several case studies in this book. However, in a crisis-ridden continent dominated by dictators, it is no understatement to conclude that the very manifestation of citizen journalism is potentially a revolution in itself. Take Zimbabwe for example. Who would have imagined that citizen-attributed comments attacking President Robert Mugabe would be published by the online edition of the state-owned *Herald*, a newspaper that prides itself on its long-standing support for the Zimbabwe African National Union–Patriotic Front (ZANU–PF) party? In a country where criticizing the president is considered taboo, the president's stumble at Harare International Airport in early 2015 will not be remembered because of how the mainstream media the world over reported the incident. Rather, it is the citizen-created comedy memes poking fun at the ageing president and circulating on social media networks that will perhaps linger in many people's memories. This incident, and several others across Africa, show that times are changing, and indeed, that technology will have a role to play in the way the continent will be governed. The time for the use of traditional letters-to-the-editor, as others have argued, is long gone (McCluskey and Hmielowski, 2011).

Several factors, including decreasing public trust in news and tumbling advertising revenues (Bruns *et al.*, 2007), have contributed to the popularity and eventual tolerability of citizen journalism. While it certainly has its own problems, citizen journalism evidently provides a powerful opposing narrative to traditional journalism. New research has also shown that, with professional journalism fast losing its credibility, citizen journalism has gained momentum (Carr *et al.*, 2014). Brown (2005) draws a clear distinction between citizen and professional journalists, suggesting that while trained journalists are obliged to respect some journalistic principles such as accuracy and fact-checking, citizen journalists do not have specific ethical standards guiding their conduct. With this distinction in mind, one can appreciate why citizen journalism has been subjected to intense scrutiny over ethical concerns. Yet in Africa, and perhaps in several other countries globally, where, due to a number of factors, reliance on traditional media is slowly becoming a thing of the past, citizen journalists are not overly concerned by the ongoing debate on whether they should consider themselves "journalists". Instead, they see themselves providing an alternative to professional journalism (Mutsvairo and Columbus, 2012): a position which allows them to challenge the conventional settings of mass media.

Conceptualizing citizen journalism

Several scholars have already delved into an array of journalistic challenges posed by the expansion of citizen journalism (Kovacic and Erjavec, 2008;

Moyo, 2009; Reich, 2008). Citizen journalists accentuate "first-person, eye witness accounts by participants" (Atton, 2003, p. 267), or "radical media offering social movements' oxygen" (Downing, 2001, p. 390). But the practice is attributable to newspapers' "loss of readers, the decline in voting, the national loss of a sense of place, declining civic membership, the rising disgust with politics, and the decay of public discourse" (Merritt and Rosen, 1995). Nip (2006) is adamant there is a clear conceptual distinction between citizen and participatory journalism. Bowman and Willis (2003) see no difference between the two, defining participatory journalism as "the act of a citizen, or group of citizens, playing an active role in the process of collecting, reporting, analyzing and disseminating news and information" (p. 9).

Yet others, like Hermes (2006), are keen to emphasize that the world stands to benefit from a more informed citizenry thanks to the emergence of citizen journalism. A key characteristic of citizen journalism, depending on geographical location, could, as already confirmed by Brown (2005), be the absence of journalistic ethics. That means, for instance, that news can be instantaneously produced and distributed, with no facts checked or verified. While some bloggers may willingly verify some of the news they publish, fact-checking is not a prerequisite for entering the largely self-regulating blogging world. The problem is, when facts are not properly and carefully checked, empowering readers with truthful and accurate information becomes an impracticable task. As noted above, several definitions for citizen journalism have been put forward by researchers in the fields of journalism and sociology. In spite of these variations, it is safe to assume that when an average, non-professional – in most cases unpaid – person voluntarily participates in the process of gathering and sharing news, then he/she can be called a citizen journalist (Carr *et al.*, 2014; Deuze *et al.*, 2007; Lacy *et al.*, 2013).

Without doubt, discussions on whether citizen journalists should possess journalistic integrity have attracted intense debate and, predictably, there is unlikely to be any consensus on this topic. Traditional and online journalism practices can be separated by the reporting element, argues Singer (2005). She is keen to draw a fine line between news reporting and discussions about news that normally frequent the online space. This is despite the fact that, as part of a global trend, traditional media organizations have also launched citizen journalism initiatives. CNN's iReport is a perfect example. For their part, Kahn and Kellner (2004) are convinced that online activists use new media initiatives, such as blogs, to promote their own agendas and interests, a view that strongly contradicts the demand for "balanced and fair" coverage embedded in traditional ethics of journalism.

Democracy in the digital age: Participatory politics

Wahl-Jorgensen and Hanitzsch (2009, p. xi) stress the importance of media in a democracy by declaring: "We should care about journalism because it's central to democracy, citizenship, and everyday life, and we should care about journalism studies because it helps us understand this key social institution." The power of the media is sometimes overrated, however. Can media alone, or access to it, instigate political change? Some have pointed to recent developments in North Africa to support the school of thought that media can indeed foster change. In sub-Saharan Africa, it could be argued that citizen journalists, and new media technologies in general, certainly help advance the democratic participation of citizens. However, it could also be argued that several factors, including (although improving vastly in some countries) poor infrastructure and accessibility to the Internet, prioritization of other issues in place of citizen journalism, indecisiveness on whether Western-styled democracy is what is needed, as well as fear of punishment for engaging in pro-democracy activism online, could be denting those prospects.

Shalom (2002), the scholar credited with coining the term "participatory politics", acknowledges the role played by a vibrant, diverse media in a functioning democracy. The diversity Shalom alludes to, one would imagine, is certainly not only restricted to mainstream media outlets, but also includes citizen-produced content, which broadly incorporates the phenomena of citizen journalism. Bucy and Gregson (2001) maintain that the emergent form of technology-based democracy is not limited to net activism only. They, rather, propose that the participatory engagement of citizens online and the comprehensive exposure to political messages play a role in defining the dynamics of participatory politics. This goes to show that technology on its own cannot effect change. It is down to people themselves to make the best of technologies. Neither is accessibility to technologies a sign of active political participation. Action is what matters, as shown by Davis' (2009) allusion to the resignation of American Trent Lott, which he attributes to bloggers actively showing discontent with the ex-senate majority leader's controversial speech. It would almost be unthinkable for something like that to happen in several African countries, given the tyrannical nature of governance, even though there is every reason to believe that deposed president of Burkina Faso, Blaise Compaoré, was forced to abdicate his post in October 2014 due to civil unrest, linked to the participatory nature of politics in the country. Further north in the continent, Harsch (2012) credits a citizen-centred initiative with starting a massive insurgency, which stopped President Abdoulaye Wade from undermining the Senegalese constitution, a development, he argues, that effectively aided Wade's electoral defeat a few months later.

Perhaps the best way to define participatory politics is by explaining what it's not. Participatory politics is not a one-man show. In their conceptualization of participatory politics, Kahne and colleagues (2014, p. 7) use Jenkins and colleagues' (2009) participatory culture as a point of departure, suggesting participation "is significantly peer-based, interactive, nonhierarchical, independent of elite-driven institutions, and social, that is, accessible to analysis at the level of the group rather than the individual" (p. vi). In the same vein Zuckerman (2013) argues that sharing data online is permissible under participatory politics, "as the large userbase for Web2.0 tools means these tools are highly discoverable" (n.p.). For the purposes of this book, citizen journalism should thus be viewed through the lens of a broader conceptualization and contextualization of citizen participation, which incorporates not just the gathering or recording of news, but also the active (participatory) involvement in producing or sharing news, or any other action leading to potential change, be it political or social. Taking a cue from Flew's (2013) view that journalism is no longer a profession for the accredited professionals only, I argue that anyone with access to the Internet is a citizen journalist, or at least potentially one. While research has shown that, in the UK, nearly half of the population has updated or joined Twitter (Dutton *et al.*, 2009), it must be noted that exact details on who is using social networks for political purposes in Africa cannot be verified. Even if figures were available, it still would be difficult to determine who is using Twitter for political purposes.

New media technologies have impacted the increasingly intertwined relationship between journalism and politics. Kluver and Banerjee's (2005) case study of China supported the use of Internet as a basis for promoting democracy. More importantly, Smith and Rainie (2008) have suggested that the traditionally elitist nature of politics would be a thing of the past thanks largely to social network sites such as Facebook, which has the capacity to provide everyone with a platform to say what they want. Mainstream outlets' ability to monopolize media is now being challenged by citizen-produced content (Benkler, 2006). However, online presence does not always come with positives, as Hindman's (2009) study showed that offline viewers echoed the same political sentiments as those online, thereby suggesting exposure to the Internet was not always beneficiary.

It is still unclear whether the participatory aspect translates into democracy. Curiously, some authors, like Carey (1997), have gone a step further by suggesting there is no difference between democracy and journalism. His thesis is that "journalism as a practice is unthinkable except in the context of democracy; in fact, journalism is usefully understood as another name for democracy" (p. 332). Carey's view is dangerous, however. It is possible to practise journalism, especially in a citizenry realm, without necessarily living in a democracy, which, by all standards, remains steadfastly a disputed term. My prime argument here, using Carey's theory as a point of departure, is that democracy in the digital age is a concept that needs to be redefined. So does journalism. To think of democracy in terms of its original definition from the Greek political and philosophical thought would be incompatible with the all-pervading confrontations of digital doctrines of contemporary times. Likewise, journalism has undergone enormous changes from the 1605 publication of what is believed to be the world's first newspaper in Strasburg to the current era of citizen journalism.

Opponents of the commonly accepted yet debatable view that the Internet sustains democracy, including Noam (2005), have sought to warn against positivist thoughts suggesting political dialogue has, in some countries, increased as a direct result of augmented digital participation. He concludes: "The Internet does not create a Jeffersonian democracy. It is not Athens, nor Appenzell, nor Lincoln-Douglas. It is, if anything, less of a democracy than those low-tech places" (p. 58). Not everyone agrees with Noam. The Internet could fundamentally provide knowledge to citizens, an aspect that is a key component of democracy (Schwartz, 1996). Ott (1998) observes that activists fighting against authoritarian regimes in Africa have loyally looked to the Internet in their quest for democracy. Norris (2001) supports this view, concluding, "potentially the role of digital technologies may be equally important in challenging authoritarian regimes" (p. 5). While digital networks such as social media are considered democratizing tools for the Internet, other forces, such email, also play a bigger role in communicating messages among activists. For instance, introduction of the Interception of Communications Bill in Zimbabwe was scuttled by a lack of technological capacity and monitoring equipment needed to intercept communication (Mutsvairo, 2013).

Chapter summaries

Chapters in the opening section of the book will separately show diverging narratives in terms of the theorization of the participatory nature of citizen media. If Antony and Thomas (2010, pp. 1284–1285) believe citizen journalism occurs when "members of the public take on the responsibility of representing common interests and actively participate in the creation and dissemination of information", Part I shows differences in the theoretical rationalization of citizen journalism in Francophone and Anglophone Africa by looking at specific cases in French-speaking central Africa and mostly English-speaking southern Africa.

Farooq A. Kperogi bases Chapter 2 on a case-study reflection of the use of social media networks such as Facebook and Twitter as alternative sources of news for Nigerians, not only for the purposes of invigorating deliberative democracy, and even democracy itself, but also for setting the agenda of the domestic mass media. This chapter opens debate on the supposedly interlocked relationship between democracy and citizen participation on the online platform? What opportunities does Facebook offer to Nigerians' quest for democracy? Highlighting the declining social and cultural capital of institutional media in a globalized and digital world, the chapter questions the objective of democracy in the African context and how the current discourse has benefited from new media revolution. Next, in Chapter 3,

Last Moyo provides a critical analysis of ethics in the context of the African blogosphere.

Everette Ndlovu, in Chapter 4, adds a voice to the ongoing debate on the role of citizen-inspired diasporic radio messages in effecting political changes in Zimbabwe. He navigates through the passage of message restriction in a supposedly undemocratic state, seeking to clarify how systematic media controls generate an environment in which underground communication strategies are nurtured (Soley and Nichols, 1987). From the south to the Horn of Africa, Terje Skjerdal's account in Chapter 5 provides an answer to one question: Why didn't the Arab Spring come to Ethiopia? He provides counter-accounts to suggestions that the citizen-stimulated political upheavals in the Middle East could find another home, this time in sub-Saharan Africa. Ending the first part is Chapter 6 by Mirjam de Bruijn; she draws upon her 14-year experience in Chad to determine the role of technology in empowering citizens politically.

Part II is a compilation of chapters that seek to reflect, in a multidisciplinary perspective, on opportunities for citizen journalism to be a potential catalyst for social, economic and democratic change in sub-Saharan Africa. Can active engagement of citizen journalism lead to political, social and economic changes in Africa? Case studies drawn from research in Kenya, South Africa and Zimbabwe are explored to tackle this question. First, foregrounded and framed within theories of democracy as well as new media concepts, Chapter 7 by Glenda Daniels introduces this part, analysing not just the prospects, but also the problems of citizen journalism's perceived entwined relationship with democracy. Following up on the suggestion that the measurement for "influence" of an editor is premised upon his or her ability to attract a sizeable number of Twitter "followers" (Verweij and van Noort, 2014), Daniels questions whether there is a connection between this "influence" and real engagement with citizenry. Acknowledging the potential of citizen media, Erika Rodrigues and Anya Schiffrin's chapter (Chapter 8) seeks to explore the relationship and use of citizen journalism in understanding Africa's economic and extractive sectors. Noting that problems limited not only to poor salaries, poor training and the highly technical nature of the sector undermine the likely success of investigative journalism in the extractive sector, they are adamant, in spite of several cited problems, that, by adding more voices, embarrassing corrupt government officials and relentlessly reporting on cases of government misdoing, citizen journalism outlets are boosting transparency and accountability in Africa. Chapter 9, by Kristin Skare Orgeret, delves into an area which has largely been ignored by journalism researchers in Africa: crowdfunding. Specifically grounding her analysis in three different models for journalism – a project-based and a subscription-based one and a "credit union" entity, Orgeret profiles activists involved in this form civic engagement, and analyses the success of their endeavours.

Two chapters conclude Part II: in Chapter 10 Bruce Mutsvairo looks at the role of propaganda in shaping the political dynamics in Zimbabwe, specifically analysing *The Herald*'s offline and online news discourses. Not to be outdone, in Chapter 11 sceptic Cleophas Muneri uses a case-study examination of Zimbabwe to postulate that, despite the opportunities they may offer and as much as they have opened up communication space around the world, new communication technologies' contribution to democratization through citizen journalism is still being held back in this southern African country.

Finally, Part III offers a chance to reflect upon differences in experiences for citizen journalism in Lusophone and Anglophone countries. What can we learn from experiences in the Portuguese-speaking countries? What lessons can be derived from Lusophone Africa, which is not normally included in comparative case studies of citizen participation? Is there any evidence that events in one country are influencing what is happening in the country next door? Starting with Susana Salgado's analysis in Chapter 12, which takes us to four Portuguese-speaking African countries: Angola, Cape Verde, Mozambique, and Sao Tome and Principe, an attempt is made to illustrate different processes of democratization and different media systems. Salgado's research shows differences among these countries in terms of levels of citizen democratic awareness and diverse modes of political engagement.

From there, Wallace Chuma's evaluation of theoretical approaches in "alternative media" in South Africa in Chapter 13 examines not just the potential, but also the limits and challenges, of new platforms to create an inclusive society within the context of an emerging democracy characterized by contradictions of freedom and inequality. Using Zimbabwe as a reference point, in Chapter 14, Joseph Mujere and Wesley Mwatwara investigate the role played by citizen journalism in Zimbabwe's elections since 2008. They question whether mobile phones and social networking forums such as Facebook, WhatsApp and Twitter are essentially providing a counter-public space to seemingly constrained state-controlled public spheres. George Ogola and Mike Owuor follow up in Chapter 15 by not only assessing the expansion of citizen journalism in Kenya and how it has sustained a discourse of executive accountability while speaking from the affective experiences of the "margins"; but also by critically reflecting on the emerging incursion by state-actors into citizen journalism, and assessing the impact of this on the character and orientation of this journalism.

The last two chapters revolve around Ebola and citizen journalists' involvement in the coverage of the scourge. First, in Chapter 16, Winston Mano and viola c. milton use a case-study analysis of citizen-centred media in Zimbabwe and South Africa to argue that, far from being victims, Africans could potentially portray and prove themselves as people with the agency and power to define and shape their own destinies. Ibrahim Shaw's chapter, Chapter 17, uses the Ebola reportages in the Sierra Leonean blogosphere to posit that the increasing tendency of citizen journalists to use mainstream media sources, or ideologically and commercially deployed sources of information limits its ability to serve as a counter-hegemonic model to conventional journalism.

References

Allan, S. and Thorsen, E. (eds.) (2009). *Citizen Journalism: Global Perspectives.* New York: Peter Lang.

Antony, M.G. and Thomas, R.J. (2010). "This is citizen journalism at its finest": YouTube and the public sphere in the Oscar Grant shooting incident. *New Media & Society* 12(8): 1280–1296.

Atton, C. (2003). What is "alternative" journalism? *Journalism* 4(3): 267–272.

Atton, C. and Wickenden, E. (2005). Sourcing routines and representation in alternative journalism: A case study approach. *Journalism Studies* 6(3): 347–359.

Barber, B. (2003) "Which Technology and Which Democracy?" In H. Jenkins and D. Thorburn (eds.), *Democracy and New Media.* Cambridge, MA: The MIT Press, pp. 33–48.

Bardoel, J. and Deuze, M. (2001). Network journalism: Converging competences of media professionals and professionalism. *Australian Journalism Review* 23(2): 91–103.

Benkler, Y. (2006). *The Wealth of Networks: How Social Production Transforms Markets and Freedom.* Connecticut: Yale Press.

Bentley, C., Hamman, B., Littau, J., Meyer, H., Watson, B. and Welsh, B. (2007). Citizen Journalism: A Case Study. In: M. Tremayne Blogging (eds.) *Citizenship, and the Future of Media.* New York: Routledge, pp. 239–260.

Bhattacharyya, B. and Hodler, R. (2012). Media Freedom and Democracy: Complements or Substitutes in the Fight Against Corruption? *CSAE Working Paper* WPS/2012–02.

Bowman, S. and Willis, C. (2003) We media: How audiences are shaping the future of news and information. *The Media Center at the American Press Institute.*

Bowman, S. and Willis, C. (2003) *How Participatory Journalism Is Taking Form. In We Media: How Audiences Are Shaping the Future of News and Information.* The Media Center at the American Press Institute, pp. 21–37. www.hypergene.net/wemedia/, Retrieved on 1 February 2015.

Brown, F (2005). Citizen journalism is not professional journalism. *The Quill* 93(6): 42.

Bruns, A. (2005). *Gatewatching: Collaborative Online News Production.* New York: Peter. Lang Publishing.

Bruns, A. (2009). "New Blogs and Citizen Journalism: New Directions for e-Journalism". In *e-Journalism: New Media and News Media*, Kiran Prasad (ed.), Delhi: BR Publishing, pp. 101–126.

Bruns, A. and Highfield, T. (2012). "Blogs, Twitter, and Breaking News: The Produsage of Citizen Journalism". In *Produsing Theory in a Digital World: The Intersection of Audiences and Production*, Rebecca Ann Lind (ed.), New York: Peter Lang, pp. 15–32.

Bucy, E. and Gregson, K. (2001). Media participation: A legitimizing mechanism of mass democracy. *New Media & Society* 3(3): 357–380.

Carey, J. (1997) "Afterword: The Culture in Question". In *James Carey: A Critical Reader*, Eve Stryker Munson and Catherine Warren (eds.), Minneapolis, MN: University of Minnesota Press. pp. 308–339.

Carlson, M. (2007). Blogs and journalistic authority: The role of blogs in US election day 2004 coverage. *Journalism Studies* 8(2): 264–279.

Carr, D.J., Barnidge, M., Byung, G.L. and Tsang, S.J. (2014). Cynics and skeptics: Evaluating the credibility of mainstream and citizen journalism. *Journalism & Mass Communication Quarterly* 91(3): 452–470.

Chari, T. (2009). Ethical challenges facing Zimbabwean media in the context of the Internet. *Global Media Journal (African Edition)* 3(1): 46–79.

Chavis, R. (1998). Africa in the Western Media. *Paper presented at the Sixth Annual African Studies Consortium Workshop*, 2 October 1998.

Cowling, J. (2005). *Digital News: Genie's Lamp or Pandora's Box? Digital Manifesto Project.* http://www.ippr.org/uploadedFiles/research/projects/Digital_Society/news _and_info_jcowling.pdf, Retrieved 13 March 2013.

Davis, R. (2009). *Typing Politics: The Role of Blogs in American Politics.* New York: Oxford University Press.

Deuze, M. (2003). The Web and its journalisms: Considering the consequences of different types of news media online. *New Media and Society* 5: 203–229.

Deuze, M., Bruns, A. and Neuberger, C. (2007). Preparing for an age of participatory news. *Journalism Practice*, 1(3): 322–338.

Domingo, D., Quandt, T., Heinonen, A., Paulussen, S., Singer, J.B. and Vujnovic, M. (2008). Participatory journalism practices in the media and beyond. *Journalism Practice* 2(3): 326–342.

Downing, J. (2001). *Radical Media: Rebellious Communication and Social Movements.* Thousand Oaks, CA: Sage.

Dutton, W.H., Helsper, E.J. and Gerber, M.M. (2009). *The Internet in Britain 2009.* Oxford: Oxford Internet Institute.

Fair, J.E. (1992). "Africa's Media Image". In *Are We Really the World? Coverage of U.S. Food Aid in Africa, 1980–1989*, B.G. Hawk (ed.), New York: Praeger. pp. 109–120.

Flew, T. (2012). The Digital Transformation of 21st Century News Journalism. Presented at the conference on *Digital Media and Journalism*. Taiwan: Taipei.

Frère, M.S. (2011). *Elections and Media in Post-Conflict Africa: Votes and Voices for Peace?* London: Zed Books.

Gil de Zúñiga, H. (2009). "Blogs, Journalism and Political Participation". In *Journalism and Citizenship: New Agendas in Communication*, Z. Papacharissi, Mahwah, NJ: Lawrence Erlbaum, pp. 108–123.

Glaser, M. (2006). *Your Guide to Citizen Journalism, Public Broadcasting Service.* http://www.pbs.org/mediashift/2006/09/your-guide-to-citizen-journalism270 .html, Retrieved 3 October 2014.

Gulvady, S. (2009). Blogging – redefining global modern journalism: An Omani perspective. *Global Media Journal* 8(13): 1–14.

Harsch, E. (2012). An African Spring in the making: Protest and voice across a continent. *Whitehead Journal of Diplomacy and International Relations* 13(1): 45–61.

Hermes, J. (2006). Citizenship in the age of Internet. *European Journal of Communication* 21(3): 295–309.

Hindman, M. (2009). *The Myth of Digital Democracy.* Princeton, NJ: Princeton University Press.

Jenkins, H., Purushotma, R., Clinton, K., Weigel, M. and Robison, A.J. (2009). Confronting the Challenges of Participatory Culture: Media Education for the 21st

Century. *Occasional Paper on Digital Media and Learning*. Chicago: John D. and Catherine T. MacArthur Foundation.

Johnson, K. and Weidenbeck, S. (2009) Enhancing perceived credibility of citizen journalism websites. *Journalism and Mass Communication Quarterly* 86(2): 332–348.

Kahn, R. and Kellner, D. (2004). New media and internet activism. *New Media & Society* 6(1): 87–95.

Kahne, J., Middaugh, E. and Allen, D. (2014). Youth, New Media, and the Rise of Participatory Politics, *Working Paper*.

Kaufhold, K., Valenzuela, S. and Gil de Zúñiga, H. (2010) Effects of citizen and professional journalism on political knowledge and participation. *Journalism & Mass Communication Quarterly* 87(3/4): 515–529.

Keen, A. (2007). *The Cult of the Amateur: How Today's Internet Is Killing Our Culture*. London: Nicholas Brealey Publishing.

Kelly, J. (2009). *Red Kayaks and Hidden Gold: The Rise, Challenges and Value of Citizen Journalism*. Oxford: Reuters Institute for the Study of Journalism.

Kluver, R. and Banerjee, I. (2005). Political culture, regulation, and democratization: The Internet in Nine Asia nations. *Information, Communication & Society* 8: 30–46.

Kovach, B. and Rosenstiel, T. (2001). *The Elements of Journalism*. New York: Crown Publishers.

Kovacic, M.P. and Erjavec, K. (2008). Mobile journalism in Slovenia. *Journalism Studies* 9(6): 874–890.

Lacy, S., Duffy, M., Riffe, D., Thorson, E. and Fleming, K. (2010). Citizen journalism web sites complement newspapers. *Newspaper Research Journal* 31(2): 34–46.

Lacy, S., Fico, F., Wildman, S., Bergan, D.E., Baldwin, T. and Zube, P. (2013). Citizen journalism sites as information substitutes and complements for United States newspaper coverage of local governments. *Digital Journalism*, 1(1): 152–168.

Lowrey, W. (2006). Mapping the journalism–blogging relationship. *Journalism* 7(4): 477–500.

Mabweazara, H. (ed.) (2015). *Digital Technologies and the Evolving African Newsroom: Towards an African Digital Journalism Epistemology*. London: Routledge.

Mabweazara, H., Mudhai, O.F. and Whittaker, J. (eds.) (2013). *Online Journalism in Africa: Trends, Practices and Emerging Cultures*. London: Routledge.

McCluskey, M. and Hmielowski, J. D. (2011). Opinion expression during social conflict: Comparing online reader comments and letters to editors. *Journalism: Theory, Practice and Criticism* 13(3): 303–319.

Matheson, D. (2004). Weblogs and the epistemology of the news: Some trends in online journalism. *New Media Society* 6: 443–468.

Merritt, D. and Rosen, J. (1995). Imagining public journalism: An editor and scholar reflect on the birth of an idea. Indiana University School of Journalism, Roy W. Howard Public Lecture.

Moyo, D. (2009). Citizen journalism and the parallel market of information in Zimbabwe's 2008 election. *Journalism Studies* 10(4): 551–567.

Mudhai, O.F. (2013). *Civic Engagement, Digital Networks and Political Reform in Africa*. New York: Palgrave Macmillan.

Mudhai, O.F., Tettey, W. and Banda, F. (2009). *African Media and the Digital Public Sphere*. New York: Palgrave Macmillan.

Mutsvairo, B. (2013). Power and participatory politics in the digital age: Probing the use of new media technologies in railroading political changes in Zimbabwe. Unpublished PhD Thesis, University of Leiden. Graduate School of Humanities.

Mutsvairo, B. and Columbus, S. (2012). Emerging patterns and trends in citizen journalism in Africa: A case of Zimbabwe. *Central European Journal of Communication* 5(8): 23–37.

Nah, S. and Chung, D. (2009). Rating citizen journalists versus pros: Editors' views. *Newspaper Research Journal* 30(2): 71–83.

Nip, J. (2006). Exploring the second phase of public journalism. *Journalism Studies* 7(2): 212–236.

Noam, E. (2005). Why the Internet Is bad for democracy. *Communications of the ACM* 48(10): 57–58.

Pippa Norris, (2001). *Digital Divide? Civic Engagement, Information Poverty and the Internet Worldwide.* New York: Cambridge University Press.

Obadare, E. and Willems, W. (2014). *Civic Agency in Africa: Arts of Resistance in the Twenty-First Century.* Oxford: James Currey.

Osborn, B. (2001). *Ethics and Credibility in Online Journalism.* Tennessee: University of Memphis.

Ott, D. (1998). "Power to the people: The role of electronic media in promoting democracy in Africa". *First Monday*, 3. www.firstmonday.dk/issues/issue3_4/ott, Retrieved 16 March 2013.

Pitts, L., Jr. (2010). Citizen journalists? Spreading like a cold. *Miami Herald*, http://www.miamiherald.com/2010/10/06/1859362/citizen-journalists-spreading.html, Retrieved 5 October 2014.

Power, E. (2006). "The Blog Revolution and How It Changed the World". In *New Media*, Albert Rolls (ed.), New York: The H. W. Wilson Company, pp. 9–15.

Reddick, R. and King, E. (1994). *The Online Journalist.* Dallas, TX: Harcourt Brace College Publishers.

Reese, S.D., Rutigliano, L., Hyun, K. and Jeong, J. (2007). Mapping the blogosphere: Professional and citizen-based media in the global news arena. *Journalism* 8(3): 235–261.

Reich Z (2008). How Citizens Create News Stories: the "news access" problem reversed, *Journalism Studies* 9(5): 739–758.

Rosen, J. (2008). "The Afterword: The People Formerly Known as the Audience". In *Participation and Media Production: Critical Reflections on Content Creation*, N. Carpentier and B. de Cleen (eds.), Newcastle: Cambridge Scholars Publishing, pp. 163–165.

Schudson, M. (2001) The objectivity norm in American journalism. *Journalism* 2 (2), August: 149–170.

Schwartz, E. (1996). *Netactivism: How Citizens Use the Internet.* Sebastapol, CA: Songline Studios.

Shalom, S. (2002). *Which Side Are You On? An Introduction to Politics.* Longman.

Shaw, Ibrahim S. (2012) *Human Rights Journalism: Advances in Reporting Distant Humanitarian Interventions.* Palgrave Macmillan.

Singer, J. (2005). The political J-Blogger: Normalizing a new media form to fit old norms and practices. *Journalism* 6(2): 173–198.

Soley, L.C. and Nichols, J.S. (1987). *Clandestine Radio Broadcasting: A Study of Revolutionary and Counterrevolutionary Electronic Communication.* New York: Praeger

Schudson M. (2003). *Sociology of News.* New York: Norton.

Smith, A., & Rainie, L. (2008). *The Internet and the 2008 Election. Pew Internet & American Life Project.* Washington, DC: Pew Trust.

Tettey, W. (ed.) (Forthcoming) *Media and Information Literacy, Informed Citizenship and Africa's Development.* Palgrave.

Thurman, N. (2007) The globalisation of journalism online: A transatlantic study of news websites and their international readers. *Journalism* 8(3): 285–307.

Tufte, T., Wildermuth, N., Hansen-Skovmoes, A.S. and Mitullah, W. (eds.) (2013). *Speaking Up and Talking Back? Media Empowerment and Civic Engagement among East and Southern African Youth.* Göteborg: Nordicom.

Verweij, P. and Van Noort, E. (2014). Journalists' twitter networks, public debates and relationships in South Africa. *Digital Journalism* 2(1): 98–114.

Volkmer, I. (2005) "News in the Global Public Space". In *Journalism: Critical Issues*, S. Allan (ed.), Maidenhead: Open University Press. pp. 357–369.

Wahl-Jorgensen, K. and Hanitzsch, T. (eds.) (2009). *Handbook of Journalism Studies.* New York and London: Routledge.

Wasserman, H. (ed.) (2010). *Popular Media, Democracy and Development in Africa.* London: Routledge.

Wasserman, H. (2011). Mobile phones, popular media and everyday African democracy: Transmissions and transgressions. *Popular Communication* 9(2): 146–158.

Wasserman, H. and Garman, A. (2012). Speaking out as citizens: Voice and agency in post-apartheid South African media. *Communitas* 17: 39–58.

Willems, W. and Mano, W. (eds.) (forthcoming). From audiences to users: Everyday media culture in Africa. London: Routledge.

Zuckerman, E. (2013). *Cute Cats to the Rescue? Participatory Media and Political Expression*, Center for Civic Media, MIT Press.

Part I
Recapturing Production Practices

2
Networked Social Journalism: Media, Citizen Participation and Democracy in Nigeria

Farooq A. Kperogi

Introduction

In this chapter, I explore the history of the struggles for democracy and inclusion by Nigeria's traditional media, and show how emergent genres of web-based journalism are supervening upon the traditional media as sites for the push and pull of democratic discourses. I then deploy case-study research to investigate how Nigerian citizens in social media networks such as Facebook and Twitter not only invigorate deliberative democracy, and even democracy itself, by serving as alternative sources of news for Nigerians, but set the news agenda of the domestic mass media. The chapter also highlights the declining social and cultural capital of the Nigerian legacy media, and shows that the profusion of citizen participation in the democratic project through social media networks isn't always benevolent. It then suggests ways the legacy media can complement, co-opt or contain the luxuriance and exuberance of the social media scene.

The institutional mass media in Nigeria, especially the country's vibrant independent newspaper press, have historically functioned as the only credible arenas for the articulation and circulation of transformative and politically consequential national discourses, and for the instigation of momentous social changes. That is why studies of political developments in Nigeria, from the colonial to the post-colonial periods, have always highlighted the role of the Nigerian press and of Nigerian journalists in energizing and galvanizing popular support for major, defining issues of the times.

However, since the restoration of constitutional rule in the country in 1999, which the newspaper press, to a greater extent than any single institution in Nigeria, helped bring about, the brand of critical journalism that characterized the anti-colonial and anti-military eras, and which found an especially concentrated expression in the guerrilla press of the 1990s

(Kperogi, 2008), dissipated considerably. The void created by this development inspired the growth and flowering of several diasporan Nigerian citizen media news sites that simultaneously hold governments to account and challenge the authority of – and sometimes set the agenda for – the institutional mass media.

In the last half decade, another crucial paradigm shift has occurred in the Nigerian journalistic landscape: former consumers of institutional news are becoming the sources, creators, co-creators, distributors and consumers of news content on such social media networks as Facebook and Twitter, thereby fundamentally challenging the age-old oligopolistic model of news production. As the traditional media, hitherto the sole purveyors of news, become increasingly dependent on citizen contributions on social media networks for their news content, they are in danger of being eclipsed. This is exacerbated by the parallel proliferation and flowering of home-based online and citizen journalism in Nigeria. The traditional news media are no longer the only informational elements in the morphology of Nigeria's democracy; they are now complemented, and in some cases supplanted, by diasporan citizen online media, a vast homeland online media formation, as well as by what one might call the journalism of the crowd on social media platforms like Facebook, Twitter and YouTube. But to understand how these emergent Internet-enabled convergent media platforms are altering media practice and democratic participation in Nigeria, it is useful to understand the history of media and democracy in Nigeria.

News media and democracy in Nigeria

To study either the newspaper press or democracy in Nigeria is to study the other. In other words, an inextricable knot ties struggles for democracy and inclusion in Nigeria and the growth and maturation of the independent newspaper press. In 1863, the *Anglo African*, the first attempt to publish an independent English-language newspaper that was not owned by Christian missionaries or the colonial government (published by a mixed-raced Jamaican émigré named Robert Campbell, who humorously described himself as "one-quarter Negro, one-quarter English and half Scotch"), was inspired by the desire to expand discursive inclusivity and encourage the evolvement of democracy and self-governance in the colonial Nigerian public sphere (Omu, 1978, p. 20).

Although *Anglo African* existed for only two years, it provided the ideological foundations and editorial template for the nationalist press that came 15 years later. On 10 November 1880, a prosperous half-Nigerian, half-Sierra Leonean journalist by the name of Richard Beale Blaize, who had worked as an apprentice in *Anglo African*, founded the bi-monthly *Lagos Times*. Blaize made it clear that his venture into newspapering was not actuated by "the hope of large pecuniary returns" (Omu, 1978, p. 31), but by the quest for opening and deepening the democratic space in what later became Nigeria and beyond. In its inaugural editorial, the *Lagos Times* declared:

> We are not clamoring for immediate independence...but it should always be borne in mind that the present order of things will not last forever. A time will come when the West Coast will be left to regulate their [sic] own internal and external affairs.
>
> (Uche, 1989, p. 93)

This declaration set the tone for the nationalist, anti-imperialist fervour of subsequent Nigerian newspapers. It, for instance, inspired the emergence of the more radical *Lagos Observer*, recognized as "one of the symbols of the intellectual aggression which characterized political developments in the two decades of the nineteenth century" (Omu, 1978, p. 30). Many more indigenous nationalist newspapers, such as the *Lagos Weekly Record*, the *Lagos Daily News*, the *Nigerian Chronicle*, the *West African Pilot* and so on sprang up in the 1900s, and committed themselves to "raising consciousness to a high level in editorials and special columns devoted to anti-colonial issues" (Falola, 1999, p. 83). Nationalist journalism thrived for decades and has been credited with being responsible for Nigeria's independence from British colonial rule in 1960.

When James Coleman wrote that "there can be little doubt that nationalist newspapers and pamphlets have been among the main influences in the awakening of racial and political consciousness [in Nigeria]" (Coleman, 1960, p. 184), he was acknowledging the central role newspapers played in expanding the democratic space in colonial Nigeria and ultimately winning independence for the country. Nigeria's first president, Nnamdi Azikiwe, who was himself an anti-colonial activist-journalist, similarly characterized the Nigerian press as "identical with the intellectual and material developments of this country" (quoted in Omu, 1978, p. vii). Nor did Nigerian newspapers' contribution to building and sustaining democracy end with the granting of independence. Although post-independence Nigerian newspapers abandoned all pretence to nationalism and engaged in long-drawn-out partisan fights on behalf of their owners, they nonetheless nourished the country's emergent democracy. That was why Frederick Schwartz asserted that the press "was probably the most potent institution supporting democratic freedom in Nigeria" (Schwartz, 1965, p. 162).

The Nigerian newspaper press also became the central bulwark in the fight against military totalitarianism, which reached a crisis point between 1993 and 1999. The emergence of a vibrant underground press in the late 1990s, often dubbed guerrilla journalism, contributed significantly to the dislodgement of military totalitarianism in 1999, which Hall considered the "most significant democratic struggle in Nigeria since colonialism ended" (Hall, 2009, p. 257). Interestingly, the inspiration for this kind of journalism derives, in large part, from the adversarial, anti-colonial journalism of the nationalist era. Nosa Igiebor, editor-in-chief editor of *Tell*, one of the most notable publications of the guerrilla journalism movement, told a Nigerian researcher that he found motivation for the kind of insurgent journalism he practised from "Nnamdi Azikiwe, Obafemi Awolowo, and other nationalists of the colonial era" (Ibelema, 2003, p. 174).

What particularly redounded to the success and wild popularity of the underground press was the fact that it practically served as the sole arena for the ventilation of popular sentiments, especially in light of the fact that the broadcast industry was controlled by the government and there was no popularly elected parliament. In the absence of the latter, as Chris Ogbonda has pointed out, the press became "the people's parliament" and the "most effective channel to express their wishes and grievances" (Ogbonda, 1991, p. 121). The major publications associated with this phase of Nigerian journalism were *Tell*, *The News*, *Tempo* and *Razor* – all news weeklies. There were many other episodic, underground newspapers that perpetually changed their names, mastheads and locations in response to repression from the military. Given the increasing precariousness of radical publishing and the ever more vicious desperation of the military junta, these news magazines decided to invent unconventional means to put out their news. *Tell*'s Nosa Igiebor told Ayo Olukotun how they did it:

> We sat down and assessed the situation. Their [the military government's] business was to ensure that we didn't publish. Ours was to ensure that we came out without fail. This meant reorganizing our approach to producing. Rather than stay on one spot and become sitting ducks for state security [operatives], we had to be several steps ahead of them, by spreading out and operating in several centers or cells. If we use [one] house this week, we change the next week and use another house. We of course had to preserve the anonymity of the owners and venues of our cells.
>
> (Olukotun, 2002, p. 322)

These perpetually migratory, unorthodox news practices that Igiebor outlined became the modus operandi of all the insurgent news magazines. The core of their strategy, according to Ayo Akinkuotu, another *Tell* editor, was the "duplication of offices.... At critical times in Abacha's five-year tenure, the magazine was forced to operate over seven 'bush offices'. Some were procured in extreme emergencies while others were evacuated without notice" (Akinkuotu, 1998, p. 33). Journalists abandoned the comfort of their newsrooms and held editorial meetings during soccer games, in sports facilities, theatres, hotel lobbies, taxicabs or other places that could guarantee a reasonable concealment of their identities. To avoid arrest by the military government's security agents, the guerrilla journalists "sometimes distributed their publication using a hired ambulance or water truck" (Ojo,

2007, p. 548). Babafemi Ojudu, an editor of *The News* and *Tempo* who is now a Nigerian senator, recalled that he basically lived a nomadic life: his bag was his office, he avoided his home and even, from time to time, camouflaged himself to escape the notice of security agents (Collins, 2001).

However, the façade of the new democratic government hid a lot of muck that needed to be raked. Although some sections of the independent media did rise to the challenge of calling attention to governmental misconduct and indiscretions, their efforts were not sufficiently robust. This is also perhaps because, since 1999, many wealthy politicians, some them elected state governors, have set up influential newspapers that compete with the independent media. For instance, one of Nigeria's most widely circulated newspapers, the *Sun*, is published by the former governor of the south-eastern state of Abia. Other influential papers published by former and current state governors are the *Independent* (owned by James Ibori, former governor of the oil-rich southern state of Delta, who is now serving time in a British prison for corruption), the *Nation* (owned by Bola Tinubu, the former governor of Lagos State, Nigeria's commercial nerve centre and most populous state) and the *Compass* (owned by Gbenga Daniel, the former governor of the south-western state of Ogun). The crowding of the media landscape with these mouthpieces of often corrupt politicians further contributed to demoting investigative journalism to the backburner, even more so since the core of the editorial staff of these newspapers are drawn from the independent, commercial, including the former guerrilla, press, meaning that several of the journalists who had investigated corruption were now in the service of the same people whose corruption they exposed. Salvation came from citizen online news sites located in the United States.

Emergence of diasporan online citizen journalism

The negligence of the mainstream institutional media in Nigeria in calling attention to corruption, misgovernance and abuse of power – in addition to their inability to stay up to speed with the dizzying pace, multimediality and interactivity of twenty-first-century news – inspired the advent and explosion of citizen media sites by Nigerians resident in the United States (Dare, 2011; Kperogi, 2008; 2011; 2012). Websites such as SaharaReporters.com (published from New York), ElenduReports.com (published from Lansing, Michigan), the TimesofNigeria.com (published from Delaware), the NigeriaVillageSquare.com (published from Chicago), PointBlankNews.com (published from New York), the AfricanExaminer.com (published from Baltimore, Maryland), USAfricaonline.com (published from Houston, Texas), IReports-NG.com (published from Noblesville, Indiana), TheWillNigeria.com (published from San Francisco, California) and many others sprouted and flowered, from 2005 onwards. The websites, especially SaharaReporters, not only challenged the dominance of the professionally run but compromised homeland institutional media, they came to occupy the centre stage of Nigerian journalism from their exilic locations.

SaharaReporters, which has emerged as the standard-bearer of Nigerian diasporan citizen journalism, in time became the go-to news site for breaking news and for news about corruption in government. It practically eclipsed the traditional media in Nigeria, and has now become such a central fixture of the Nigerian media landscape that it has attracted the attention of the US government, renowned philanthropic organizations and Western international news organizations (Kperogi, 2011). The *New York Times*, for instance, profiled the site, describing it as "one of a growing number of New York-based journalists in exile taking advantage of cheap and easy Web-publishing technology, and the growing access in the developing world to the Web, to report with impunity from afar" (Spiegel, 2011). In another laudatory profile of the site titled "Africa's WikiLeaks", the *Daily Beast*'s Philip Shenon reported that SaharaReporters' "impressive muckraking has drawn the support of that most august of American philanthropies – the Ford Foundation, which has given SaharaReporters $175,000 over the last two years". He quoted Calvin Sims, a former *New York Times* foreign correspondent who now works for the foundation and who is overseeing the grant, as saying, "I hadn't seen anything like this. The impact it's having – holding political leaders to account – is very impressive", pointing out that SaharaReporters could be a model for similar sites throughout the developing world (Shenon, 2010).

The NigeriaVillageSquare.com, although not strictly a journalistic enterprise in the way that SaharaReporters is, has also emerged as a robust site both for citizen reporting and for news-inflected community and discursive participation. As Bill Kovach and Tom Rosenstiel have observed, the "concept of journalism", since its materialization in seventeenth-century Europe, has always been wedded to the "concept of community and later democracy" (Kovach and Rosenstiel, 2001, p. 18). The NigeriaVillageSquare shares this discursive democratic preoccupation with SaharaReporters, and the success of both sites shows that they provide a model for the future of journalism in transitional societies with similar media and political systems to Nigeria's.

There are at least three reasons why exilic citizen media outfits have become an integral part of Nigeria's media ecology. The first, as was pointed out in the second section of this chapter, is the loss of Nigeria's time-honoured critical press tradition – especially the adversarial guerrilla press tradition that reigned in the 1990s – in the face of the profound moral putrescence that the restoration of democratic rule has paradoxically inaugurated since 1999. At a time when billions of dollars are brazenly stolen and salted away in foreign bank accounts by political office holders, and when bald-faced cronyism and avarice have taken over the public sphere, the national media, for the most part, have either looked the other way or have been actively complicit. This is inconsistent with the progressive, agitational and inquiring disposition that had defined the character and performance of much of the Nigerian press since its founding in the mid-1800s.

The second reason for the ascendance of Nigerian diasporan citizen online journalism is the backward state of the Web presence of the homeland news media. Most Nigerian newspaper websites lack multimedia and hypertextual capabilities, and are therefore incapable of telling twenty-first-century stories which are increasingly not only video- and audio-based but also "networked" and interactive.[1] For instance, the story of a northern Nigerian "Sharia" governor who furtively danced with prostitutes at a nightclub in Dubai, United Arab Emirates, while harshly punishing similar activities in the state he governed could only be told with a video post. SaharaReporters told the story videographically to maximum effect (Kperogi, 2011; 2012). But it is not only the capacity to report on stories with multimedia and interactive corroborations that give the diasporan media an edge: it is also their ability to report them in real time. Although Nigerian newspapers have improved their technical capabilities over the years, they still lag behind diasporan citizen media sites like SaharaReporters in technical sophistication and speed, and do poorly in search engine optimization. Fringe, marginal but SEO-savvy Nigerian websites that steal or spin content from the institutional, mainline newspapers' websites even beat them in searches on major Nigerian news keywords.

The third factor that has contributed to the vigour and attractiveness of the Nigerian diasporan citizen media is the comparative richness and reliability of their sources of information, which has been made possible by the willingness of privileged but disgruntled or conscientious Nigeria-based sources to confide in the citizen reporters of the diasporan media. The diasporan citizen media built their credibility by publishing apparently off-the-wall stories about corruption and influence-peddling in high places in Nigeria that readers either initially doubted or scoffed at, but which turned out to be mostly true. In many cases, otherwise improbable stories are accompanied by vividly telling pictorial and documentary corroborations. Perhaps the biggest gain in the credibility of the online diasporan news media happened in December 2010, when cables released by the whistle-blowing, secret-spewing WikiLeaks confirmed most of the stories that the diasporan online media had published. SaharaReporters, for instance, ran a series of articles comparing its previous stories about corruption in the Nigerian presidency with new revelations that came out in WikiLeaks cables (Kperogi, 2011).

The geographical distance of the practitioners of diaspora citizen online journalism confers many advantages on them. First, it assures would-be whistle-blowers in Nigeria that their identities would be concealed and protected since US-based citizen reporters are unlikely to be under pressure to reveal their sources to Nigerian authorities. Nigerian traditional journalists, on the other hand, cannot give such guarantees even if they wanted to practise adversarial journalism because they have to contend with the ever-present reality of libel and sedition laws. They can also be subpoenaed by the courts to reveal their sources.[2] Although two diasporan citizen journalists were arrested and detained when they travelled to Nigeria in 2009, there was no indication that they were forced to reveal their sources, even though they were both charged with "sedition" (Kperogi, 2011; 2012). They were ultimately released after international pressure was brought to bear on the Nigerian government.

Domestic online media, social networked journalism and participation

Inspired by the success, popularity and impact of the diasporan citizen online media, a slew of home-based online sites have emerged in the last five years. Many mimic the editorial template of SaharaReporters, but they have not been able to replicate its success, and seem condemned to vegetate on the margins of the Nigerian journalistic landscape. But one home-based online news site that has shaken the foundations of Nigerian journalism and rivals SaharaReporters in impact and hard-hitting investigative reporting is Premium Times, which was established in 2011 by home-based, professional, award-winning investigative journalists, some of whom were associated with the guerrilla journalism of the 1990s. According to Alexa Rank, Premium Times is the 37th most visited website in Nigeria, and the 4th most visited news site, outranked only by *Punch*, *Vanguard* and SaharaReporters (http://www.alexa.com/topsites/countries;1/NG).

Coterminous with the growth of home-based online journalistic sites has been the rise of social media networks as independent sources of news, as co-creators of news for the traditional media and as amplifiers of news from traditional sources. This development has been made possible by the exponential growth of Internet usage in Nigeria over the last decade. According to Internet Live Stats, as of July 2015, there were nearly 80 million Internet users in Nigeria, meaning there are more Internet users in the country than there are people in the UK or France. Internet penetration went from a measly 0.06% in 2000 to nearly 40% in 2014.

It is not just that Nigeria has the largest population of Internet users in Africa and the eighth largest in the whole world; it also has one of the world's fastest growing Internet usage. For instance, between 2011 and 2012, over 9 million new Internet users were added in the country, and between 2013 and 2014, a whopping 10 million new users were added, representing a 16% increase. This fact explains why nearly 40% of all Internet traffic from Africa originates in Nigeria (Malakata, 2010). This enormous growth in Internet usage is fuelled largely by the proliferation of Internet-enabled mobile devices in the country. The explosion of Internet usage via mobile devices isn't exclusive to Nigeria; it is happening all over the African continent, prompting Erik Hersman, co-founder of the open-source, crowdsourcing platform Ushahidi, to characterize Africa as the "mobile continent" (Hersman, 2013). Similarly, a 2014 report in the (London) *Guardian* quoted researchers as predicting that Internet usage on mobile phones in Africa "will increase 20-fold in the next five years – double the rate of growth in the rest of the world", while pointing out that "People in Africa use mobiles for online activities that others normally perform on laptops or desktop computers as the technology overcomes weak or non-existent landline infrastructure in large swaths of the world's poorest continent" (*Guardian*, 2014). A 2015 Pew Research Center study also showed that "cell phones are as common in South Africa and Nigeria as they are in the United States" (Pew Research, 2015).

This unprecedented mobile-enabled Internet penetration has afforded Nigeria the opportunity to digitally leapfrog from what Manuel Castells once called the "black hole of informational capitalism" (Castells, 1998, p. 162) to the emergent, horizontal, self-directed, socially networked information age that is often called "the network society". At the symbolic core of the social morphology of the network society are such social media sites as Facebook and Twitter, in which Nigerians now increasingly participate. As StatCounter's Global Stats show, more than 88% of Nigerian social media users have accounts on Facebook, while about 10% use Twitter (StatCounter, 2015). Predictably, Facebook has emerged as the biggest site for online sociability, discursive engagement and social media journalism. Nevertheless, although "Nigeria is among the top ten countries with the fastest increase in Facebook membership" in the world (Olukoya, 2014), with more than 11 million subscribers as of January 2014, Nigeria's traditional media have yet to take central roles in guiding and influencing community conversations on the platform.

Of Nigeria's prominent daily newspapers, only the *Vanguard* had over 1 million likes on Facebook as of April 2015 (see Figure 2.1); SaharaReporters, the New York-based citizen media platform, outpaced it with 1,531,519 likes. *Punch*, Nigeria's most widely circulated newspaper, had 837,476 likes; the *Nation* had 783,191 likes; *ThisDay* had 640,355 likes; *Daily Trust*, northern Nigeria's pre-eminent newspaper, had 587,075 likes; Premium Times, the Nigeria-based online-only newspaper, had 430,000 likes; the *Nigerian Tribune*, Nigeria's oldest surviving private newspaper, had 253,642 likes; the *Sun* had 495,860 likes; the *Daily Independent* had 362,416 likes; *Leadership* had 344,010 likes; the *Guardian*, Nigeria's newspaper of record, had 229,238 likes; *Daily Times*, Nigeria's oldest surviving newspaper, had 110,785 likes; and *PM News*, Nigeria's only evening newspaper, had 84,000 likes. The news media's Twitter following isn't any better. As of April 2015, *Punch* had 751,000 followers; *Vanguard* 668,000 followers; SaharaReporters 557,000 followers; the *Guardian* 369,000 followers; *ThisDay* 308,000 followers; *Daily Trust* 214,000

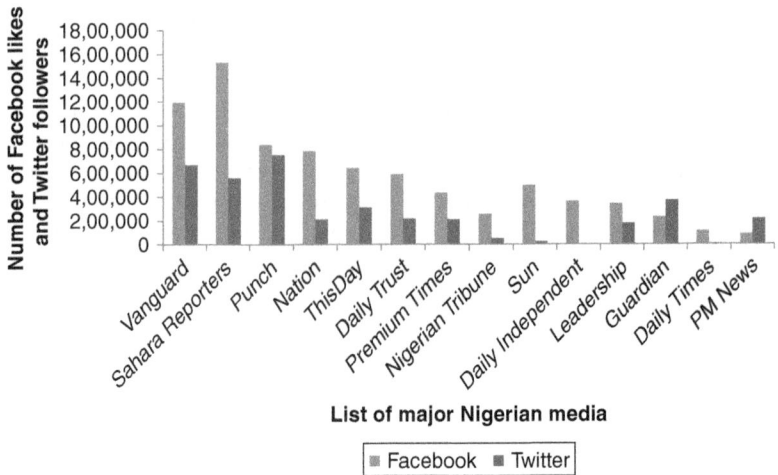

Figure 2.1   The social media following of Nigerian news media

followers; *PM News* 214,000 followers; *Premium Times* 209,000 followers; the *Nation* 209,000 followers; *Leadership* 177,000 followers; the *Sun* 22,000 followers; the *Nigerian Tribune* 50,000 followers; the *Daily Times* 6,097 followers; and the *Daily Independent* 3,553 followers.

But it is not the modest numerical strength of Nigeria's traditional news media's social media presence that vitiates their influence; the social ecology of the Nigerian social media space vests more power and authority in trendsetters, digital influencers and other everyday users with vast and engaged followers than it does in legacy media institutions and their journalists. In other words, social media gives more editorial powers to the crowd than it does to the mass media. That is why most defining national conversations on social media now take place outside the spaces of the Nigerian traditional news media or their social media streams.

For example, in more ways than the traditional news media, social media networks, particularly Facebook and Twitter, played central roles in Nigeria's 2015 presidential elections that saw an opposition candidate, Muhammadu Buhari, defeat incumbent President Goodluck Jonathan. That marked the first time in Nigeria's electoral history that an opposition candidate would trounce a sitting president. While the political party in power exploited and relied on its control of state-run broadcast stations to appeal to the hearts and minds of the Nigerian electorate, the opposition party took to social media to drum support for its candidate, since it was denied airtime in the state-run broadcast media, which typically have a wider reach than newspapers. Although there is no firm empirical proof to make the case that the opposition party won the election because it deployed social media

more artfully than the then incumbent president's party (the then dominant People's Democratic Party also robustly used social media in addition
to its monopoly over the broadcast media), all observers agreed that such
social media platforms as Facebook and Twitter did play remarkable roles in
ensuring transparency in the electoral process. As Quartz noted:

> The consensus from all sides is that while social media didn't decide
> the vote it had a significant influence on perception, expectations and
> a demand for transparency. All in all it seemed that social media was
> a winner with the #NigeriaDecides hashtag resulting in citizens pro-
> claiming that Democracy is alive and well in Africa's most populous
> nation.
>
> (Quartz, 2015)

Hours before the Independent National Electoral Commission announced
the official results of the presidential poll, Nigerian social media users had
accurately predicted it, and the traditional media's reporting of the election
was almost entirely reliant on social media feeds from ordinary citizens. This
was possible because millions of Nigerians with smartphones shared the
results of the elections from their polling units on Twitter and Facebook.
They not only shared the results of the elections in their polling units
in real time, they also took pictures of the official results, and videotaped
instances of electoral malpractices, which they shared on Facebook, Twitter
and YouTube. The ubiquity of smartphones and the unceasing flow of social
media updates on the processes and immediate aftermath of the election had
the effect of what Michel Foucault called the panoptic gaze on government-
appointed superintendents of the election, and forestalled the scale and
kinds of voter frauds typical of past elections in Nigeria. Foucault described
the panoptic gaze in the following way:

> There is no need for arms, physical violence, material constraints. Just a
> gaze. An inspecting gaze, a gaze which each individual under its weight
> will end by internalizing to the point that he is his own overseer, each
> individual thus exercising this surveillance over, and against, himself.
> A superb formula: power exercised continuously and for what turns out
> to be a minimal cost.
>
> (Foucault, 1980, p. 155)

But while traditional scholarship on the mass surveillance industry customarily talks of the panoptic gaze in Orwellian terms, where Big Brother's
ever-present and intrusive gaze over citizens constrains them, in the Nigerian
case, it was an inverse, contra-directional, many-to-many, collaborative
panoptic gaze on the state and its institutions by politically conscious,
smartphone-wielding Nigerian citizens. In other words, Big Brother wasn't

watching the citizens; the citizens were watching Big Brother and using their hand-held devices and social media status updates to report his actions. The traditional news media didn't have such powers; their reach was limited since they couldn't be at every polling station. They didn't have the collective intelligence of the social media crowd, and came to depend on it for their own reportage. This phenomenon is called the backdraft, which, according to Seol Jin-ah, occurs "when the traditional media such as newspapers or television news receive and use such things as Twitter feeds or individually created content in their reporting" (Jin-ah, 2011, p. 5).

The backdraft is not limited to the coverage of elections. On many other issues of national importance the news media have, on several occasions, lifted stories directly from social media feeds and run them on their pages and websites, sometimes without verification. For instance, *Saturday Vanguard*'s 10 May 2014 cover story titled, "Chibok: American Marines Locate Abducted Girls in Sambisa Forest", with a rider that read, "Joint Operation with Nigerian Military Leads to Arrest of Leader of Abductors", complete with a photo of the alleged leader of abductor, was sourced entirely from unverified social media chatter. The story, which alleged that the whereabouts of more than 200 schoolgirls abducted by Boko Haram in 2014 had been found by American Marines and that the brain behind the abduction had been arrested, turned out to be a completely fictitious story which, nonetheless, went viral on Nigerian social media circles before it was picked up by *Saturday Vanguard*, the weekend edition of *Vanguard*. The paper was forced to apologize and eat humble pie when it emerged that a Nigerian social media user with a large, engaged audience made it up, and that the photo the paper used to illustrate the story was an old picture of a man who had been arrested by French soldiers in the Central African Republic (Kperogi, 2014).

This social-media-induced journalistic misadventure is not an exception; it is increasingly becoming normalized in Nigerian journalism. Typically, news now starts from social media chatter, percolates into online news networks, and then to the mainstream news media, from where it is further shared by social media users to create social stories. It sometimes takes a different route: it may start as social media gossip, get picked up by the traditional media, get republished on the slew of fringe Nigerian online news sites, and be amplified even further by social media sharing. At other times, the propaganda and chatter of individual Nigerian digital trendsetters, some of whom have a more numerous social media following than the traditional media, define the news agenda.

This role reversal, where the audience of news becomes both the source and audience is inflicting tremendous damage on the professional authority of Nigeria's institutional media. What the traditional media still have going for them, however, at least for now, is their symbolic power to give professional imprimatur to social media chatter, which the social media chatterers then quote to support their positions. But when mendacious social media rumours find their way to the traditional media and their accuracy is called into question, as happened with regard to *Saturday Vanguard*, the traditional media's credibility is eroded. In the long term, this will vitiate the professional authority and symbolic capital of such media.

Conclusions

In the fast-paced, discursively robust era of social media, the traditional media in Nigeria, more than ever before, need to stand out from the crowd by sticking to the time-honoured journalistic ethos of scepticism and verification before publication if they are to remain relevant. Most importantly, as the realm of social news is becoming more salient and central to journalism, as social media sites are becoming the landing pages for news, the media must understand their role not merely as reporters of the news but as managers and guides of news conversations. This requires that they increase their presence on social media, provide robust platforms for citizen social media conversations on their media platforms, and not be mere echoes of citizen social media chatter.

Notes

1. Network journalism is multimedia, hyperlinked journalism targeted at specific audiences. For an analysis of what "network journalism" entails in practice, see Jo Bardoel and Mark Deuze (2001).
2. To be sure, this is also the case in most advanced democracies in the world. Journalists can be subpoenaed by the courts to reveal their sources before a grand jury (see Fargo, 2003). However, it is highly improbable that a subpoena from a Nigerian court against an online diasporan citizen journalist, say in the USA, can be enforced.

References

Akinkuotu, Ayo. (1998). *Tell*, 31 August 1998, p. 33.
Bardoel, Jo and Deuze, Mark. (2001). Network journalism: Converging competences of media professionals and professionalism. *Australian Journalism Review* 23(2): 91–103.
Pew Research. (2015). Cell Phones in Africa: Communication Lifeline. *Pew Research Center*. Last modified 16 April 2015, http://www.pewglobal.org/2015/04/15/cell-phones-in-africa-communication-lifeline/.
Castells, Manuel. (1998). *End of Millennium*. Malden, MA: Blackwell.
Coleman, James S. (1960). *Nigeria: A Background to Nationalism*. Los Angeles and Berkeley, CA: University of California Press.
Collins, Anthony. (2001). *Words of Fire: Independent Journalists Who Challenge Dictators, Drug Lords, and Other Enemies of a Free Press*. New York: New York University Press.
Dare, Sunday. (2011). *The Rise of Citizen Journalism in Nigeria: A Case Study of SaharaReporters*. Reuters Institute for the Study of Journalism, Oxford University.

http://reutersinstitute.politics.ox.ac.uk/sites/default/files/The%20Rise%20of%20
Citizen%20Journalism%20in%20Nigeria%20%E2%80%93%20A%20Case%20
Study%20of%20Sahara%20Reporters.pdf, Retrieved 21 April 2015.

Falola, Toyin. (1999). *The History of Nigeria*. Westport, CT: Greenwood Press.

Fargo, Anthony. (2003). Evidence mixed on erosion of journalists' privilege. *Newspaper Research Journal* 22(2): 50–63.

Foucault, Michel. (1980). "The Eye of Power". In *Power/Knowledge: Selected Interviews and Other Writings 1972–1977 by Michel Foucault*, C. Gordon (ed.), Sussex: Harvester Press, pp. 146–165.

Hall, Philippa. (2009). "Think Imperially": The private press mediation of state policy and the global economy within colonial and postcolonial Nigeria. *Journal of African Media Studies* 1(2): 247–262.

Hersman, Erik. (2013). The mobile continent. *Stanford Social Innovation Review*. http://www.ssireview.org/articles/entry/the_mobile_continent, Retrieved 4 April 2015.

Ibelema, Minabere. (2003). The Nigerian press and June 12: Pressure and performance during a political crisis. *Journalism Communication Monographs* 4(4): 163–209.

Guardian (2014). Internet use on mobile phones in Africa predicted to increase 20-fold. *TheGuardian.com*. http://www.theguardian.com/world/2014/jun/05/internet-use-mobile-phones-africa-predicted-increase-20-fold, Retrieved 5 June 2014.

Jin-ah, Seol. (2011) Social media and the evolution of journalism. *Korea Journalism Review* 5(1): 1–124.

Kovach, Bill and Rosenstiel, Tom. (2001). *The Elements of Journalism: What Newspeople Should Know and the Public Should Expect*. New York: Crown Publishers.

Kperogi, Farooq A. (2008). Guerrillas in Cyberia: The transnational alternative online journalism of the Nigerian diasporic public sphere. *Journal of Global Mass Communication* 1(1): 72–87.

Kperogi, Farooq A. (2011). Webs of resistance: The citizen online journalism of the Nigerian digital diaspora. PhD Dissertation, Department of Communication, Georgia State University, Atlanta. *Communication Dissertations. Paper 27*, http://digitalarchive.gsu.edu/communication_diss/27.

Kperogi, Farooq A. (2012). "The Evolution and Challenges of Online Journalism in Nigeria". In *The Handbook of Global Online Journalism*, Eugenia Siapera and Andreas Veglis (eds.), Oxford: Wiley-Blackwell, pp. 445–461.

Kperogi, Farooq A. (2014). Journalism is dying a slow death in Nigeria. *Weekly Trust*. http://www.farooqkperogi.com/2014/05/journalism-is-dying-slow-death-in.html, Retrieved 21 April 2015.

Malakata, Michael. (2010). Nigeria claims top internet spot in Africa. *SaharaReporters*. http://saharareporters.com/2010/08/13/nigeria-claims-top-internet-spot-africa, Retrieved 20 April 2015.

Ogbondah, Chris. (1991). The pen is mightier than the "Koboko": A critical analysis of the Amakiri case in Nigeria. *Political Communication and Persuasion* 8: 109–124.

Ojo, Tokunbo. (2007). The Nigerian media and the process of democratization. *Journalism* 8(5): 545–550.

Olukotun, Ayo. (2002). Authoritarian state, crisis of democratization and the underground media in Nigeria. *African Affairs* 101: 317–342.

Olukoya, Sam. (2014). Facebook growing fast in Nigeria. *Deutsche Welle*. http://www.dw.de/facebook-growing-fast-in-nigeria/a-17408466, Retrieved 15 April 2015.

Omu, Fred I. (1978). *Press and Politics in Nigeria 1800–1937*. London: Longman.

Schwartz, Frederick. (1965). *Nigeria*. Cambridge, MA: The MIT Press.

Shenon, Philip. Africa's WikiLeaks. *The Daily Beast*. http://www.thedailybeast.com/ blogs-and-stories/2010-08-12/sahara-reporters-uncovering-nigerias-corruption/2/ m, Retrieved 18 April 2015.

Quartz. (2015). Social media was the other big winner at Nigeria's historic elections. *Quartz*. http://qz.com/377777/social-media-was-the-other-big-winner-at -nigerias-historic-elections/, Retrieved 7 April 2015.

StatCounter (2015). Top 7 desktop, mobile & tablet social media sites in Nigeria from July 2014 to July 2015. http://gs.statcounter.com/#desktop+mobile+tablet-social _media-NG-monthly-201407-201507-bar. Retrieved July 31, 2015.

Spiegel, Brendan. (November 2011). From safety of New York, reporting on distant home. *New York Times*. http://www.nytimes.com/2011/11/20/nyregion/from-safety- of-new-york-reporting-on-a-distant-homeland.html?_r=0, Retrieved 12 April 2015.

Uche, Luke U. (1989). *Mass Media, People and Politics in Nigeria*. New Delhi: Concept Publishing Company.

3
Crossing Taboo Lines: Citizen Journalism Ethics in Political Crisis Settings

Last Moyo

Introduction: The ethical gaze

The advent of the Internet and social media has arguably opened up and democratized journalism as a social and professional practice. Most recently, newer online and mobile phone practices, variously referred to as "citizen journalism", "participatory journalism", "citizen-generated media", "unfiltered journalism", "hyperlocal journalism", "networked journalism" and "grass-roots journalism", have entered the journalism landscape, albeit constituting themselves mainly as subaltern, deprofessionalized, deinstitutionalized and radical counterhegemonic spaces (Allan, 2013; Atton, 2002; Gillmor, 2006; Moyo, 2014). Over time, these practices have crystalized around the term "citizen journalism", identified by the leading alternative and digital media scholars as:

(a) journalism that is often associated with narratives of the ordinary people;
(b) journalism that is often associated with crises, be it social, political or even environmental;
(c) journalism that is shaped by the history and society in which in obtains (Allan, 2013; Atton, 2002; Gillmor, 2006).

This chapter attempts to extend this characterization of citizen journalism by focusing on the ethical dimensions of the practice. Most academic work on citizen journalism has ignored this aspect, as focus has mainly been on its affordances in opening up journalism and creating a voice for the marginalized classes. However, some scholars and practitioners have focused on the subject of ethics, albeit indirectly, so criticism is mostly implied and rarely explicit. Most have tended to be critical of citizen journalism as a grossly irresponsible and dangerous practice in news production and dissemination

(Grant, 2007; Keen, 2007; Safran, 2005). Citizen journalism is perceived as "amateurish", "phony" and a "bad imitator" of mainstream journalism (Hogg, 2009). Most significantly, other critics have even contested the view that citizen journalism merits being referred to as journalism. They contend, "we are all citizens, but not all of us are journalists" (Safran, 2005, p. 3). A good and caring neighbour, they caution, is not a citizen social worker, just as someone who helps to dose flames in a neighbour's house gutted by fire does not walk away a proud citizen firefighter (Simon, 2009). Interesting as this may sound, it is clear that the debate on citizen journalism ethics has not only been about the norms and values of the profession, but also about ownership and control of the journalism profession (Singer and Ashman, 2009). The debate on ethics is also tied to a power struggle where ethics have been used to delimit the boundaries of who is accepted or rejected with regard to practising journalism. The "label journalist and who is entitled to use it is a prominent site of [power] contestation [in the debate]" (Campbell, 2014, p. 5). Missing in the debate is a positive constructivist critique of journalism's demotic turn, where citizen journalism ethics are seen as definitive of a new journalistic practice that, while at times converging with mainstream journalism, may actually constitute an entirely new philosophy of the practice.

This chapter breaks away from the negative critique by endeavouring to construct a moral and ethical characterization of citizen journalism on its own terms. It argues for an ontological critique of citizen journalism ethics where the practice is not always judged in relation to the moral taboos of mainstream journalism. It perceives most of the negative characterizations of citizen journalism ethics as not only misplaced, but also based on critics who hide the fact that their locus of enunciation is actually mainstream journalism itself. As the reader shall see in the section on citizen journalism criticism what is often presented as an objective ontological critique of citizen journalism ethics is actually subjective criticism that is informed by the interests, norms and values of mainstream journalism as, if you like, a brand that feels threatened at many levels. The chapter's main arguments on citizen journalism ethics are empirically grounded on the Zvakwana–Sokwanele case study from Zimbabwe. Ancillary cases from Africa from the so-called Arab Spring are also used to broaden the scope.

The online practices of Zvakwana–Sokwanele bloggers are seen through the prism of citizen journalism obtaining in restrictive, politically volatile and authoritarian media environments (Moyo, 2014). Critically reflecting on deontological and teleological moral frameworks, citizen journalism ethics in crisis settings are seen as emergent, nascent, fluid, liquid and sometimes contradictory, albeit generally underpinned by a humanist moral obligation that seeks to wrestle journalism from the publishing monopolies and recast it to serve public good, free speech, and a politics of life and not death in the country. In Zimbabwe's usually violent political crises, civic virtue often intersects with the citizens' conversational impulse to expose injustice as a moral obligation. In the age of pervasive new media technologies, this conversational impulse is what Ong (1982) has dubbed "secondary orality": evidenced by the ever nagging need to connect with community through social networks, sharing stories and images, and expanding locality to globality and vice versa. In crises, this has often been done through citizen media practices that can be perceived as ethically and aesthetically radical and subversive to the mainstream habits, but perhaps brutally honest to their own emerging value system and identity. Citizen journalism therefore confirms the advent of an era of personalized ethics characterized by ambivalence, personal responsibility, morality without an ethical code, and what I have referred to as the "higher-order ethics" of freedom, social justice, and human rights.

Citizen journalism is examined within the context of an electoral crisis in the presidential run-off campaign in 2008. Specifically, the focus is on Zvakwana–Sokwanele's Album of Terror: a graphic photojournalism streaming of the most gruesome murders and inhuman torture that characterized the run-off elections after the first election allegedly failed to produce a clear winner. Judging from what local and international election observers said, the run-off election was largely violent and brutal towards citizens. The Pan African Observer Mission (PAOM), a group that was made up of African members of parliament from various countries, reported, "the prevailing political environment throughout the country was tense, hostile and volatile" (PAOM, 2008, p. 54). It stated that there were "high levels of intimidation, hate speech, violence, war rhetoric, displacement of people, abductions, and loss of life and many abuses of other rights and freedoms" (Ibid., p. 34). These claims were corroborated by, among other African regional groupings, the Southern African Development Community Parliamentary Forum Observer Mission, which also noted that the conduct of the ruling party was not consistent with the principles of free and fair elections.

Zvakwana–Sokwanele: Citizen journalism as rhizomatic

Zimbabwe has many news blogs that are run by professional journalists, often based in the diaspora. However, blogging by ordinary citizens is not a very common exercise, mainly because of the digital divide, especially at the levels of access to smart technologies with higher capabilities for content production. In that context, Zvakwana–Sokwanele arguably represents one of Zimbabwe's most interesting case studies of how citizen journalism has developed in the country. Zvakwana–Sokwanele is a civic organization that uses cyber activism to highlight democracy and human rights issues in the country. It is an underground social movement that uses innovative guerrilla and multimedia strategies online and offline. Apart from its online media, it also uses graffiti, leaflets, CDs, videos and condoms inscribed with messages of resistance that aim to wake up the masses through conscientization. The Zvakwana–Sokwanele civil society context suggests that citizen journalism in Zimbabwe has developed largely within institutional settings of civic activism, where citizen media are used to either counter state media propaganda or create independent conversations and reading publics about the crisis. Again, the broader context of political activism may have a direct influence on how radical citizen journalism is in terms of not only form and content, but also the moral philosophy guiding its journalistic practices.

The fact that citizen journalism in Zimbabwe has developed within the institutionalized context of civil society also raises legitimate concerns around the participation of the real marginalized and poor people in urban and rural areas. This brings to the fore structural, ideological and moral issues that are not mutually exclusive to the debate on ethics. Following Atton (2002, p. 267), citizen involvement is foundational to the character of citizen journalism as a "practice that is embedded within the everyday lives of citizens" and "media content that is both driven and produced by those people". While civil society in Zimbabwe sometimes endeavours to be as inclusive as possible, it cannot escape the fact that many ordinary citizens are excluded structurally, as most civic organizations are located in urban areas and served by mostly middle-class members who are structurally isolated from the poor. This obviously carries the risk that the poor majority will continue to be talked for and about, never directly mediating their experiences themselves. This renders the concept of the citizen in citizen journalism somewhat contestable (see Campbell, 2014). However, this chapter perceives citizen journalism as rhizomatic, that is, an entanglement of variegated spatial news practices and discourses from citizens of different walks in life, such as social activists, development workers, journalist bloggers (j-bloggers), academics, students, housewives, the unemployed and the diasporans (see Bailey, Cammaerts and Carpentier, 2007). While, in its most ideal form, citizen journalism must directly involve the poor majority of citizens who are often ignored in elite media spaces, it can also be embedded on or even driven by people sitting in formal structures such as civil society and informal spaces such as social movements, or even traditional media itself. The metaphor of a rhizome helps to highlight the fact that citizen journalism cannot be singular, but a plural and diverse web of citizen news media production and dissemination strategies using smart technologies. It is a diffused expanse and web-like network of information sharing, with specific nodal points that converge and diverge at various levels of society. The rhizome must not be limited to structural convergences and divergences, but should be seen as extending to values and ethics, the moral philosophy that guides practices of citizen journalism's blogosphere. As this chapter will demonstrate, the Zvakwana–Sokwanele blogosphere is an ethical mixed bag, a mishmash and melange of utilitarian ethics, virtue ethics, humanist ethics and duty ethics.

The genre of citizen journalism that emanates from civil society can be seen as originating from a vantage point of citizens who may be combative having civic consciousness and the ability to speak truth to power with intellectual clarity and moral authority that is at once vernacular and globally entrenched. They also may have institutional resources to create strategic alternative online platforms that rhizomatically labyrinth their way to the masses, thus directly or indirectly giving a voice to the real marginalized citizens in the country. As I demonstrate in the section on emerging citizen journalism ethics, this appears to be the case with Zvakwana–Sokwanele. In the context of Zimbabwe's unending political crisis, the citizen journalism that is embedded in civil society's real and virtual spaces can also be said to enjoy relative autonomy from the state and the market, while also, as implied earlier in this chapter, appropriating the radicalness of political activism normally associated with civic activism. Hence, in crisis settings, citizen journalism is more amenable to civil society as "a sphere of public life beyond control of the state" (Colas, 2002, p. 25) and "a buffer zone strong enough to keep both state and market...from being too powerful and dominating" (Giddens, 2001, p. 15). In principle, civil society's vanguard role in democratization and human rights in Zimbabwe makes it ideal for citizen journalism, which speaks against the excesses of power while drawing its power from the participatory politics of activism in civic organizations.

Morally blind: Overview of citizen journalism criticism

Apocalyptic predictions of the death of the journalism profession have increased with the advent of new media such as the Internet and social media like Twitter and Facebook. The focus of the crisis critiques has been twofold: on the one hand, some scholars analyse the threat of the new media on traditional media economics and business models (Luengo, 2014; Pavlik, 2010; Picard, 2014) while, on the other hand, others have preoccupied themselves with the crisis in professional ethics and moral values (Keen, 2007; Siegel, 2008; Whitaker, 1999). Some of the scholars in the former group, to be fair, have provided some of most critically informed analysis, especially in the context of the developed or industrialized countries of the North. It is the latter group, which focuses on journalism ethics, that is less convincing. This is why van Der Haak, Parks and Castells (2012, p. 27) advise that there is a need to distinguish between the two perceived threats on journalism by new media technologies. The business threat must not be conflated with the journalism profession threat because these are different scenarios. In these authors' view, the new ecology of journalism that is occasioned by citizen news and informational practices "does not represent a crisis of journalism but rather an explosion of it [through the democratization and pluralization of spaces of practice]" (Ibid., p. 28). They argue that concerns about the impact of new technologies on the quality of journalism are somewhat misplaced, as they believe that "the current developments, may in fact, be paving the path toward better journalism and more independent journalists" (Ibid., p. 29). This section throws light on the concerns of the former group of scholars who raise moral panics around the end of journalism ethics. The point here is to quickly map the scope of the general criticism of citizen journalism before the discussion of the concerns through case studies.

1) In Africa, many cases are used to demonstrate moral reservations about citizen journalism. Take, for example, the case of Tunisian Mohamed Bouazizi, who set himself on fire in 2011 to protest alleged endless state persecution for illegally setting up a vegetable stall. This incident was recorded by a citizen journalist, and when it eventually went viral it sparked the revolution that would end Ben Ali's 23-year rule.

2) Closely interwoven with the above case is the recording by another citizen journalist of the callous murder of the Libyan leader, Colonel Muammar Gaddafi, by rebels the same year. Numerous other examples of citizen journalism's photo and video recordings of xenophobic attacks on foreigners in South Africa – grim and horrifying scenes of torture and death – exist.

In view of these cases and many others, the criticism of citizen journalism ethics has been wide and varied. Concerns have been raised about its capacity for respect of privacy, human dignity, grief and mourning, honesty and truth, public interest and so on. Writing from the perspective of Surveillance studies, Whitaker (1999) long envisaged the digital technologies, and by implication citizen journalism practices, as heralding the end of privacy. He argued that "capitalist enterprise ... has been and continues to be a primary site not only for the exercise of surveillance, but also a site for technological and organisational innovations in surveillance" (Whitaker, 1999, p. 40). New media technologies and their attendant practices are not "technologies of freedom" as argued by Morisett (2004), but rather "political technologies" of surveillance and control, "inducing in the subject a state of conscious and permanent visibility that assures the automatic function of power" (Ibid., p. 33). In many ways citizen journalism represents the outsourcing of surveillance from the state to the private individual, since one can be photographed or recorded anytime, anywhere, by someone, somewhere, somehow. The technologies of citizen journalism, like smartphones and the Internet, and digital platforms like blogs, Twitter and Facebook, make surveillance a seductive and participatory exercise where people even willingly provide personal data, information, and images of themselves, their families and their homes. The pervasiveness of these seductive technologies render individuals "visible to multiple gazes coming from many different directions looking for different things" (Whitaker, 1999, p. 140).

The long- established image of a citizen journalist is that of an amateur-ish accidental reporter whose personal naivety, technological obsession and desire for fame overrides respect for the integrity and privacy of others in a very dangerous and insidious way. These "non-professional journalists" (Grant, 2007, p. 44) are always ready to wield mobile cameras, blog, tweet or video stream at the slightest excuse to serve their own self-interest, outside of any tangible moral purpose. More recently, in Zimbabwe, the images of the fall of President Mugabe at the airport have been used as a good example of the moral bankruptcy of citizen journalism. The photographing of the falling of an elderly "statesman" is seen as being against the values of "ubuntu" (humanism) and really serving no public interest at all. In such instances, citizen journalists becomes an extension of the sadistic "paparazzi delight" that feeds off the pain and misfortunes of others. In a hard-hitting critique on how citizen journalism has destroyed "moral values, cultural standards, and [indeed the journalism profession]", Keen (2007, p. 3) argues that citizen journalism is:

> Corrupting and confusing popular opinion about everything from politics and commerce, to arts and culture. Blogs have become so dizzingly infinite that they have undermined our sense of what is true and what is false, what is real and what is imaginary. These days kids can't tell what the difference between credible news by objective professional journalists and what they read [from blogs].

Dismissing claims about the democratization of journalism, Keen portrays citizen journalism and new media technologies as morally decadent and as a neurosis that is eating into the core of the culture and moral fibre of modern society. The established tried and tested norms of traditional journalism are being violated in a case of "the blind leading the blind – infinite monkeys providing infinite information for infinite readers, perpetuating the culture of misinformation and ignorance" (Ibid., p. 7). In concurrence, Siegel (2008) also sees the Internet and social media as a source of rumours, lies and fabrication sanitized through buzzwords like "user-generated content" and "citizen journalism". The perceived threat to journalism ethics has even forced others to recommend that the "courts and legislature [must] create laws on who is a journalist" (Grant, 2007, p. 135). Clearly, from the view of the pessimists, citizen journalism is fundamentally a disruptive practice that is attacking the foundations of professional journalism and established traditional news cultures. Melissa Wall's new book, *Citizen Journalism: Valuable, Useless or Dangerous*, also, at least according to one review, commits the fallacy of perceiving citizen journalism as disruptive to the mainstream oligarchy. In the absence of a "journalistic background, editing, and quality control [citizen journalism] has often led to biased, inaccurate, low quality pieces" (Culbertson, 2012, p. 191). Granted, mistakes and oversights take place in citizen journalism just as they are abound in the mainstream, but perhaps that is not even what the debate must focus on. Allan (2013, p. 25) frames citizen journalism in crises as "citizen witnessing", a concept that is more helpful in the discussion of citizen journalism ethics. "What does it mean to bear witness in a moment of crisis?", he asks, in ways that invite reflections on the question of what motivates citizen journalists to do what they do and whether, if at all, they even perceive themselves as journalists in the manner the so-called professional journalists do? It's important to notice that, as van Der Haak, Parks and Castells (2012, p. 29) advise, citizen journalism "tools and practices [may] offer possibilities of the new identity of the journalist". With a new identity must come a rethink of ethics which acknowledges the new sociological realities of networked practices that sometimes converge and diverge with established mainstream norms in ways that still remain crucially relevant to the main public functions of journalism, which are to inform and educate.

Ethics as normative theory

A panoramic overview of theories of ethics is necessary at this point to lay the foundation for the final analysis and discussion of citizen journalism ethics in the Zimbabwean and other African contexts, such as those alluded to in the previous section, "Morally blind: Overview of citizen journalism criticism". The objective is mainly to draw a picture of the existing moral frameworks before discussing the case studies that are specific to this chapter. The subject of ethics or moral values is a very old one. According to Sanders (2003), in the Western genealogy, key figures identified with ethics include Socrates (*c*.470–399 BC), Plato (427–347 BC), Aristotle (384–322 BC), Kant (1724–1804), Mill (1806–1873) and others such as Hobbes, Bentham and Nietzsche. While these figures have influenced wide conceptions of ethical conduct, it is important that the reader realize that there are other schools of thought on ethics, such as African ethics (Afriethics), which emphasize ubuntu (humanism), that can also be easily applied to the practice of journalism.

The most important traditional approaches to ethics comprise, among others, deontological ethics (Kant), teleological ethics (Mill) and virtue ethics (Aristotle). I do not intend to discuss each of these at length, suffice to say that an in-depth analysis of these would show that, at one stage, they intersect and interlock in a way that makes their separation artificial.

Deontological ethics are duty-based ethics. Human agents, for example, must always pay fidelity to the duty or obligation of telling truth, defending justice, exposing evil and so on. Obligation must always take precedent over all other considerations, including one's personal happiness and pleasures, and even that of society. Consequences, good or bad, beautiful or ugly, are immaterial in this approach, as what matters is what Kant referred to as the "categorical imperative", that is, the ability to identify what is good and do it for its own sake as a duty. Kant (1785/2008, p. 35) argued: "an action done from duty derives its moral worth not from the purpose which is to be attained by it, but from the maxim by which it is determined". In line with this, utilitarian concerns of self-interest and community happiness are not central in deciding what must be done. Transcendental considerations such as God are not important here either, as the principle of duty is the principal fundamental based on human reason based on free will: "obligation is the necessity of a free action when viewed in relation to a categorical imperative of reason" (Ibid., p. 45). Duty is morally binding in and by itself.

It is easy to think Kant advocated for a pragmatist ethics, a Machiavellian approach where the end determines the means. On the contrary, humanism was central to his theory, as duty was always understood in the context of humanity not outside it. For instance, in the *Groundwork of Metaphysic of Morals*, Kant (1785/2008, p. 760) also states that: "Act in such a way that you treat humanity, whether in your own person or in the person of any other, never merely as a means to an end but always at the same time as an end." Loosely interpreted, Kant here seems to allude to religious deontology's golden rule of doing unto others as you would have them do unto you. Other scholars, such as Ross (1930), developed the moral philosophy of deontology by arguing that there are always multiple duties for every person and the primary duty of, for example, any journalist is to strike a balance between the duties. The principal duty for everyone is to do no harm, even as they pursue the duty to do good. In essence, not all duties are equal in status, as some are prima facie duties (such as telling the truth) while others are circumstantial or duty proper, such as lying to save an innocent friend from murder by evil people in a war. In essence, duty or obligation in this perspective is an area of contestation or relativity subject to context and the situations facing human beings as moral agents.

The second category of ethics is called teleological ethics. John Stuart Mill, a British scholar, is one of the most well-known exponents of this theory. Teleological ethics are consequentialist in orientation, emphasizing the results or outcomes of anything we do in life. Ward (2015, p. 34) asserts that teleological "ethics is primarily about the aims or telos of actions: the 'goods' to be pursued, including the impact of actions on individuals or groups". Here, what brings happiness and pleasure to the majority of people is what matters, and action is judged to be right if its consequences are, for example, in the public interest. Unlike in deontic ethics, one's duty, obligation or rights are subordinated to, and determined by, that which maximizes the collective good. Utilitarianism is, arguably, one of the best examples of teleological ethics as it posits that it is the results of our actions that matter, not just the action itself. Act utilitarianism focuses on human action in specific circumstances where one has to intuitively decide what one must do where there are no known guidelines. Act utilitarianism is closer to what may be called situational ethics, where the truth may not always be seen as sacrosanct or ultimate. Rule utilitarianism is about cases where there may already be some established rules that may help us decide what to do in a situation. Here, there would be grounds to reasonably expect any rational person to have acted in a particular way for the collective good. For example, disclosing that you have been to a country affected by Ebola may have you detained at the airport clinics, but may serve the collective good by ultimately saving many lives.

Virtue ethics have mostly been associated with Aristotle through his popular work *Nicomachean Ethics*, where his emphasis is human character. Aristotle believed that evaluative judgements or moral pronouncements needed to focus on the individual as the source of action. The act itself or its outcome is inconsequential: what matters is character, which is underpinned by virtue. In *Nicomachean Ethics* Aristotle discusses many virtues that are foundational to good character, such as courage, temperance, truthfulness, liberality, magnificence and magnanimity. Take courage, for example, as the "capacity to confront fear in the face of pain, danger, uncertainty, or intimidation" (Aristotle, 1893/2002, p. 62). The virtue of "courage ensures firmness in difficulties and consistency in the pursuit of the good" (Ibid., p. 74). Aristotle divided courage into physical and moral. While "physical courage is courage in the face of physical pain, hardship, or threat of death, moral courage is the ability to act rightly in the face of popular opposition, shame, scandal, or discouragement" (Ibid., p. 89). The list of Aristotelian virtues suggests that good character is the basis for good actions and good outcomes in society. However, he could be criticized for overlooking the dialectical relationship of the three factors of character, action and outcome. It may indeed be a fallacy to assume that good outcomes are always a result of virtue, since the relationship between virtue and vice is fluid if not altogether problematic.

Work in progress: Emerging citizen journalism ethics

This section analyses citizen journalism practices from the Zvakwana–Sokwanele blog during the Zimbabwean electoral crisis mentioned in the 'Introduction' to this chapter. The aim is not to cut and paste the deontological, teleological and virtue ethics onto citizen journalism practices in the crisis, but rather to problematize the entire discourse of ethics in relation to citizen journalism practices, especially in unstable authoritarian political environments such as that in Zimbabwe. In order to do that critically, three questions on citizen journalism are inescapable:

(1) Do the deontological, teleological and virtue ethics as outlined apply to citizen journalism? Should they apply, how and to what extent?

(2) Has the practice of citizen journalism evolved and crystallized so as to have its own ethics or even be judged on the moral values of mainstream journalism?

(3) Are digital media technologies deprofessionalizing journalism and democratizing it into just a social activity or social practice in which journalism ethics, as we know them, are no longer of any critical relevance?

Put differently, is citizen journalism breaking mainstream journalism taboo lines or simply inventing a new philosophy and practice of journalism? I have already hinted that the new tools and new practices by citizen journalists may imply the need for new values of moral judgement, a radical departure that takes cognizance of the new social and technological realities out there. In *Ethics of Emerging Media*, German (2011, p. 256) advises that the "current models of professional responsibility build on journalistic and legal strictures do not address the [new] conditions of [digital citizen] communication" and that "we need to explore the ethical practices of new media users like citizen journalists amid the sociological changes induced by new media". In other words, a new sociological hermeneutics that problematizes the nexus between technology, society and ethics can help us to unlock some of the fundamental questions facing the transformations in journalism practice today.

One of the ways to do that is through the analysis of the user-generated content (UGC) produced by citizen journalists online, and the kinds of social relations such content is producing, including its intended and unintended effects on people. As Bauman (1993, p. 17) authoritatively argues, ethics are not only about following morally sanctioned codes and duties, but also principally about our responsibility to others because "what we and other people do may have profound, far reaching, and long-lasting consequences which we can neither see directly nor predict with precision". He continues to discuss the side effects of our actions, equally applicable to citizen journalism, that may result in "unanticipated consequences which may smother whatever good purposes [were] intentioned and bring about disasters and suffering neither we nor anybody ... contemplated" (Ibid., p. 19). Bauman's observation straddles the arena of the intersection between ethics and rights, where we expect ethics, as institutionally agreed and voluntary moral principles or codes of conduct, to serve in balancing the competing rights of citizens. This observation lays a perfect foundation for the analysis of the ethical and moral conundrums faced by citizen journalists who witnessed some of the worst atrocities from the electoral violence in Zimbabwe. Examples 1 and 2 are descriptions of the Zvakwana–Sokwanele Album of Terror available on Flickr.com, on which this discussion will be partially based:

Example 1: The Album of Terror (Online: https://www.flickr.com/ photos/sokwanele/sets/72157600853440301

The album is a visual narrative of the gruesome experiences of pain, torture and death of some Zimbabwean citizens in the electoral crisis of 2008. According to the album, most of these human rights abuses were allegedly perpetrated by the state and government militia. Pictures on the violence at Friedewal farm show a man and a woman with deep cuts on forehead and head respectively. Blood gushes out onto their clothes, which are already dripping with blood. Part of the Friedewal picture stream shows a grim trail of destruction of farm workers' houses and huts by the state and its militia.

Example 2: The Album of Terror (Online: https://www.flickr.com/ photos/sokwanele/sets/72157600853440301

Pictures of Wilson Jori, 65, who was allegedly beaten at Chimkoko militia base. The pictures show the horror the old man went through. He has a deep cut on both his buttocks that are horrific and unsightly. Next to this are pictures of Gift Mutsungunu whose rear is also badly damaged. It is not clear whether this is from burns or beatings. Below that picture is a photo of a 70-year-old woman lying in a hospital bed, allegedly dying from the burns. The fire has consumed her back and legs. The rest of the album tells of untold suffering that the people went through. Some lie dead as charred corpses while survivors have bodily injuries beyond description.

The Album of Terror has over 120 pictures, mostly depicting the violence meted out on ordinary people, farmers and opposition leaders in the electoral crisis of 2008. It seems to be an open platform where any blogger that witnessed the suffering of the people could upload pictures, but with some authorization from Zvakwana–Sokwanele. However, Zvakwana–Sokwanele bloggers appear to be the main citizen journalists, providing most of the content. The album has been viewed by over 50,000 people so far. Looking at the Album of Terror, there are obviously moral and ethical issues about the way the blog splashes the pictures of torture, mutilated and charred bodies, death and grief online. One is tempted to ask if the right to free speech weighs too much in favour of the social movement at the expense of the privacy and dignity of the victims and survivors? What about the rights of the children, especially the bereaved ones, to protection against traumatic content from the blog? There is no warning or even age restriction against viewing what many may regard as morally offensive and disturbing content.

The Album of Terror resonates well with other cases of citizen journalism highlighted earlier in this chapter: the Mohamed Bouazizi case (Tunisia), Muammar Gaddafi (Libya) and xenophobia killings (South Africa). Could these incidents of citizen journalism be confirmative of claims by some postmodernists that modern information and network societies "represent a post-deontic epoch where our conduct has been freed from the last vestiges of [modernity's] infinite duties and absolute obligations?" (Lipovesky, 1992, 31). This line of argument would, therefore, have us believe that citizen journalists owe no one, not even children, any moral responsibility or obligation. This categorical rejection of the value of ethics to social practices like citizen journalism would obviously take modern society back to the dark ages – a dialectic of enlightenment of sorts. I think the critical agenda for Media Studies then must be to examine the transformations in journalism ethics in ways that explain their reconfiguration, transformation and reformulation in the age of new media technologies and platforms. Below are two more examples from Zvakwana–Sokwanele bloggers that suggest that deontological, teleological and even virtue ethics have a place in citizen journalism, albeit perhaps, as I shall demonstrate in the section "No end of ethics: Citizen journalism as liquid journalism" with profound changes on the need for their institutionalization and enforcement due to the deprofessionalization and democratization of journalism by the new smart technologies.

Example 1: The Human Stain, 29 June 2008

In an attempt to cow and intimidate people into voting, Zimbabwe's state security agents yesterday launched Operation Red Finger to identify if people had voted by checking if they had indelible ink stains on their finger. Those who had not voted are being beaten and forced to vote.

Example 2: Farm attacks taking place in Chegutu today, 30 June 2008

Update from this morning: Mike, Angela and Ben were dumped in Kadoma at around 01h30 this morning. This update was from last night – a forwarded email. Police at Chegutu have now provided six armed personnel after receiving instructions from PROPOL...

Both the Album of Terror and the last two examples demonstrate an undeniable moral impulse from Zvakwana–Sokwanele citizen journalists. It is self-evident that the pictures expose serious violations of human rights, allegedly by the state, and that the stories serve a moral purpose: not only to expose injustice, but also to inform and educate other citizens who may be equally vulnerable. These acts can be viewed as obligatory, virtuous and with potentially good consequences in terms of serving the higher ideal of social justice. As Pojman (1993, p. 59) rightly observes: "there is something inherently right or good about such acts as truth telling [against power]" and that "it is important to develop a virtuous character, for if, only if we have good people can we ensure habitual right action". Beyond the everyday personal characters of the bloggers, there is civic virtue, as citizen journalists dutifully act as responsible citizens, expressing relations of "deep horizontal comradeship" (Anderson, 1983, p. 144) with fellow citizens and netizens. One Zvakwana–Sokwanele citizen journalist blogger alerted fellow citizens of the ruling party reprisals before the run-off election: "Zanu PF thugs torturing people in re-education meeting where... 6 men died because of their injuries" (Sokwanele, 19 May 2008). Another wrote "...the MDC national youth chairman is battling for his life in intensive care unit after armed Zanu PF militia attacked him yesterday" (Sokwanele, 28 June 2008). The intertextuality between the Album of Terror and these news reports is further evidence of the virtues of citizen journalists. Virtue ethics are amenable to citizen journalism because "it goes beyond rules to connect with people's character and habits... [and] humility" (Craig, 2015, p. 15). Character is seen as seminal to the newer digital journalism practices like that of Zvakwana–Sokwanele. Sanders (2003, p. 31), however, cautions that: "To every virtue corresponds two vices: one of excess and one of deficiency." In many ways, this summarizes the debate on the moral dilemmas that are countenanced by citizen journalists, especially in relation to sensitive stories and photographs in politically unstable societies. Sometimes these can be perceived as insensitive and sensationalistic and likely to escalate conflicts into war or even cause genocide. How much truth and how much graphic visual details can citizen journalists show online before crossing the ethical lines of duty, virtue and care? As a spatial practice within a conservative society like Zimbabwe, how far can citizen journalists go before they are labelled as culturally insensitive and morally blind? Indeed, Allan (2013, p. 55) observes that there is a tendency by advocates of citizen journalism "to reveal an array of virtues" about the practice while "conceal[ing] a multitude of sins in the eyes of the critics".

Three critical points are important to understand the radical ethics in the Album of Terror, and indeed the other African case studies, with regard to graphic content. First, as an underground movement, Zvakwana–Sokwanele is an activist and radically oriented entity that is more likely than traditional media to produce radicalized citizen journalism practices that push the moral, cultural and ethical boundaries. Downing believes that social movements as networks are the most conducive for radical media, as news and information are always tied to some form of praxis or social action seeking social change (Downing *et al.*, 2001, p. 34). It can be argued that Zvakwana–Sokwanele represents a radicalized civic context where the role of citizen journalists as witnesses to violence and death blends and blurs with political activism in ways that recast it as a new form of journalism that at once informs, educates, conscientizes, networks and also mobilizes citizens to some form of praxis driven by networked politics and cyber activism. Indeed, Van De Donk and colleagues (2004, p. 34) envisages the many spatial citizen news production and dissemination practices that are executed through new media in social movements as amounting to "newer levels in the way [social movements] mobilise, build coalitions, inform, lobby, communicate, and campaign".

Second, a political crisis like that of Zimbabwe always produces media that are radical in form, content and even ethics. This radicalness is often prefigured through presentation, broad participation, epistemic attitude and, most notably, in the change of news cultures and practices from those that privilege elite voices to those in favour of the poor and marginalized, and social movements (Atton, 2002). As such, the kind of citizen journalism that is born out of such a crisis politics cannot be expected to embrace loyal citizenship as its identity, but is acutely rebellious and counterhegemonic, almost, as Atton observes, of all alternative media, in the Foucauldian fashion of "the insurrection of subjugated knowledges" (Foucault, 1980, p. 81). The polarized and radicalized political environment in Zimbabwe has produced a radicalized kind of citizen journalism that pushes ethical restrictions in pursuit of its humanistic goal. If mainstream journalism represents a disciplined profession in terms of its elitist moral and ideological alignment, then citizen journalism can be said to represent that which is still undisciplined ideologically and ethically, as seen through its counterhegemonic attitude. In the context of an absence of supportive public media and a censored private media, citizen journalists in Zvakwana–Sokwanele push the moral boundaries of conventional journalism. For example, the end determines the means in the defence of human rights that ethically can be characterized as a "perfect duty that must be done unconditionally" (Kamm, 2000, p. 205). As consequentialists would say: "We may harm to aid" (Ibid., p. 205). As such, if read in context, the Album of Terror streams a semiotics of death, grief and somatic disfigurement so as to create a better Zimbabwean society whose body politics is underpinned by a politics of life and not death. The Album resembles the Nyamata Genocide Museum in Rwanda, where a dense forest of human skulls tell a story that must and had to be told despite the strictness of African traditions on death and burial. Just as those who walk the corridors of the museum hardly imagine it to be a tourist attraction in the sense of the Great Wall of China, the Album of Terror also represents a higher ideal that not only demonstrates citizen journalism's power, but also shows how that power has been executed with moral responsibility as a categorical imperative.

Last but not least is the issue of liquid modernity and its concomitant liquid journalism and liquid ethics (see Bauman, 2000; Dueze, 2008). Bauman's theory of liquid modernity is an "attempt to explain the current state of modern society, its changes and position in the history of modernity" (Priban, 2013, p. 1). Briefly, modernity is perceived as characterized by very fast changes captured through the metaphors of liquidity, fluidity, temporality and uncertainty affecting identities, professions, morality and ethics. Here things change at lightning speed, are unstable, and uncertainty and risk are part of social life. In the following section, "No end of ethics: Citizen journalism as liquid journalism", I use Bauman's theory of liquid modernity to critically engage with the changes that it has occasioned, especially to the journalism profession. Framing citizen journalism as liquid journalism, I shall return to answer in depth the question asked earlier in the section "Emerging citizen journalism ethics": Has the practice of citizen journalism evolved and crystallized so as to have its own ethics, and have digital media technologies democratized journalism into a social activity or social practice (i.e. citizen journalism) in which professional ethics as we know them are no longer of any major relevance? The next section, "No end of ethics", is therefore very important because it seeks to characterize the profound social and technological changes underlying citizen journalism as a new form of practice. It acknowledges these huge changes as central in driving citizen journalism ethics, but rejects the apocalyptic claims of the demise of journalism ethics and death of the profession in its civic and democratic sense.

No end of ethics: Citizen journalism as liquid journalism

In earlier work, I have argued that citizen journalism is evidence of a postmodern turn in journalism (Moyo, 2011). This turn is characterized by a number of factors, chief among them the rejection of the old models of mainstream journalism practice based on the illusions of truth, objectivity, balance and accuracy. Postmodernity essentially represents an assault on modernity's illusions on many things, including the hypocrisy behind the façade of an ethical and moral society as seen through pervasive Judeo-Christian values. As the reader knows only too well, postmodernism rejects modernity's illusory and superfluous claims on being, identity, morality and so on. Hence, Bauman (1993, p. 32) has described postmodernity as "modernity without its illusions", or put differently, "modernity is postmodernity refusing to accept its own truth" (Ibid., p. 32). This section of the chapter argues that citizen journalism represents a radical rejection of the mainstream's codes of practice. We are, even by the sluggish pace of

Africa, entering interesting times with regard to the journalism of personalized ethics, morality without ethical codes, and moral ambivalence and ambiguity around what is right or wrong. The dividing line between wrong and right is increasingly blurred and "responsibilities such as seeking the truth and minimising harm...are sometimes in tension with each other" (Craig, 2015, p. 15).

However, this does not represent an end of ethics in the sense of total collapse, but a transformation to higher-order ethics, such as liberation, justice and pluralism, that are yet to crystallize to something very futuristic and not yet fathomable in everyday practice. This is how Caputo (2000, p. 112) puts it:

> The end of ethics does not mean all hell has broken loose. [It] does not mean anything goes which now can be taken as official...The end of ethics means instead that the business as usual of ethics has given out the ethical verities that we all like to think are true, the beliefs and practices we cherish, are now seen to be a more difficult spot than we liked to think...The discourse on the end of ethics means setting off the ends, limits, and boundaries of ethics. It means to insist on their provisionalness and temporality, the inaccessibility of the singular to ethical universals.

The technologically induced changes underlie most of these transformations in ethics, but most notable is the role played by liquid modernity. As such, Bauman's theory of liquid modernity is strategic in illuminating what exactly might be happening in relation to the transformations of ethics in journalism. I use it partly to add flesh to a concept of liquid journalism, a concept on which Dueze (2008) has already done some groundwork. The theory of liquid modernity does not really raise something radically new as most of its tenets are adjunctive to claims that were made in postmodernization, or what others are now referring to as "second modernity", "late modernity" or "reflexive modernity" (Priban, 2013, p. 6). Bauman (2005, p. 1) described liquid modernity as "a society in which the conditions under which its members act change faster than it takes the ways of acting to consolidate into habits and routines". It's a condition of most contemporary society "where uncertainty, flux, change, conflict, and revolution are the permanent conditions of everyday life" (Dueze, 2008, p. 851) because "all that is solid [is] melting into air" (Bauman, 2000, p. 7), due to, in part, "the diminishing role of spatial dimensions of social life" (Priban, 2013, p. 6).

The relationship between time and space is increasingly confusing because of the new communication technologies leading to a reconfiguration of many things, among them culture, identity, morality and ethics. Things are constantly in the state of becoming and flux. There is no stable social or moral order. In the "space-time duality it is [increasingly] time that is associated with change, flexibility, mobility and the overall lightness of the liquid society" (Priban, 2013, p. 3). New media make communication in space instantaneous and, in the process, disrupt and unsettle, through the processes of distanciation, deterritorialization and decentring, old habits, spaces and practices representing our zones of comfort, such as "our culture", "our identities", "our professions", "our ethics" and so on. Therefore, liquid modernity can also be seen as a critique of the social and moral crisis characterizing modern networked societies, which has been portrayed by some scholars as "post-human", "moral enclosure" and "an end of ethics" (Caputo, 2000; Fukuyama, 2003). It is a theory that, at the same time, provides a window of opportunity to at least explain contemporality in journalism, if not even suggest solutions to the crisis. There are further characterizations of liquid modernity, but, for purposes of time, these will be more usefully dealt with in the discussion of citizen journalism ethics that follows below.

In liquid modernity, sociality is increasingly a network not a structure (Bauman, 2000). Digital networks created through various citizen practices such as citizen journalism are ideal with regard to fluidity and liquidity, where witness accounts, news and information flow unfettered by the constraints of time, space and power. In its mundane and rhizomatic form, citizen journalism is arguably a product of those networks where professional journalists, non-professional journalists, accidental journalists, academicians and activists now partake in what was previously a ritual for the chosen few: to break news and tell stories often as they happen. While I do not agree that liquid modernity is necessarily substituting ethics with aesthetics in journalism, I believe that there is a change of journalism from a profession to a social activity, as seen through the rise of open participatory platforms for citizens such as the Zvakwana–Sokwanele blogosphere. Add to this the micro-blogging sites such as Twitter, Facebook, YouTube and others, and it can be seen that citizen journalism, as a new practice, represents a radical change in communicative democracy and its ethics. This multifarious and diverse practice is not synonymous with what others see as too many cooks spoiling the broth, but, on the contrary, represents the rise of personalized ethics due to the deinstitutionalization and deprofessionalization of journalism leading to the rise of non-institutionalized ethics. Whereas conventional journalism has articulated itself through institutional frameworks such as media, publishers and advertisers ideal for an ethos of institutionalized ethics, citizen journalism is predicated on the ethics of personal responsibility described by Bauman (1993, pp. 33–35) as: "morality's last hold and hope" against "socially sanctioned [ethical] demands" that are "merely functional and procedural" and "untrustworthy, morally doubtful" often "traceable to the interests of power". In this vein, the Album of Terror does not demonstrate the end of ethics in journalism, but rather a rebellion against a moral crisis in Zimbabwe which goes far beyond journalism, although is largely reflected through it. At the societal level, it's a crisis epitomized by the betrayal of the ideals of national liberation as a foundation for social justice, equality and the respect for human rights. It is always the case that, in all societies in crisis, "the moral crisis rebounds in an ethical one" (Ibid., p. 21). What we are witnessing through the Album of Terror as a visual form of citizen journalism is a repudiation of rule utilitarianism by Zvakwana–Sokwanele bloggers, who reject the belief that "an act is permissible if and only if, it is allowed by a code" (Frey, 2000, p. 165). The fact that showing excessively graphic content probably violates the Zimbabwe Union of Journalists Code of Ethics is immaterial to the bloggers, who might believe their acts enjoy a superior moral ideal. However, because citizen journalism as networked personal reporting is generally open and participatory, this makes its moral philosophy exist in a continuously liquid, fluid, ambivalent, dynamic and unpredictable state. The new realities of (citizen) journalism are those of multiple authorship (e.g. Wikinews), crowdsourcing and data mining, thus making previously codified ethics difficult or impossible to administer.

One of the characteristics of citizen journalism practices in all modern societies is the rise of morality without an ethical code (see Bauman, 1993; Bauman and Donskis, 2013; Priban, 2013). The new media technologies have repopulated the agora with so many online civic practices that it is difficult to regulate these through ethical codes and regulations sanctioned from above by professional bodies or the state itself. In fact, the speed and fluidity of things means that the traditional sources of moral authority often find themselves at a loss as what to do, or completely caught unawares, or simply lagging behind the juggernaut of translocal and global networks of citizen practices that have decentred and deterritorialized the newsroom. A good example is President Robert Mugabe falling at the airport in early 2015. While the state agents and the police forced all journalists to delete the pictures at the scene, citizen journalists had already circulated the pictures instantaneously, and in just hours the story of the big fall was headline news in most news media around the world. Outside Africa, another embarrassing incident of citizen witnessing was when the Iraqi government presented the hanging of Saddam Hussein as dignified and respectful. However, an unofficial version of the execution by citizen journalists showed that he had actually been treated in the most primitive and barbaric way, thus drawing a global outcry about not only this, but immorality of capital punishment in general. Both these examples are a typical example of liquid modernity, where things are "light", "liquid", "movable", "instantaneous" and "speedy", and journalism itself is "user-generated", "liquid", "fluid", "unfiltered", "pure" and individualized, possibly representing the practices that are closest to the ontology of news in contrast to the routinized standardized news from the mainstream media (Pavlik, 2010; Schudson, 2011). A good example of this strong sense of immediacy and speed in transmitting first-hand accounts of events through citizen journalism is that by a Zvakwana–Sokwanele blogger (30 April 2008):

This is taking place right now. Please can you all call the press in your area and pass the information onto them. We believe that the family are in real danger. Include the message to the press to contact SWRadio Africa for more information. Their website has contact details. Wayne Munroe, a farmer in Nymandlovhu (just outside Bulawayo in Matabeleland North, Zimbabwe), has been under siege since early this morning. His property has been encircled by in excess of 100 "war veterans". He phoned the police in Nymandlovhu to inform them of the problem and was on the phone to them when 4 "war veterans" entered his office. He immediately told the member in charge that they were there and that a 303 gun was being pointed at his chest. He was forced to hang up.

This quotation demonstrates certain important qualities about citizen journalism that are relevant to questions of morality and ethics. As a performance of public citizenship, citizen journalism encompasses the virtues of courage and responsibility by providing real-time descriptions of violence and conflict, often at great risk to citizen journalists' lives. Allan (2013, p. 16) has a very helpful moral and utilitarian characterization of citizen journalism as a practice that seeks "to bear witness in a moment of crisis". To him, citizen journalism must be understood as a type of "first person reportage in which ordinary citizens temporarily adopt the role of a journalist in order to participate in news making, often spontaneously during a time of crisis". Thus, as seen in the Zvakwana–Sokwanele quote, citizen journalists can be seen as role players who are driven by a moral impulse to do something good, a goodness that may far transcend the ethical codes that are often seen as rigid, solid, heavy and inimical to the pluralism and diversity of practice. For example, the story about the Nymandlovhu farmer may not strike anyone as objective and impartial reporting and need not be, but it is likely to save the life of the farmer, who is allegedly besieged by hundreds of war veterans. Bauman (1993) argues that we should understand humans as inherently moral beings. It's not the rules or codes of ethics that make good people, but what Kant (1785/2008, p. 67) referred to as "the mystery of morality inside me". Therefore, observes Bauman (1993, p. 32), "it is the personal morality that makes ethical negotiation and consensus, not the other way round". By implication, as a moral framework to witnessing, citizen journalists probably see themselves as human beings and/or citizens first, before being (if at all) journalists. Elsewhere, Bauman (2013) seems to argue that we live in modern societies, which are obsessed with the codification of ethics, resulting in the overemphasis on rules at the expense of the moral responsibility we owe each other as human beings and citizens. In authoritarian environments such as Zimbabwe, rules and ethical codes are often prescribed by power as a strategy to contain the news media rather than to empower journalists as moral agents. This ethical quandary creates moral uncertainty where even "in … situations in which the choice of what to do is ours alone, we [still] look in vain for the firm and trusty rule which will reassure us that we have followed them and that we could be right" (Ibid., p. 20). The Zvakwana–Sokwanele Wayne Munroe case shows citizen journalists' moral decisiveness to "strive to engage in a form of eye-witness reportage … to record and share … personal experience of what is happening in front of them" (Allan, 2013, p. 17). Allan shows that eyewitnessing ethically and practically, "is a formidable challenge [that is] fraught with difficulties", but that the benefits include "the authority of presence, a situational imbrication of here and now [that is] a precarious achievement" (Ibid., 2013, p. 19). In crisis situations, the motivation for citizen journalists is not to be professional journalists or even compete with them, but to share and connect in a society that is fragmented, brutal and immoral. Yet as Bauman (1993, p. 16) says, moral and ethical behaviour is about the simple fact that "we live and act in the company of other human beings … whose life and actions depend on what we do, what we can do, and what we ought to do". From the Zvakwana–Sokwanele blog, it's clear that bloggers keep the public informed about many things, but, most critically, the violence and murder affecting the public in the election.

Last but not least, citizen journalism represents the disappearance of a single narrative in the public sphere that is epitomized by discourses from public and private publishing monopolies which always privilege elitist frames of reference. Liquid modernity, as evidenced by citizen journalism practices, celebrates higher-order ethics of "the emancipatory effect of pluralism" (Bauman, 1993, p. 23). It rejects the homogenizing tendencies of mainstream media by exposing the dangers of a single narrative and that of one storyteller – the so-called professional journalist. The practice is fluid and flexible, occurring in multidirectional, convergent and divergent multimodal flows that promote lateral engagement among citizens and vertical flows between citizens and power. However, it is also counterhegemonic, where higher-order ethics of liberation and freedom constitute its epistemic foundations as well as its chief concerns. Citizen journalism therefore takes morality back to the individual and deregulates ordinary people's conduct in ways that are not only empowering to the individual, but also broaden their freedom choice and expression as citizens. In the process, journalism ethics, as sanctioned by the external mainstream tradition, is simultaneously modified, adapted, adopted or completely rejected. Citizen journalism therefore "lets morality out of the stiff armour of artificially constructed codes, [thus] repersonalis[ing] it" (Bauman, 1993, p. 34). The move can also be seen as a movement from institutional ethics to personal morality, and a hybridized aesthetics that expresses not only the freedom of the new journalist and the new practice of citizen journalism, but also the subversion of the old myths that defined journalism. For example, the Album of Terror epitomizes this creativity, showing how photojournalism or visual journalism can be used to tell a story in ways that are dramatic to the viewer and undeniable to the perpetrators of violations.

What is clear from the Zvakwana–Sokwanele stories is not only the concern over human rights abuses, but also the mundanely written and stylized news narratives that fall within the idiom of everyday speech. The "deprofessionalized" nature of the news is one of the primary characteristics of citizen journalism, also dubbed by van der Haak, Parks and Castells (2012, p. 25) as "point of view journalism" because of the mixing of fact, opinion and advocacy in the story. In most cases, Zvakwana–Sokwanele bloggers use no sources, no bylines, and have no pretentions towards objectivity and balance. Although they perform an important role – informing and educating the public about the crisis – they do not, however, perceive themselves as objective and disinterested mediators, because they tell stories about everyday life of which they are part. For example, extrapolations from the blogs depict the journalists as citizens who are equally frustrated by the alleged rigging of the run-off election by Mugabe. For example, in the story titled "The results of a sham election", one blogger states that:

> On March 29th 2008, Robert Mugabe polled total votes of 1,079,730. Somehow, despite mass intimidation, gross violence, increasing poverty, murders, and hyper-inflation, Robert Mugabe's popularity accelerated faster than our inflation figures (which is quite something) and he managed to secure himself an extra 1,070,539 votes on 27 June 2008. He has effectively doubled his vote.
>
> (Zvakwana-Sokwanele, 29 June 2008)

This hybridization of opinion and facts, a mishmash of conventional journalism and advocacy journalism does not amount to a nihilist ethical ethos, but rather a new kind of journalism that does not operate within an illusion of freedom from society. The storytelling of such journalists is based on a realistic acceptance of the fact that they are situated interpreters of reality in terms of class, gender, race, ethnicity and worldview. In that sense, citizen journalism, as opposed to mainstream journalism, is reflexive and conscious of its ideological baggage. To a certain extent, the advent of citizen journalism also means that the epistemes of mainstream journalism are being challenged and an alternative liquid form of journalism is emerging as networked, individualized, autonomous, self-referential, participatory, convergent and morally ambivalent (Dueze, 2008). While traditional mainstream journalism is predicated on the epistemologies of empiricism, realism and objectivism as philosophies that see the truth and reality as largely ontological and something to be observed and gathered in space, citizen journalism is moving away from these epistemes and embracing a hermeneutic, constructivist, liquid and postmodern approach to journalism where the notion of objective truth or objective reality is contestable and a universal, totalizing journalism ethical code is rejected.

Conclusion: back to the future

This chapter sought to discuss citizen journalism ethics using the Zvakwana–Sokwanele blogs in Zimbabwe. It argued that citizen journalism does not herald the end of ethics, but transformations that are associated with liquid modernity and networked journalism. The new ecology of ethics is that which is largely underpinned by digital networks, flows, fluidity, flux, uncertainty, ambivalence, anxiety, impulse and everyday moral contractions. The Album of Terror and other sampled stories demonstrated that these characteristics resonate with the condition of citizen journalism, as its moral philosophy is fluid, ambivalent and unpredictable. Liquidity also means that citizen journalism ethics are constantly in "a state of becoming", thus making traditional sources of moral authority in journalism irrelevant as they are often overtaken by this dynamic practice. As a result, most contemporary societies in the developed and developing world are witnessing the rise of an ethos of morality without an ethical code in journalism, where ethics are highly individualized, subjective, intrinsic and based on personal impulse than rigid rules. As with the crisis of modernity in other spheres of life, such as the rejection of a universal Cartesian subject, the notion of a universal journalism that is applicable everywhere and at all times is also beginning to crumble. From it is developing the notion of journalism as a multiversal and pluriversal social activity that captures a range of experiences and practices from particular and specific people in space and time. In liquid modernity, Enlightenment's wave of universalization, as in the "universal man", "universal culture" and "universal journalists", has been rebuffed by a new wave of particularization where journalism is no longer just the property of institutionalized elite practices, but also of the subaltern and marginalized. The triumph of the particular over the universal means that moral ambiguity and ambivalence will continue to characterize citizen journalism ethics. Particularization also means that the traditional journalism codes of the deontic, virtue and teleological also shift from codes to moral impulses in a complex melange that is informed by the higher-order ethics of freedom, human rights, social justice, equity and citizen participation. As such, citizen journalism represents something that, while presently practised, remains deeply futuristic, as ethics are likely to crystallize around personal responsibility rather than remain codes that are sanctioned by power. Dueze (2008, p. 863) rightly observes that the value of future journalism "will be increasingly determined by the interactions between users and producers rather than the product (*news*) itself". To conclude, there are basically "three places that ethical practice should emerge for [citizen journalism] – the self (individual), interaction of self and community, and the practices of power that limit the self" (German, 2012, p. 259). These changes may radically shift journalism ethics as we know them to something that is deeply futural – only time can tell.

References

Allan, Stuart. (2013). *Citizen Witnessing: Revisioning Journalism in Times of Crisis.* London: Polity.

Anderson, Benedict. (1983). *Imagined Communities.* London: Verso.

Aristotle. (1893/2002). *Nichomachean Ethics*, trans. Sarah Broadie and Christopher Rowe. Oxford: Oxford University Press.

Atton, Chris. (2002). *Alternative Media.* London: SAGE Publications.

Bailey, O.G., Cammaerts, B. and Carpentier, N. (2008). *Understanding Alternative Media.* Buckingham: Open University Press.

Bauman, Zygmunt. (1993). *Postmodern Ethics.* Oxford: Blackwell Publishers.

Bauman, Zygmunt. (2005). *Liquid Life.* Cambridge: Polity Press.

Bauman, Zygmunt. (2000). *Liquid Modernity.* Cambridge: Polity Press.

Bauman, Zygmunt and Leonidas, Donskis. (2013). *Moral Blindness: The Loss of Sensitivity in Liquid Modernity.* London: Polity.

Campbell, Vincent. (2014). Theorising citizenship in citizen journalism. *Digital Journalism.* DOI: 10.1080/21670811.2014.937150

Caputo, John. (2000). "The End of Ethics". In *The Blackwell Guide to Ethical Theory* 1st Edition, LaFollette, H. (ed.), Malden: Blackwell Publishing, pp. 111–128.

Colas, Alejandro. (2002). *International Civil Society.* London: Polity Press.

Craig, David. (2015) "Journalism Ethics and Best Practices". In *Ethics for Digital Journalists: Emerging Best Practices*, Lawrie Zion and David Craig (eds.), New York: Routledge, pp. 15–30.

Culbertson, H. (2012) Review of *Citizen Journalism: Valuable, Useless, or Dangerous?* by Melissa Wall. *Journalism and Mass Society Quarterly* 91(1): 190–192.

Downing, John, Ford, Tamara, Gil, Genev, and Stein, Laura. (2001). *Radical Media: Rebellious Communication and Social Movements.* Thousand Oaks, CA: SAGE Publications.

Dueze, Mark. (2008). The changing context of News Work: Liquid journalism and monitarial citizenship. *International Journal of Communication* 2(3): 848–865.

Dushrel, Bruce, and German, Kathleen. (2012). *The Ethics of Emerging Media.* London: A&C Black.

Foucault, Michel. (1980). *Power/Knowledge: Selected Interviews and Other Writings, 1972–1977.* Brighton: Harvester Press.

Frey, Raymond. (2000). Act-Utilitarianism. In *The Blackwell Guide to Ethical Theory*, H. LaFollette (ed.), Malden: Blackwell Publishing. pp. 183–195.

Fukuyama, Francis. (2003). *Our Posthuman Future: Consequences of the Biotechnology Revolution.* New York: Picador.

German, Kathleen. (2012) "Citizen Journalists and Civic Responsibility: Decorum in an Age of Emerging Media". In *The Ethics of Emerging Media*, Bruce Dushrel and Kathleen German (eds.), London: A&C Black. pp. 251–273.

Giddens, Anthony. (2001). *The Global Third Way Debate.* Cambridge: Polity Press.

Gillmor, Dan. (2006). *We the Media: Grassroots Journalism by the People, for the People.* New York: O'Reilly.

Grant, Scott. (2007). *We Are All Journalists Now.* New York: Focal Press.

Hogg, Chris. (2009). Did the internet kill journalism. *Digital Journal.* http://www.digitaljournal.com/article/271696, last visted 6 August 2015.

Kamm, Frances. (2000). "Nonconsequentialism". In *The Blackwell Guide to Ethical Theory*, H. LaFollette (ed.), Malden: Blackwell Publishing. pp. 227–238.

Kant, Immanuel. (2008). *Fundamental Principles of the Metaphysics of Morals*, trans. Abbot Thomas. New York: Arch Manor.

Keen, Andrew. (2007). *The Cult of the Amateur: How Today's Internet Is Killing Our Culture and Assaulting Our Economy*. Britain: Nicholas Brealey Publishing.

Lipovesky, Gilles. (1992). *Le Crépuscule du devoir: l'éthique indolore des nouveaux temps démocratiques*. Paris: Gallimard.

Luengo, Maria. (2014). Constructing the crisis of journalism. *Journalism Studies* 15(5): 576–585.

Morisett, L. (2004). "Technologies of freedom". In *Democracy and New Media*, H. Jenkins & D. Thorbun (eds.), Cambridge, MA: MIT Press. pp. 21–32.

Moyo, Last. (2014). "Beyond the Newsroom Monopolies: Citizen Journalism as the Practice of Freedom in Zimbabwe". In *Citizen Journalism: Global Voices*, Einar Thorsen and Stuart Allan (eds.), London: Peter Lang. pp. 273–288.

Moyo, Last. (2011). Blogging down a dictatorship: Human rights, citizen journalists, and the right to communicate in Zimbabwe. *Journalism* 12(6): 745–760.

Ong, Walter J. (1982). *Orality and Literacy: The Technologising of the Word*. London: Routledge.

PAOM. (2008) *Report of the Pan African Parliament Election Observer Mission: Presidential Run-off Election and House of Assembly By-elections*. Republic of Zimbabwe, Harare: 27 June 2008.

Pavlik, John. (2010). The impact of technology on journalism. *Journalism Studies* 1(2): 229–237.

Picard, Robert, G. (2014). Twilight or new dawn journalism. *Journalism Studies* 15(5): 500–510.

Pojman, Louis. (1993). "The Defence of Ethical Objectivisim". In *Moral Philosophy*, Louis Pojman (ed.), Cambridge: Hackett Publishing Company, pp. 38–52.

Priban, Jiri. (2013). *Liquid Society and Its Law*. London: Ashgate.

Ross, David. (1930). *The Right and the Good*. Oxford: Oxford University Press.

Safran, Steve. (2005). *How Participatory Journalism Works: A Journalist Describes Why and How "A News Organization Works with Its Audience to Have That 'Conversation' That Is News"*. Cambridge, MA: Harvard University Press.

Sanders, Karen. (2003). *Ethics and Journalism*. London: SAGE Publications.

Schudson, Michael. (2011). *The Sociology of News*. London: Routledge.

Siegel, Lee. (2008). *Against the Machine: Being Human in the Age of the Electronic Mob*. London: Spiegel & Grau.

Simon, David. (2009). *Future of Journalism*, ed. Senator John Kerry. Democracy Now, New York.

Singer, Jane, and Ashman, Ian. (2009). "User-Generated Content and Journalistic Values". In *Citizen Journalism: Global Perspectives*, S. Allan and E. Thorsen (eds.), New York: Peter Lang, pp. 233–242.

Van De Donk, Wim, Loader, Brian, Nixon, Paul, and Rucht, Dieter. (2004). "Introduction: Social Movements and ICTs". In *Cyberprotest: New Media, Citizens and Social Movements*, Wim Van De Donk, Brian Loader, Paul Nixon and Dieter Rucht (eds.), London and New York: Routledge. pp. 1–22.

Van Der Haak, Bregtje, Parks, Michele, and Castells, Manuel. (2012). The future of networked journalism. *International Journal of Communication* 6(5): 20–31.

Ward, Stephen. (2015). *Radical Media Ethics: A Global Approach*, Oxford: John Wiley and Sons.

Whitaker, Reg. (1999). *The End of Privacy: How Total Surveillance Is becoming a Reality*. New York: The New Press.

4

The Positioning of Citizen-Influenced Radio in the Battle for the Control of Minds

Everette Ndlovu

Introduction

Zimbabwe is an illuminating case study that glaringly shows how radio, as a powerful medium, plays a role in the battle for the control of minds in a conflict-ridden environment. As a medium that has a significant impact on politics and power, it remains a preferred medium of hegemonic projects that are of great service to the status quo. It is effective in facilitating the ideological manipulation of the masses. This explains the interest that has been shown with regard to the control of radio by both the colonial governments and the Zimbabwean government, leading to the emergence of alternative voices from outside the country that have been offering the masses an alternative voice to that churned out by the state. These radio stations emerged during the time the state was named Rhodesia as a tool to fight against colonialism. Most interestingly, they have re-emerged after independence, their focus though, no longer being the liberation from colonial occupation, but what Moyo (2012) sees as a new form of liberation from emerging forms of oppression perpetrated by the former liberators on the people they are supposed to have liberated. This chapter therefore seeks to examine the impact of radio both in pre- and post-independent Zimbabwe, with the aim of creating an understanding of why voices are still emerging from the diaspora in a country which is a signatory to the 1991 Windhoek Declaration, which upholds freedom of expression and access to information as a constitutional and democratic right for all citizens.

The nature of broadcasting in pre-independent Zimbabwe

The use of radio for hegemonic purposes can be traced right back to the colonial days when, according to the then Director of Information in Northern Rhodesia, Harry Franklin (Moyo, 2005), radio broadcasting for Africans in Rhodesia was established to help in the dissemination of government policies to the natives, most of whom were illiterate and could only be communicated to through the spoken word in their own native languages. This also helped to make them employable in the new economies as skilled labour (van der Veur, 2002, pp. 82–86).

Franklin stressed the importance of getting to the masses in time to avoid a situation that he saw emerging in other states, where, according to him, the underprivileged and excluded masses were being easily misled by a few agitators from the intelligentsia class. He expressed the view that the black mind was getting thirstier for knowledge. It was therefore at risk of picking up the wrong knowledge – knowledge that could be dangerous to the colony, especially knowledge propagated by the communists.

This was at a time when the powerful nations were battling for influence over Africa through information warfare, which was pivotal in the battle for the control of minds. Some had already started broadcasting communist ideologies into Africa. Most of them were from the communist bloc. By 1958, Radio Moscow was broadcasting to Africa on a regular basis followed by Prague Radio and Radio Peking, which began regular African transmissions in 1959 (see Mosia and colleagues, 1994, p. 4). By the following year, East Germany, Poland, Romania and Bulgaria started broadcasting into the continent as well. The continent was in the thick of an international "war of words", the main themes of which were colonialism, white minority regimes, apartheid and capitalism. The colonial powers were getting concerned by the impact of these broadcasts, which were countering their ideologies and threatening their hegemonic powers.

The political climate as a catalyst to the emergence of revolutionary radio

The attempt to keep the natives under control through information warfare was met with formidable challenges which eventually changed the political landscape in Southern Africa. This was a time when nationalism was taking root in the continent. The quest for independence from colonial powers was getting stronger by day. In 1961, Dr Hastings Kamuzu Banda's Malawi Congress Party (MCP) gained a majority in the Legislative Council elections. In 1963 Banda became Nyasaland's prime minister. The Federation of Rhodesia and Nyasaland was dissolved in 1963. On 6 July 1964, Nyasaland became independent from British rule and renamed itself Malawi. Under a new constitution, Malawi became a republic with Banda as its first president.

Northern Rhodesia followed suit. It became the Republic of Zambia on 24 October 1964, with the United National Independence Party (UNIP) assuming power under the leadership of Dr Kenneth David Kaunda, who became its first president. However, in Southern Rhodesia, which later became Rhodesia, the prime minister Ian Douglas Smith refused to embark on any negotiations about black rule, arguing that "Never in a thousand years will Africans be able to rule themselves," (see *The New York Times*, November 21, 2007). "No African rule in my lifetime," he said. "The white man is the master of Rhodesia. He has built it, and he intends to keep it." Mr Smith argued that Black Africans were not ready for self-government.

Mr Smith resisted black rule and maintained control of the wealthy part of the former federation. He broke away from Britain under his unpopular unilateral declaration of independence (UDI) in 1965.

The Rhodesian government began to limit foreign communication. It intensified its control of Rhodesian Broadcasting Corporation (RBC). It introduced a weekly radio broadcast prepared by the Ministry of Information, whose content slanted towards building up a bleak picture of the independent African states to the north, combined with an image of Rhodesia, South Africa and the adjacent Portuguese territories as havens of good government and fair play.

Smith drastically narrowed the communicative space in the country by introducing the 1965 Emergency Regulations Act, which prohibited turning on a radio in a public place, "if it picked up broadcasts that might endanger public safety or interfere with public order" (Moyo, 2008, p. 15). According to Zaffiro (1984), anyone found guilty of making it possible for others to hear an objectionable broadcast or speech, statement, poem or song could be jailed for up to two years and fined the equivalent of $1,400. All those who were seen to be engaged in political activities inspired by these so-called illegal broadcasts were imprisoned in high security jails like *Khami* Prison, *Hwahwa* Prison and *Gonakudzingwa* Prison. There are reports of some of the prisoners being castrated in those jails. Others were tortured to death. Some were never accounted for. In Rhodesia, the media had to serve the interests of the state.

Smith ensured radios were fitted with frequency modulation (FM), as opposed to long-range short wave (SW) and medium wave (MW), which could pick revolutionary broadcasts. These radio sets were manufactured by Supersonic and World Radio System (WRS). These short-range FM radio sets were branded with the name "Chief" and given to traditional black chiefs who lived in rural areas and who, Smith hoped, would sway their subjects into turning against the guerrillas, whom he referred to as "terrorists". Chiefs would then distribute these radio sets to their subjects to make sure everyone listened to RBC's propaganda messages (Moyo, 2008). Batteries for these radios were made easily accessible to those living in rural areas. The natives were being communicated to and not afforded the opportunity to contribute to political and social debate in the country. The African language broadcasters did not have any input to the news content. According to a former broadcaster, Japhet Masuku (interviewed 20 January 2010), they translated English news scripts into Shona and Ndebele word for word. People could only get to hear alternative perspectives on any story if they listened to revolutionary radio stations domiciled outside the country.

A batch of radios named "Commando" was also manufactured and distributed to soldiers in the battlefield in an attempt to keep their spirits high. RBC had programmes dedicated to the fighters, through which they could send greetings to their families, request favourite songs and relay messages about their welfare to loved ones. Their families and friends could also send them greetings and song requests to cheer their spirits.

The Rhodesian government implemented a coordinated strategic information and public diplomacy campaign, which included propaganda, censorship and psychological operations aimed at maintaining the support of the country's black majority in the face of infiltration and indoctrination by the Zimbabwe African National Liberation Army (ZANLA) and the Zimbabwe People's Revolutionary Army (ZIPRA), who were seen as linked to communist states. The government stated that the terrorists [freedom fighters] were scared of the government forces, and were therefore pursuing "soft targets". It claimed that the villagers were dying in a war they did not want, waged to further a political creed they did not understand or care about.

As the war progressed and the Rhodesian government's control diminished, Smith's Psychological Operations Unit (POU) implemented "Operation Split-Shot". It started spreading information that instilled fear among the population. The campaign was focused around the theme of "Terror and death is the way of the communist terrorists in Rhodesia." Information about ZANLA/ZIPRA recruiters forcing black Rhodesians into training camps, raping women in front of their children, spreading sexually transmitted diseases and killing defenceless civilians was spread through radio. Military recruits were depicted as being mistreated and killed by opposition forces. These propaganda efforts backfired when blacks who had voluntarily joined the liberation forces returned to their villages unharmed and told the people a different story.

The emergence of revolutionary radio in Rhodesia

According to Ziegler and Asante (1992), once governments begin to control the media and compel them to serve primarily as instruments of official propaganda the media eventually loses its rightful role. Media control is seen as an onslaught on democracy, a situation that can actually encourage oppositional message creation and propagation by disenfranchised masses.

Ian Smith's dictatorial approach led to the intensification of nationalism in the country. This led to a protracted guerrilla war led by the Zimbabwe African National Union (ZANU) and its associated guerrilla army, ZANLA, and the Zimbabwe African People's Union (ZAPU) and its armed wing, ZIPRA.

The nationalists also understood that military warfare alone could not win the support of the masses. There was a need for information warfare which could win the minds and hearts of the people, and subsequently their approval. They understood why the colonial powers were keen to control information and the media in the country. They therefore understood that the voices of the nationalists would never be permitted on media controlled by the white regime. This resulted in them starting radio stations outside the country, which broadcast revolutionary messages on SW and MW back into the country.

According to Mosia and colleagues (1994) and Windrich (1981), the Nasser regime in Egypt gave airtime to Zimbabwe nationalists over its external service as early as 1958. Radio Tanzania had granted airtime to both ZANU radio Voice of Zimbabwe (VOZ) and ZAPU radio Voice of the Revolution (VOR) from as early as 1963. Kwame Nkrumah also extended use of the new Ghana Broadcasting Corporation shortwave transmitter to ZANU until his fall in 1966.

These stations broadcast in English, Shona and Ndebele, the three main languages used in the country. Their role was to counter the regime's propaganda and to appeal to the emotions of the masses in order to mobilize them against the colonial powers. This, according to Mosia and colleagues (1994, p. 1), helped African liberation movements report their activities and broadcast information that counteracted what was considered to be the false and malicious propaganda broadcast by colonial radio stations. Whilst RBC tried to project Africans as happy under the colonial rule, the nationalist radio stations exposed the plight and suffering of the Zimbabwe masses under the yoke of colonialism and racialism. They mobilized public opinion and support for their cause from friendly countries, organizations and individuals. They gave the natives an alternative political perspective to that of the colonial powers, thereby affording the masses an opportunity to engage intellectually and emotionally in the fight against white domination.

These radio stations were crucial in the battle for the minds. They helped to mobilize public opinion and support for the liberation cause, which resulted in a massive resistance to white domination. They mobilized people to embark on a massive resistance to white rule and to join hands with the liberation movements. The commanders of the liberation fighters also used radio to give information to the combatants in the battlefield in special codes only understood by the freedom fighters.

For instance, according to ZANU, VOZ was aimed more at the fighters than at the masses:

VOZ was the only common thing every combatant could listen to. It was often used to convey battle objectives and military orders ... in a way understood only by the officers. Each guerrilla unit was required to have a radio. Of particular significance was the frequent use of VOZ for speeches by comrade Mugabe on any subjects we felt the people had to be briefed on. General Togongara often used VOZ to pass instructions.

(Tichatonga interview, July 1983, in Mosia and colleagues, 1994)

The radio stations created a two-way information flow between the black people in the country and those outside the country, unlike RBC, which communicated to the people without accommodating their views:

We wanted to get people to rally behind the war and form a link with the fighters, so that whatever they did was played back in a 2-way flow of information. Those inside Zimbabwe could get news of the outside and those outside got news of the movement.

(ZAPU Publicity Secretary Willie Musarurwa interview, 1983, in Mosia and colleagues,1994)

The broadcast content for these revolutionary station consisted of news, commentary, letters from the listeners and revolutionary song requests. Addresses and announcements by the revolutionary leaders were very inspirational, to both the forces and the black masses. The military wings of the liberation movements provided continuous reports and sent correspondents into the war zones, for interviews with fighters. The voices of the fighters and the people working with them struck a devastating blow to the propaganda churned out by the settler regime. In ZANU, Charles Ndlovu [Webster Shamu], Eddison Zvobgo and Richard Hove were the main VOZ staff, along with Rugare Gumbo, Henry Hamadziripi and Mark Marongwe (*aka* Grey Tichatonga).

Towards the end of the war of liberation, ZAPU's VOR broadcast mainly from Lusaka. Their prominent voices included those of Japhet Masuku, Joseph Masuku and Saul Gwakuba Ndlovu. Their broadcasts were instrumental in the recruitment of fighters and supporters. Joseph Masuku was known for his inspirational poetic voice, which would be punctuated by revolutionary songs from ZIPRA forces. He would invite the youth to cross into Zambia where ZAPU had its base, to take up arms against the stubborn Rhodesian government. He is remembered for saying:

Wozani bantwana benhlabathi!
Wozani! Izikhali zisemsamo!
Zililindile! Wozani!
[Come children of the soil! Come! The weapons are waiting for you! They are stacked here at the back of this very room! Come!]

(Ndlovu, 2014)

As the commander-in-chief of ZIPRA, Joshua Nkomo also directed their operations through coded messages over the radio. VOR was a platform that linked the people, the fighters and the revolutionary leaders through unsanctioned engagement. Revolutionary radio stations were therefore a vital tool in the protracted war of liberation, where ideation worked alongside military combat within the restricted political environment of the then Rhodesia.

These radio stations gave the natives an alternative political voice to that of the colonial powers, thereby affording them an opportunity to engage intellectually with issues affecting their land. Not everybody had access to radio broadcasts. As a tradition, word of mouth, commonly referred to as *radio troittor*, would then help to disseminate messages far and wide.

Broadcasting in independent Zimbabwe

Revolutionary radio stations closed down when Zimbabwe attained its independence in 1980. They had achieved their purpose and maintaining them was unnecessary. However, as Moyo (2009) notes, the government of Zimbabwe inherited broadcasting which, for many years, had been used to serve the narrow interests of the settler regime at the expense of the indigenous majority. There had been a lot of interference in the operation of broadcasting in the country. Of concern was how the colonial regime had used radio to propagate ideologies that would consolidate the authority of the illegitimate regime.

The new black government engaged a BBC taskforce to look into the future needs of broadcasting in the newly independent country. (see Moyo, 2005, p. 5). As Moyo explains, the brief of the taskforce was to evaluate the existing transmission, training, management, editorial and financial aspects of ZBC so as to make recommendations on how public broadcasting services could be expanded to serve all parts of the country. The taskforce recommended that the most important requirement was for the broadcasting service to be properly insulated from government, party, commercial or any other pressures. The report urged ZBC to structure its programming in such a way that its service became responsive to the interests of its audiences and that it acted as a unifying, educational and informational force.

The government did not totally embrace all the advice it was given by the taskforce. To the contrary, it immediately changed ZBC into an institution that would serve the interests of the ruling party by turning it into its ideological tool. The government established a communication policy and legislative infrastructure whose main purpose was to complement the construction of the ruling party's hegemony through media (Chuma, 2010, p. 91).

The ruling party immediately focused on media control and denied oppositional voices equal access to the media. Broadcasting was kept under direct control of the Ministry of Information. ZBC stifled the oppositional voices and dominated the country with ZANU philosophy, something which immediately created unequal power relationships and dissatisfaction among other sectors of the populace, who felt excluded from the democratic process.

The government staffed ZBC with former cadres of the ruling party to ensure the successful propagation of the ruling party's ideologies to the masses, who lived mainly in rural areas where newspapers were difficult to come by, due to the country's poor infrastructure, which had been ravaged by years of conflict. The first Zimbabwean Minister of Information, Dr Nathan Shamuyarira justified the ruling party's media control by saying:

> The comrades we've brought in from Maputo, who were running the VOZ, were put into key posts at ZBC, so they are in a position where they can direct policy.
>
> (Moyo, 2005:7)

Broadcasting became reflective of the linguistic and cultural diversity of the Zimbabwean nation, with indigenous languages given prominence. Radio proved to be the dominant means of communication, as the broadcasts were predominantly in vernacular languages that were understood by the masses.

As Moyo observes, despite claims of neutrality, broadcasting was turned into a tool of mass manipulation right from the onset. Mugabe vehemently opposed media plurality, just as his predecessor Ian Smith, arguing that, "You don't know what propaganda a non-state radio might broadcast" (quoted in Maja-Pearce, 1995, p. 123). Mugabe saw media plurality as having the potential to cause discord in the governance of the new state. This enabled the ruling party to ensure that none of the other political parties gained access to the airwaves. It banned all songs that made reference to other political parties, as they considered this to have the potential to divide political allegiance and make it difficult to introduce a one-party state.

Ian Smith's division of broadcasting for blacks along ethnic lines was a tactical move which would later impact on the unity of the country after independence. In 1975, the government of Ian Smith had established a solely Ndebele-speaking radio station at Montrose Studios in Bulawayo, the capital city of Matabeleland. This region was also a ZAPU stronghold. At independence, ZAPU deposited vast quantities of media material at Montrose Studios, which comprised of a large archive of tapes and musical records from VOR in Zambia. Among these materials were records by the ZAPU's choir, Light Machine Gun, popularly known as LMG.

By default, VOZ broadcasters from Maputo in Mozambique deposited their archive material at Mbare Studios in Harare. During the build-up to independence, Montrose Studios and Mbare Studios were polarized in the way they played these revolutionary songs and tapes, with Mbare being evidently pro-ZANU while Montrose was evidently pro-ZAPU. Despite these two parties having been compatriots during the liberation struggle, tensions that had been suppressed for sometime began to appear.

When ZANU won the elections with a landslide victory, the party embarked on a project which would see its influence dominate the programming policy for ZBC. At Montrose Studios, this large archive of revolutionary songs and tapes from ZAPU is reported, by former employees of the station, to have been physically destroyed by former ZANU cadres, who had been deployed to the station to eradicate any material that made any reference to ZAPU's contribution to the war of liberation (Ndlovu, 2014). All songs by groups like LMG were completely destroyed. One former music librarian in the station said in an interview on 17 June 2011:

I watched helplessly as the ZANU thugs deployed to Montrose studios went through the catalogues pulling down every record and tape that made reference to ZAPU or Joshua Nkomo. They put them on the floor and danced on them, breaking them into pieces. They did so while at the same time singing ZANU songs that despised the contribution of ZAPU in the liberation struggle. After what seemed a lifetime, they left the music library for us to clean the mess. My heart sobbed as I started cursing myself for not having predicted that such a barbaric act was going to take place. I would have hidden this material and smuggled it out of the station for safe keeping.

The station, which had been situated in the opposition ZAPU stronghold since 1975, was left with no material about ZAPU. ZANU immediately changed the programming of this station by forcing it to play songs and programmes that praised Robert Mugabe and his ZANU and denigrated Joshua Nkomo and his ZAPU. The ruling party filled the airwaves with derogatory songs from the likes of Thomas Mapfumo, Harare Mambo Band, Elijah Madzikatire and many other musicians whose songs described the contribution of ZAPU in the liberation struggle as insignificant. One of the divisive songs that dominated the charts was that by Thomas Mapfumo entitled *Nyarai kana makundwa*, translated "Losers must shut up", a direct reference to ZAPU which had lost to ZANU in the first democratic elections in 1980. Any song that praised Robert Mugabe and that spoke against Nkomo and his ZAPU was guaranteed air play and hopefully good sales. Many artists capitalized on this and churned out song after song that attacked the compatriots of the ruling party. The songs described ZAPU as a party of dissidents who should accept defeat, or face destruction by the ruling party. This psychological and information warfare served to guarantee ZANU's hold on power.

Some well-trained broadcasters from ZAPU were forced to leave broadcasting because of the ill-treatment they received from the ruling party cadres who were in charge of ZBC, despite some of them having little or no broadcasting credentials. Others had to be taught the job by ZAPU cadres who they later replaced or who they were later elevated above. According to one former broadcaster, all one needed to be promoted in broadcasting was a ZANU card, not an academic certificate. This former broadcaster lamented:

> I was transferred from Bulawayo to Harare where I would sit in the office for days doing nothing. The only time when I was called to the broadcasting booth was when I was forced to read propaganda about ZAPU to the nation. I knew that all I was reading was a lie and a calculated move to humiliate my people through me for our political convictions. I couldn't stand it. I resigned from broadcasting.
>
> (Interview, 19 January 2011)

According to the respondent, that act was a calculated exploitation of the communication infrastructure: broadcasters were forced to give a one-sided view of events at the expense of truth and democracy so as to eradicate the contribution of the rest of the nation in the fight for the country's liberation, making ZANU look as if it was the only party to liberate Zimbabwe (Ndlovu, 2014). This alone created insecurity and mistrust, and made some people, especially those that were aligned to ZAPU, feel that their efforts to liberate their country had been fruitless.

ZANU inherited, developed, implemented and perfected legislation that restricted and sought to close down the democratic space, while the trend in other countries like Zambia and Botswana, and later South Africa for example, had been to do the opposite (Lush and Kupe, 2013). According to Lush and Kupe, ZANU proliferated legislation that impacted on the free flow of information and the engagement of the masses in political debates. One such unpopular legislation is the Access to Information and Protection of Privacy Act (AIPPA) (2002), which requires journalists to be licensed and accredited by the state-run Media and Information Commission (MIC). Those who violate its provisions, mainly in the private media or among foreign journalists, face fines and up to two years in prison. Many journalists have been charged under the AIPPA, accused of publishing false information. Interestingly, none of them are part of the state media, something which raises concerns about the selective application of this law in a land where democracy and equality are expected to prevail. This has led Windrich (2010, p. 74) to argue that the legacy of Rhodesia Front's censorship and propaganda has come to define broadcasting control and uses under Mugabe's ruling ZANU-PF Party.

By 2005, at least 90 Zimbabwean journalists, including many of the nation's most prominent reporters, had been forced out of the country and were living in exile in South Africa, other African countries, the United Kingdom and the United States. According to the Committee to Protect Journalists (19 October 2005), this made Zimbabwean journalists one of the largest groups of exiled journalists in the world. Since then, Zimbabwe has witnessed the emergence of oppositional radio stations formed by Zimbabweans domiciled in America, South Africa and the United Kingdom.

Among them are Short Wave Radio Africa (SWRA), Studio 7, Nehanda Radio and Mthwakazi Radio. These alternative radio stations broadcast back into Zimbabwe and gave the population a platform to engage with each other and express their views on the country's political and economic state.

As Moyo (2012) says, the aim of these stations is not the liberation from colonial occupation, but a new form of liberation from emerging forms of oppression perpetrated by the former liberators on the people they are supposed to have liberated. The people are thus reacting to the replacement of one form of oppression by another. They have consciously created dialogical spaces on which to deliberate on ways to change their circumstances through creating alternative dialogical spaces from environments far away from the controls of the state, which is unsympathetic to democratic participation.

Oppositional radio stations were thus established offshore to give the disenfranchised sectors of the populace a platform where they could be heard. The opposition parties also needed to reach the people to explain their policies so that people could make informed political decisions. In the light of this, Zimbabwean radio stations domiciled outside the country are giving power to the masses to freely debate on issues that impact on the governance of the country.

These unsanctioned radio stations, like their predecessors, contribute to the dialogical engagement by sourcing information from the country, processing it outside the country and transmitting it back to the land with the aid of digital technologies accessible to the general public (see Ndlovu 2014, p. 122). This engagement is aimed at empowering people, and enabling them to use their uncensored voices to influence the country's democratic landscape. This is alternative media, which Hyden and colleagues (2007) describe as having a role in disseminating information in an environment where officials try to hide facts from the citizenry. Such a situation makes citizens address issues in different ways to bridge the gap left by government-controlled media institutions. This media empowered the marginalized sectors of the community to oppose the dictatorial regime through ideas and thought processes.

As Moyo (2012) observes, these radio stations beaming into Zimbabwe have made a massive contribution to public debate on the constantly shifting Zimbabwe crisis. Just as during the liberation struggle, these radio stations have the ability to provide counter-discourses to the propaganda churned out by the state-controlled media. The Zimbabwe government no longer enjoys a monopoly on the power to define the political and economic crises facing the nation, thanks to the re-emergence of diasporic radio as another form of alternative media. There is now interaction between Zimbabweans inside and outside the country as well as a link with the international community, so alternative perspectives from those propagated by the Zimbabwean government-controlled media on what is happening in the country are able to be accessed. Alternative radio stations, as part of the emancipatory project, play an important role in Zimbabwe's social transformation process, by seeking to involve citizens as key players in message production and propagation, a situation which empowers the populace in a restrictive political environment.

As Ndlovu (2014, p. 243) explains, such alternative stations have formed a human and technological agency that has a bearing on how the people think and respond to the disenfranchisement that characterizes a political environment like Zimbabwe where a few dominate the majority. There is evidence that this disenfranchisement is being challenged by these poorly resourced radio stations. Divergent voices that are offering a formidable challenge to the status quo's hegemonic influence are being enabled by these radio stations. These media are proving to be an emancipatory force which has empowered the masses to challenge the status quo in full view of the international community, something which has reduced the ability of the ruling party to exert its dominance on the populace of Zimbabwe without challenge. They play what Curran (2010, p. 38) refers to as the watchdog role, which exposes the abuse of power by the government.

The information warfare generated by such media activity through critical information gathering, processing and dissemination is conducted via avenues that are not sanctioned by the Mugabe regime. These media are succeeding in going around information barriers to establish a new public sphere that is crucial in dialogically engaging people in an activity that has a bearing in creating a democratic environment in which every citizen has a voice. Even if they are domiciled outside the country, there is evidence that these media get their feed from Zimbabweans on the ground through active citizen participation and the deployment of modern media technologies that transcend political boundaries and statutes, something that gives them power, credibility and authenticity. There is evidence that the voices heard on diasporic media are the voices of the citizens and not the elite whose focus is controlling the minds of the people to stay in power which gives them unlimited privileges.

The state's response to alternative radio stations

The government of President Mugabe is critically aware of the power of radio in the struggle over the shaping of the minds of its citizens as well as influencing public opinion abroad. He is therefore unsympathetic to alternative media that seeks to undermine the sovereignty of his state. This has led to his relentless attack on post-independence alternative radio stations, which he argues are focused on regime change.

In 2000, the first independent station to be established in Zimbabwe, Capital Radio, was closed down at gunpoint at its hideout at the top of

Monomotapa Hotel in Harare, forcing the founders of the station to relocate to the UK to start SWRA.

On the night of 29 August 2002 the Voice of the People Radio (VOP), a Netherlands-sponsored alternative radio station, had its Harare offices raided. Vast amounts of material were looted. The offices were then destroyed by a bomb that was widely attributed to state security forces (Windrich, 2010, p. 83). The blast destroyed a modern digital studio, computers, furniture, project documents, tapes and compact discs worth more than US$120,000. The perpetrators of this act were never brought to book. The government's slow pace of the investigation led critics to point fingers at security agents who were suspected of seeking to silence the so-called clandestine radios. As Windrich later argued, the dismissive response from the then Information Minister Jonathan Moyo, that "Something went wrong and they bombed themselves so they could blame the government," (p. 83) while in the same breath describing the station as a pirate radio sponsored by Western imperialists to cause disharmony in the country, partly justifies the belief that the government was behind this act of silencing divergent voices which are impacting on governance.

When Jonathan Moyo was Information Minister he accused Western nations of creating clandestine radio stations, which he described as inflammatory and as fanning tribal divisions and ethnic hatred among Zimbabweans in order to make the country ungovernable (Moyo, 2010). He likened these radio broadcasts to those of the Rwandan station Radio Télévision Libre des Mille Collines (RTLM), which is accused of having promoted the tribal hatred that led to the 1994 genocide. On this basis, the government criminalized these radio stations, threatening their staff with punitive action should they be caught.

On 3 November 2005, the government-run *Herald* newspaper published an article that referred to broadcasters and journalists working for Studio7 in Washington, DC, and SWRA in UK, respectively, as clowns, puppets and sell-outs who were determined to advance the agenda of Western imperialist propaganda. The then Minister of Mines and Mining Development Obert Mpofu also expressed concern about what he called "the invasion of the airwaves" by the so-called "hostile broadcasts" (*Daily News*, 5 July 2012). At the official opening of ZBC TV2 in Bulawayo, Mpofu expressed concern that Zimbabwean airwaves continued to be invaded by hostile broadcasts that fed the people with what he described as outright lies and half-baked truth about the Zimbabwean government. Just as was observed by the Southern Africa Report (2011), which says that the stridently partisan ZBC is rapidly losing its audience, Mpofu acknowledged that more and more people relied on external stations, especially what he described as pirate radio stations.

The former VOZ radio broadcaster, and also former Minister of Information Webster Shamu said, "They [diasporic radio stations] will never win the war against Zimbabweans. We advise all those employed by them, wherever they are, to come back home in a proper channel than to continue peddling foreign policies, which will never succeed" (SWRA, 14 August 2012). He also claimed that these stations are operated by enemies of the state, and that they are being used to reverse the gains of the liberation struggle.

As Ranger (2004) pointed out, the state-owned media have placed the blame for the economic malaise facing the country on "Western imperialists", "illegal (targeted) economic sanctions", the "pirate" or foreign-funded radio stations and an unpatriotic, intransigent, puppet opposition, Movement for Democratic Change (MDC), which ZANU-PF argues, is doing everything to please its perceived handlers, the British, at the expense of the national interest (see *The Herald*, 9 August 2013). They describe the opposition as sell-outs and puppets of the West.

Talking about the poor ZBC quality and coverage in the country the presidential spokesperson George Charamba once said: "You will note that radio trades on sound quality, but what we are getting here is a raw deal. Foreign radio stations are performing better than ZBC, and this is not good at all" (*The Herald*, 4 October 2012).

The government of Zimbabwe is believed to have sourced equipment from China to jam the signal from SWRA and other external radio stations, which include Voice of America's Studio 7 and VOP. SWRA director, Gerry Jackson (interview, 18 January 2011), confirmed the interference on SWRA's frequencies, which has been linked to jamming from the Zimbabwe government since March 2005. This has forced the station to operate on multiple frequencies to evade what Biener (2008) refers to as "Bob's Fire Dragon" – the Chinese-sourced jamming technology used by Mugabe (see http://www.evrel.ewf.uni-erlangen.de/pesc/peaceradio-ZBW.html).

According to Biener, in the report "Radio for Peace, Democracy and Human Rights" (2008), BBC Monitoring (BBCM) observed what appears to be interference specifically targeted at both the 15145 and 12145 kHz frequencies used by SWRA from 2005. According to the report, typical of the results observed by BBCM were those of the 18 April, when the 1630 GMT English transmission from SW Radio Africa was jammed from 1630 until 1644 GMT and then again from 1659 to 1714 GMT on 15145 kHz. On 12145 kHz jamming is reported to have been observed from 1645 until 1659 GMT and also 1715 until 1729. The deliberate interference was again noted on 15145 kHz from 1729 until 1743 GMT, and on 12145 kHz from 1744 to 1758 GMT. Also, according to Jackson (interview, 18 January 2011), the jamming of the SWRA programme, Newsreel has been repeated several times since then.

BBCM confirmed the deliberate interference on the 4880 kHz frequency, forcing SWRA to use an alternative frequency. Periodic checks have shown the continued use of rotary type jammers against transmissions. In March

2005, Paris-based organization Reporters Sans Frontières reported that the Media Monitoring Project Zimbabwe (MMPZ), a Harare-based independent watchdog, said the jamming of SWRA's broadcasts is being carried out from Thornhill airbase, located outside the south-western town of Gweru, between Harare and Bulawayo, where the government has a transmission station. According to the International Broadcasting Bureau (IBB), a US federal government entity, the equipment being used for the jamming comes from China, which has close trade links with Zimbabwe, especially in the telecommunications domain (Biener, 2008).

The government admitted that it was behind the jamming of clandestine radio frequencies when the then deputy Information Minister Bright Matonga told parliament that Zimbabwe was not going to allow foreigners to invade its airwaves without authority.

As a way of further countering the "anti-government rhetoric" from diasporic radio and of influencing international public opinion, the government of Zimbabwe started News 24, which was meant to be a 24-hour external news service whose primary mission was "to tell our own story", as the then Information Minister Sikhanyiso Ndlovu reportedly put it.

The government has also tried to put pressure on regional governments to condemn the diasporic radio broadcasts. They called upon the Southern African Development Community (SADC) to take a stand against these broadcasts. The Botswana government was accused of allowing the erection of transmitters that were relaying the clandestine radio signal into Zimbabwe. The government of Botswana has, however, consistently denied hosting such transmitters, and has even invited Zimbabwean authorities to come and verify their claim, something which the Zimbabwean government hasn't been able to do (Newzimbabwe.com, 6 September 2011).

The Zimbabwean government has also approached South African authorities to find and close down South African-based Zimbabwean community Internet radio station Radio Mthwakazi FM, run by a group of Johannesburg-based Zimbabweans from the country's western region of Matabeleland.

Non-governmental organizations (NGOs) have been attacked for supplying radio sets to the people. Government officials accuse the British and Americans of sponsoring a "radio for free project", which is seen as a way of encouraging rural people to listen to anti-government messages from external broadcasts. Security agents have been confiscating radio sets distributed by NGOs. Writing on Radio Netherlands Worldwide (RNW), Africa Desk Nkosana Dlamini said:

> Even 33 years after Zimbabwean independence, President Mugabe remains a harsh critic of the white colonial government's system. But through the latest radio ban, he is imposing the same oppressive tactics that he himself once fought against to liberate his people.
>
> (2 April 2013)

VOP radio reported, on 22 January 2007, that at least 42 radio sets had been confiscated by state security agents from locals (www.evrel.ewf.uni-erlangen .de). These wind-up radio sets are an excellent way to help cash-strapped Zimbabwean villagers access information.

On 1 March 2013, authorities in Zimbabwe raided the production studio Ingwe Studios, confiscating over 180 wind-up solar powered radios distributed by NGOs (*Zimbabwe Mail*, 2 March 2013). Deputy Police Commissioner Innocent Matibiri told a Parliamentary Committee on Defence and Home Affairs that some of these NGOs pose a serious security threat to the country (SAPA, 25 February 2013):

> People are just distributing them [radios] but they are not telling where the gadgets came from and how they got into the country. Under such an environment we can only suspect that whoever is doing that has some intentions that are not good for the country and until we get satisfactory answers, we will continue to confiscate those gadgets.

National police spokeswoman Charity Charamba also added to the voices against these radio sets, claiming that the radio equipment was from Western countries and was intended to be "used for hate speech" and to discredit the 2013 elections.

Article XIX of the agreement signed on 15 September 2008 between President Robert Mugabe's ZANU-PF and rival Morgan Tsvangirai's MDC on resolving the challenges facing Zimbabwe focused on freedom of expression (see http://www.ft.com/cms/s/0/d84c07b2-836e-11dd-907e-000077b07658. html#axzz3hwFEBlb8). It paid particular attention to broadcasting. The article carried the ruling ZANU-PF's demand for the immediate disbandment or demobilization of foreign-based and foreign government-funded external radio stations, which had been beaming into Zimbabwe since the beginning of the crisis in 2002. The ZANU-PF government promised to ensure the immediate processing of all applications for re-registration and registration (of broadcasters) in terms of both the Broadcasting Services Act as well as the AIPPA. The opposition, in turn, pledged to call upon the governments that are hosting and/or funding external radio stations broadcasting into Zimbabwe to cease such hosting and funding. It pledged to encourage the Zimbabweans running or working for such external radio stations to return to Zimbabwe (Moyo, 2012).

Of interest, though, is the denial of some of these radio stations that they are funded by foreign governments, claiming that they generate their funding from advertisers and human rights organizations. Whilst SWRA claims that it got its funding from human rights and media freedom groups, a report by Chris McGreal in the *Guardian* in 2002 suggested that the American government, through the Office of Transition Initiatives (OTI), was giving large sums of money to the station. SWRA has denied that. A 2012 report by

Source Watch (www.sourcewatch.org) also indicated that diplomatic sources say OTI pays for the studios, equipment and airtime on the transmitters of SWRA. By the time this chapter was written, the station was still adamant that the information was untrue, even though, when MDC lost to ZANU-PF in the 2013 elections, funding for the station stopped. The station blamed MDC for letting it down, something that affected its funding. Of interest is also why these stations emerged just when Mugabe was embarking on his unpopular land distribution policy. Could this have been a coincidence? An English saying is: "Who pays the piper, calls the tune."

Conclusion

Radio is therefore a very powerful medium for the control of minds in a polit-ical environment. In Zimbabwe radio has been used as a hegemonic tool by all the regimes that have ever ruled the country. There has always been a protracted battle for the control of minds of the vulnerable by the powerful. Once in control, the powerful have always prevented oppositional forces from having access to the medium. This has consistently led to the emer-gence of alternative voices from outside the country, which, after reaching the country, create political waves that challenge the establishment. Silenc-ing of the masses in an environment that is expected to be democratic is the surest predictor that alternative discourses will emerge from environments beyond the controls of the repressive regime. In Zimbabwe this has led to history repeating itself. Alternative offshore voices have emerged in the form of diasporic radio. The citizens have established alternative spheres through which they are able to challenge domination by those who are supposed to have liberated them. Until democracy is achieved, the battle for the control of the minds will continue.

References

Biener, H. (2008). "Radio for peace, democracy and human rights: Zimbabwe". http://www.evrel.ewf.uni-erlangen.de/pesc/peaceradio-ZBW.html. (Accessed 03/06/ 2012)

Cowell, Alan. "Ian Smith, Defiant Symbol of White Rule in Africa, Is Dead at 88." *The New York Times*, November 21, 2007, International News sec. Accessed July 17, 2015. http://www.nytimes.com/2007/11/21/world/africa/21smith.html?pagewanted=all&_r=0.

Chuma, W. (2010). "Reforming the media in Zimbabwe: Critical reflection". In Moyo, D. & Chuma, W. (eds.) 2010. *Changing Southern Africa: Critical Reflections on Media Reforms in the Global Age*. 1st edition. Pretoria: Unisa Press, pp. 90–107.

Curran, J. (2010). *Media and Society*. Bloomsbury Academics, 5th edition. London: Bloomsbury.

Hyden, G., Lesslie, M., and Ogundimu, F.F. (2007). *Media and Democracy in Africa*. London: Translation Publishers.

Lush, D. and Kupe, T. (2013). "Free expression and access to information in Zimbabwe". In *International Conference on Media*, Johannesburg: International Media

Support (IMS), The Netherlands Institute for Southern Africa (NiZA), Media Institute for Southern Africa (MISA) and the Open Society Institute. pp. 4–15.

Maja-Pearce, A. (1995). "Zimbabwe". In Article 19 and Index on Censorship, *Who Rules the Airwaves? Broadcasting in Africa*, London: Article 19. p. 123.

Mano, W.(2005). "Press Freedom, Professionalism and Proprietorship: Behind the Zimbabwean Media Divide", Westminster Papers in Communication and Culture, Special Issue, November, pp. 56–70.

Mosia, L., Riddle, C. and Zaffiro, J. (1994). From revolutionary to regime radio: Three decades of nationalist broadcasting in southern Africa. *Africa Media Review* 8(1): 1–23.

Moyo, D. (2005). *"From Rhodesia to Zimbabwe: Change without Change?"* Broadcasting Policy Reform and Political Control. In *Media, Public Discourse and Political Contestation*, Henning Melber (ed.), Uppsala: Nordic Africa Institute.

Moyo, D. (2009). Citizen journalism and the parallel market of information in Zimbabwe's 2008 elections. *Journalism Studies* 10(4): 1–20.

Moyo, D. (2010). Reincarnating clandestine radio in post-independence Zimbabwe. *Radio Journal: International Studies in Broadcast and Audio Media* 8(1): 2–16.

Moyo, L. (2012). Participation, citizenship, and pirate radio as empowerment: The case of radio dialogue in Zimbabwe. *International Journal of Communication (IJoC)* 6(484–500): 1–17.

Ndlovu, E. (2014). The re-emergence of diasporic radio in independent Zimbabwe. *Ecquid Novi: African Journalism Studies*, 35(3). http://www.tandfonline.com/eprint/6KJDrJREKwQ7gXKeUzYu/full. Accessed25/07/2015.

Ndlovu, E. (2014) The Role of Diasporic Media in Facilitating Citizen Journalism and Political Awareness in Zimbabwe. Doctoral Thesis. University of Salford. Manchester. UK.

Ranger, T. (2004). Nationalist historiography, patriotic history and the history of the nation: The struggle over the past in Zimbabwe, *Journal of Southern African Studies* 30(2): 215–234.

Rheingold, H. (1994). *The Virtual Community: Surfing the Internet*. London: Minerva Publishing.

Van der Veur, P. R. (2002). *Colonial Broadcasting Philosophies in British Africa, 1924–1968* [Unknown Binding].

Windrich, E. (1981). *The Mass Media in the Struggle for Zimbabwe: Censorship and Propaganda under Rhodesian Front Rule*. Gweru: Mambo Press.

Windrich, E. (2010). "Broadcasting in Zimbabwe". In *Media Policy in a Changing South Africa: Critical Reflections on Media Reforms in a Global Age*, D. Moyo and W. Chuma (eds.), Pretoria, South Africa: UNISA. pp. 85–87

Van der Veur, P. R. (2002). *Colonial Broadcasting Philosophies in British Africa, 1924-1968* [Unknown Binding].

Zaffiro, J. (1984). *Broadcasting and Political Change in Zimbabwe, 1931–1984*. Unpublished doctoral dissertation, University of Wisconsin-Madison.

Ziegler, D. and Asante, M. (1992). *Thunder & Silence: The Mass Media in Africa*. New Jersey: Africa World Press.

5
Why the Arab Spring Never Came to Ethiopia

Terje Skjerdal

Introduction

The potential impact of citizen journalism depends on its socio-political context. While a conducive climate can accommodate participatory media, a restrictive society has barriers that might be imperceptible to an outsider. These barriers are not just political: they are likely to be technological, economic and cultural as well. Despite the fact that citizen journalism is often believed to depend little on formal policy, in reality alternative journalistic forms also hinge on a supportive social and political environment. This is all too well known in Africa, where people-driven journalism is applauded by many commentators but in actuality occupies limited space in the continent's media activity (and is close to non-existent in some societies).

Understanding citizen journalism in a society therefore requires an examination of its political and cultural setting. Relevant indicators in this regard are the legal framework, the level of transparency in the public administration, the functioning of civil society and the application of informal control vis-à-vis the media. On top of this, citizen journalism might also require a sense of support from the media environment itself, implying that attitudes in the professional media has a bearing on the viability of alternative, non-institutionalized journalistic forms.

Against this backdrop, the underlying question which motivates this chapter is why citizen journalism thrives in some societies but not in others. This will be discussed in relation to a case study of Ethiopia, which is a society where citizen journalism cannot be said to be widespread. More specifically, the case concerns the attempt to bring the Arab Spring to Ethiopia in 2011 using new media technology along the lines of citizen engagement which had been observed in Egypt and Tunisia. For Ethiopia, the attempt turned out to be a failure, and this despite seemingly growing support among parts of the public ahead of the announced rallies in Addis

Ababa in May 2011. The current contribution, although acknowledging that the reasons for political developments are complex, argues that formal and informal restrictions in Ethiopian media governance became a major impediment for the public's engagement in a movement for political change.

Current developments in the Ethiopian mainstream media

Although the Ethiopian government has introduced various liberalizing measures in the media sector, the mainstream media remain largely government-controlled. This is especially evident in broadcasting, where all television stations and most radio stations are state-owned. Restructuring of the state media from approximately 2008 onwards has led to a more decentralized broadcasting structure where regional mass media agencies are in charge of content in various local languages. The restructuring has led to significant expansion not only in media infrastructure but also in the number of journalists throughout the country. By 2015 the total number of reporters in Ethiopia is likely to have exceeded 2,000, where most (roughly 80%) work in the federal or regional state media.

Depending on how one counts the different services and networks, the state-organized media structure counts at least five television stations and 11 radio stations which are on air most of the day. On the private side, there are five radio stations (all urban), plus another two which have obtained a licence but are not yet on air. Licences have also been given to a number of community radios, but community broadcasting is in its infancy in Ethiopia and these stations are low-capacity ventures which typically broadcast only one to two hours a day.

The print media sector is the only area where private channels outnumber the state-owned ones. Of approximately 20 newspaper titles, four are government-controlled and the rest are private. Newspapers in Ethiopia are mostly distributed in urban areas (notably in Addis Ababa, the capital city), and the circulation figures are low. The print media are mainly a channel for the urban and educated class.

The use of the Internet as a news medium, on the other hand, is steadily rising. Ethiopia has for long been one of the least connected countries in Africa, and out of a population of 90 million, only 2 million are regular Internet users.[1] This, however, represents rapid increase and three times as many users than just two years earlier. The use of mobile phones and smart phones is growing quickly too, and the first 4G network in the country was launched in Addis Ababa in April 2015.

In respect of media freedom, Ethiopia is frequently accused of suppressing independent voices. The country is usually placed in the latter half among African countries on general press freedom indexes, and scores especially poorly when it comes to assaults on journalists and media surveillance (e.g. Fortin, 2015). Although independent and critical media channels do exist, the outlets are constantly scrutinized by the authorities. Critical channels risk repercussions of various kinds, such as denial of access to public documents, verbal attacks in the government media, or revoked printing contracts at the government-owned printing press.

Ethiopian media governance has nevertheless also displayed liberal achievements since the mid-1990s. A new media law in 2008, despite occasionally being portrayed as a step in the wrong direction (Ross, 2010), marked important progress for the press in several areas. Pre-trial detention of journalists was prohibited; licensing of newspapers ended; professional association became a legal right; and Ethiopia became one of the first countries in Africa to pass legislation securing access to government information. With the new law, media legislation was no longer an effective tool to persecute journalists, as had been the case with the repealed 1992 press law until 2008.

However, the year after, in 2009, the Ethiopian parliament passed legislation which since has been a key instrument against critical reporting; specifically the 2009 Anti-Terrorism Proclamation. The first of its kind in Ethiopia, the law is instituted to prevent and fight terrorism. However, at the same time the law gives the authorities a wide room to interpret what constitutes incitement and support for terrorism. With regard to the media's role, a clause which targets "encouragement of terrorism" has been particularly critiqued. The clause declares that

> Whoever publishes or causes the publication of a statement that is likely to be understood by some or all of the members of the public [...] as a direct or indirect encouragement [...] of an act of terrorism [...] is punishable with rigorous imprisonment from 10 to 20 years.
> (Ethiopian Anti-Terrorism Proclamation, No. 652/2009, clause 5)

The clause gives wide space to the judiciary to interpret what constitutes a transgression. The offender could be anyone involved in the production and dissemination of sensitive material, and is not restricted to the distributor. Likewise, when the verification of what constitutes encouragement of terrorism is left to the perception of "some or all of the members of the public", the prosecutor has an opportunity to argue that nearly all references to terrorism constitute a criminal act, since a member of the public who sees such publicity as an inspiration to extremist acts can always be found. Experiences from several court cases confirm that broad interpretation of the legislation has become the order of the day. Mentioning an organization which is deemed a terrorism network by the Ethiopian parliament in a media report is risky if it in any way could be perceived as favourable publicity for the organization. The Ethiopian court system has consequently had several cases concerning journalists and charges of support for terrorism. The most famous is the case against Eskinder Nega, who was sentenced in 2012 to 18 years in prison for provoking violence and for supporting the Ginbot 7 group which is banned in Ethiopia on legal grounds with reference to the anti-terrorism law. Eskinder Nega was active as a critical columnist and blogger until he was detained in 2011.

The use of the anti-terrorism law against journalistic activity has reinforced self-censorship in Ethiopian newsrooms (Binyam, 2013; Skjerdal, 2010). Reporters adopt a culture of care, where they learn how far they can go in critical reporting until they risk repercussions. The constraints, however, could also be attributed to self-imposed restrictions which are intensified by internal newsroom discourses rather than actual recorded consequences (Skjerdal, 2013). Self-censorship mechanisms are not only a phenomenon in the private media, but in the state media as well. Thus, although a degree of disparity between state media journalists and independent journalists can be observed (Birhanu, 2014), the journalistic culture is also a common one and transgresses the political dichotomy between state media and private media.

Traces of citizen journalism in Ethiopia

There is little talk of citizen journalism in Ethiopia. Two possible reasons can account for this: first is that the concept is not yet adopted locally, and secondly citizen journalism as a practice is not prevalent. That the concept has not gained popularity is evident, and should not come as a surprise. Even if the global research literature has embraced citizen journalism and other alternative journalistic frameworks, the notion is still a novel one in sub-Saharan Africa (Mutsvairo and Columbus, 2012). In Ethiopia, the scholarly discussion about journalistic form is limited and, arguably, less driven by trends in global research. The most debated journalistic framework in the local environment is development journalism, which largely ceased as a concept globally in the 1990s (Xu, 2009), but was revitalized in Ethiopia in the 2000s (Skjerdal, 2012).

The second explanation for the few references to citizen journalism in Ethiopia could be that the practice has not gained ground. In comparison with other societies where people-driven journalism is vibrant and widespread, Ethiopia has a less visible arena where regular citizens can exchange material and ideas which look like journalism in one way or the other. The most obvious reason for this is the limited diffusion of digital technology. With less than 3% of the population as Internet users (as of 2015), the use of digital media is still considered exclusive rather than ordinary; elitist rather than popular; and costly rather than affordable. The political climate is not supportive either. While the country had a number of news blogs prior to the 2005 elections, the number went down rather than increased in the year which followed, according to research reports (Helen, 2011; Skjerdal, 2014).

That said, it is fully possible to find traces of citizen journalism in Ethiopia. The local blogosphere, although small in size, accommodates some of the leading commentators and reporters in the country. Among these is Horn Affairs (www.hornaffairs.com), which contains daily news reports and comments. The blog is run by a team of voluntary writers, although it is mostly the work of one person, Daniel Berhane. In contrast to pure commentary blogs, Horn Affairs produces news and investigates its own stories. The site appears to have key contacts within the ruling party, and has exposed internal views and disputes more than once. Though leaning towards the incumbent, the blog is not particularly prejudiced towards one political view, as reflected in its slogan "The extreme lies between the two sides". Horn Affairs is not institutionalized, yet it produces something that comes close to journalism. It is a good example of locally produced citizen journalism in Ethiopia.

The bulk of participatory journalism concerning Ethiopia, however, is actually not produced in the country, but abroad (see Hafkin, 2006). A high number of blogs and social media content emanating from the Ethiopian diaspora around the world may qualify as citizen journalism in the broad sense. The greater part of these are politically motivated, especially against the ruling coalition in Ethiopia. Among the three prototypes of participatory journalists defined by the US-based National Association of Citizen Journalists – accidental journalists, advocacy citizen journalists and citizen journalists (Ross and Cormier, 2010) – the contributors to the Ethiopian diaspora media largely belong to the advocacy type. Their online engagement is motivated by a desire of political change back home. A number of the reports and contributions are aggressive and lack decency. As a result, many of the websites are blocked from access in Ethiopia by Ethio Telecom, the national (and only) telecommunications company.

There are examples of Ethiopian-related citizen journalism which has had political impact. The most famous of these, at least among journalism scholars, is a series of articles that were published on the American blog the McGill Report (www.mcgillreport.org) and involved a mass murder of 425 persons in Western Ethiopia in 2003 (McGill *et al.*, 2007). It is unlikely that the massacre would have reached the media and the international community as quickly if it hadn't been for that particular blog in the US. Doug McGill, a former reporter with the *New York Times* and *Bloomberg News*, published stories on his blog about mass killings in the remote town of Gambella in Western Ethiopia based on reports that he received from Ethiopian immigrants who kept in touch with their families through mobile phones. The details they told were horrific, but the reporter had no chance of double-checking the news apart from the many direct accounts that he received through Ethiopian immigrants to the US. He still chose to publish the story on his blog, only to find that the mainstream media in the US would not follow up because there was no mention of the massacre by reputable organizations such as Human Rights Watch and Amnesty International. Ironically, the professional media were not satisfied with the reports of McGill even though he quoted various eyewitness accounts. Two months after the first blog entry, a rights organization published an investigative report which confirmed the slaughter, and the mainstream media eventually began to report on the incident. The massacre, which had been unknown even in the central parts of Ethiopia, subsequently became an issue in local public debate and was used by the opposition to confront the government prior to the 2005 elections. The official media in Ethiopia continued to ignore the incident, but visitors in Internet cafeterias made printouts of the blog reports and distributed the material among citizens. Not long after, the Gambella massacre had become an issue in Ethiopia's foreign relations.

In discussing the role of the McGill Report in the Gambella incident, Bala Musa and Franklin Yartey (2014) point to the double-sided aspects of citizen journalism. While such reporting allows the public to set the agenda, it also easily runs into a problem of partisanship. This is because the reporters are often stakeholders of the community which they report on, leading citizen journalism to become "point-of-view journalism" (Musa and Yartey, 2014, p. 261). Keeping a certain distance to the events reported on could make it easier for the reporter to tell things as they are without advocating a certain agenda (cf. McGill *et al.*, 2007, p. 290). The greater part of the transnational Ethiopian blogosphere, however, is motivated by advocacy and a desire for political change.

Failed attempts to bring the Arab Spring to the Horn of Africa

Inspired by the political demonstrations in North Africa and the Middle East in the first half of 2011, potent forces sought to awaken a similar reform movement in Ethiopia. The initiative did not spring out of an established political party, but was the result of mainly young campaigners who saw an opportunity to instigate change through public gatherings and citizen engagement akin to the Arab uprisings. Like the demonstrations in, for example, Tunisia and Egypt, the movement had a grassroots image with a less defined leadership structure. Although the campaign was clearly aimed at the local Ethiopian public, the initiative itself was largely transnational and relied heavily on the Ethiopian diaspora, especially in the US and Western Europe.

The campaign took a name which at the same time functioned as an effective slogan: "Beka!" – meaning "enough" in Amharic. To spread the message, the campaigners made strong use of the social media, particularly Facebook. Numerous Ethiopians changed their profile picture to the "Beka!" logo, visualized by the colours of the national flag overwritten by the slogan.

On 28 May 2011, the campaign was intended to move to a whole new level when a large rally was scheduled in Addis Ababa. The demonstration was supposed to resemble a momentous rally that took place six years earlier when 1 million people or more gathered in Meskel Square in downtown Addis Ababa to show their support for the political opposition in the run-up to the 2005 elections. The plan this time around was to turn Meskel Square into an Ethiopian Tahrir Square, and maximize the event by engaging the global Ethiopian diaspora in simultaneous demonstrations throughout the world. This would be made possible by effective use of new media technology, connecting Addis Ababa with the global community through interlinked protests throughout the world. The organizers promised that the rally would be "the greatest demonstration for freedom and democracy in the history of our nation".[2] The choice of 28 May was not accidental; it marked the 20th anniversary of EPRDF rule in Ethiopia. The time had come to put an end to Meles Zenawi's Tigray-dominated regime.

However, the anticipated Arab Spring spin-off in Ethiopia never occurred. The protests in Addis Ababa on 28 May 2011 came to next to nothing. Very few of the 3,000 people who had confirmed their attendance in one of the Facebook groups actually appeared. Instead, the ruling party seized the day to make their own celebrations of 20 years of EPRDF rule, and gathered tens of thousands of supporters at Meskel Square. The announced worldwide "Beka!" protests were insignificant, despite massive social media campaigning which extended far beyond the local websphere, engaging Ethiopians and supporters around the globe. Even serious commentators who noted that the political opposition in Ethiopia was weak cautioned in advance that the "Beka!" movement could take everyone by surprise (Lefort, 2011). Soon after it became clear to everyone that there would be no surprise. Instead of marking a new beginning, 28 May 2011 effectively marked the end of any attempt to institute an Arab Spring in Ethiopia, and, with that, growing scepticism of political change through citizen journalism (Endalkachew, 2011).

A society opposed to citizen journalism?

In order to understand the incompatibility of citizen journalism in the "Beka!" campaign in 2011, it is helpful to consider the recent history of digital media in Ethiopia. The 2005 elections represented a watershed, as the nation for the first time got thorough experience with the use of new media platforms in electoral politics (Kibnesh, 2006). A number of news and commentary blogs surfaced, challenging the previous situation where the communication landscape consisted of traditional, controllable media channels. For the country as a whole, the size of the digital readership was low. However, among opinion leaders, the use of the Internet as a news medium was already significant and created a new arena for exchange of ideas. Furthermore, digital technology played a pivotal role by means of informing people about time and place for political rallies through SMS. Such events, which previously depended on slower media channels (posters, weekly news-papers, etc.), could now be announced much more efficiently and on short notice. The situation left the authorities powerless, it seemed. In the weeks which followed after the election day 15 May 2005, the atmosphere grew tense as the announcement of the final results dragged out and preliminary data were questioned. On 8 June, the tensions erupted in violent clashes between security forces and the opposition in Addis Ababa. In an attempt to control the situation and avoid public gatherings, the authorities closed the SMS service through the only telecommunications provider in the country, the state-owned Ethiopian Telecommunications Corporation. The ban lasted for more than two years and later became known as the longest obstruction of the SMS service in Africa ("SMS message", 2010).

The restrictions imposed on digital technology in the aftermath of the 2005 elections later transpired as only the first step in intensified restraints on both professional and participatory media activity in Ethiopia. In 2006, the first five websites containing controversial material were blocked. By 2015, the total number of sites which have been reported blocked amounts to more than a hundred, although some of the sites have been periodically available. The filtering of web content is particularly distressing for the oppositional diaspora, which is significantly hampered from communicating their message to Ethiopians in the homeland. In Africa as a whole, Ethiopia is still in a league on its own when it comes to Internet filtering and is one of very few countries on the continent which engage in Internet censorship (Matschke, 2015).

With the anti-terrorism law of 2009, bloggers and participatory journalists faced yet another hurdle. In April 2014, six bloggers from the Zone 9 network were detained for allegedly inciting public disorder via social media and for receiving support from two officially designated terrorist organizations. Created in 2012, Zone 9 is an informal community of young bloggers focusing on democracy and human rights. The contentious nature of its activities is revealed in its name: "Zone 9" refers to the Kality prison in Addis Ababa where most journalists with long-term sentences end up. The prison has eight zones, while "Zone 9" alludes to the imaginable zone where all other Ethiopians are "imprisoned". The Zone 9 bloggers were detained for more than a year before the first two of them were released prior to US President Barack Obama's state visit to Ethiopia in July 2015. During that year, their court case had been adjourned no less than 27 times. Beyond the legal process, the effect of the Zone 9 case is that it has a chilling effect on other bloggers and independent reporters who focus on issues such as political criticism and democracy in Ethiopia.

The reporting of the Arab Spring and its possible offspring on the Horn of Africa in the local media illustrates the sensitive nature of political uncertainty in Ethiopia. The state media did report on the events that were spreading in the Arab world, but the reporting was undramatic and presented in distanced manner (Asmeret, 2013). The news reports were framed in such a way that it became clear to the viewer that the protests were something that happened "there" and were unrelated to anything locally. When reports of the "Beka!" movement began to appear on blogs and in the social media, it was largely ignored by the professional media – both in private and state-owned channels. The movement was still known to the informed Ethiopian public, thanks largely to online channels such as Facebook, which remained open. However, behind the scenes, the authorities watched the developments closely and were prepared to take action if necessary. Less than a month after the failed "Beka!" rally, two journalists, Woubshet Taye and Reeyot Alemu, were arrested, accused of taking pictures of "Beka!" graffiti in a bus terminal in Addis Ababa, among other charges. They were later sentenced to 14 and five years in prison respectively on terrorism-related charges (Reeyot Alemu was released ahead of President Obama's visit in July 2015). The even more renowned case, the one against the previously mentioned blogger Eskinder Nega (18 years sentence), began with an article that he wrote in February 2011 where he discussed the possibility of an Arab Spring in Ethiopia (Eskinder, 2011). The article was never posted in the mainstream media, whether state-owned or private, hence demonstrating – in the eyes of the government – the feared potential of the alternative media as a vehicle for political transformation.

Concluding discussion

The actual role of citizen media during the Arab uprisings is debated. While the political changes which followed, especially in Egypt, are popularly referred to as a "Facebook revolution" (Harlow, 2013; Smith, 2011), researchers generally hold that the social media were only one among several factors that contributed to the transformation (Howard and Hussain, 2013; Khamis and Vaughn, 2013). This is underscored by analyses which emphasize the interdependence between the uprisings and general political transformation (Bogaert, 2013; Wolfsfeld *et al.*, 2013). However, the social media, in different forms, functioned as catalysts and accelerators in a special way in the regime overthrows that took place in North Africa in January 2011 onwards (Khamis, 2013; McGarty *et al.*, 2014). Illustratively, the people who began to take to the streets in Egypt in January 2011 were active social media users (Tufekci and Wilson, 2012).

Certainly, the Ethiopian authorities followed the events in North Africa closely. Even if the local opposition was weak and seemed incapable of a revolt, the 2005 election rallies had demonstrated that it was able to mobilize the public in a relatively short time. In contrast to the situation in 2005, as uprisings were unfolding in North Africa and on the Arab Peninsula in the first half of 2011, the media were much more an inherent part of the Ethiopian governance strategy. That strategy included both proactive use of the government media, as well as application of media policy which served to curb the independent media, especially the online media. The state-owned media were employed to portray the events in the Arab countries in a favourable way for Ethiopian interests. Contrary to perceptions of international rights organizations and some foreign commentators (Keita, 2011; Lefort, 2011), the Ethiopian government media did not silence the Arab uprisings, but provided daily reports of the events, not least in the local language media. A coherent study of three Amharic newspapers found 83 articles concerning the Arab Spring in the government-run *Addis Zemen* in the period January to April 2011, compared with 32 and 23 articles respectively in the private publications *Reporter* and *Feteh* (Asmeret, 2013). The tone of the coverage in the three newspapers differed. While the two private newspapers – especially the opposition-minded *Feteh* – speculated that the Arab Spring could spread to Ethiopia, the state-owned *Addis Zemen* had a negative portrayal of the uprisings and maintained that the pretext for the demonstrations was not present in Ethiopia. The findings are corroborated by a study of English-language newspapers which concludes that the private press depicted the Egyptian protests positively while the state-owned *Ethiopian Herald* softened and downplayed the events (Desalegne, 2014). However, by the time of the announced "Beka!" rally in late May 2011, the coverage of the Arab Spring had largely ended. Characteristically, the government media duly acknowledged the events as long as they took place abroad, but were not interested in giving space to potential dissent at the Ethiopian end.

While coverage of the Arab Spring transpired in the mainstream media, the engagement was more challenging for the alternative (citizen) media. Ethiopian authorities applied policy measures – primarily informal – which largely stifled amateur and activist media. The diaspora media were particularly targeted. Oppositional websites run from the US and Europe, such as Ethiomedia.com, Ethiopianreview.com and Ethsat.com, are customarily blocked in Ethiopia, which meant a cumbersome mobilization of the Ethiopian public in the "Beka!" campaign. The campaign did not get much support from local opposition-minded blogs and websites, simply because there are so few of them. Local people who do contribute to diaspora websites either do it anonymously or know that they risk repercussions if they write under full identity. The social media, on the other hand, were unrestricted and represented an arena for sharing news and opinions. The role of Facebook in particular is noteworthy, insofar as the channel each day engages far more people than the number of people who relate to the printed press. As argued by Tesfaye Alemayehu (2013), Facebook has attained a position as an alternative platform in Ethiopia where the public can discuss a wide range of issues, including political controversy (cf. Sileshie, 2014). The full availability of Facebook, however, did not result in any mobilization of note in the Arab Spring-inspired "Beka!" campaign. Of course, the possibility that most of the wired Ethiopian public simply did not support the sentiment of the "Beka!" initiative should not be excluded.

In conclusion, the failed Arab Spring protests in Ethiopia may underscore a broader lesson in regard to citizen journalism. While one of the tenets of citizen journalism is its autonomy from established media structures and policy, it is bound to relate to its political surroundings. Although there is no licence required to start a blog in Ethiopia, once a blog is live it risks being subject to security assessment, terrorism consideration, political scrutiny and so forth. Citizen journalism is certainly possible in a tightly controlled society, but it can be demanding, and it is less likely to be clamped down on if it represents more than merely activism for political change.

Notes

1. www.internetworldstats.com as of 31 December 2014
2. https://www.facebook.com/events/103675769714614/

References

Note that Ethiopian authors are listed according to the local naming tradition, which means that the first name rather than the last name is used for reference. The first name is the proper reference in Ethiopia, while the second/last name is the father's name and is listed for clarification purposes.

Asmeret Hailesilassie. (2013). Ethiopian print media coverage of the Arab uprisings: The case of Addis *Zemen, Fetehe,* and *Reporter.* MA Thesis, Addis Ababa University.
Binyam Tamene. (2013). The impact of Ethiopia's anti-terrorism proclamation on freedom of the press: The case of the Ethiopian private press. MA Thesis, Addis Ababa University.
Birhanu Olana Dirbaba. (2014). Pride versus humility: The self-perceived paradoxical identities of Ethiopian journalists. *Sage Open* 4(1). http://classic.sgo.sagepub.com/content/4/1/2158244014528921.short.
Bogaert, Koenraad. (2013). Contextualizing the Arab revolts: The politics behind three decades of neoliberalism in the Arab world. *Middle East Critique* 22(3): 213–234.
Desalegne Tadesse. (2014). Framing of the 2011 Uprising in Egypt: Content Analysis of the *Ethiopian Herald* and the *Reporter.* MA Thesis, Addis Ababa University.
Endalkachew Hailemichael. (24 June 2011). "What happens on Facebook remains on Facebook: The 'Beka' revolution evangelists on Facebook revisited." https://endalk.wordpress.com/2011/06/24/what-happens-on-facebook-remains-on-facebook-the-%E2%80%9Cbeka%E2%80%9D-revolution-evangelists-on-facebook-revisited/.
Eskinder Nega. (2011). Egypt's and general Tsadkan's lesson to Ethiopian generals. http://www.ethiomedia.com/above/2092.html.
Fortin, Jacey. (2015). Conflating terrorism and journalism in Ethiopia. https://cpj.org/2015/04/attacks-on-the-press-conflating-terrorism-and-journalism-in-ethiopia.php.
Hafkin, Nancy J. (2006). "Whatsupoch" on the net: The role of information and communication technology in the shaping of transnational Ethiopian identity. *Diaspora: A Journal of Transnational Studies* 15(2–3): 221–245.

Harlow, Summer. (2013). "It was a Facebook revolution": Exploring the meme-like spread of narratives during the Egyptian protest. *Revista de comunicación* 12(1): 59–82.

Helen, Yosef. (2011). Backfiring repressions: The polarization of Ethiopian blogs. MA Thesis, Costa Rica: University for Peace.

Howard, Philip N. and Muzammil M. Hussain. (2013). *Democracy Fourth Wave? Digital Media and the Arab Spring.* Oxford: Oxford University Press.

Keita, Mohamed. (18 February 2011) . Sub-Saharan Africa censors Mideast protests. News report, Committee to Protect Journalists. http://cpj.org/x/41be.

Kerina, Kakuna. (October 1996). Clampdown in Addis: Ethiopia's journalists at risk. Report, Committee to Protect Journalists. http://www.cpj.org/reports/1996/07/ethiopia-journalists-at-risk.php.

Khamis, Sahar. (2013). "Cyberactivism" in the Arab spring: What social media can and cannot do. *International Affairs Forum* 4(1): 104–106.

Khamis, Sahar and Vaughn, Katherine. (2013). Cyberactivism in the Tunisian and Egyptian revolutions: Potentials, limitations, overlaps and divergences. *Journal of African Media Studies* 5(1): 69–86.

Kibnesh Chala. (2006). The use of Internet as a medium for disseminating information by Ethiopian newspapers. MA Thesis, Addis Ababa University.

Lefort, René. (26 May 2011). "Beka!" ("enough"). Will Ethiopia be next? *OpenDemocracy.* https://www.opendemocracy.net/ren%C3%A9-lefort/beka-enough-will-ethiopia-be-next.

McGarty, Craig, Thomas, Emma, F., Lala, Girish, Smith, Laura, G.E. and Bliuc, Ana-Maria. (2014). New technologies, new identities, and the growth of mass opposition in the Arab Spring. *Political Psychology* 35(6): 725–740.

McGill, Douglas, Iggers, Jeremy and Cline, Andrew, R. (2007). Death in Gambella: What many heard, what one blogger saw, and why the professional news media ignored it. *Journal of Mass Media Ethics* 22(4): 280–299.

Matschke, Alexander. (29 April 2015). Freedom House interview: Press freedom declines drastically. http://www.dw.de/freedom-house-interview-press-freedom-declines-drastically/a-18414325.

Musa, Bala, A. and Franklin Nii Amankwah Yartey. (2014). "Citizen Journalism and Emerging Perspectives on Conflict Transformation." In *From Twitter to Tahrir Square: Ethics in Social and New Media Communication*, Bala A. Musa and Jim Willis (eds.), Santa Barbara, CA: Praeger. pp. 251–264.

Mutsvairo, Bruce, and Columbus, Simon. (2012). Emerging patters and trends in citizen journalism in Africa: The case of Zimbabwe. *Central European Journal of Communication* 5(1): 121–135.

Ross, Ron, and Carson Cormier, Susan. (2010). *Handbook for Citizen Journalists.* Denver, CO: National Association for Citizen Journalists.

Ross, Tracy J. (2010). A test of democracy: Ethiopia's Mass media and freedom of information proclamation. *Penn State Law Review* 114(3): 1047–1066.

Sileshie, Semahagne. (2014). Challenges and opportunities of Facebook as a media platform in Ethiopia. *Journal of Media and Communication Studies* 6(7): 99–110.

Skjerdal, Terje. (2010). Justifying self-censorship: A perspective from Ethiopia. *Westminster Papers in Communication and Culture* 7(2): 98–121.

Skjerdal, Terje. (2012). "Development Journalism Revived: The Case of Ethiopia." In *Press Freedom in Africa: Comparative Perspectives*, Herman Wasserman (ed.), London: Routledge. pp. 67–83.

Skjerdal, Terje. (2013). Competing loyalties: Journalism culture in the Ethiopian state media. PhD dissertation, University of Oslo.

Skjerdal, Terje. (2014). "Online Journalism under Pressure: An Ethiopian Account." In *Online Journalism in Africa: Trends, Practices and Emerging Cultures*, Hayes Mabweazara, Okoth Fred Mudhai and Jason Whittaker (eds.), New York: Routledge. pp. 89–103.

Smith, Catharine. (11 February 2011). Egypt's Facebook revolution: Wael Ghonim thanks the social network. *The Huffington Post*. http://www.huffingtonpost.com/2011/02/11/egypt-facebook-revolution-wael-ghonim_n_822078.html.

"SMS message ban in Mozambique raises difficulties operators and government will have to deal with". (17 September 2010). Balancing Act, newsletter no. 522. http://www.balancingact-africa.com/news/en/issue-no-522.

Tesfaye Alemayehu. (2013). Social media as an alternative political forum in Ethiopia: The case of Facebook. MA Thesis, Addis: Ababa University.

Tufekci, Zeynep, and Wilson, Christopher. (2012). Social media and the decision to participate in political protest: Observations from Tahrir Square. *Journal of Communication* 62(2): 363–379.

Wolfsfeld, Gadi, Elad Segev and Tamir Sheafer. (2013). Social media and the Arab Spring: Politics comes first. *The International Journal of Press/Politics* 18(2): 115–137.

Xu, Xiaoge. (2009). "Development Journalism". In *The Handbook of Journalism Studies*, Karin Wahl-Jørgensen and Thomas Hanitzsch (eds.), New York: Routledge. pp. 357–370.

6

Citizen Journalism at Crossroads: Mediated Political Agency and Duress in Central Africa

Mirjam de Bruijn

> March 2013: Y. is working in the nearby hotel where there is semi-permanent electricity and Wi-Fi, to get the things done he has to do. He rents a room in a house in Ndjamena, capital city of Chad, in a neighbourhood that is not electrified, not tarmacked.
>
> January 2015: G. records his engaged songs in the new studio of a friend and peer, who buys the equipment for this studio with the salary he gains as a journalist and the extra work he does for national TV or for the presentation of a certain award. His studio is one of the most modern in town.
>
> May 2009: Before these two young men became part of my research we were already confronted with the advancement of internet access by young people in a central Chadian town from where a Facebook group became the connection between young people from central Chad spread over the world, and for whom identity politics seemed to be an important topic to discuss.
>
> (Seli, 2014)

These three examples show the connectivity of young people in Chad since 2010, during which time Facebook was appearing on cheap phones and the Internet became available to more people. As we will see in the different (hi)stories of the young people, individual adoption of technology is narrowly related to the connectivity environment, and it is especially related to the individual's skills and eagerness to connect. Who are the young men and women who are eager to connect? And what are the circumstances that make this possible?

The literature suggests that, with the advancement of the Internet, social spaces are created that allow people to express themselves differently and to join debates which they would not have been able to join in an "ordinary" public setting. The virtual creates a public but "anonymous" space. The role of media and politics is a widely discussed chapter in social science research, but we are still discovering much about the role of the Internet in political action G (Fahlenbrach *et al.*, 2014; Hands, 2011; Miller, 2013). The expectations of new information and communication technologies (ICT) and their connectivity to the political field are high among non-governmental organizations (NGOs) and more activist-minded scientists. Indeed, as Rheingold (2002) and later Ekine (2010) have shown, ICTs – including the simple mobile phone – have the power to organize movements and protests, merely by communicating dates and short messages in order to recruit people. A far more difficult question is how such exchanges, and the more extensive exchanges on Facebook and other internet fora, lead to action. What is the relationship between the world of discussion in cyberspace and the action of individuals on the ground? And how is this mediated by, for instance, mobile phone communication and social media? Before we can answer such questions we need to delve into the practice of political acting (political agency, Chabal, 2009) and new media use, which I will do in this chapter in relation to a few individuals in Chad.

Researching this question in Chad brings another variable into the puzzle. Chad is one of the least connected countries in Africa. A couple of the huge problems for the Chadian citizen wishing to find their way onto cyberspace are the high costs of internet access and the lack of constant power/electricity, which means there is a huge difference in the relationship between political actions and ICTs in Chad, and in Europe and USA. However, as the stories of the young people in this chapter show, there is also the question of who is eager to connect and the depth of their social and political engagement? In the oppressive and dictatorial political environment of Chad, an environment of duress, this is a daring endeavour.

Some methodological notes

This chapter should be understood as being the result of a long follow-up of Chadian society in different parts of Chad. The approach to the field of technology and society is qualitative and became almost organically part of my research since 2001, when I visited Chad for the first time. It simply happened that new communication technology was entering my field and people started using it in diverse ways, influencing our relationship and my relation to the field. It also imposed a different topic on my research that, previously, had been concentrating on the effects of the long periods of conflict and political turmoil in central Chad and among migrants from Ndjaména (see de Bruijn and van Dijk, 2007). With Djimet Seli, I began research on the relation between conflict mobility and communication technology among the Hadjeray, a group from central Chad with specific conflict mobility. This research started in 2007, when the capital city Ndjaména was able to access the new technology of communication, but large parts of the interior of Chad still had to become connected.

The government's policy is, on face value, very open to internet connectivity. The organization of the ICT fair in September 2014, however, illustrates the deeper significance of this openness. Behind the high fence of the Palais du Congrès, those invited were able to take a look at the future cyber revolution of Chad: discussions with celebrated Chadian artists, high-tech people from telecommunication companies, and highly placed officials seemed to be paving the way to internet access for all. This fair was, however, only accessible for elites, which is the reality of Chad. Rapid internet connections are denied to the general population: the reason being the government's obvious fear of allowing them access to the net. The President of the Republic, Idriss Déby, made an allusion to the Arabic Spring after the government arrested people accused of attempting a coup d'état in May 2013, making it clear that such a "spring" would not be allowed in Chad. As one of my colleagues declared: "la peur a changé du camp". Nevertheless, even today the Internet is not easily accessible and is still expensive. If one wants to connect, it should be possible considering the technology of mobile modems for computers, or the new models of mobile smartphones, often produced in China.

I did not interview any highly placed individuals and my interpretation of the ICT event is a shared experience with observers outside the fence. However, there is reason to interpret it in these terms. Chadians have experienced civil war since 1965, and have been subjected to highly repressive regimes that do not allow freedom of speech. Djimet Seli makes it clear, in his ethnographic study among the Hadjeray, that fear is an important emotion, informing the way people operate with regard to communication and to expressing their political opinions. They simply do not speak in public. This fear environment may be a form of self-censorship (as was suggested by G. in an interview held in November 2014 (in Holland)); it is therefore also a lived reality. This makes researching political agency quite difficult.

On the other hand, over the past decade, collective action in the form of protests such as strikes, student protests and also rebellions have been recurrent in urban Chad. The most recent examples have been the student protest of March 2015, which was followed by a strike by medical students at the end of April 2015. How do such actions relate to the fear environment? I decided therefore to delve into the lives and experiences of people who are manifesting a wish for social change, and who seem to have gone beyond the sphere of fear.

The only way to understand changes in political agency in the Chad environment is to interact closely with people, hold conversations and probably involve informants in the research (see van Stapele, 2015). Consequently, my links to politically active young people in Chad became a conscious step in this research. They present themselves "leaders" who want to inform and unite citizens to change this environment, either through political action or by helping others understand the situation better. The intimate knowledge sharing against the background of what we already (thought) we knew about Chad helped us to understand the interaction between the presence of new ICT and the political agency of these social actors.

Young men in Ndjaména

Y. (mid-20s), orphan, is an ICT worker and law student especially interested in human rights and injustice. He is an angry young man who would love his environment to change. His explicit wish to be a political activist is probably different from the goals of his peers. Young people in Ndjaména form the majority of the population, as is the case in many African countries, where over 60% of the population are under 30 years old. Y. clearly wants to inform them. He also wants to get the message out of Ndjaména, and beyond Chad. But before all this he wishes to develop himself:

> Le travail me permettait pas de vivre comme je voulais (...) j'ai tout construit de mes propres mains Jusqu'à aujourd'hui ce n'est pas facile, mais... je me bats.... Il y a beaucoup de choses qu'il faut dénoncer... c'est comme ça que je suis en train d'étudier le droit. Je suis optimiste, je crois à l'avenir, même si les réalités exigent le renoncement, je crois, j'aime le travail et j'aime être occupé,... c'est d'apprendre, j'ai toujours envie d'apprendre.
>
> (Interview, 23 September 2014)[1]

G. is an artist and a medical doctor. In this chapter I cited and described G.'s daily life as a representative of a newly appearing scene of engaged artists in Chad. G. started as a rapper and gradually turned to the literature genre of slam poetry. His poems are short essays that analyse the conditions of life in Chad. As he says himself: "I want to analyze, not push people into action. They can do with my analysis what they want" (interview, November 2014). G. and Y. are good friends.

I will share two experiences that I had with both: Y.'s wish to put up a blog. G.'s creation of engaged songs. And with them I followed the student protest of March 2015 that got special coverage through the social media used by the students to gain ground in their protest.

Blogging

Blogging is a new technique/medium increasingly embraced by young people in Africa to make their voices heard. Blogs made by Chadians who live in Chad are rare. A well-known blog (in Chad) is Maikala.com. The creator of the blog, finally expelled from Chad, lived in Senegal, and now has asylum status and is living in France. The writers for the blog are anonymous citizens of Chad. I know a few of them, but they do not want their names to appear. Especially after the arrests of journalists/participants in the blogs of diaspora others in May 2013. Why would Y. start up a blog while living in Ndjaména? Isn't it dangerous? He admits that his environment did make him think twice. But Y. was determined and took a course in Yaoundé to improve his blogging skills.

In-between sharing his ideas with me on FB text-messenger, Y. also confides that he is feeling quite depressed. It is not easy to be a student without work, to be young in Chad, without a family support network; no generous uncle or other relative. He is fed up with the situation in Chad, and his uncertain future. He has decided to live on his own. He spends quite a lot of time alone in his room, working on some ICT work on demand, or just idling. He likes to read, but now and then goes out with his friends for a beer. He also goes alone to a bar next door, and works on his computer there. His computer and smartphone are practically always with him.

For Y. new ICT, Internet and mobile telephony, have been part of his life since this new technology entered Ndjaména. He was born around 1990, the moment President Déby took power and gradually installed a "democratization" in Chad. Y. witnessed the arrival of the new ICTs in Chad and told me that he was so eager to be part of that new development. He queued for hours in order to buy the relevant equipment, and since then he spent a lot of money to access Internet. He was one of the early adopters of this new technology. After his training as a graphic designer he was able to find jobs in publishing houses and so on. But, more importantly, he was involved in the first youth movements, if we may call them so, from Chad on the Internet. *Rafigi*, a youth journal, was one of the first youth-focused platforms on the Internet. G., one of the founding members, invited Y. to be part of that enterprise and he was asked to develop posters, the look of the website and so on. That was in 2009. In 2011 Y. started his first blog, "Tchad est possible". It did not satisfy him fully, so he took a course in Yaoundé, Cameroon. He is now one of the writers for another blog. He started his own new blog in 2015: Haadji Platform. In an interview we held in February 2015 he expressed his wish to be a blogger; it is intrinsic to his being:

> Etre bloggeur n'est pas facile, le travail, et mes études. A un moment donné être bloggeur ça demande l'électricité. Je suis dans un endroit ou l'accès de l'électricité n'est pas à la portée de tout le monde; la connexion je ne l'ai pas tout le temps; j'achète la connexion qui me coute extrêmement cher, un tiers de mon salaire; je ne gagne rien, mais ça me permet de m'exprimer, de faire parler les gens qui ont envie d'exprimer leur joie, mécontentement; mais ça te sert à rien; il y a de bloggeurs qui ont les gens autour qui leurs protègent, la sécurité avant tous, mais j'en ai pas, ... je le fait par amour parce que je suis comme ça, avec ou sans blog toute ma vie,tout mon quotidien c'est ça, je suis né revendicateur.

> Mon blog ça me tient tellement que.. milité.. ça se paye pas, militer ce n'est pas un métier, mais il y a de choses dans la vie, on le fait par amour, ...

> Le Tchad n'est pas connu ailleurs malheureusement, et ça fait mal.[2]

However, his new blog has not yet been published in full. Until now it is more a Facebook platform, where Y. posts short texts in which he expresses his observations of present-day Tchad, football and politics. His wish is to finally focus his blog on artists who, according to him, are the "porte-paroles" of this society, like his friend G.

Engaged musician in Chad

G. was, like Y., an early adopter of the new technology. He is about ten years older than Y. His first engagement with "modern" technology was when he was a boy and asked his uncle to bring him a game computer from France. His family were not rich, but some uncles did study abroad.[3] G.'s interest in technology has never waned, and he is ready to spend money on accessing the Internet and buying the necessary equipment.

G. is, first and foremost, a writer. His texts are indeed subtle and literary. He has embraced the style of "slam poetry", an urban form of poetry that was born in Chicago. It is part of urban popular culture. The lyrics of his songs speak of the difficulty of life in Ndjaména, indicating lack of governance and appealing to the "innocence" of Chadian political leaders. His songs talk also to the aspirations of the youth, who are unemployed and struggling to survive, as well as asking deeper philosophical questions, in which he ponders the very fact of human existence. As one of his supporters, director of the Institut Française Tchadien (IFT) in Ndjaména said: he is subtle and erudite. His use of language is his "arm".[4] G.'s songs have a large audience in Chad. His CDs sell well and, most importantly, probably his lyrics and songs have been sent to others through Bluetooth, and, more recently, can be accessed through the Internet, as some of his songs have been posted on YouTube.

G. only could flourish in this way because of new technology: use of the newly appearing modern studios; the spread of his songs among the population via mobile devices and CDs made with modern technology in the studio; the transmission of his songs on both national and international radio. But, probably foremost, because of the access new technology has given him to a wider world and information about that world, enabling him to reflect on his own position and on his country. He also travels, leaving and returning to "his village". As he himself comments, that is part of gaining the necessary knowledge to know who one is: "Ndjaména ce n'est pas la civilisation: ce n'est même pas 18ième siècle... être civilisé c'est connaître plein de truc... dont les trucs de village aussi. Il faut toujours avoir un repère... "[5] In the same interview,[6] he comments on his life in Ndjaména, where electricity and water are scarce goods:

> Aujourd'hui je vais créer ma condition de vie, et travailler comme je veux (...) je crée la modernisme; technologie est être moderne. Aujourd'hui si quelqu'un veut communiquer avec le monde, il faut la technologie (...) sacrifier deux trois bouteilles de bière et ça se fait (...) créez vous-même vos conditions de vie![7]

The student protest on Facebook

What seemed a small issue had the potential to change the political landscape in Chad. The student protest on 9 March 2015 was, according to my informants, provoked by the police. The police entered the school pretending a measure of control. The students reacted with their protest. The reason for the protest was a new law: the obligation for motorbike drivers to wear a helmet. The students might not have been against protecting their craniums, but they were revolted by the injustice that went with the imposition of this law. Helmet dealers exploited the situation, raising prices to impossible amounts; consequently, there were numerous arrests of unhelmeted young people by the gendarme, who then would fine them, and often take bribes. This was not the first law that had resulted in profit for the gendarmes and the population was no longer simply willing to accept the status quo. It could have been left there. But what made this protest really different was the death of three students. They were shot by police – an ugly death. Subsequently, some teenagers were arrested and tortured by the police. This was shown on a short film that was published on YouTube, and subsequently found its way to other social media, particularly Facebook. Chadian opposition press also picked up the film.

The following three posts are an example of the way the news was circulating:

Figure 6.1 Facebook posts with YouTube film about the police torture of students after March 9 protests

Translation: Peace be with your soul, Daouda, a young student who lost his life as a consequence of the police action in Chad. We are shocked and it is inacceptable. The video attached to this message shows what happened. The devil wears a uniform and is called our national police. This video is only the tip of the iceberg, it is an illustration of the lack of professionalism and lack of humanism in the acts of the Chadian forces. We will again cry out and cry: in God we trust.

Figure 6.2 Facebook post, picking up the YouTube film about the police torture of students after March 9 protests

Translation: Tchad/barbary of the police: Watch this video. What do the Police authorities have to say about this video that shows how the police tortures these youngsters like animals? These images make us aware that the politically responsible who lie to the people/population day and night need to be interrogated. The accountable of the political parties....

Figure 6.3   Facebook post in reaction to the YouTube film about the police torture of students after March 9 protests
Translation: Chad: the procureur of the republic opens a survey in relation to the video showing the tortures....

The sequence of these three posts shows how the posting of the film on the news Facebook site (fan Ndjaména-matin) was picked up by Facebook activists, which resulted in a public debate, that certainly also fed into the measures taken by the Chadian government, who then started an investigation and subsequently fired the head of the police force responsible.

What followed after the March 9 Student Protest

The funeral of one of the students, whose family lived in one of the popular quarters of Ndjaména, led to another act of protest. The students sent SMS messages around to call for a march on the 11 March to accompany the deceased to his resting place. Y. also joined this march, despite his family's opposition. He shared his observations with me, and later posted on Facebook as well. It was a quiet march, the students giving signs of peace (walking with their hands on their heads), nevertheless the police started to shoot and used gas to disperse the students.

After this march, the students continued organizing protests (...); such as a general refusal to go to school which led in practice to the closure of schools and several attempts to organize other manifestations. Most of these, announced via Facebook, were never to become reality, as they were suppressed before they got going. But finally, it appeared that the students gave in to the repeated requests of the government and university and schools opened again. When the government distributed helmets for free for the students, the queues were long. Y. detested the lack of protest spirit: he wrote to me on messenger; *"proteste échoué*, a missed chance!"

Y. and G. undertook actions on Facebook and in cyberspace, and on the ground in their own ways. Y. went out to protest and posted several posts, linking the protest to a larger social problem in Chad.

Later we invited Y. to publish a longer text on our website (see: www .connecting-in-times-of-duress.nl; rubrique journalistique).

Figure 6.4 Post of Y. while protesting, and a comment of G. to this post (11 March)
Translation: Y.: I am expressing my discontent together with the students of Ndjaména. A peaceful march to remember a child/citizen of Chad: Hassan Daouda, slaughtered by the illiterates of the Chadian republic. G.: He did not even ask to be listened to; The students did not really protest. These policemen....

G. did not join the students, even criticizing them in a way, as they were not very reflective in their actions. He manifested himself as a caretaker for

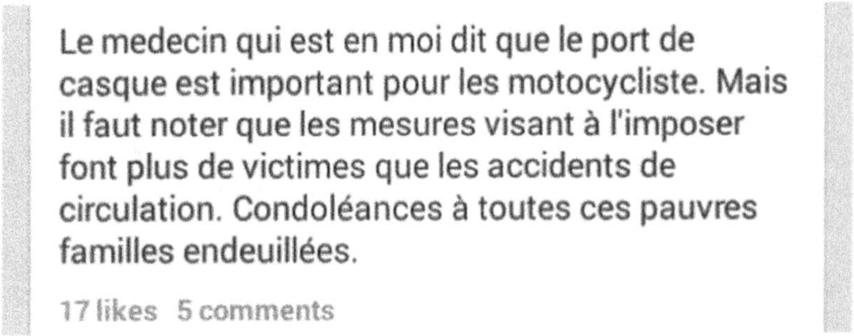

> Le medecin qui est en moi dit que le port de casque est important pour les motocycliste. Mais il faut noter que les mesures visant à l'imposer font plus de victimes que les accidents de circulation. Condoléances à toutes ces pauvres familles endeuillées.
>
> 17 likes 5 comments

Figure 6.5   G.'s first post

Translation: The medical doctor in me says that it is important to wear a helmet. But it is clear that the measures inflicted make more victims than the traffic accidents. My condolences to all the families who lost beloved members.

the Chadian population. He was very angry, and not the least because the randomness of the violence (see Figure 6.5).

During the protests on 9 March, G. started composing a song in which he comments and analyses the situation in Chad. The song was posted on YouTube, first by anonymous people, and later by ourselves (see blogpost Mirjamdebruijn.wordpress.com). An excerpt from the song's text (translated from French) follows:

> I would like to wear a helmet
> One that protects me against traffic accidents
> To avoid head wounds
> Or to be completely crushed
> To avoid blowing up my cherished brain
>
> I would like to wear a helmet
> That protects me against the electricity cuts
> Of the grimy streets in my neighbourhood
> To be able to watch TV
> One that protects against our discharged computers
> And our closed petty trades
>
> I would like a helmet
> One that fights against the police atrocities
> And the violence at schools
> All the students who were beaten
> While writing their exams at the faculty
> Who will end up traumatized
> The emergency rooms overcrowded
>
> *I would like to wear a helmet*
> *Not just a kind of mask*

A final stage in this Facebook and internet activity was the calls for actions published on Facebook: calling for meetings to discuss the situation and define further action. These were organized most probably by the university students. However, the meetings had no effect. Finally, the students returned to school and university and many accepted the gift of helmets from the government, which was commented upon by Y. as a weakness: this whole protest was a missed chance and the death of the three young men without any meaning.

Discussion

The (ICT) actions of Y. and G. are not exceptional for youth in Central Africa today. From Senegal, to Congo (DRC) and recently Burkina Faso, protest marches and youth movements have been on the rise. The use of the Internet and SMS in these movements must be similar to the situation sketched in this chapter for Chad. Research in Mali of the situation in the northern part in 2012, when it was the scene of several opposing groups and conflicts, also revealed the importance of ICTs in conflict, and the way "ordinary" citizens gain access to these conflicts through these new means of communication (see de Bruijn *et al.*, 2015, fc.).

What is ICT action? In the case of Chad we can discern two "sorts" of action: the very practical organization of protest with the help of ICT by sending messages through SMS, or calling for meetings through Facebook posts. Part of this "enabling" factor is also the "easy" music production by studios equipped with digital cameras, computers, and so on. The second way is the use of the (social) media to exchange ideas about what is happening, or to ventilate one's frustration and so on. Such posts/videos are often seen and "liked" or commented upon by others, which then creates a discussion and exchange on the situation surrounding these protests or events. Further analysis of these messages, likes and comments could give us more insight into the opinions and emotions around these topics.

Those posting on Facebook are not the uneducated of society. The two persons we presented here are clearly highly educated young men. They do not come from very rich backgrounds, but they do both have a high level of education. And remarkably, in an environment where new technology is very expensive and difficult to access, they were both eager and able to access the new technology, even at a young age. The hunger for information is another common thread. It needs many more "information" biographies of young people who are active in the political field and use ICTs to say something general about the character and "features" of these young men. This is research we still need to develop.

Political agency, understood as political action in everyday life, is changing for these two men with their access to new ICTs. It seems that the violent and restrictive environment of Chad does not (yet) extend to the Internet, and that a more "anonymous" space is indeed created, where online activity seems to be "harmless". As we have also seen for the two men presented in this chapter: their online activity cannot be separated from their offline actions. Y. was active in the protests and manifests himself as an active blogger (online activity with an offline action), and G. created a song (offline) that was also posted on YouTube and announced on Facebook (online). The Internet and mobile communication made their offline activities far more effective.

Will this combination of online and offline engagement lead to changes in political agency and hence in the political landscape of Chad? It is far too early to draw any such conclusions. Gergen (2008) foresaw a reformulation of the political organization in which power would shift to the younger generation. Both Y. and G. show a new political activity on Facebook and YouTube, the Internet (blogs) reaching out to a young public. Support for their actions may grow with time, when the government provides high-speed Internet and a reliable supply of electricity. However, even without these services people do access the information these young men send into the ether, picking it up in their own ways, which hopefully helps them to develop their own opinion. Political agency is certainly changing, but the effects this will have on the scale or form of movements or large-scale protests is not yet clear.

When I asked G. if there would be an Arabic Spring in Chad, he was very clear in his answer: "No! That would not be possible, because of the deep poverty and illiteracy of the large majority of the Chadian population" (interview, March 2014).

A word on methodology can conclude this discussion. The data I presented in this chapter are part of ongoing research. I try to find out about the lives of young men and women in the age of new ICTs and in a condition of duress, political oppression and conflict, by using the ethnographic method and reconstructing their biographies in context. This is qualitative research. Interestingly, though their actions on Facebook are related to many more actions by others, their actions feed into Facebook data, relate to other posts and so on. This creates quantitative sets of data. The analysis of these sets of data in relation to the actions of the individual actors that are central to this research could provide us with insights into the larger meaning of changes in political agency.

Notes

1. My work did not allow me to live the life I had wanted (...) I did all by myself until today, it is not easy, but ... I do not give up. There is a lot I have to denounce ... it is in this way that I follow my studies in law. I am an optimist, I believe in the

future, even if not supported by the lived reality, I believe, I love to work and
to be really busy,... that is learning/studying, I always want to learn ... (interview,
23 September 2014).

2. Being a blogger is not easy, my job, my studies. At a certain moment to be a blogger
one needs access to electricity. I live in a place where access to electricity is exclusive, it is not everybody who has access. I am not constantly connected; I have to
"buy" connectivity, which is extremely expensive, it costs one third of my salary.
I gain nothing (with blogging) but it gives me room for free expression, and also
allows others to say what they want, their happiness or their sadness; but it does
not bring me anything (money wise); there are bloggers who are protected by people around them, security *avant tous*, but I don't have,... I do this blogging because
I love it, and because it is me, with or without blog my whole life, all my daily
activities that's it: I am born a revolutionary.
   My blog is very important for me, being militant...does not pay; it is not a job,
but there are things in life that one does out of love...
   Chad is not at all known to the world, which is painful.
3. His family were from the south. His father studied in England and trained as a
teacher; while his uncle went to France for his studies. This was the end of colonialism and the beginning of independence. At the time, the situation was much
better in Chad and life was good.
4. Interview, February 2015, in Ndjaména.
5. N'djaména is not civilized, it did not even reach the stage of the eighteenth century. Being civilized means that you know a lot of things...as well as the things
from the village. It is important to have a point of reference...
6. Interview in the Netherlands, November 2014; present: Mirjam, Sjoerd (film-
maker) and G.
7. Today I want to create my own conditions of life and work as I want (...) I create
modernism; technology means being modern. Today if I want to communicate
with the world, I need technology (...) just the sacrifice of two or three bottles of
beer (i.e. not drinking them, hence saving money) will do it (...) create yourself
your own life condition!

References

Chabal, P. (2009). *Africa: The Politics of Suffering and Smiling*. London and New York:
   Zed Books.
De Bruijn, M. and van Dijk, H. (2007). The multiple experiences of civil war in the
   Guéra region in central Chad. *Sociologus* 57: 61–98.
De Bruijn, M., Pelckmans, L. and Sangaré, B. (2015). Communicating war
   in Mali (2012), on-offline networked political agency in times of conflict.
   JAMS 7 (2):
Ekine, S. (ed.) (2010). *SMS Uprising: Mobile Activism in Africa*. Nairobi, Cape Town,
   Dakar, Oxford: Pambazuka Press.
Fahlenbrach, K., Sivertsen, E. and Werenskjold, R. (eds.) (2014). *Media and Revolt,
   Strategies and Performances from the 1960s to the Present*. New York and Oxford:
   Berghahn Books.
Gergen, Kenneth J. (2008). "Mobile Communication and the Transformation of the
   Democratic Process". In *Handbook of Mobile Communication Studies*, J.E. Katz (ed.),
   Cambridge, MA: The MIT Press, pp. 297–309.

Hands, J. (2011). *@Is For Activism: Dissent, Resistance and Rebellion in a Digital Culture.* New York: Pluto Press.

Miller, D. (2013). *Tales from Facebook.* Cambridge: Polity Press.

Rheingold, H. (2002). *Smart Mobs: The Next Social Revolutions, Transforming Cultures and Communities in the Age of Instant Access.* Cambridge: Basic Books.

Seli, D. (2014). *(Dé)connexions Identitaires Hadjeray: Les enjeux des technologies de la communication au Tchad.* Leiden and Bamenda: ASC/Langaa.

Van Stapele, N. (2015). Respectable "illegality": Gangs, masculinities and belonging in a Nairobi ghetto. Unpublished Doctoral Thesis.

Part II
Prospects, Promises and Pitfalls

7

South African Arab Spring or Democracy to Come? An Analysis of South African Journalists' Engagement with Citizenry through Twitter

Glenda Daniels

Introduction and theoretical framing

This chapter explores to what extent social media – particularly Twitter – deepens democracy through engagement between journalists and the public. The promise of social media to further the ends of democracy, as in more voices for diversity and more inclusion of those on the margins, is like a rose not yet in full bloom. Nothing illustrates and depicts this more than a quantitative analysis of the usage of Twitter in the Johannesburg newsroom. An analysis of Twitter in the newsroom shows that only 5% of all tweets under analysis were disseminated specifically for engaging with citizenry (Daniels, 2014b, p. 304); journalists say they spend an average of 15 minutes out of every hour on Twitter (Ibid.) and concede that this 5% is a low number. In 2015, subsequent qualitative investigations – namely, interviews – into this 5% result found that the majority of journalists and editors were not surprised that such a small percentage of their tweets were deliberately written to engage with citizenry. Before a full explication of the research data and conclusions, we need a theoretical framing and an explanation of the concepts: What do we mean by "soliciting engagement"? What are "Twitter" and "radical democracy" and "how was this research carried out?"

The concept of "soliciting engagement" was developed for the report *State of the Newsroom (SoN), South Africa Disruptions Accelerated*,[1] published by the department of Journalism at Wits University in 2014, to ascertain or quantify how much journalists were trying to engage with citizenry in an attempt to create robust debate and inclusion of diverse voices in the public sphere. Twitter is an online social network site for sending and receiving messages of up to 140 characters; these are called tweets. It is the most used social media platform in the newsroom. More specifically, soliciting engagement indicated how much journalists and editors were eliciting – from the citizenry – views and opinions, discussion and debate about issues in the public domain.

According to several theorists (Hermida, 2012; Jordaan, 2013; Stassen, 2010; Twitter has changed how journalists work today. In its 2013 World Press Trends report, the World Association of Newspapers (WAN) asserted that the digital first transition has already happened; namely, putting the digital product ahead of traditional media, which includes the incorporation of social media strategy (2013, p. 17). In Johannesburg, this transition is progressing, but the research in this chapter strengthens the theories about access and the networked society (Mudhai, 2011; Paterson, 2013), as mainstream media tap into a space as a way of creating an impression about close links with citizenry and call this public engagement (Moyo, 2009). However, this chapter's qualitative component also shows that journalists accept that their contribution to democracy via engaging with citizenry is limited. Before an explanation of methodology is given, let us turn to the theoretical framing.

Theoretical framing

This research is framed through the radical democracy theory lens, particularly in Chantal Mouffe's works in *The Democratic Paradox* (2000) and *On the Political* (2006). The concept of democracy, albeit contested, is still commonly acknowledged to have its origins in ancient Greece – more than 2,500 years ago – with the terms "demos" and "kratos" (Held, 2006). This relates broadly to people and rule. However, at that time, many important voices – more than half the citizenry consisted of slaves and women – were excluded, even though the system of rule was still called "democracy" (Daniels, 2012). Then there were advancements to deliberative democracy rule (Shapiro, 2003) by the people, and participatory democracy (Gutmann and Thompson, 2004) to include citizens' voices. This chapter prefers the "radical democracy" model because it appears to demand the greatest possible inclusion of voices and diversity in the many public spheres, with fights, contestations and difference or dissension in action rather than unity and consensus. This is the radical democracy model as defined by Mouffe (2000; 2006). Indeed, it is the democratic paradox: the conceptual impossibility of a democracy, as a perfect democracy would destroy itself and this is why it should be regarded as a goal that exists as long as it cannot be achieved. Therefore, to this extent, Mouffe accepted Jacques Derrida's postmodernist philosophy that democracy can never be fully realized. It was "always becoming"; hence, "democracy to come" (Derrida, 2004, p. 323).

The pertinent question posed here, using the radical democracy model as the background, is: Can the now widespread use of Twitter in the newsroom be regarded as some form of bottom-up democracy, engaging citizenry in debates surrounding their everyday concerns, which could then be incorporated in the news agenda? The research is indicative of trends at a particular time and context in the Johannesburg newsroom; namely, 2013 to 2015. Clearly, the full extent of the social media landscape (for example, Facebook, Snapchat, LinkedIn and WhatsApp) is not explored. Rather, this chapter uses the example of Twitter in the newsroom, hailed as the most used social media for breaking stories, life sharing, opining and commenting, and engagement with the public to examine any possible contributions to deepening democracy, and possibly even an Arab Spring. The theoretical framing in this chapter moves beyond the role of the media in a democracy in the liberal pluralist tradition to a much more expansive view of democracy; namely, Mouffe's view of many more voices and many more fights and contestations, in an imperfect democracy. So, while the framework for this chapter supports the premise that the more media the better (for diversity and plurality of views) and that a free press is intrinsic to any democracy – its characterization as that of the fourth estate and more (Berger, 2004; Ibelema, 2012; Jacobs, 1999; Keane, 1991; Tomaselli, 2004) – it demands more.

The literature around and about Twitter and journalism (Hermida, 2012; Lasorsa *et al.*, 2011; Paterson, 2013; Stassen, 2010; Vis, 2013) continues to expand apace, but it does not deal with Johannesburg's newsrooms as specific locations. However, a recent article by Verweij and Van Noort (2013), "Journalists' Twitter Networks, Public Debates and Relationships in South Africa", argues that Twitter contributes to pluralism and more open engagement with the public spheres. This chapter accepts that there is a contribution to democracy but, after analysing evidence from the quantitative data and the discourse of journalists' and editors, argues that, at this moment in time, it is not very great.

The radical democracy theoretical framework expounds a multiplicity of public spaces; the noisier and more inclusive the better. The aim is for a more expansive democracy than that currently on the table in the Western world (Daniels, 2012, p. 16). As mentioned, in today's journalism, which incorporates social media, it is argued by some theorists that this enables public participation and "noise" and opens up previously elite spaces. However, this chapter questions what kind of noise this is: Is it the tamer rational consensus model of democracy or the more inclusive, robust model? The premise is that it is better for the news to include a more all-encompassing, more inclusive and plural democracy which can come from a greater participation of all kinds of citizens, genders and different ideological perspectives and class strata, lending diversity. The radical democracy model argues against an elite space full of consensus, with the like-minded engaging and reaffirming each other.

The radical democracy model accepts "agonistic pluralism" (Mouffe, 2000, p. 104), with the central argument that social division is constitutive of democracy. Antagonism, therefore, is ineradicable and pluralist democratic politics will never find a final solution. In Derridean fashion, it was "democracy to come". A well-functioning democracy calls for "a vibrant clash of political positions" (Ibid.). The radical democratic model is more receptive to the multiplicity of voices that contemporary pluralist societies encompass, advocating a positive status to differences while questioning homogeneity. In terms of the significance for the research here, social media signals potential for a radical democracy; that is to say, more noise, more diversity and more inclusion of voices otherwise excluded from mainstream media. This conceptual theorizing frames this analysis of a reflection on some of Johannesburg's journalist engagement with social media. How does this theoretical framing of radical democracy relate to the main issues here: Twitter and Journalism and Democracy?

The thesis on radical democracy incorporating the media's role was elucidated in an interview with Carpentier and Cammaerts when Mouffe commented: "Ideally, the role of the media should precisely be to contribute to the creation of agonistic public spaces in which there is the possibility for dissensus to be expressed or alternatives to be put forward" (2006, p. 974). For her, however, new media was not the answer to all the problems. But it does have potential: "I am also not one of those people that automatically see the new media as a solution" (Ibid.). She observed that there are many people claiming that, through new media, "you can realise direct democracy" (Ibid.). On the contrary:

> In fact, it perversely allows people to just live in their little worlds, and not be exposed any more to the conflicting ideas that characterise the agonistic public space. New media are making it possible to only read and listen to things that completely reinforce what you believe in.
>
> (Ibid.)

This chapter, through quantitative data and interviews with Johannesburg editors and journalists through discourse analysis, elucidates these theoretical matrixes. Meanwhile, social media landscape's rate of expansion in South Africa appears quite phenomenal if one accepts World Wide Worx statistics in 2014: Twitter use had grown by 129% from the year before, showing the highest percentage growth of all social networks – from 2.4 million to 5.5 million users. But an obvious word of caution relating to access is that this figure must be seen in the context of a population of approximately 50 million people.

Methodology

The quantitative component of the methodology consists of the fact that raw data and empirical research from *State of the Newsroom South Africa, 2014*

Disruptions Accelerated (2014) were used for this chapter. They were then combined with discourse analysis from qualitative interviews in 2015 to reach some analysis. Discourse analysis is important for this research if one considers that editors and journalists are interviewed about the quantitative data findings. What do their words reveal, and how are meanings constructed? Diane Macdonell (1986, p. 45) argues that discourse is social and that the "statement made, the words used, and the meanings of the words used, depends on where and against what that statement was made". Using the works of Pêcheux, she elucidates that conflicting discourses develop even when there is supposedly common language. For example, in conservative discourses, the concepts of "liberties", "rights" and "natural" are tied to inheritance. Indeed, liberty can be regarded as a noble freedom, and rights are synonymous with privilege. Pêcheux found that there were ideological effects in all discourses because words and expressions "change their meanings according to the positions held by those who use them" (1982, p. 111).

This multipronged methodological approach (theoretical, quantitative and discourse analysis) worked well when making an assessment of the contribution of Twitter to facilitate democratic change at this point in time. The journalists/editors were selected on the basis of their relatively high Twitter activity; for example, numbers of tweets and followers. A coding structure identifying the purpose of the tweet was used: Was it for "work" or was it "personal"? Then, of the "work tweets", were they for breaking news or broadcast, promotion of brand and promotion of self, disseminating opinions and comments, and, importantly for this research, what quantity was for soliciting engagement, namely, asking questions and initiating debate? Eight Twitter accounts from three newsrooms at two newspapers and one radio station were chosen for analysis. The data was collected via the Twitter application programming interface (API), which provided information such as content of the tweet (the actual 140-character message), the favourites, and the number of tweets, retweets and hyperlinks.

A total of 200 tweets per journalist were extracted over a two-week period in August 2013. This research must therefore be considered as a snapshot at a particular point in time. About 1,800 tweets were analysed. The newsrooms of Eyewitness News (*EWN*), *Mail & Guardian* (*M&G*) and *City Press* were deliberately chosen as they were considered to be frontrunners in South Africa's transition from traditional platforms to digital first. At the time this research was conducted, there was high Twitter usage among journalists in all three of these newsrooms: both the *M&G* editor-in-chief, Chris Roper, and editor-in-chief of *EWN*, Katy Katopodis, said that 100% of their journalists use Twitter in their work. Liesl Pretorius of *City Press* said about 90% of workers for this Sunday weekly used the platform.

The following journalists'/editors' tweets were chosen for analysis at *EWN*: Katy Katopodis (editor-in-chief), Mandy Wiener (journalist) and Barry

Bateman (journalist). At the *M&G*, Chris Roper (online editor at the time of analysis),[2] Ben Kelly (special projects editor) and Mmanaledi Mataboge (senior political journalist) were selected, and at *City Press* we analysed the tweets of Carien du Plessis (senior political journalist), Natasha Joseph (news editor) and Adriaan Basson (deputy editor at the time of analysis).[3]

The big question: What were journalists and editors tweeting about?

The category, "soliciting engagement", emerged as the smallest percentage of all: 5% of the total number of tweets dispersed was used for engaging with citizenry.

The majority of journalists used Twitter to tweet about work issues (which included broadcasting of news, breaking stories, promoting news brands and sharing opinions) rather than tweets about personal matters ("it's so hot"; "just saw a movie"). "Broadcast" meant headlines that were tweeted or retweeted by the user; the "Opinion/Comment" category meant tweets or retweets that expressed an opinion; the "For Promotion" category meant those tweets that encouraged further consumption of material by the audience; and "Soliciting Engagement" (asking questions, hoping for debate) were tweets/replies that invited comment from followers. The following graph illustrates the breakdown (see Figure 7.1).

Twitter was used primarily for disseminating opinion and comment, broadcasting news and "other" – such as promotion of brand – with a

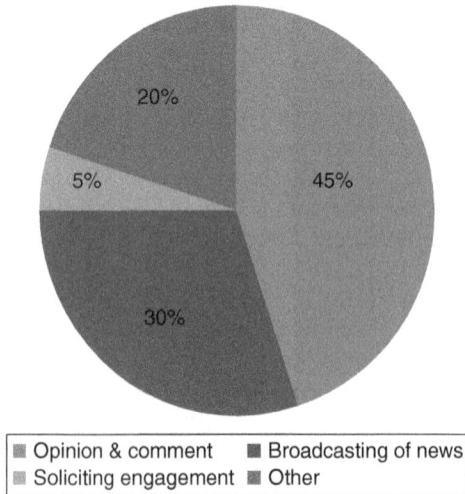

Figure 7.1   Public engagement versus other tweets

significantly smaller percentage for directly soliciting public engagement (Daniels, 2014, pp. 53–61). It is the latter category that would contribute to deepening democracy by adding more voices to the public domain. If there was a greater percentage for soliciting engagement, then there could be an argument for citizen journalism facilitating democratic change, or, in the angle taken by this chapter, there could be an argument for journalists encouraging citizen engagement as a first step. The most important point here is that the proportion of tweets, which constituted engagement, was in fact far too small to make any valuable contribution to a radical democracy. In fact, it was the smallest percentage of all categories, indicating that while journalism spaces were opening up, these spaces were not wide or deep enough to be described as a radical democracy in the making. This research returns to this finding in the "Concluding reflections" section. Now, we turn to insights from the journalists themselves with regard to this 5% finding.

Do the editors/journalists accept these findings?

This section highlights the responses of the editors and journalists to this low "engagement" finding. The two questions posed to the journalists/editors for comment were: First, from an analysis of your tweets the smallest percentage, 5%, of all tweets was found to be for "soliciting engagement", your comment? Second, what was the value of Twitter (if any) for getting comment or public opinion, and do these feed into news diaries in any way? To what extent does this happen? The majority of the editors/journalists were not surprised or defensive about the 5% finding. There were mainly similarities, with a few nuances, in the way they attempted to explain the result. In an interview, editor of *Beeld*, Adriaan Basson, articulated thus:

> I don't find it surprising that the majority of journalists don't engage the public in debate on Twitter. It is a public podium and it will be difficult to cover subjects if you have expressed a view on them on Twitter. I also think the "once bitten twice shy" principle is relevant – too many journalists have been personally insulted, even threatened on Twitter. I think there has been a chilling effect that keeps them away from robust debate.
>
> (Basson, 2015)

Basson expressed two important reasons for the low 5% in the articulation. First, journalists were protecting themselves from expressing too strong a view as they would have to try and cover the same issue in a fair and balanced way. Second, it was hard to take the heat of robust debate, which often turned into verbal fights, which sometimes degenerated into insults and threats. In the theory of radical democracy, he was articulating that journalists prefer to avoid conflict, robust fights and contestations rather than engage. He then explained what he thought most journalists use Twitter for, and this was, "to push their content and build their brands":

> Social media, particularly Twitter, is a good and effective way to push traffic to your website, where the full story is published. Twitter can never replace traditional ways of seeking comment from subjects through personal contact. I do find it useful as a reporting tool in soliciting information, tip-offs, photos and videos about news events. I've also gained valuable insights from Twitter debates, e.g. the Zelda la Grange debacle, that feed into my own views on life.
>
> (Ibid.)

In the theory delineated Basson's discourse indicated that he was interested in views that were not dissimilar from his own. It could be argued that he felt more comfortable in a space he knew and understood, rather than engaging with something that was too removed from his comfort zone. Twitter was used to tease readers with the mainstream product's full story.

Joseph, similar in discourse to Basson, was practical about the value of twitter and was not envisaging any Arab Spring or Damascus revolutionary potential regarding debate with citizenry on Twitter. However, she did gain information and she helped her readers find her newspaper, and, as she articulates, she appreciated the diversity of views it offered:

> Twitter is a wonderful tip-off space and it's a good way to, for instance, find totally different voices talking about a big national issue. But I think it's bloody lazy of journalists to write stories that are entirely premised on what's happening on Twitter. If I see one more "Twitter was abuzz today" intro in a South African newspaper I may revert to using a typewriter in protest. I use Twitter to track unfolding stories or pick up something fresh and unique (my colleagues at City Press's Trending are very clever at spotting these nuggets of gold), but it doesn't feed the news diary in any major way.
>
> (Joseph, 2015)

The last comment by Joseph is valuable: what happens on Twitter does not feed the news diary in any way. Unlike Basson and Joseph, Chris Roper, editor-in-chief at the *M&G*, felt that the statistic did not really apply to him as, in fact, he had the opposite view of his tweets to what the statistics showed:

> I would think that around 80% of my tweets are for soliciting engagement. I might be wrong, but that's certainly the aim I have in my head. I hardly ever just retweet something – I prefer to add something to it, and to then take part in discussions around it. I think if you're not involved in Twitter as a properly shareable, social platform, you shouldn't be there.
>
> (Roper, 2015)

Upon closer examination, Roper's discourse suggests that he would like 80% of his tweets to be for soliciting engagement. He calculated that Twitter prompted approximately eight to ten stories per week. The newspaper employed the help of an analyst who tracked the trends on social media on a daily basis: "This way we make sure we know what our readers are doing, and respond accordingly if the news agenda warrants it" (Roper, 2015). His last comment indicated that he was keen to respond to and engage with his audiences, readers or the citizenry, even though the analysis of his tweets did not turn up a different statistic from any of the other journalists. Clearly, Roper was engaging less than he imagined he was.

Senior political journalist at *City Press*, Carien du Plessis, thought the 5% an "interesting finding" which she "did not really have an opinion on" (Du Plessis, 2015). However, she too, like Joseph and Basson, disclosed that she did not like to "purposefully engage in debate on Twitter because the return I get from it news-wise isn't worth the amount of time that is invested in such engagement" (Ibid.). It is clear from this comment that the professional side of journalism, the news diary, is what Du Plessis prioritized. Then there were practical considerations, but within this an acknowledgement, which reinforces the argument in this chapter – regarding who was on Twitter. It was the "chattering classes" (Ibid.):

> Also, if we are working on a story for Sunday, we wouldn't want to give away the angle on Twitter. The people who are on Twitter are also not representative, especially in SA and Africa – they are usually the chattering classes and other journos. For real engagement, it is still better to go out and talk to people the old-fashioned way. I also believe people in Africa prefer to engage on Facebook, so locally I don't think Twitter in itself is as great a tool for engagement as it might be in the US for example.
>
> (Ibid.)

This discourse reveals that Du Plessis was keenly aware of the issue of access and the limitations of Twitter, and therefore she preferred to talk to people the "old-fashioned" way. Nonetheless, she found Twitter useful in this sense: sometimes she would need someone to interview on a topic, and would send out a tweet, but this had only happened about two or three times. Sometimes the noise on Twitter does have an effect on the particular angle she would take on a story, but by and large she did not have the time or energy to solicit engagement on Twitter. She disclosed:

> As for engaging public debate, I sometimes gauge a news angle for an online story on the tweets on which I get the most feedback. E.g. if I go to a press conference and people seem to be outraged about a certain point raised there, I might use that as my angle even if I didn't consider doing so before. This will only happen if there isn't an angle which I think

is stronger or more important. I try to stay away from soliciting public opinion or debate on Twitter. I don't have time or the energy to engage in that way.

(Ibid.)

The last comment is worth noting apropos soliciting public opinion. Du Plessis did not have the time or energy to engage in debate on Twitter. Similarly, *EWN* senior reporter, Mandy Wiener, had a clear view about what she used social media for and why. Indeed, she was also unsurprised by the low finding on engagement with the citizenry:

I'm not surprised by this statistic at all as in the past I have always approached social media from the viewpoint that I am "informing" or disseminating information to my followers. This is usually the norm when I'm "live tweeting" a court case or tweeting links to articles or columns that I've written.

(Wiener, 2015)

However, she had experienced a change in this "of late":

I find that journalists are using social media to crowdsource more often now, to find people to interview and to solicit engagement on opinion pieces. More journalists are also using Twitter to answer followers' questions about topics they are reporting on – for example, people often ask about the nuances of a court case and I try and explain it to them whereas that would not have been possible in the past.

(Ibid.)

From this comment, Wiener, reflecting on her own work, felt she was fulfilling a civic duty in journalism by explaining to citizens what was happening; for example, in a complicated court case. She also found that Twitter had value in "getting comment, both from the public and from newsmakers. Politicians' tweets are often used as statements on breaking news events." She added that the same applied to an organization such as Eskom regarding its announcements on loading-shedding cycles. On occasion, Wiener disclosed that she sometimes aggregated a report based on public sentiment from social media in reaction to a story:

That report would include a cherry-picked selection of tweets so it's quite difficult to actually accurately reflect public sentiment. Usually it's through the journalist's jaundiced view of a story and they'll select the tweets that appropriately fit what they believe the sentiment is.

(Ibid.)

From this discourse, it is clear that the traditional role of the journalist as mediator or "cherry picker" still abides, showing the limited role of social media: in this case, Twitter. It must be noted that the interviewed journalists were not asked directly about the role of Twitter in a democracy. To take a slight detour from these reflections on the 5% findings, this chapter turns to one last interview, a self-reflection on tweeting, before drawing some conclusions. This interview deals directly with the contribution of social media to democracy – in this case, Twitter. Inadvertently, the journalist articulates some of the Mouffian expositions elucidated in the theoretical framework section of this chapter, and it is argued here that this is an apposite interview to tie up the qualitative component of this research.

Spotting the deficiencies of Twitter

Sam Mkokeli, then *Business Day* political editor and subsequently *Sunday Times* parliamentary correspondent, found Twitter "fun" but also a "sort of a newswire" where he scrolled through the feeds of the people he knew to see what was happening in their world. This is where he picked up the latest current affairs trends. Mkokeli asserted that Twitter was "totally useful", but one had to be "aware of its shortcomings". It allowed everyone to tweet whatever they liked, "unedited", he stated. That means, that as a reader of the tweets, you have to be careful and circumspect about the authenticity of the information and the veracity of opinion, he cautioned.

> Twitter is also good to gauge the mood out there – but even there you have to be careful not to take that as a balanced reflection of society. The people I follow are mostly well-to-do professionals, who look at the world from their middle class perspectives. You just got to understand that they don't speak for the rest of SA. So the views I get from Twitter are not truly reflective of the broad sentiment in SA. Twitter is still a useful outlet for those who live in the Twitter world.
>
> (Mkokeli, 2013)

Twitter was important "but not everything", according to Mkokeli. In a similar vein to Mouffe's argument, his discourse reveals that social media was not the ultimate saviour. It was interesting that he scrolled through feeds of the people he knew; once again summoning the theorizing here that Twitter's engagement is more akin to the like-minded seeking the views, or reinforcing the views, of the like-minded. In fairness to Mkokeli, he spotted the deficiency: that while it was a useful medium for those who live in the Twitter world, this was in reality a middle-class, "well-to-do" world of professionals. It was a small world within a big world. It was not the Mouffian all-encompassing, inclusive, open and noisy one of robust debate.

Mkokeli tweeted from press conferences and other political events because it was "fun". "I love it. It can be a disruption in the sense that it's difficult to live-tweet and take proper notes at the same time." He felt that journalists needed to "embody this information superhighway and live in it. If we don't adapt, our trade will suffer." Herein resided the contradiction – you need to live in the superhighway. However, this highway was the networked and the connected highway of a minority. In terms of the theoretical reflections deployed in this chapter, Mkokeli was clear when asked about the kind of contribution social media engagement was making in South Africa:

> Democracy – the aspect of access to information – benefits from the presence of journalists in the social media sphere. The problem arises when journalists allow themselves to be dictated to by social media trends. Journalists must guard against being told by Twitter what areas to focus on and what should be covered. It is easy for that to happen. People on Twitter easily get outraged or excited – and in 140 characters – that snowballs into a "trend". Then journalists, especially editors take that cue as the reflection of what is important, with their papers effectively allowing themselves to be dictated to by the social media sphere as to what is important... Twitter is no substitute for the real world out there.
>
> (Ibid.)

Mkokeli valued the social media platforms he engaged in, but he hones in to the insight that it was not the "real world". He saw the potential but recognized the inadequacies and limitations. The Twitter public sphere was an elitist public sphere in action, the networked society, rather than a broader, more inclusive, radical democratic space. The majority of journalists appeared to be well aware of this and did not take the Twittersphere too seriously in their work, although an inordinate amount of time was spent on Twitter – 15 minutes each hour (Daniels, 2014) – which appears to be a bit of a contradiction, given that many of the interviews cited in this chapter point to an almost dismissive view of Twitter.

Discourse analysis revealed that journalists and editors who were interviewed were well aware of the limitations ("not the real world", for example) of Twitter, were not defensive or surprised that the percentage for "engagement" was as low as 5%, and finally they clearly steered away from overly robust discussion with citizenry. These findings are elaborated on in the last section "Concluding reflections: A "democracy to come", deploying the conceptual framework of the chapter.

Concluding reflections: A "democracy to come"

This section concludes that when we use the radical democracy model – namely, more noise, more voices, more diversity and inclusion in the public sphere – to analyse the finding of 5% of tweets for soliciting engagement, and couple this with the discourse analysis, then a radical democracy is not in action. From the content analysis, the majority of tweets related to breaking news, promoting the news organizations' brands, and the dissemination of opinion and comment. The smallest percentages of tweets, a mere 5%, related to soliciting public engagement; namely, getting the views of those outside the journalism network. The pattern of journalists' and editors' discourse revealed acceptance of the finding, and they were neither surprised nor defensive that "soliciting engagement" with the public was low. They explained their reasons for not wanting to engage too deeply with the public. They also often acknowledged that Twitter was "not the real world".

In all fairness, using the radical democracy model lens is demanding of Twitter and journalists in the newsroom. Nonetheless, one of the key findings in this research is that journalists' public engagement on Twitter appears to be neither widespread nor particularly deep. This was revealed from the quantitative data findings and the discourse analysis, and from the self-reflective interviews.

Deploying the conceptual framework explicated at the beginning of the chapter about Derrida's democracy to come, or an unrealized and imperfect democracy, the research here suggests that the potential for greater reach between journalism and Twitter exists but has not yet been realized. Social networks do not appear to be setting the news media's agenda, although there are sporadic pockets of it influencing angles on stories. In some instances, it appears as though journalists would like to believe that the majority of their tweets are aimed at soliciting engagement from citizenry, even though the quantitative data does not support this. Also, in some instances, journalists were conscious of a civic duty in their work when they used social media to explain what was happening in the news, for instance regarding complicated court cases.

Finally, journalists' use of Twitter in the Johannesburg newsroom has been deconstructed here through discourse analysis which revealed little evidence, if any, of a revolutionary use of social media; namely, a South African Arab Spring. Just as radical democracy articulates pluralism which must include antagonism and engage with differences, so too must journalists' use of Twitter for a deepening of democracy to occur.

In terms of the theoretical conceptual deployment to understand Twitter and journalism in Johannesburg, it appears that there is a more rational consensus model of democracy (downplaying differences) in action rather than a more robust radical democracy matrix of dissensus, as explicated by Mouffe. The pattern of the discourse revealed that the journalists appeared to be wary and cautious about engaging with the public too much on Twitter, afraid that they would give their stories away, and fearful of a backlash in the form of an avalanche of harassment and threats from citizenry.

Some reflections on the process of tweeting (for instance, by Du Plessis and Mkokeli) reinforce the view the Mouffian theory that the public engagement on Twitter was not all encompassing, expansive and inclusive. To put it simply, it was a small and tight little world. The journalists, in a self-reflexive process and without realizing it, conceded that their engagements were not competing and robust but more the case of the like-minded enjoying reaffirmation. Mkokeli was clear that the social media contribution towards democracy was not obvious as this was not the "real world"; it was engagement by the middle class, or as Du Plessis articulated: "the chattering classes".

Through this research, it appears then that there is a rather elite public sphere engagement model in action in Johannesburg, rather than a Mouffian robust and more inclusive deepening of democracy at work. Coupling the Twitter analysis with the interviews, framed against the theoretical conceptual formulations developed here, one has to conclude that the new trajectory presents an opportunity for the deepening of democracy, but it is limited in access and content. This chapter has argued that the democratic potential for this particular social media has not yet been realized, as Mkokeli insightfully expounded: "Twitter is an exciting world for journalists", but is "no substitute for the real world out there". Journalist spaces may be opening up, but they are far from the expansive, inclusive and wide-open spaces that are in the radical democracy model. And yes, social media, especially Twitter, has the potential to create opportunities for democracy, by bringing in more diverse voices into the public sphere, à la Mouffe's radical democracy, but perhaps its rose-petalled promise will only be in bloom once all have access and all are connected in a networked society. Even then, there is no certainty, as the chattering classes may still prefer the company of each other. However, as Derrida so optimistically pronounced, democracy is never fully realized; it is always becoming. In conclusion, this chapter explored the role that Twitter plays in deepening democracy through engagement between journalists and citizens. The chapter finds that, while the potential exists for this social media space to deepen democracy through greater engagement with citizenry, it is far from realized – it is a democracy to come.

Acknowledgements

Thanks are due to the Wits Journalism honours students who performed the Twitter extraction for analysis.

Notes

1. The author of this chapter was the lead researcher/writer who conceptualized the research for SoN 2014 for tweet analysis.
2. Roper became editor-in-chief after the analysis was concluded.
3. Basson moved to *Beeld* as editor in September 2013.

References

Basson, Adriaan. (2015). Reflections on tweeting. Email interview by Glenda Daniels. Johannesburg, March 2015.

Berger, Guy. (2004). "More Media for Southern Africa?" The place of politics, economics and convergence in developing media density. *Critical Arts, South-North Cultural and Media Studies* 18(1): 42–75.

Carpentier, Nico, and Cammaerts, Bart. (2006). "Hegemony, Democracy, Agonism and Journalism", an interview with Chantal Mouffe. *Theory Review. Journalism Studies*, 7: 78–84.

Daniels, Glenda. (2012). *Fight for Democracy: The ANC and the Media in South Africa.* Johannesburg: Wits University Press.

Daniels, Glenda. (2013). *State of the Newsroom, South Africa 2013: Disruptions and Transitions.* Johannesburg: Wits Journalism.

Daniels, Glenda. (2014a). *State of the Newsroom, South Africa 2014: Disruptions Accelerated.* Johannesburg: Wits Journalism.

Daniels, Glenda. (2014b). How far does Twitter deepen democracy through public engagement? "An analysis of journalists' use of Twitter in the Johannesburg newsroom". *Journal of African Media Studies,* 6(3): 299–311.

Derrida, Jacques. (2004). The last of the rogue states: The democracy to come. *South Atlantic Quarterly.* Project Muse, 103: 2, 3. Spring/Summer. 323–341.

Du Plessis, Carien. (2015). Reflections on tweeting. Email interview by Glenda Daniels. Johannesburg, March 2015.

Gutmann, Amy and Thompson, Dennis. (2004). *Why Deliberative Democracy?* Princeton, NJ: Princeton University Press.

Held, David. (2006). *Models of Democracy.* Cambridge: Polity.

Hermida, Alfred. (2012). Tweets and truth: Journalism as a discipline of collaborative verification. *Journalism Practice* 6 (5–6): 659–668.

Ibelema, Minabere. (2012). The press as a watchdog of the people: Revisiting a theoretical triad. *Ecquid Novi* 33(2): 4–15.

Jacobs, Sean. (1999). Tensions of a Free Press: South Africa after Apartheid. Research Paper, John F. Kennedy School of Government, Harvard University.

Jordaan, Marenet. (2013). Poke me, I'm a journalist: The impact of Facebook and Twitter on newsroom routines and cultures at two South African weeklies. *Ecquid Novi: African Journalism Studies* 34(1): 21–35.

Joseph, Natasha. (2015). Reflections on tweeting. Email interview by Glenda Daniels. Johannesburg, March 2015.

Keane, John. (1991). *The Media and Democracy.* Cambridge: Polity Press.

Lasorsa, Dominick, Lewis, Seth C. and Holton, Avery E. (2011). Normalizing Twitter: Journalism practice in an emerging communication space. *Journalism Studies* 13(1): 19–36.

Macdonell, Diane. (1986). *Theories of Discourse: An Introduction.* New York: Basil Blackwell.

Mkokeli, Sam. (2013). Reflections on tweeting. Email interview by Glenda Daniels. Johannesburg, January 2013.

Mouffe, Chantal. (2000). *The Democratic Paradox.* London and New York: Verso.

Mouffe, Chantal. (2006). *On the Political: Thinking in Action.* London and New York: Routledge.

Moyo, Dumisani. (2009). Citizen journalism and the parallel market of information in Zimbabwe's 2008 elections. *Journalism Studies* 10(4): 55–67.

Mudhai, Okoth F. (2011). Immediacy and openness in a digital Africa: Networked-convergent journalisms in Kenya. *Journalism* 12(6): 674–691.

Paterson, Chris. (2013). Journalism and social media in the African context. *Ecquid Novi: African Journalism Studies* 34(1): 1–6.

Pêcheux, Michel. (1982). *Language, Semantics and Ideology.* London: Macmillan.

Roper, Chris. (2015). Reflections on tweeting. Email interview by Glenda Daniels. Johannesburg, March 2015.

Shapiro, Ian. (2003). *The State of Democratic Theory.* Princeton, NJ, and Oxford: Princeton University Press.

Stassen, Wilma (2010). Your news in 14 characters: exploring the role of social media in journalism. *Global Media Journal*, African edition, 4(1): 1–6.

Tomaselli, Keyan. (2004). Transformation of the South African media. *Critical Arts: South-North Cultural and Media Studies* 18(1): 1–6.

Verweij, Peter, and Van Noort, Elvira. (2013). Journalist Twitter networks, public debates and relationships in South Africa. In *Digital Journalism*, 2:1, 98–114.

Vis, Farida. (2013). Twitter as a reporting tool for breaking news. *Digital Journalism*, 1:1, 27–47.

WAN (World Association of Newspapers and News Publishers). (2013). *World Press Trends 2013.* Darmstadt, Germany: WAN-IFRA Washington Platz.

Wiener, Mandy. (2015). Reflections on tweeting. Email interview by Glenda Daniels. Johannesburg, March 2015.

World Wide Worx. (2014). The South African Media Landscape 2014. *World Wide Worx*, Johannesburg, http://worldwideworx.com, Retrieved 15 May 2014.

8
Digital Technologies and the Extractive Sector: The New Wave of Citizen Journalism in Resource-Rich Countries

Erika Rodrigues and Anya Schiffrin

Introduction: New media technology and the extractive sector

Almost 20 years after the arrival of the Internet in Africa and the birth of the modern citizen journalism movement, it is time to assess what impact these powerful phenomena have had on one of the most critical and intractable problems in Africa today: the disappointing way that governments and corporations on the continent use the revenue they make from the oil, gas and mining industries, and the distortions this corruption and misuse have caused to the political system.

In countries where resource extraction is well developed, governments depend on it for their revenue and to spur growth. In countries where oil and gas are newly discovered, citizens naturally hope that the extraction will make them prosperous. For journalists and citizen journalists who want to change the world, hold government and business to account, expose wrongdoing and help their fellow citizens, there is no better subject than covering oil, gas and mining. Indeed, some of the most passionate journalism of the nineteenth and twentieth centuries was written by campaigning and investigative reporters who exposed the brutal treatment of workers gathering rubber in the Belgian Congo and in the Amazon area, and the misdeeds of Standard Oil in the USA (Schiffrin, 2014).

Journalists in Ghana, Uganda, Mozambique and Tanzania – just a few of the countries where oil and gas have been found – look to Nigeria as an example of what can go wrong when oil wealth is misused. In Nigeria, corruption, as well as oil theft and sabotage, has led to an estimated loss of 7 billion dollars of oil revenue annually since 1973 (International Energy Agency, 2012). The tenth-largest oil producer in the world, oil revenues make up 70% of total government revenue in Nigeria. Another example is South

Africa. Mining continues to be a key industry in the country, contributing 18% to the GDP and employing more than 1 million people, directly and indirectly (Mining Intelligence Database, n.d.). Even so, the overall unemployment rate is still at 24.7%, and 31.3% of the population lives below the poverty line. The prevalence of poverty and unemployment has contributed to recent violent conflicts – the worst since the end of apartheid – between mining workers, their unions and their employers, three of the largest platinum producers in the world (CIA WorldFactbook, n.d.). In other cases, fighting over resources such as "blood diamonds" or "conflict minerals" fuelled decades of civil wars in Congo, Liberia and Sierra Leone.

The problems caused by the "resource curse" are well known, and across the continent non-governmental organizations (NGOs), activists, citizens have mounted efforts aimed at boosting corporate social responsibility and transparency, and creating shared value. International organizations such as Global Witness (based in London), the Natural Resource Governance Institute (originally funded by George Soros and the Open Society Foundation) and activists from Human Rights Watch such as Arvind Ganesan, Lisa Misol and Nisha Varia and Ian Gary from Oxfam, to mention a few, also play a major role in supporting local players. Open Society Foundation and Global Witness have supported investigative reporting about the extractives in Africa, including a lengthy piece on Guinea by Patrick Radden Keefe (2013) and work by journalist Ken Silverstein (2014). Another recent expose is *The Looting Machine* by Tom Burgis (2015).

Any understanding of citizen journalism in Africa must be grounded in an understanding of the journalism climate and traditions of the continent. It's not possible to view citizen journalists as separate from the journalism context in which they work. Some citizen journalists worked *for* media houses before becoming citizen journalists. As well, citizen journalists report in a way that draws on and articulates traditional journalism conventions, including language and reporting practices. Further, journalism is a wide term that, throughout its history, had a close and rich involvement with citizen journalism even if this term is a modern one. The pamphleteer of the eighteenth century or the crusading reporting done by freed slave George Washington Williams about conditions in King Leopold's Congo are certainly examples of early forms of citizen journalism (Hochschild, 1998).

However, it must be said that legacy media (i.e. newspapers, radio, television) in Africa has generally not been able to take on the large extractive sector companies or investigate their activities and finances in an informed and detailed way. Poorly paid and poorly trained, unfamiliar with the complex and technical information that solid coverage of the extractive sector requires, African journalists, with some notable exceptions, have found it difficult to undertake meaningful long-form reporting on the sector's effects on the environment, economy and society.

This chapter will look at some of the new citizen journalism efforts on the continent that try to examine economics, corruption and the extractive sector. We will describe how these journalists gather and disseminate information and assess their effect (if any). We will argue that their effects are limited and that they have not been able to bring about the large, systemic structural changes that are needed and for which they aim. However, there are cases where journalists and citizen journalists, with the help of digital technology, are able to embarrass government officials publicly and relentlessly cover some cases of corporate misdoing. We argue that their efforts boost transparency in the sector and add another perspective to stories that are either ignored by state-owned or state-censored traditional media or covered with a pro-government slant. In many cases, the citizen journalists are journalists who use social media and digital technology not just to gather information but to disseminate it. This allows others to comment, creating and connecting communities of outrage and engagement. Says Namibia-based journalist John Grobler, who writes on mining and corruption: "I mostly use Facebook and then local reporters pick [my stories] up. The only way I can move things forward is through social media."

In this chapter, we look at examples from around the African continent, drawing on extensive and ongoing research done at Columbia University, and make use of fieldwork carried out by the authors in Uganda, Mozambique and South Africa, as well as secondary research on Angola and Nigeria.

The Resource Boom and its curse

The extractives sector (oil, gas and mining) continues to be an important subject for journalists, particularly in developing countries. Revenues from oil, gas and mining contribute substantially to GDP, and in many cases make up the bulk of government revenue.

Indeed, among 29 nations that, in 2011, were implementing the Extractive Industries Transparency Initiative, 10 reported extractives revenues totalling over one-quarter of their respective government budgets (6 of which were actually over 50%) (EITI, 2011). Among the broader global community, 30 countries reported natural resource rents representing over one-fifth of their entire national economies, with 6 whose natural resource rents constituted more than half of their GDP (Iraq, the Republic of Congo, Saudi Arabia, Mauritania, Kuwait and Gabon) (World Bank, 2011).

The way revenues from the extraction of natural resources are spent affects economic growth, domestic security and social well-being. Often, the results are negative. In many countries, revenues are wasted or lost due to corruption and/or financial mismanagement. Managing large and sudden inflows of resource wealth is notoriously difficult as it can create high inflation from increased spending, overvalued currencies and an unbalanced economy, as investment and skilled labour is often drawn away from other economic sectors.[1] The process of extraction itself can also create severe environmental damage, hurting the lives and livelihoods of the people living in the surrounding areas. A Resource Boom can tear at the social and moral fabric of societies. The influx of job- and opportunities-seekers to regions where extraction takes place can lead to conflict over land and resources, as well as an increase in illicit activities, such as the use of drugs and trade in contraband and prostitution, and other crimes. These can cause increased tensions between ethnic groups and/or classes, which sometimes escalate or prolong conflicts and civil wars. It is not surprising that the abundance of natural resources can lead not only to a lack of growth in the overall economy but also an increase in economic and social inequality, and to societies marked by poverty and underdevelopment.[2]

Reasons for weakness in media coverage of the extractives

Inside the newsroom: Lack of resources

There are many reasons why the extractive sector is not covered as comprehensively as it could be (Canonge and Purcell, 2009). These include lack of resources to spend on developing experienced beat reporters who can cover a subject in depth, lack of funding to send reporters out on stories and lack of access to the far-flung places where extraction often takes place. Covering oil, gas and mining can be far more complex than other kinds of business reporting, as journalists on the beat need to track a range of companies and players with different kinds of tax regimes, labour conditions, and environmental and contractual agreements. Moreover, although transparency has been increasing in the last few decades, the sector remains obscured by the interests of the many players who want to exploit it away from the public eye.

In developing countries and emerging markets (within which a large part of the natural resources reside) poorly funded news outlets with overstretched editorial staff simply do not have the time, money, will or expertise to cover these stories in sufficient detail. Because the challenges to good reporting are so well known to anyone working in the world of journalism we will not detail them further here. We will just give one example from our research on press coverage of the extractives found in Ghanaian, Nigerian and Ugandan newspapers in 2009. Having multiple sources is a tenet of good journalism as a diversity of sources can provide balance and perspectives to reporting. Studies of US media have found that US newspapers have three or more sources 90% of the time (2006) and four or more sources 48% of the time (Project for Excellence in Journalism, 2005; 2006). A 2008 study found that online US newspaper articles have an average of 3.64 sources, while online citizen journalism stories have an average of 1.37 sources (Carpenter, 2008). By contrast, a 2009 study of African newspapers found that only 21.45% of the African newspaper articles surveyed had three or more unique sources. Nearly 50% of articles had one unique source or less. By far the most prevalent types of sources were those from government or business outlets (Canonge and Purcell, 2009).

Outside the newsroom: Pressures and information asymmetries

As well as the constraints inside the newsroom, there are the problems of the larger ecosystem. The oil, gas and mining companies tend to be rich and well connected. They have friends and allies in government and in business who are able to shape and control the character of the stories that appear about them. Typically. these companies are able to outspend media outlets and so can put pressure on journalists in many ways, including soft pressure, smear campaigns, threats to withdraw advertising and, of course, costly and drawn-out lawsuits.

Further, because in many countries the extractive sector is the major source of revenue there is at times widespread support from governments and/or companies benefiting from the sector.[3] NGOs, civil society and journalists who question their practices are viewed as marginal and find it hard to be heard. These critics may face litigation, and, in more severe (but not uncommon) cases, be attacked or killed. Another problem, journalists and activists note, is that when corruption is pervasive – Nigeria and Angola come to mind – watchdog media reports lose their novelty and have little impact, as society, government and companies shrug off the criticism.[4,5] The "naming and shaming" approach to covering companies can have an effect (Dyck and Zingales, 2002), but only when the company or government is concerned with its reputation, locally, nationally and internationally.

Despite these power asymmetries, the last few years have seen a general trend towards transparency. There is now far more data available than ever before, including data produced by members of the Extractive Industries Transparency Initiative (EITI) and companies affected by the passage of the (still-contested) Dodd–Frank Act in the USA. There has also been a push from the international community, including the United Nations and the European Union, in the areas of transparency, open contracts and tax evasion. Websites such as Document Cloud and ResourceContracts.org make contract information publicly available. According to Bard College law professor Peter Rosenblum, the opening up of contracts to the public has already led national governments to negotiate far better deals. By seeing what kinds of environmental protections countries are negotiating, other governments learn what to ask for. "Governments are getting better at renegotiating opportunities", says Rosenblum (interview, 6 September 2013).

Although more information is available, it can still be difficult to make use of the data. When numbers are shared, it's often not in a consistent way. Different institutions, governments and companies publish different data, in different formats and at different times. Often, the information made available is incomplete or not comparable. Companies and governments may disclose overwhelming amounts of unusable data, a strategy well known as a "data dump", with the intent to complicate any analysis of information that might shed light on what companies are doing or the terms at which they have been able to obtain the resources.

Despite these obstacles, there are many cases of journalists and citizens around the world circumventing the limitations of traditional media and making use of new technologies and social media to expose problems associated with the extractives sector.

Examples of citizen reporting on the extractives

Angola: Bloggers and legal pressures

Maka Angola, an Angolan investigative website founded in 2008, publishes articles, cartoons, radio programming and videos, in Portuguese and in English, denouncing corruption, power abuses, socioeconomic exclusion and human rights violations in the country by the government. The website also receives and publishes complaints, tips and investigations from Angolan citizens.

Angola's extractive sector is prominently characterized as the fourth-biggest diamond-producing country by value and the second-largest oil producer in Africa. Gruesome cases of the torture of workers in the Angolan diamond mines and the acquisitiveness of the president and his family and associates, who have benefited from the extractive sector, have been exposed relentlessly by journalists and citizen journalists at Maka Angola. However, these exposures of corruption and other forms of malfeasance can have consequences. Rafael Marques de Morais, the founder and executive director of Maka Angola, and a fearless investigative journalist and human rights defender, has been imprisoned and sued several times throughout his career, including for calling the Angolan president "a dictator", and has been subjected to illegal surveillance and hacking more than once (in 2010 and 2013) (Maka Angola, 2013). On 20 September 2013 Marques was again incarcerated because of his 2011 book *Blood Diamonds: Corruption and Torture in Angola*, which accused private security companies and diamond mining companies, with the complicity of the government, of routinely killing and terrorizing villagers deemed to have interfered in mining operations in Northern Angola (Marques, 2011). Marques subsequently filed a criminal complaint with the Attorney General of Angola against nine top Angolan generals, part of the directorship of the two diamond mining companies he accused in his book.

In 2015 Marques was again put on trial after a suit brought by seven of the Angolan army generals and directors of the Cuango Mining Company, whom he exposed as responsible for the killings, torture and farmland grabs that took place in the lucrative diamond fields, between June 2009 and March 2011. In solidarity, his editor, Barbara Bulhosa from Tinta da China, made his book available online for free, "so everybody can read it and understand what is at the basis of a process that can put the author behind bars". She was also persecuted and sued for publishing the book when it was first released. In relation to the possible incarceration of Rafael Marques, Bulhosa stated: "At the time, naively, I thought this book would serve to at least mitigate the daily violence in the mining areas in Angola. How I was wrong. The book only served to trigger a chase on the author"[6] (Esquerda.net, 2015).

Marques' travails have not been in vain though. As well as exposing corruption in Angola and human rights violations, one of Marques' incarcerations, in 1999, eventually resulted in positive changes to Angola's Press Law. This came after a long process, which included lobbying from international organizations concerned with press freedom including Interights, Open Society Institute and the Committee to Protect Journalists.[7]

Mozambique: The need for balanced reporting

In Mozambique, with recent discoveries of significant mineral and hydrocarbon reserves – "one of the most important natural gas fields discovered in the last 10 years", investigative, balanced and informed coverage of the extractive sector is still quite limited.

The lack of resources in the newsroom, discussed in an earlier sub-chapter, *Inside the Newsroom*, means understaffed and underfunded newsrooms often can't send journalists on the extensive training sessions that could help them better cover the extractives. In the case of Mozambique, language barriers present another challenge. Although there is a lot of information available online that can be used by reporters and researchers, most of this is only available in English (Oliveira, personal communication, 2014).

There has been interest from extractive companies in projects that train journalists and citizens in better analysing information regarding this specific sector, as companies also struggle with the expectations that the media help raise in the country, especially when the media provides information that is based on speculation rather than on a balanced and in-depth analysis. However, corporate involvement in training is sometimes seen as a plan to "buy" or influence reporters and shape public opinion to the advantage of the companies and governments, thereby exacerbating the power asymmetry between government, companies and citizens.

Despite the limited quality of reporting in Mozambique on the extractive sector, citizen reporting has helped get information out. Text messages and WhatsApp messages of protests against resettlements of farming communities in the mining areas, which was picked up and enhanced by traditional media, helped spur government to issue new legislation on resettlements (Human Rights Watch, 2013a).[8] Civil society organizations pushed Mozambique to join the EITI, holding EITI workshops for government officials at the beginning of 2011 (Nombora, 2012). After a number of ups and downs, and a great deal of back and forth about what conditions Mozambique had to fulfil, it finally became compliant on 26 October 2012.

Nigeria: Motivating citizens to act

SaharaReporters.com is perhaps the most well-known example of anti-corruption citizen journalism on the continent.[9] Founded by Omoyele Sowore and based in New York City, SaharaReporters has more than 1.5 million Facebook likes and depends on citizen whistle-blowers who send in documents, videos, tips, text messages and blog postings. The site's credo is "Report Yourself",[10] and as Sowore says, "We challenge people to act, we're not just a media platform" (personal communication, 2014). SaharaReporters has been funded by Ford Foundation, and in 2011 received a $450,000 grant from the Omidyar Network. It has been the subject of studies authored by Simon Dare and a group of students at Columbia University's School of International and Public Affairs in 2014.[11]

SaharaReporters published more than 5,000 stories between 2006 and April 2014, revealing numerous accounts of corruption and raw reports of groundbreaking news.[12] The site has been referred to as the "thorn of political corruption".[13] SaharaReporters published five years of reporting on the former Delta State Governor James Ibori, who committed crimes of theft, embezzlement, money laundering, bribery and abuse of public office. Another famous case reported on by SaharaReporters was that of Sanusi Lamido Sanusi. Sanusi became governor of the Central Bank of Nigeria (CBN) in 2009 after working for years as a banker. During his time as governor, Sanusi exposed a $20 billion shortfall in the accounts of the Nigerian National Petroleum Company (NNPC). He was also responsible for bailing out several banks in Nigeria and implementing an anti-corruption campaign, firing all of the managers.[14] In September of 2013, Sanusi wrote to President Goodluck Jonathan, stating that up to $50 billion was missing in crude oil shipments from the NNPC. During the next year, reports surfaced of Sanusi using CBN money to pay for his mistress's trips. In February 2014, President Jonathan suspended Sanusi from his post, accusing the governor of "financial recklessness and misconduct". In the weeks following the suspension, Nigeria's currency took a downward spiral and prompted uncertainty on the Nigerian stock exchange; Sanusi has denied any wrongdoing. It is hard to know exactly what impact SaharaReporters had – the *Premium Times* first broke the story – but it's clear that by relentlessly reporting on the subject and keeping it in the public mind it increased the pressure on the government to act.

Uganda: Towards greater transparency

Uganda's situation is similar to that of Mozambique in that oil has been discovered only recently (BBC News, 2015). According to Reuters, oil was discovered in 2006 in the Albertine Rift Basin and drilling is expected to begin in 2017.[15] Press freedom is not assured in Uganda, as there are periodic government crackdowns, but civil society and some vocal journalists have actively pushed for more disclosure.

In June 2012, the government disclosed information contained in the oil contracts, purportedly due to the pressure from various civil society organizations and the non-state-owned media. Nonetheless, civil society groups argued that only limited information on petroleum royalty rates had been released and more was needed. Several details of the agreements remained confidential due to "commercial interests", sparking speculation that Uganda may have received a raw deal (Kasita, 2012).

In Uganda, the Kampala-based African Centre for Media Excellence (ACME), committed to improving journalism in the country and continent, trains journalists to cover the recently booming oil sector and assist civil society in effectively regulating the sector.[16] However, Executive Director Dr Peter Mwesige notes that there is still much to be done: "despite some progress, there is too little serious investigation and too much reporting without supporting evidence (especially about land issues)".

In Uganda, information on the extractives is still dominated by official statements, mainstream newspapers and radio stations (Young, 2013). However, organized "citizen" journalism alternatives include some local research organizations that are mostly donor-aided groups working with communities (personal correspondence with Angelo Izama).

Citizen journalism plays an important role in contributing to shared knowledge. Angelo Izama, a Ugandan journalist and media analyst, explains:

> *Since news circulates within the entire media ecosystem, citizens catch it one way or another. Their participation appears to me to have increased considerably with the availability of phones, cheaper internet and social networks. Many traditional media have also expanded their investment to include this participation through websites and social media platforms ... the shared nature of news between the originator (news organization or so) and its growing audience online and outside as a powerful addition to the consumption of news in the extractives. In some areas I can say citizen journalists consider whistleblowing as what one does on Facebook, WhatsApp or sharing a blog in order to get word or an issue into the mainstream.*

(Izama, 2014)

South Africa: Challenging the single story

Mining in South Africa is a key industry for the country: it accounts for 20% of all investment, 18% of the GDP (Smit, 2013), and employs more than 1 million people (Mining Intelligence Database, n.d.). On the other hand, social and economic well-being for the majority of the population is still very low, including for mining workers and their families.

The notorious "Marikana Massacre" in 2012 was the most violent mining workers' strike since the end of Apartheid (Dolan and Herskovitz, 2012).

Pushed by their unions, workers at one of the largest platinum companies embarked on an illegal strike, demanding a 300% salary increase. The strike resulted in the deaths of 6 miners, 2 security staff and 2 policemen during clashes between two competing labour unions (the result of political power struggles); then 34 miners were gunned down in clashes with the police. The dominant narrative within the public discourse was that the strikers had provoked their own deaths by charging and shooting at the forces of law and order. The narrative was fed to the public by the police, various state entities and by the media.

At the time, a few journalists, bloggers and academics, frustrated with this one-sided narrative, sought out the other side of the story. Jared Sacks, executive director of Children of South Africa (CHOSA) and a young citizen journalist, recounted that, with the few resources he had at the time, he headed to Marikana, where he spent time establishing trust with members of the community and hearing their side of the story. According to Sacks, there were others doing the same: September National Imbizo, an advocacy initiative, and academics such as Peter Alexander, a professor at the University of Johannesburg, dedicated themselves to bringing the story of the victims and witnesses to the public. *Amandla!* magazine, for example, produced by the Alternative Information Development Centre in South Africa, wrote about the experiences of "the Marikana women" in the mines and during the clashes, expanding on reports from bloggers (Hefez, 2013).

Even professional journalists were frustrated with the official story told by the media. Greg Marinovich, writing for the *Daily Maverick*, spent two weeks at Marikana developing an investigative piece. He concluded that police had in fact trapped the workers and community to make it seem as if they had acted in self-defence from a raging crowd. In 2014, video footage showed Marinovich's assessment was accurate (Marinovich and Nicolson, 2014).

In South Africa, because the blogosphere and citizen journalism are more developed, there are various content producers, and so news consumption and audiences are fragmented, limiting the impact of news reports. Several blogs, including "Africa is a Country" and "GroundUp", focus on getting the views of common citizens on various issues and trying to provide alternatives to the one-sided story presented by some legacy media (Jared Sachs, personal communication). Prosecutions of journalists are not common but media freedom is not completely encouraged: a Secrecy Bill was passed by the South African parliament in 2013, which allows the government to choose, at its discretion, not to disclose certain state information.

Impact or no impact? The importance of "global journalism"

Despite the pressures and challenges, in some cases crusading citizen journalists have had a discernible effect on government policy, as seen in some of the cases described in this chapter (Mozambique, Angola, etc.). Often, however, government and companies continue with their plans in the face of critical press coverage, leading to frustration from journalists and activists, who wonder why their work has not had more impact.

When bloggers/journalists are effective, there can be several reasons. One is the amplification effect: bloggers and traditional media can provide new information and then reinforce each other's points by broadcasting this information, so that it comes to the attention of larger groups. Bloggers and the media (including social media) can also draw attention to criticism of, say, government policies, and help reframe how the debate is cast. There is, of course, a tremendous fluidity between different platforms. In countries where heavy-handed governments try to control the media, the blogosphere and social media can open up discussion about policy options in a way that legacy media are often unable to do. The reporter who writes for state-owned media by day may blog anonymously by night and report the information s/he could not reveal in the official media.

This is perhaps the promise of the Web: that it can help connect different people and organizations that had not previously been connected. When there is accurate information to be found, teaming up with other voices and the unblocking of information flows can lead to far more comprehensive reporting. The journalist working in isolation does not necessarily know what is happening in other parts of the world. The hope of Information and Communications Technology (ICT) is that it will facilitate the communication between different entities across time and place, circumventing national blockages, even in the face of local resistance (Keck and Sikkink, 1998).

Further, it's encouraging to see that, for the moment, donors and a range of media development and civil society organizations are interested in helping reporters undertake serious work on oil, gas and mining. For example, the following training courses have been set up: Economic Journalism Mentorship by IREX in Mozambique, Extractive Sector Journalism by ACME in Uganda by the Natural Resource Governance Institute and the Data Journalism Course by the Tanzania Media Fund. Organizations like the Global Investigative Journalism Network, the International Consortium of Investigative Networks, SCOOP, the Organized Crime and Corruption Reporting project and the 100 Reporters project are essential because they connect different groups to each other and help journalists report stories across international borders.

Craig Hammer from the World Bank, which, along with partners such as Code for Africa and the International Center for Journalism, has sponsored "Data Literacy Bootcamps" in a number of countries, notes that, in Ghana, there is already a strong local community (partly supported by Google among others) interested in accessing, analysing and spreading data about such topics. There is also a growing chorus of voices calling for greater government transparency, including release of data through the Ghana Open Data Initiative, particularly concerning government-mandated royalty payments for communities that arise from extractives sales. Part of Hammer's job is to support and amplify data-driven work that is already being done. "There are ways for the international donor community to support and scale homegrown solutions, as well as leverage each other's technical and financial resources for improved coordination and complementarity, to achieve more meaningful and lasting impact", says Hammer (personal communication, 24 April 2015).

Conclusion

Thirty years ago, it was simply *assumed* that the discovery of natural resources would be a blessing. "Dutch Disease" was one of the first maladies that showed that this might not be the case, and its analysis enhanced understanding of the macro-economic consequences of natural resource abundance. In subsequent years, there has been a greater understanding of other aspects of the resource curse, the low growth, high inequality and weak institutions systematically associated with resource abundance and lack of improvement in the standards of living of a majority of the population. In many countries, domestic and international NGOs and the press have raised public awareness of these issues, and many countries have enacted legal frameworks that attempt to mitigate the risk of the resource curse. In heavily fought battles, some developed countries, not wanting to be accused of aiding and abetting corruption, have passed legislation facilitating transparency.

But these are ongoing struggles. There are those whose interests are served by lack of transparency. Extractive industries make more profit if they pay less for obtaining resources; and paying even a large bribe is a cost-effective way of reducing overall payments – if they can get away with it. Sometimes paying a fine is cheaper than following the rules. Those in the industry have systematically fought against legal frameworks that would ensure transparency, and against regulations that would effectively implement the legislation that has been passed in law.

Moreover, transparency in itself has proved insufficient as it has not been accompanied by greater accountability from governments and companies. According to Human Rights Watch, although transparency initiatives such as the EITI have pushed successfully for more availability of data, such actions need to be complemented by a push for human rights to improve governance: "Transparency can be transformative in an environment when freedoms are respected because the combination of the two is what provided accountability" (Human Rights Watch, 2013b, p. 2).

Journalists and citizen journalists on their own cannot transform corporate structures or solve the many problems of countries developing their extractive sector. But strong media outlets can do their part, and powerful, well-researched pieces of journalism can help bolster NGOs working on transparency or human rights. The media provides the most effective counterweight to the pressures from industry: investigative journalism into acts of corruption and poorly designed auctions and contracts; stories of what has happened in other countries; and analyses of the adverse role that the extractive sector has so often played, as well as the positive role it plays in the few that have managed to tame the resource curse.

There are ample opportunities for investigative reporters and citizen journalists to use the new tools and data to deepen their reporting. New technology has dramatically changed how reporting is happening around the world and can help journalists overcome some of the difficulties they face in getting access to sources and information, and reaching audiences.

Vast amounts of data are being published online but it will take some time for people to understand how to use it. Much of the data is hard to find, hard to read and not of a uniform standard that can be easily compared.

Further, it is expected that the work that donors and media and civil society organizations are doing in training journalists and citizens in better understanding the sector will create a more balanced and informed reporting that will correctly adapt people's expectation to what an actual Resource Boom can bring about to a country, and what needs to be done to enable better opportunities over negative consequences.

Acknowledgements

We would like to acknowledge the help of Karen Attiah, Sheila Coronel, Tom Glaisyer, Hollie Russon Gilman, Misha Glenny, Eliza Griswold, Rob Howse, Lisa Sachs, Joseph E. Stiglitz, Michael Vachon and Jo Weir. Research on SaharaReporters was conducted by Inas Abbas, Erin Banco, Kelsey Buchbinder, Jillian Housman and Vianey Luna.

Thanks too to our interviewees, who kindly and generously gave us their time over Skype, on the phone, by email and in person: Adérito Caldeira (@Verdade), Nelson Charifo (e-magazine: *Energia e Indústria Extractiva em Moçambique*), Tom Glaisyer, Craig Hammer, Gavin Hayman, Antoine Heuty (Ulula, USA), Angelo Izama, Lise Johnson, Nicholas Koch, George Lugalambi, Lisa Misol, Peter Mwesige (ACME, Uganda), Dayo Olopade, Ory Okolloh, Katharina Pistor, Nicholas Phythian, Jenik Radon, Peter Rosenblum, David Sasaki, Nisha Varia (Human Rights Watch), Dionisio Nombora (*Centro de Integridade Pública*, Mozambique), Arild Drivdal, Paulo Oliveira and Patrick Brock (IREX, Mozambique), Fernanda Lobato (*Olho do Cidadão*, Mozambique), Milton Machel (*SAVANA*, Mozambique) and Jared Sacks (CHOSA, South Africa).

Disclaimer

Portions of this paper have appeared in papers by the authors that were presented at the Global Investigative Journalism Network conference in Rio in 2015 as well as at the Power Reporting Conference at University of Witwatersrand in Johannesburg in 2015.

Notes

1. Also known as Dutch disease, a theory that stemmed from the Netherlands example in the 1960s when the manufacturing sector withered as the gas industry grew (*The Economist*, 1977).
2. These perverse results have collectively been referred to as "the resource curse", originally named by Stanford professor Terry Karl, or the "paradox of plenty".
3. Note the "diplomatic apology" in autumn 2013 from the Portuguese Foreign Relations Minister Rui Machete to the Angolan president, his family and government for the ongoing investigations by the Portuguese Attorney General in response to several accusations by renowned investigative journalist Rafael Marques and others.
4. For a discussion of "graft fatigue" in Nigeria following the major Halliburton bribery scandal see: http://saharareporters.com/column/graft-fatigue?page=1
5. Articles questioning and investigating the wealth of Isabel dos Santos, the daughter of Angolan President José Eduardo dos Santos, who has also been declared the richest woman in Africa, have appeared several times in the Angolan newspapers and blogosphere in the past five years but have never received much attention from the wider Angolan community and media nor attention from Isabel dos Santos herself (Cristóvão, 2013).
6. Legalized threats to the press happen everywhere. The July 2013 article in the *New Yorker*, by Patrick Radden Keefe, about corruption in the allocation of mineral rights in Guinea describes a series of angry letters and lawsuits from BSGR, the shadowy company run by the notoriously litigious and aggressive Benny Steinmetz. The article itself provoked an aggressive response from the BSGR, although not a lawsuit or threat of lawsuit against Keefe.
7. http://cpj.org/2000/03/attacks-on-the-press-1999-angola.php. April 2015.
8. Mining giants Rio Tinto and Vale, in the coal-rich west-central region of Mozambique, have been uprooting self-sufficient farming communities and resettling them to arid land with difficult access to food, water, health and education facilities, and work, since 2009. In January 2012, approximately 500 people in the remote mining area blocked the railway and citizen reports finally made the national news. Local and international pressure then followed and led to the adoption of a new resettlement decree on 8 August 2012 (Human Rights Watch, 2013a).
9. This section is drawn from an unpublished paper written by a group of students at Columbia University's School of International and Public Affairs in the spring of 2014, and edited by Anya Schiffrin and Matthew Purcell. Thanks to Erin Banco, Kelsey Buchbinder, Jillian Haussman, Vianey Luna and Inas Abbas for their research.
10. http://www.saharareporters.com. August 2015.
11. Unpublished report by Erin Banco, Kelsey Buchbinder, Jillian Haussman, Vianey Luna and Inas Abbas.
12. Omoyele Sowere. Interview with Global Voices. "Nigeria: SaharaReporters: Africa's Wikileaks". Posted May 2011. https://globalvoicesonline.org/2011/05/12/nigeria-saharareporters-africas-wikileaks/, Retrieved 24 March 2014.
13. Musikilu Mojeed, Sahara Reporters: A thorn in the flesh of corruption. 21 November 2010. http://www.gbooza.com/m/group/discussion?id=5506827%3ATopic%3A52206, Retrieved 24 March 2014.
14. The Banker's Editors, "Central Bank Governor of the Year 2011", *The Banker*. 23 December 2011. http://www.thebanker.com/Awards/Central-Bank-Governor-of-the-Year/Central-Bank-Governor-of-the-Year-2011?ct=true. April 2015.

15. Biryabarema Eliyas, Uganda ups oil reserves estimate by 85 pct, finds natural gas. *Reuters.* 29 August 2014. http://www.reuters.com/article/2014/08/29/uganda-oil -idUSL5N0QZ1EW20140829. April 2015.
16. A training programme offered by the Revenue Watch Institute and the Thomson Reuters Foundation teaches journalists to report effectively on oil and gas issues and promote public debate on the sector. ACME also launched, in 2012, a prize for the best reporting on oil, gas and mining. Submissions were scored for originality, sourcing, relevance, depth and clarity.

References

BBC News. (2015). *Uganda Country Profile.* http://www.bbc.co.uk/news/world-africa -14107906. March 2015.

Burgis, Tom. (2015). *The Looting Machine: Warlords, Oligarchs, Corporations, Smugglers, and the Theft of Africa's Wealth, Public Affairs.* New York: PublicAffairs. 320 pp.

Behrman, Michael, Canonge, James, andPurcell, Matthew. (2010). "Watchdog or Lapdog: Limits of African Media Coverage of the Extractive Sector". In *Initiative for Policy Dialogue.* School of International and Public Affairs, Columbia University. 74 pp.

Carpenter, Serena. (2008). Source diversity in US online citizen journalism and online newspaper articles. In *International Symposium on Online Journalism.* http: //online.journalism.utexas.edu/2008/papers/OnlineCitizenJournalism_Carpenter .pdf. Arizona State University. August 2015.

CIA World Factbook. (n.d.). South Africa. *The World Factbook.* https://www.cia.gov/ library/publications/the-world-factbook/geos/sf.html. March 2015.

Colmery, Ben, Diaz, Adriana, Gann, Emily, Heacock, Rebekah, Hulland, Jonathan and Kircher-Allen, Eamon. (2009). *There Will Be Ink: A Study of Journalism Training and the Extractive Industries in Ghana, Nigeria and Uganda.* New York: Revenue Watch Institute and Columbia University's School of International and Public Affairs. http://policydialogue.org/images/uploads/There%20Will%20Be%20 Ink%281%29.pdf. August 2015.

Cristóvão, Cláudio. (2013). When Forbes starts asking questions about the wealth of Angola's ruling family .... *Africa Is a Country.* http://africasacountry.com/when-forbes-starts-asking-questions-about-the-wealth-of-angolas-ruling-family/. April 2014.

Dolan, David, and Herskovitz, Jon. (2012). Wildcat strikes up stakes in South Africa. *Reuters.* http://www.reuters.com/article/2012/10/07/us-safrica-unions -idUSBRE89607Y20121007. April 2015.

Dyck, Alexander, and Zingales, Luigi. (2002). "The Corporate Governance Role of the Media". pp. 107–141. In *The Right to Tell: The Role of Mass Media in Economic Development*, Roumeen Islam (ed.), Washington, DC: World Bank.

The Economist. (1977). The Dutch disease. 26 November 1977, pp. 82–88.

EITI (Extractive Industries Transparency Initiative). (2011). Extracting data: an overview of EITI reports published 2005–2011. *EITI.* https://eiti.org/files/2012-02 -10_Extracting_Data_0.pdf. April 2015.

Esquerda.net. (2015). *Editora oferece livro de Rafael Marques para download gratuito.* http://www.esquerda.net/artigo/editora-oferece-livro-de-rafael-marques-para-download-gratuito/36329. August 2015.

Hefez, Jeanne. (2013). After the massacre: the women's solidarity forum. *Amandla!* http://amandla.org.za/after-the-massacre-the-womens-solidarity-forum/. April 2015.

Hochschild, Adam. (1998). *King Leopold's Ghost*. New York: Houghton Mifflin.

Human Rights Watch. (2013a). *What Is a House without Food: Mozambique's Coal Mining Boom and Resettlements*. http://www.hrw.org/reports/2013/05/23/what-house -without-food. March 2014.

Human Rights Watch. (2013b). *A New Accountability Agenda: Human Rights and the Extractive Industries Transparency Initiative*. http://eiti.org/files/A%20New%20 Accountability%20Agenda%2C%20Human%20Rights%20and%20the%20EITI.pdf. March 2014.

International Energy Agency. (2012). U.S. $7 billion lost annually to oil theft in Nigeria. *AllAfrica.com*. http://allafrica.com/view/group/main/main/id/00020867 .html. April 2015.

Kasita, Ibrahim. (2012). Government discloses oil deals. *New Vision*. http://www .newvision.co.ug/news/632457-government-discloses-oil-deals.html. October 2013.

Keck, Margareth E. and Sikkink, Kathryn. (1998). *Activists beyond Borders: Advocacy Networks in International Politics*. Ithaca, NY, and London: Cornell University Press, pp. 19–21.

Keefe Radden, Patrick. (2013). "Buried Secrets". *The New Yorker*, 8 and 15 July, pp. 50–63.

Maka Angola. (2013). *Rafael Marques de Morais alvo de espionagem informática*. https:// www.facebook.com/maka.angola/posts/177606762403600. August 2015.

Marinovich, Greg, and Nicolson, Greg. (2014). Marikana Commission: Police defense collapsing. *Daily Mavericks*. http://www.dailymaverick.co.za/article/2014-09-09- marikana-commission-polices-defence-collapsing/#.VTSGZJMwB81. April 2015.

Marques, Rafael. (2011). Diamantes de Sangue; Corrupção e tortura em Angola. Tinta da China: 240 pp.

Mining Intelligence Database. (n.d.) *Mining in South Africa*. http://www.projectsiq.co. za/mining-in-south-africa.htm. April 2015.

Nombora, Dionisio. (2012). *Extractive Industries Transparency Initiative: Mozambique Moves towards Compliant Status*. http://publishwhatyoupay.org/ sites/publishwhatyoupay.org/files/Mozambique%20moves%20towards%20 Compliant%20Status%20DN%20(2).pdf. March 2013.

Project for Excellence in Journalism. (2005). *The State of the News Media 2005: An Annual Report on American Journalism*.

Project for Excellence in Journalism. (2006). *The State of the News Media 2006: An Annual Report on American Journalism*.

Revenue Watch Institute. (n.d.). Oil and mining companies on global stock exchanges. *RWI*. http://data.revenuewatch.org/listings/. April 2015.

Schiffrin, Anya. (2014). *Global Muckraking: 100 Years of Investigative Journalism from Around the World*. New York: New Press.

Silverstein, Ken. (2014). *The Secret World of Oil*. New York: Verso.

Smit, Carel. (2013). The role of mining in the South African economy. *KPMG South Africa Blog*. http://www.sablog.kpmg.co.za/2013/12/role-mining-south-african -economy/. April 2015.

World Bank. (2011). Total natural resources rents (% of GDP). *The World Bank*. http://data.worldbank.org/indicator/NY.GDP.TOTL.RT.ZS?order=wbapi_data_ value_2011+wbapi_data_value+wbapi_data_value-last&sort=desc. April 2015.

Young, Nick. (2013). Media deserve only five out of ten for promoting oil trans- parency. *Oil in Uganda*. http://www.oilinuganda.org/features/interviews/media- deserve-only-five-out-of-ten-for-promoting-oil-transparency.html. October 2014.

9
Crowdfunding: A Harambee for African Journalism?

Kristin Skare Orgeret

Fifteen years into the new millennium, at a time marked by an ongoing struggle to find new revenue streams for serious journalism, both in Africa and globally, the advent of crowdfunding has been welcomed with curiosity and expectations, and also with some scepticism around the world. As a new community-funding model, crowdfunding is the process of convincing a relatively large group of people to contribute relatively small sums of money towards a specific project via the Internet. A focal question is whether the crowdfunding model proposes an alternative to corporate–commercial control and whether it may serve as a platform from which political changes may be initiated. The empirical backdrop of the research on crowdfunding is the general lack of resources in contemporary journalism, which is often argued to undermine the quality of reporting and fact-checking practices. Fewer news correspondents and the abuse of information received from agencies are merely a few consequences of this situation (Brogan, 2008; Carvajal *et al.*, 2012). A core challenge is how to make media businesses profitable without compromising the investigative reporting, as well as how to take advantage of digital economies for providing quality journalism. As traditional news outlets dedicate a decreasing amount of resources to investigative reporting, freelance journalists have fewer options for working on these kinds of projects and funding their costs. Hence, since 2010, a growing number of journalists have turned to crowdfunding, creating a platform for obtaining support from users.

This chapter will examine the potential of the crowdfunding model in relation to citizen journalism from and about Africa. With reference to the Swahili concept of "harambee" – literally "pulling together" – the chapter will discuss some possibilities of linking crowdfunding platforms to African traditions. The analysis is based on a case study of three different crowdfunding platforms – Beacon Reader, Contributoria and Kickstarter – and their stories on Africa. The main research question is whether it is possible to see any of these models approaching ideas of citizen or participatory journalism, and whether such platforms have the potential to be a base from which political changes in Africa may be initiated. Through these discussions, the chapter's findings aim to feed into ongoing debates over the democratic potential of alternative media in Africa.

Methodology and selection of cases

The case-study approach has been chosen to investigate crowdfunding platforms, as it emphasizes detailed contextual analysis of a limited number of phenomena and their relationships. All case-study research starts from the same convincing feature: the desire to derive a(n) (up-)close or otherwise in-depth understanding of a single or small number of cases, set in their real-world contexts (Bromley, 1986, p. 1). The closeness aims to produce an invaluable and deep understanding – that is, an insightful appreciation of the "case(s)" – hopefully resulting in new learning about real-world behaviour and its meaning. The distinctiveness of the case study, therefore, also serves as its abbreviated definition:

> An empirical inquiry about a contemporary phenomenon (e.g., a "case"), set within its real-world context – especially when the boundaries between phenomenon and context are not clearly evident.
>
> (Yin, 2009, p. 18)

For this project, the cases have been selected and studied primarily because of each one's intrinsic interest. Furthermore, the three cases are also quite diverse, with different historical trajectories and varying funding and ownership structures. They will be studied as potential tools for civic engagements by looking at presentation, who participates and with what outcome.

Kickstarter.com is the world's largest general crowdfunding initiative, which is also used by journalists, whereas Beacon Reader and Contributoria are crowdfunding initiatives exclusively for journalists. Contributoria was selected mainly because it was launched by one of the largest British media groups, the Guardian Media Group (GMG), as a new collaborative platform for journalists and writers. Beacon Reader was selected for its subscription-based model. Rather than funding a once-off project by a particular writer, Beacon Reader is a platform for writers to collect paid subscribers who will offer an ongoing stream of support. While a normal crowdfunding project only succeeds if a minimum amount of money is raised, a Beacon Reader crowdfunding campaign succeeds if a certain amount of people (normally 25–100) pledge to pay a journalist $5 a month on an ongoing basis, in exchange for continued access to his/her stories, but also access to all the other stories on the site.[1]

It may be a methodological challenge for case-study research to approach the selected cases in a way that make their contents comparable across the embedded cases. However, analysing the three different crowdfunding cases through the prism of citizen journalism and in light of the need for new platforms from which political changes in Africa may be initiated, makes it possible to draw preliminary conclusions across the board.

The observations presented here are based on a small sample and should be considered initiative findings. Still, they are believed to be valuable as they raise some important questions linked to the possibilities and challenges crowdfunding has as a mechanism in general, and in increasing journalism from and about Africa in particular. These observations may be treated as hypotheses that can inform, and possibly be tested in, further studies. The three specific crowdfunding tools looked at here were studied in April 2015. In addition, what was probably the very first journalistic project in Norway to use crowdfunding tools to enable travelling and reportage, in 2014, will be referred to.

Key concepts and background

Crowdfunding is the practice of funding a project or venture by raising monetary contributions from a large number of people, typically via the Internet, whereas crowdsourcing is the activity where tasks are outsourced to a large network of people, recruited through an open call (Muthukumaraswamy, 2010, p. 48).

As early as in October 2007, the *Guardian* embarked on a goal to develop the impoverished community of Katine in rural Uganda in collaboration with the non-governmental organization (NGO) Amref. The newspaper used its website as a platform to stimulate discussion, and drew from its large diversity of readers and their intellectual capital. The editor, Alan Rusbridger asked the pertinent question: "Would it be possible to find a way of connecting the ideas, goodwill, resources and expert knowledge of 15 million readers around the world and focusing them on one problem?" (Muthukumaraswamy, 2010, p. 56). The answer was yes, and the Katine site became a "veritable goldmine of proposals for development issues that range from electricity to education" (Muthukumaraswamy, 2010, p. 56). *Guardian* reporters were observing livelihoods in the Ugandan village, interacting with its residents, and allowing them to share their stories through videos and blogs on the website. The media development organization Panos worked with the *Guardian* to train local journalists to be better able to convey the story of Katine. The *Guardian* managed to draw in readers from around the world in its effort to enhance livelihoods in rural Africa. People from all walks of life were contributing their time and expertise to address the issues involved. The news organization could stress that they aided citizen participation to make this a more democratic process, while they also attracted and activated large group of readers. This was one of the first projects in crowdsourcing's infancy, although Rick Davies, who was called upon to evaluate the project, was reluctant to call the exercise a crowdsourcing project, insisting that that would entail the conversion of suggestions on the site to real progress in Katine (Davies, 2008; Muthukumaraswamy, 2010).

A couple of crowdfunding initiatives for journalists were launched in 2006 (Spot.us and chitowndailynews.org), but the real breakthrough for crowdfunding initiatives came around 2010–2011. The very first crowdfunding platform, Spot.us, was launched in 2008 to support reporting, and helped publish stories on partner sites from the *New York Times* to the *Cleveland Free Press*. Most crowdfunded journalism projects have raised modest amounts – measured in the thousands or tens of thousands of dollars – but there are some noteworthy big successes. The Global Investigative Journalism Network (2015) describes how, during a period of two years from 2013, three European campaigns have raised over 1 million euros each. These projects were initiated by De Correspondent in Netherlands, Krautreporter in Germany and El Español in Spain.

At an early stage of the development of crowdsourcing, Jay Rosen was explicit about the differences between citizen journalism and crowdfunding. Whereas citizen journalism facilitates a greater role for citizens in the democratic process through contribution of their thoughts, stories and photos, crowdsourcing, according to Rosen, "is a collaborative effort between a news organization and its audience, one where the roles of citizen contributors are clearly defined" (2007). However, as crowdsourcing initiatives have rocketed since 2010, it may be easier to see some links to citizen journalism in its current form, as journalism itself no longer necessarily has to be attached to an institution of the media.

The role of the citizens or "the people formerly known as the audience"

Journalism and the press shape the way we understand and think about the world, the way we perceive ourselves and our surroundings, and the way we relate to one another and society at large. Furthermore, journalism and the press shape the way in which core societal concepts like "democracy" and "freedom of expression" are understood and practised. Journalism and the press therefore function as a cultural prerequisite for societal change at large, and for the dissemination and communication of ideas of democracy and freedom of expression in particular. The traditional role of journalism and the press is today under pressure as new technology and new media practices facilitate new cultural conditions, which enable societal change and shape new practices and understandings of democracy and freedom of expression. This potential hegemonic shift between journalism and the press on the one hand, and new media institutions and actors with no prior affiliation to professional journalism on the other, is not only promoted by the rise of new, social media, but by other effects of political, economic and technological developments influencing society at large and the media industry in particular. The media industry is increasingly marked by the blurring of borders between producers, distributors and consumers of information. This blurring affects media institutions on both a micro level of individual agency as well as on a macro level of ownership and control. Concerning the micro level of individual agency, journalists, for instance, increasingly base their production on the consumption of other journalists' production (Boczkowski, 2010); consumers of journalism become producers through practices of "participatory journalism"; anyone with Internet access can be a distributor of information to a potential mass audience. Professional ideology might therefore become what separates the journalist from the blogger, the press agent, the spin doctor and other professionals and non-professionals, who select, interpret, frame and distribute information to an audience. Consequently, journalists may increasingly be defined not by what they *do*, but by "the degree to which they choose to adhere to the normative goals of their professional culture", according to Singer (2006, p. 13).

The role of the public, or the citizens, is also crucial here. Those who Rosen referred to as "the people formerly known as the audience" (2006):

> [A]re those who *were* on the receiving end of a media system that ran one way, in a broadcasting patter, with high entry fees and a few firms competing to speak very loudly while the rest of the population listened in isolation from one another – and who *today* are not in a situation like that *at all*.

As processes of convergence happen, one might argue that globalization has made geographical locations and spaces less significant. An increasingly globalized world also demands intercultural communication skills on both a global, and progressively also on a local, level. As some of the most pressing challenges of our times – climate change, global inequalities, migration, terrorism – cannot be fully solved or understood solely at a national level, serious journalism is increasingly becoming an international phenomenon with global networks, no longer able to operate solely within national or cultural borders (Löffelholz *et al.*, 2008). Concurrently, more news media content becomes global, and it becomes harder to categorize news texts as either solely domestic or foreign news. However, many digital notifying networks and critical websites worldwide are censored by authoritarian regimes through filtration or blocking (Al-Saqaf, 2010). The role of citizen journalism may be even more important in such authoritarian regimes.

Stuart describes how, despite its ambiguities, the term *citizen journalism* appears "to capture something of the countervailing ethos of the ordinary person's capacity to bear witness" (2011, p. 97). He argues that the changing dynamics of technological convergence and divergence will necessarily "entail thinking anew about the social responsibilities of the citizen as a journalist while, at the same time, reconsidering those of the journalist as citizen" (2011, p. 98). Clemencia Rodríguez (2011) draws on new social movement theories that understand power and resistance as tightly connected with issues of recognition of identity, voice, agency and narration, as key elements of political representation. According to such approaches, "citizen media" are those media that facilitate the transformation of individuals and communities into citizens, that "trigger processes that allow individuals and communities to recodify their contexts and selves" (2011, p. 101).

African journalism and "harambee"

Roland Robertson was one of the first scholars to describe how globalization and localization are interrelated, and state that "globalization involves the universalization of particularism, not just the particularization of universalism" (1992, p. 130). Similarly, whereas the term "African journalism" is highly contested, a growing body of academic literature recognizes that African journalism is indeed unique and different in terms of how it is practised (e.g. Bosch, 2015; Skjerdal, 2015; Shaw, 2009). Despite the notion of universality in journalism as an ideology (see, for instance, Deuze, 2004), Bosch argues that academic researchers turning their focus to African journalism, should "keep in mind the geographical and cultural peculiarities of the continent and adapt their approaches accordingly" (2015, p. 18).

The increased use of new media technologies, particularly social media, has been a prominent change for African journalism (Bosch, 2015, p. 19). This makes it even more relevant to discuss the potential of crowdfunding initiatives for African journalism. Moreover, in many African societies there are long traditions for defining individuals in reference to their community and valuing community processes. Language and social rules bind people with other community members and with ancestors; furthermore, the community plays an important role in the individual's transformation into personhood (Menkiti, 1984). The Bantu word "ubuntu", which means "human-ness" and that a "person is a person through other people", reflects this. According to ubuntu, there exists a common bond between all human beings, and it is through this bond, through interaction with fellow human beings, that we discover our own human qualities. The Swahili word "harambee" – meaning "all for one" or "pulling/working together" – also reflects the value of joint efforts and of community belonging. Harambee is a form of communal work, where a gathering takes place to accomplish a task – everyone does what they can, through their personal effort, or through donations in cash or in kind – "all for one". It is against this background that we go on to analyse crowdfunding initiatives and their potential for African journalism.

The case studies: Three crowdfunding initiatives

Kickstarter: Project-based crowdfunding

The first crowdfunding platform to be analysed here, Kickstarter is an initiative for all types of people and projects, which is also used by journalists. It was launched in April 2009 as a platform to initiate all types of creative projects. Kickstarter is equally crowdsourcing *and* crowdfunding, as it is both a mechanism to pledge funding, and also to initiate input to the projects in hand. The funding goal is the amount of money that creators need to complete their project. Funding is "all-or-nothing", which means that no one will be charged for a pledge towards a project unless it reaches its funding goal. This way, creators always have the budget they need before moving forward (http://www.kickstarter.com). Kickstarter has its own journalism section, where about 568 successfully funded journalism projects, which have raised a total of 6 million dollars, were launched during from April 2009 to April 2015. In April 2015, there were 22 journalism projects on Africa on Kickstarter, they may be written stories, podcasts, videos, or photojournalism or multimedia productions. The writers do not need to have any links to a traditional media institution and some of them may thus be seen as citizen journalists in the sense that they are actors promoted by the rise of new, social media.

If we take a closer look at the focus of the journalism projects (see full list at the end of the chapter) it is clear that most of them are concerned with social justice, in a similar manner to many citizen journalism projects (see e.g. Orgeret, 2013; Radsch, 2011). While it is media professionals who physically construct the stories, the choices they make in their news-gathering and news-writing routines are actually guided by a much broader social and political context. Some campaigns at Kickstarter are more projects than journalistic reports, for instance, "The Speak Out Citizen Journalism Training Project", which aims to return the power of a free and fair press to the people of Tunisia. Other examples are "Loud Silence Media", a small team of young people, mostly from Ghana, which covers local stories from cities and villages; "The Toronto Globalist" (Project Tahir), a non-profit publication that aspires to engage in international dialogue on world issues; and "Project Survival Media", a global youth journalism network dedicated to broadcasting stories of survival and ingenuity in the face of climate change.

As of April 2015, Kickstarter is open to backers all over the world; meanwhile, project creation is only available to individuals in the USA, UK, Canada, Australia, New Zealand, the Netherlands, Denmark, Ireland, Norway and Sweden. As a result, the majority of reporters are journalists from the Western world proposing to travel to Africa to undertake the journalistic projects, although some are based in Africa (namely in Egypt, Ghana, South Africa and Sudan), and a few are actually from the countries they propose to report from (Ghana and Kenya), with a link to a project creator based in the West. Hence, the "African journalism" we find here is more "journalism about Africa" than "African journalism" in the sense of being reports initiated by African journalists, even though some reports are a mixture and some do originate from African journalists.

A total of 18 journalism projects about Africa, or 44% of the totality of such projects, have been successfully funded by Kickstarter (with between 44,856 and 2,095 USD).[2] For 19 out of the total of 41 projects, funding was unsuccessful or was cancelled. Four had not yet received any funding by the time this analysis had been completed, and had between 54 hours and 21 more days to go. Kickstarter estimates the success rate in the journalism section to be of 25%,[3] hence the findings here indicate that there is a significantly higher success rate when proposing a project relating to Africa and journalism, than relating to journalism in general. Of all the journalists launching African projects on Kickstarter in April 2015, 16 were women and 13 men. This an interesting finding, as female journalists are often presumed to be more conservative when it comes to trying out new technological possibilities, echoing the myth that women are more fearful than men of new technology (see, for instance, Mitra, 2010, for a discussion of this myth).

Potential Kickstarter supporters are promised different rewards according to how much they donate. For instance, in Trevor Clark's project – about an US doctor and kayak professional who opened five clinics focusing on malaria education in Uganda – for a 10 USD donation to the project one receives a "shout-out" on the reporter's Facebook page. For 20 USD a personal Thank You card made from an image in the project will be given in addition to a special "Thanks" on the reporter's own blog. For a donation of 50 USD one receives a special T-shirt and a "behind-the-scenes" DVD of the project. For 100 USD the reward is "local arts and crafts" from the villages the reporter visits. For 500 USD he adds a personal phone call and a signed print from the project. The 1,000 USD support reward is everything mentioned so far, three signed prints and a "Special Thanks" in the final multimedia piece. These rewards also function to create links between the journalists and the supporters of their project.

Furthermore, when the backers are urged to "tell us what you want the journalists to investigate", the link between the readers and journalists is strengthened. Or, as a group of writers at Kickstarter put it: "We hope to get rid of the barriers between journalists and readers – to move past the old model of us writing and you reading, toward the modern era of interaction and collaboration."

Beacon Reader: Subscription-based crowdfunding

Beacon Reader (http://www.beaconreader.com) is a subscription-based crowdfunding initiative exclusively for journalists. In 2013, founders Dan Fletcher, Dmitri Cherniak and Adrian Sanders launched Beacon as a different kind of crowdfunding platform, one that focuses on writers more than their stories, and takes a collective approach by sharing revenue across different projects.

Users subscribe to their favourite of Beacon's 150 writers for a minimum of $5 a month, and in return receive access to all the content produced by all writers on the site. About 60% of the subscription fee goes to the chosen writer, while the rest is shared between the other Beacon writers. Backing a particular writer on Beacon is thus a gateway into a broader subscription of the work of the whole Beacon writer collective. It has been described as a kind of writers cooperative, but it is a competitive one in which writers have to earn their place (and a share of the resultant income stream) by securing a certain number of new subscribers (and to continue building more subscribers over time). Writers get 70% of their subscribers' cash, and the surplus goes into a collective bonus pot to reward those whose stories receive the most recommendations, thereby incentivizing consistent high-quality writing.

Significantly, the writer still owns the rights to the pieces produced, and they can publish them elsewhere or sell them on to media outlets. The writers use the money to publish stories and the readers get an email update whenever the writer posts a new story.

On 23 April 2015, Beacon had 11 potential projects about Africa that readers were asked to support (see end of chapter for the total list). "With Beacon, you can enable journalism all around the world" (http://www.beaconreader .com/projects). The writers describe how the money will be spent, and frequently argue that travelling and reporting from the ground in Africa is expensive. For instance, Tyrel Bernardini promises the top-level backers postcards from the road. Caitlin Kara promises her top-level backers a souvenir from Tanzania – handmade crafts and exclusive access to the first cuts of the documentary film about youth and refugees in Kigoma. There is a lot of focus on how the financial support will enable journalists to undertake investigative projects and make "more fearless stories"; furthermore, the community aspect is frequently stressed through the need to allow the stories to get back to the people from whom they stem.

For Beacon, the relationship between the reporters and their audience seems rather traditional, in the words of Beacon itself: "Journalists have stories to tell, readers are listening" (http://www.beaconreader.com/about). Beacon describes itself as a simple platform that lets "writers connect with readers that value their work".

Similarly to the findings from Kickstarter, the gender equality in terms of reporters who propose journalistic projects about Africa is quite balanced: the initiators are six men and five women. Whereas it is not completely clear from the website instructions whether Beacon operates with any restrictions on where the writers are from, in the selected material of proposed projects related to Africa, all writers originate from the global North. The distance between those who initiated the projects and the focus of the articles in several of the cases seems to echo the claim that the emergence of global citizens' compassion and responsibility largely takes place in sanitized, depoliticized, media-constructed spaces (Chouliaraki, 2006; Moeller, 1999).

Contributoria: The "credit union" for journalism approach

Contributoria (http://www.Contributoria.com) is an independent journalism community, which describes itself as "a platform for journalists, by journalists". It is a place designed to help people help each other, to improve the writing process with transparency, and to support quality journalism through collective funding. Of the three cases discussed in this chapter, it is the one where the readers are given the largest role in the creation of articles. When one becomes a member, you get the right to pitch articles to be funded, but also to financially support another's articles, and to offer editorial advice to those whom you've backed. As one of the users explained: "As a user of the platform I am thus a hybrid between a receiver of funding, and giver of funding, a receiver of editorial services and giver of editorial services" (Scott, 2014).

Contributoria is a network where a writer can cooperate with other writers over a cycle of three months. If a project does not receive enough funding during the first month it will not go through. If it has received sufficient, however, the journalist will use one month to undertake the project: the last month of the cycle is dedicated to editing and proofreading. When the project is finished and published on Contributoria's website, the journalist gets paid from the pool of subscribers. During the process, the journalist gets input, ideas, contacts and suggestions for editing from the global members. Registered members (10,000 as of March 2015) receive a certain amount of points each month that they may use as currency to support whatever project they would like to see realized.

Citizen journalism has been described variously as "networked journalism" (Allan, 2011, p. 97), and the concept fits well in here. During a seminar in Oslo in March 2015, co-founder of Contributoria, Matt McAlister, explained how the members can collaborate on early versions of the writers' draft and are hence involved in the writing process. This model is thus closer to the idea of citizen journalism, although experienced writers are still in charge of the final product. This model has great potential to let people participate in the creation of stories of interest to their lives. There are some similarities to citizen journalism in the way the stories "progressively ingratiate themselves into the differentiated news ecology, and may reconfigure, or simply bypass traditional hierarchies and relations of communicative power" (see Allan and Thorsen, 2009, p. xii). However, a relevant question asked by Brett Scott is whether Contributoria can become a vibrant self-sustaining community of writers, readers and editors, or whether members' dues need to be supplemented with money from external sponsors? (Scott, 2014)

Contributoria produces a monthly online magazine: in the April 2015 issue, four articles were about Africa: three were written by women and one by a man. Three of the writers are South Africans and the other an American living in South Africa (for details about the articles, see list at the end of this chapter).

Discussion: This time for Africa?

The three different cases discussed in this chapter have a number of common themes. First, they set themselves against corporate-backed media (in developed countries) and state-backed media (in developing countries) by offering a technological way to decentralize funding, and, in so doing, to "democratize journalism". McChesney and Schiller describe how underlying the new communication technology has been a political force – the shift to neoliberal orthodoxy – which relaxed or eliminated barriers to commercial exploitation of media, and concentrated media ownership. However, they argue "there is nothing inherent in the technology that required neoliberalism; new digital communications could have been used, for example, to simply enhance public service provision had a society elected to do so" (McChesney and Schiller 2003, p. iv). The examples presented here show how crowdfunding may be used for public, as opposed to corporate–commercial, control.

At the same time, crowdfunding for journalism raises some important questions in terms of the integrity and independence of journalism. Is it only the taste of the audience that shall decide which projects to be funded? Do the audience always know what they need?

The fact that alternative communication and journalism's practices are often formed by characteristic political–economic limits and pressures is of importance here. Hence, it is necessary to take into consideration the context of the country in each case, when discussing the potential of alternative journalism models. In many African societies, news with a grass-root perspective is excluded for the benefit of more upmarket commercial stories. When this development coexists with a politically motivated reassertion of media control, where loyalty is rewarded and critics side-lined, the result is often a narrowing of the communication space. Hence, important public issues are, to a large degree, excluded from the public agenda and important groups of the population are excluded from important discussions (Gumede, 2008; Orgeret, 2010). New platforms driven by the wish to create good journalism and cover stories that otherwise would not be heard could be important for African journalism. Introducing crowdfunding may involve new exchanges and play an active role in disseminating news and information from sectors of society, or even the world, that usually have little or no access to the formal channels of communication.

It has been argued that citizen journalism may challenge the traditional concepts of the journalist (see, for example, Turner, 2010). One aspect of this challenge, as Turner sees it, is that "the once privileged position occupied by journalists has been reclaimed, as it were, by those who wish to enable ordinary citizens to participate more directly in the construction of the public sphere" (2010, p. 72). Questions linked to traditional journalistic practices are therefore also relevant here, as some scholars argue that only trained journalists can understand the exactitude and ethics involved in reporting news (e.g. Lemann, 2006). A striking result of crowdfunding initiatives for journalism is that the editorial power is diminished. In countries where the public sphere is challenged by pressure on freedom of speech, challenging editors loyal to not-so-democratic regimes may be a good thing. However, there are some immediate challenges to introducing such an alternative model within the African context: the first one is related to the fact that if the community's funding is decisive for the type of media content it receives, an inherent danger is that media content may be bought. As crowdfunding initiatives allow donators to choose which story they find most interesting and relevant, there might be a hidden danger related to the fact that this potentially opens the door for money deciding the news agenda. This is particularly relevant with regard to countries with authoritarian regimes, and many questions could thus arise about the independence and autonomy of working journalists. How to go forward while avoiding bipartisanship (Carvajal *et al.*, 2012, p. 645) is a relevant question here. The undermining of editorial control is also challenging, and raises questions linked to the basis on which decisions related to journalistic frames and content are going to be made.

On the level of the individual journalist's work, a crowdfunding model also involves some challenges. There may, for instance, be a risk involved in publicly revealing a journalistic story idea, as somebody might steal the idea. This means that it is a balancing act for the journalist, between getting funders interested and convincing them to donate, while at the same time not giving away too much to competitors. Writing a good pitch has been described as an art form (Aitamurto, 2011, p. 436). For freelance journalists this is nothing new: there are many stories circulating about freelancers pitching to a newspaper, and being refused, just to find out, at a later stage, that the paper has written the story anyway (Aitamurto, 2011, p. 436). It has been argued that the crowdfunding journalistic process creates new conditions for the journalist's role. Whereas in the traditional, mainstream journalism model, the journalist concentrated on getting the story told and did not have to market it, many journalists today are used to promoting their stories through social media and are even expected, by their institutions, to tweet and use Facebook to enhance awareness of their stories or programmes. Hence, many journalists already have experience of marketing their own stories – the new aspect in the crowdfunding process is that even the pitch is to be sold, and that it is not just the editor, but the community, who have to be convinced about the importance of the story topic. Crowdfunding is thus about funding people who are providing a service for the community.

It is assumed that crowdfunding can be a sustainable model, but not a substitutive model (Carvajal *et al.*, 2012, p. 645). It is uncertain whether such models of financing can offer the predictability that journalism demands. It is of interest here to discuss how journalists could benefit from this model in the field of African journalism. Crowdfunding seems to be a good opportunity for investigative journalism to discover new ways to obtain resources, and this may be of particular importance in countries where the mainstream media are censored or under heavy political pressure. There is also great potential for shedding light on stories that are ignored or forgotten in mainstream media, including outside the African continent, such as a focus on alternative aspects of African societies, rather than the traditional Cs that guide much of the media industry's news values – Catastrophe, Crisis, Crime and Celebrity – or the sunshine stories of the "struggling but smiling African" (Orgeret, 2010, p. 48). A case in point here is how Norwegian journalist Maren Sæbø, in 2014, initiated a crowdfunding project for going to Nigeria and covering the conflict with Boko Haram. The project was a reaction to the lack of quality journalism from Nigeria in the Norwegian press, although Nigeria is Africa's second largest economy and home to almost a fifth of the African population. Sæbø stressed the fact that there are highly competent journalists in Nigeria and from elsewhere who are covering the conflict, but stated that these stories seldom make it to Norway (Kampanje, 2014).

We see that, in some of the cases, crowdfunding indeed places the audience at the very heart of the journalistic process in the way it engages users and involves them in the creative development. The different formats give users the chance to participate in the creative process through voting, commenting, sharing, twittering or enjoying a direct connection to creators. Earlier research has shown that the connection created by donations causes a strong sense of responsibility to develop in the journalists, a feeling different from the professional one found in a more traditional story assignment (see, for example, Aitamurto, 2011). Instead of replacing the journalism professional with citizen journalists, crowdfunded journalism gives users "the role of producers without endangering content quality" (Carvajal *et al.*, 2012, p. 645). Cohn, the founder of the very first crowdfunding initiatives specifically for journalists (Spot.us, founded in 2006), believes that journalism is a process in which users and journalists should have an equal relationship (Carvajal *et al.*, 2012, p. 645).

In all three of the models looked into here, the community members' power lies in donations, through which donors get to define which pitches succeed, and hence, which stories will be reported upon. Donating as part of the crowdfunding process is, in the words of Aitamurto, "a significant act that bonds the reporter to the community members, or donors, in the crowdfunded, journalistic process" (2011, p. 434).

Possibilities of contributing to the betterment of the community echo the ideas of traditional African values of ubuntu or harambee. Whereas the traditional normative African journalism models appear to be in collective conflict with Western journalism paradigms (see Skjerdal, 2012), the crowdfunding format, and particularly the ones which invite members of the community to actively take part in the journalistic process, seem to be less at odds with African normative models.

However, in terms of linking crowdfunding to "citizen media" in the way Rodríguez uses the concept, as communication spaces where men, women and children learn to manipulate their own languages and gain power "to name the world in their own terms" (2011, p. 101), there is still a long way to go. Nonetheless, it is possible to imagine that the crowdfunding model could suit such processes, aimed at activating communication processes that shape local communities and that allow individuals and communities to recodify their contexts and selves, and even combining these processes with dissemination to a larger scale. Perhaps it is in the role of the reader that the link between the different crowdfunding models and the concept of citizen journalism is the strongest:

> People who have prepaid for content in the knowledge that they are helping to bring forth unique critical voices, are also people who wish to move past being mere passive consumers of media. Instead, they are hybrid producer–consumers with an interest in critically engaging with the content they helped bring to life. And perhaps it is in the development of this new type of participatory reader that the true democratic potential of crowdfunding lies.
>
> (Scott, 2014)

In Africa, as Internet connections rapidly increase, new models that take advantage of digital economies for providing quality journalism become more relevant. The added value provided by users seen in the examples in this chapter, gives users the chance to participate in the creative process. If the potential that lies in the cases selected here to be an alternative platform from which political changes in Africa may be fully exploited, the crowdfunding models need to open up to creators from more countries than the currently selected few. There is further a need to open up to opportunities where teams of reporters may cooperate to report on issues for importance for several countries or a region in a "harambee", where one joins forces around a specific challenge or topic. Theoretically, crowdfunding works as the perfect place for connecting audiences and reporters (Carvajal *et al.*, p. 646). The analysis of this chapter indicates that it may also be a great tool in creating stories within the field of African journalism, with connectedness to the community and of importance to citizens.

There is definitely need for more research within this field, particularly with regard to those who donate to journalistic stories and their engagement with the stories. Do those who donate for African stories donate mainly for altruistic or instrumental reasons? Is it appealing for them to participate in story production or are they happy with providing financial resources only? What could this mean for the perspectives of an African journalism? The relationship with the traditional media is also of interest here, as one could envision that the crowdfunding reports challenge the traditional media to be more outspoken. What seems certain at this stage is that including crowdfunding models in discussions about the future of African journalism allow for interesting dimensions, both in relation to how old mediated stereotypes may be challenged, and to how new bases from whence political change may be initiated may be created.

As this chapter has shown, crowdfunding journalism may variously enter into and inform the news ecology with its corresponding formations and flows of stories, sometimes overlapping with alternative media and the principles of citizen journalism and with new, interactive technologies of news dissemination. Though still, in large part, structured by Western establishments and flows from the "West to the rest", the crowdfunding model has great potential to strengthen new dimensions of citizen journalism and a plethora of new views and voices, from the local to the global, from "the rest to the West", as platforms from which political changes may be initiated.

Overview of the crowdfunding platforms' stories on/from Africa:

Name, gender and where possible nationality of the journalist/creator in brackets.

Kickstarter:

- Nuba Reports (Ryan Boyette, male)
- Speak Out Tunisia, A citizen Journalism Training Project (Anne Medley, female and Tunisian PaCTE)
- Journalism without walls goes to Kenya (Ilana Ozneroy, female)
- Michael J. Totten's Dispatches from Libya (Michael J. Totten, male)
- GUMMIE: first urban magazine in Johannesburg (Ksenia Mardina, female)
- Kayaking doctor working for good (Trevor Clark, male)
- The Delta project (Eric Knecht, male, Nicholas Hilgeman, male and Megan Larcom, female)
- Loud silence media (Marisa Scwartz, female)
- Project Tahir (Project Tahir)

- 2011 UN Climate Negotiations in Durban (Project Survival Media, 4 female, 2 male from Kenya, India, the Netherlands and the United States)
- GEARS of change: a youth climate change media project (Lindsey Gillies, female)
- Slum rising (The Seattle Globalist aka Alisa Reznick, female)
- On a boat to raise awareness on plastic pollution (Carolynn Box, female)
- The face of Maar (Laurie Michaelson, female)
- Worlds apart (Megan Egbert, female)
- Tunisia after the revolution (Jabeen Bhatti, female)
- Documenting the struggle and resilience of Dakar youth (Bennett Barthelemy, male)
- The love of Libya (Timothy Jagielo, male)
- Last of the Northern White rhino (Chad Copeland, male)
- Why to help refugees where they live (Arvid Haag, male)
- Tanzania Community Journalism Project (Khalid Magram, male)
- South Africa Mission Possible (Princess Wilkes and Erik White, female and male)

www.beaconreader.com:

- East Africa's Shifting Societies (Will Swanson, male Australian based in Kenya)
- South Sudan in Crisis (Armin Rosen, male American, Washington DC)
- After Ebola comes Hunger (M. Sophia Newman, female, American)
- South Africa's next generation (Adam Sege, male American reporter, Emily Jan, female American photojournalist)
- Booming Southern Africa (Andrea Dijkstra, female Dutch)
- Hitchiking to Africa (Tyrel Bernardini, male, American)
- Oral Histories of African migration (Kate Thomas, female, British-American)
- Pirates, Poachers and Palm Oil (Adam Mc Cauley, male Canadian)
- Building a Better Africa (Caitlin Kara, female American)
- Promise and Peril in Somalialand (Rachel Williamson, female, New Zealand)
- Egypt's Refugee Exodus (Rom Rollins, male British)

Contributoria:

- A South African photographer: pictures of art, politics and protest (Madi Hanekom, female, South African).
- No wine before its time: The impact of climate change on South Africa's vineyards (Rebecca L. Weber, female, American based in South Africa).
- King Arabic sandwiches: a taste of Palestine in Johannesburg (Kim Harrisberg, female, South African).
- Rainbow nation (Brada Tease, male, South African).

Notes

1. https://contributoria.com/issue/2014-04/52fb61421035cc010b000081.
2. See the list of all projects at the end of the chapter.
3. https://www.kickstarter.com/learn?ref=nav.

References

Aitamurto, Tanja. (2011). The impact of crowdfunding on journalism. *Journalism Practice* 5(4): 429–445.
Al-Saqaf, W. (2010). "Internet Censorship Challenged". In *Increasing Transparency and Fighting Corruption through ICT*, C. Strand (ed.), Spider ICT4D Series No. 3, Stockholm: Universitetsservice, pp. 71–93.
Allan, Stuart. (2011). "Citizen Journalism" In *Encyclopedia of Social Movement Media*, S. Allan (ed.), Thousand Oaks, London, New Delhi and Singapore: Sage.
Allan, Stuart and Thorsen, Einar. (2009. *Citizen Journalism: Global Perspectives*. New York: Peter Lang.
Boczkowski, P.J. (2010). *News at Work: Imitation in an Age of Information Abundance*. Chicago: University of Chicago Press.
Bosch, Tanja. (2015). Research in African journalism: Trends and projections. *African Journalism Studies* 36(1): 18–21.
Brogan, Daniel. (2008). Good journalism can be good business. *Nieman Reports*.
Bromley, D.B. (1986). *The Case Study Method in Psychology and Related Disciplines*. New York: Wiley.
Carvajal, Miguel, Garcia-Avilés, José A., and Gonzalez, José L. (2012). Crowdfunding and non-profit media. *Journalism Practice* 6(5–6): 638–647.
Chouliaraki, Lilie. (2006). *The spectatorship of suffering*. London. Thousand Oaks, CA & New Delhi: Sage Publications.
Davies, Rick. (2008). *Crowdsourcing and International Aid Programs*. https://evaluatingkatine.wordpress.com/, Retrieved 12 April 2015.
Deuze, N. (2004). Journalism studies beyond media: On ideology and identity. *Equid Novi* 25(2): 275–293.
Global Investigative Journalism Network (2015). *Crowdfunding for Journalists* http://gijn.org/2015/02/17/crowdfunding-for-journalists/, Retrieved 1 March 2015.
Gumede, William M. (2008). Mbeki, Zuma: A Political Earthquake, *Pambazuka News* Issue 401, October. www.pambazuka.org/en/category/features/51032, Retrieved 5 August 2015.
Kampanje (2014). Kroneruller for å dekke bortføring. http://kampanje.com/archive/2014/06/kroneruller-for-a-dekke-bortforing/, Retrieved 9 April 2015.
Lemann, Nicholas. (2006). Amateur Hour: Journalism Without Journalists. *The New Yorker*. 7th and 14th August 2006.
Löffelholz, Martin *et al.*, (2008). *Global Journalism Research. Theories, Methods, Findings, Future*. Blackwell Publishing.
McChesney, Robert W. and Schiller, Dan (2003). *The Political Economy of International Communications*. Geneva: United Nations Research Institute for Social Development.
Menkiti, Ifeanyi A. (1984). *Person and Community in African Traditional Thought*. http://www2.southeastern.edu/Academics/Faculty/mrossano/gradseminar/evo%20of%20ritual/african%20traditional%20thought.pdf, Retrieved 6 April 2015.
Mitra, Ananda. (2010). *Alien Technology, Coping with Modern Mysteries*. New Delhi, Thousand Oaks, CA, and London: Sage Publications.

Moeller, Susan D. (1999). *Compassion Fatigue. How the Media Sell Disease, Famine, War and Death.* London: Routledge.

Muthukumaraswamy, Karthika. (2010). When the media meets crowds of wisdom. *Journalism Practice* 4(1): 48–65.

Orgeret, Kristin Skare. (2010). Mediated culture and the well-informed global citizen: Images of Africa in the global North. *Nordicom Review* 31(2): 47–61.

Orgeret, Kristin Skare. (2013). "16 Days of Activism Citizen Journalism in South Africa". In *Media Interventions*, K. Howley (ed.), Peter Lang Publishers.

Radsch, Courtney. (2011). "Arab bloggers as citizen journalists". In *Encyclopedia of Social Movement Media*, C. Atton (ed.). Sage.

Robertson, Roland. (1992). *Globalization: Social Theory and Global Culture.* London, Newbury Park: Sage.

Rodríguez, Clemencia. (2011). "Citizen Media". In *Encyclopedia of Social Movement Media*, C. Atton (ed.), Sage Reference.

Rosen, Jay. (2006). The people formerly known as the audience. *Press Think.* http://archive.pressthink.org/2006/06/27/ppl_frmr.html/ Retrieved 20 April 2015.

Rosen, Jay. (2007). *What I Learned from Assignment Zero.* http://archive.pressthink.org/2007/10/09/what_i_learned.html/, Retrieved 15 April 2015.

Scott, Brett. (2014). Crowdfunding critical thought: How alternative finance builds alternative journalism. *Contributoria.* https://contributoria.com/issue/2014-04/52fb61421035cc010b000081, Retrieved April 2014.

Shaw, I.S. (2009). Towards an African journalism model: A critical historical perspective. *International Communication Gazette* 71(6): 491–510.

Singer, J.B. (2006). The socially responsible existentialist. *Journalism Studies* 7(1): 2–18.

Skjerdal, Terje. (2012). The three alternative journalisms of Africa. *International Communication Gazette* 74(7): 636–654.

Skjerdal, Terje. (2015). Why the "African" still matters in African journalism studies. *African Journalism Studies* 36(1): 57–64.

Turner, Graeme (2010). *Ordinary People and the Media. The Demotic Turn.* London and Th. Oaks: Sage.

Yin, R.K. (2009). *Case Study Research. Design and Methods,* 4th edition. Thousand Oaks, London, New Delhi and Singapore: Sage Publications.

10
Politics of Passion and the Pursuit of Propaganda in Zimbabwe's State Media: A Study of the Case of *The Herald*

Bruce Mutsvairo

Introduction

In this chapter, the author has endeavoured to first problematize *The Herald* newspaper's role in Zimbabwean society. The first issue lies within the institution itself. Its role and responsibility to provide citizens with reliable news content have all been severely questioned by critics at home and abroad because of its traditional, openly pro-government stance. The second issue, which is related to the first, is associated with the newspaper's ownership structure, which presumably forces editors to pointedly paint a positive picture on stories involving Zimbabwe African National Union – Patriotic Front (ZANU-PF) officials even when unprejudiced scrutiny is needed, while anything that seeks to dehumanize, discredit or demonize the opposition attracts instant attention and is decidedly disseminated at whatever cost. The author, therefore, decided to formulate one central research question: To what extent do *The Herald's* historical ties with ZANU-PF contribute to its perceived biased coverage of news events?

Propaganda is commonly associated with Adolf Hitler during the Second World War even though it should be traced back to 500 years BC, to Alexander the Great in the ancient world, according to Jowett and O'Donnell (2006). Since the aftermath of the nineteenth-century Industrial Revolution, there has always been propaganda, argues Pratkanis and Aronson (1991), who link propaganda to the invention of human civilizations. Jackall (1995) opines that propaganda's origins can effectively be found in religion, arguing that, between 1621 and 1623, a propaganda office was set up by Pope Gregory XV. Ngoa (2006) is adamant there is a strong connection between advertising and propaganda, suggesting that, with the coming of the Industrial Revolution, lifestyles changed, automatically creating the need to guide the consumer.

Lasswell (1927), one of the most influential scholars in the field, has defined propaganda as "the control of opinion by significant symbols, or to speak more accurately by stories, rumors, reports, pictures and other forms of social communication" (p. 627). Contemporary scholars Jowett and O'Donnell (1999) have opted for a more cautious approach, defining propaganda "as the deliberate, systematic attempt to shape perceptions, manipulate cognitions, and direct behavior to achieve a response that furthers the desired intent of the propagandist" (p. 7). Manipulation is thus very central in both definitions, supporting an observation by Ross (2002) that propaganda is based on the manipulation of symbols. Persuasion is a key characteristic in Ross's (2002) definition, which concludes that propaganda aims to "persuade a socially significant group of people on behalf of a political institution, organization or cause" (p. 24), while Pratkanis and Turner (1996) attempt to illustrate how propaganda effectively works by proposing that it turns to "simple images and slogans that truncate thought by playing on prejudices and emotions" (p. 190).

Bernays (1928), another leading scholar in the field, concludes: "Modern propaganda is a consistent, enduring effort to create or shape events to influence the relations of the public to an enterprise, idea or group" (p. 25). Even though he believed that, in spite of its negative connotations, propaganda was not always ruthless, he pointed out that the propagandist's intentions have always been to convince he is right even if it means that he has to deceive. Thus, propaganda does not necessarily have to be outright lies. There has to be an element of truth in everything that is reported. However, not everything has to be accurate, as suggested by Cunningham (2001), who – paying tribute to the earlier works of Ellul (1957) and Coombs (1993) – concludes: "We now understand that propaganda is a far more diversified and complex phenomenon than just uttering lies and the slick manipulation of beliefs and language" (Cunningham, 2001, p. 138).

Tactics and techniques used in propaganda vary. Sproule (1994) pinpoints the fact that propaganda operates clandestinely and therefore the sender will not openly admit that his messages carry manipulative elements. Propaganda rarely relies on authority (Petty and Cacioppo, 1986). Jowett and O'Donnell (2006) also consider fabrication and distortion of information to be among the most commonly used techniques of propaganda. Smith (1989) concurs, arguing that, apart from using distortions, the propagandist may also use deliberate falsehoods and omissions. The propagandist can also calculatingly withhold vital information (Pratkanis and Aronson, 1991). Lee and Lee (1972) credit the then New York-based Institute of Propaganda Analysis (IPA) for its instrumental role in detecting techniques used in propaganda. These include bandwagon, which appeals to the audience by creating an impression that everyone else is supporting the idea or policy; therefore, presumably anyone who chooses not to take part is automatically isolated. Name-calling attaches negative symbols to a person or idea in order to discredit it, while glittering generalities are manipulative in the sense that they attach highly valued societal concepts such as democracy to a policy, potentially forcing people, including those who do not know what it means, to support it based on a generalized view that it is positive.

One of the most commonly accepted norms to the success of democracy is the system's inseparable relationship to a free press. It has been repeatedly claimed that freedom of expression is the lifeblood of democracy (Bhattacharyya and Hodler, 2012; Fog, 2004; Wahl-Jorgenson and Hanitzsch, 2009). We are made to believe that media and democracy are inseparable, which perhaps explains why the two words are often used interchangeably. The media provide citizens with information essential to the decisions they make, especially when choosing the country's political leaders (Fog, 2004). The media is a source of power that influences, controls and promotes new standards in society or reinforces existing ones (Lal *et al.*, 2007). During his decades-long rule, President Mugabe, deliberately or not, has had a dependable mouthpiece for disbursing information. At the same time, critics, especially his opponents in the Movement for Democratic Change (MDC) Party, have dismissed the broadsheet as a cheap propaganda platform. The availability of several weekly newspapers, including those fiercely critical of President Mugabe, has failed to hold back *The Herald*'s market dominance. With the exception of the *Daily News*, which doubled its circulation from an initial 60,000 to 120,000 within a few months of its 1999 launch, *The Herald*, with 90,000 readers, has been the overwhelming force on the Zimbabwean media scene (Moyo, 2005). Nor did the arrival of several other post-independence political parties, including the MDC, destabilize the newspaper's powerful support for ZANU-PF and authoritative market dominance.

The Herald's role in Zimbabwean politics

Propaganda, for right or wrong reasons, is often associated with negative connotations. It is frequently perceived that propaganda techniques can only be employed by autocratic and despotic regimes. However, it has been argued that practically all governments, including the ones that affirm democratic values, use some form of propaganda to bolster their support from other nations and citizenry (Pratkanis and Aronson, 1991). In its quest to discredit and disavow President Mugabe's rule in Zimbabwe, the British government has also used propaganda techniques, one may argue. Continuously labelling President Mugabe a dictator, with a distasteful "human rights" record, is an established propaganda technique associated with glittering generalities and name-calling, especially when one considers the fact that it was Mugabe who introduced basic "human rights" in Zimbabwe when he took over in 1980. There is no agreed definition of "dictator", even though it is quite clear that the term carries negative connotations, which the British government used to help convince its allies in the European Union, Australia, Canada, the USA and New Zealand to impose sanctions against the Zimbabwean leader and his closest associates in 2002. That Mugabe had rigged national elections, as was suggested at that time as the justification for launching a sanctions regime, is debatable, because the Southern African Development Community (SADC) concluded in its assessment that the elections had been free and fair.

However, while very few can doubt the newspaper's unshaken loyalty to ZANU-PF, it is important to explore the ways through which Zimbabweans consider the daily to be a credible source of reliable news. Without the media, "people in societies would be isolated, not only from the rest of the world, but from governments, lawmakers, and neighboring towns and cities" (anon) *The Herald's* approach to reporting, one can conclude based on an analysis of its content, could potentially damage its position as a harbinger of fair-minded, impartial coverage of news. Indeed, the newspaper often fails to provide an accurate picture of Zimbabwean news by continuously supporting ZANU-PF policies regardless of the impact they may have on the people. However, as Fog (2004) argues, how different is *The Herald's* reporting from that of other media outlets, which adopt an editorial line aligned with their advertisers or sponsors? If *The Herald* has failed to provide a fair and balanced coverage of developments in Zimbabwe, has any Western newspaper been able to achieve that goal? Several studies have documented the deep distrust and debilitating disapproval among Africans of the West's institutionalized media coverage of their continent (Fair, 1992; Maynard, 1974). Ebo (1992) even went as far as hypothesizing that Africa is depicted in the Western media as "a crocodile-infested dark continent where jungle life has perpetually eluded civilization" (p. 15). Willems (2005) unearthed evidence of systematic framing on the part of the British press coverage of the Zimbabwean crisis.

A closer analysis of the newspaper's ownership helps explain its perceived bias towards ZANU-PF. The newspaper is majority-owned by Zimbabwe Newspapers Group, Zimpapers, which holds 51.09% of the shares (Munyuki, 2005). The remaining shares are owned by the nation's leading financial firm, Old Mutual, and several other government-connected private companies (Open Society Institute, 2009). It is not surprising, then, if *The Herald* takes orders from its masters. Yet it is the newspaper's failure to give a platform to a variety of voices and its deliberate decision to label anyone who criticizes ZANU-PF a "traitor" that may potentially help undermine its authority.

The Herald's relationship with the government is symbiotic. While faithfully disseminating the ruling party's political, social and economic agenda, it has been guaranteed exclusivity to news, ensuring that it secures "scoops" away from independent journalists and maintains its journalistic edge against competitors. President Mugabe historically travels with a reporter from *The Herald* on most of his foreign trips. This favour is not extended to journalists from the private media. Accordingly, the newspaper has always had an unchallenged access to the president. Thus, the reports may be dismissed as manipulative propaganda though its coverage may actually be informative, despite the fact that the main objective, like most forms of propaganda, is to create a favourable public response. Though its content is one-sided, the paper has long been a vital and occasionally credible source of Zimbabwean news. For instance, while various foreign media incorrectly reported that President Mugabe had left the country in the aftermath of his first-round defeat to Tsvangirai in the 2008 elections, *The Herald* had it right: the president had not left the country. In 2012, Western media outlets, including *The Sydney Morning Herald*, incorrectly speculated that President Mugabe may have died during a trip to Singapore (Levy, 2012). As it turned out, *The Herald*, which had a reporter travelling with Mugabe, rebuffed these reports, stating what later turned out to be the case – that Mugabe was alive.

Historical overview

Among several challenges faced by any new nation, Hobsbawm (1992) introduces the question of loyalty to, and identification with, the state and ruling system. A carefully crafted ZANU-PF art of dominance has seen the nationalistic party controlling Zimbabwe's political landscape uninterrupted over the past three decades. *The Herald*'s pro-state stance can be traced back to the heyday of its predecessor, the *Rhodesian Herald*, which was then a powerful propaganda platform for the Rhodesian Front in 1963, according to Windrich (1981). The flagrant control of the press is an entrenched characteristic of the legacy of colonialism in post-colonial Africa, argues Mukasa (2003). Determined to discontinue foreign ownership of the press, President Mugabe's government created the state-controlled Zimbabwe Mass Media Trust (ZMMT), a watchdog that eventually took overall ownership of *The Herald* and its sister papers, according to Nyahunzvi (2001).

Chikuhwa (2004) points to Henry Muradzikwa, Musarurwa's replacement, who was removed from his job over a story that claimed that 60 Zimbabwean students had been deported from Cuba for unspecified health reasons (p. 61). The story implied that the students had AIDS, which was seen as potentially damaging to Zimbabwe's relations with the communist island Cuba. While enjoying its monopoly during the first years of independence, *The Herald* undoubtedly carried a compound of challenges that included serving a racially and ethnically divided nation fresh from the horrors of war. Satisfying the believers of press freedom could not have been tougher. However, it appears the lack of independent media players at independence proved detrimental to the overall government media policy over the years.

While Mukasa (2003) argues that ZANU-PF's media control resolve was tested in the 1990s with the rise of weekly newspapers such as the *Zimbabwe Independent*, *The Standard* and the *Daily News*, it goes without saying that *The Herald*'s political and social influence has remained steadfast. Before its unexpected return in 2010, the *Daily News*, which claims to be the first independent Zimbabwean daily newspaper, had been encumbered by plenty of problems, falling victim to a catalogue of new media laws introduced by the government under Jonathan Moyo's five-year reign as Information Minister. Moyo's period in office witnessed one of the most unalleviated propaganda campaigns in post-colonial Africa (Chitando, 2005). The Access to Information and Protection of Privacy Act (AIPPA) introduced a rigorous licensing system for media outlets, restricting foreign ownership of the media and prolonging *The Herald*'s monopoly, since the other privately run newspapers were weeklies. Despite their influence, they could not challenge *The Herald*'s circulation figures. Intimidation against journalists regardless of their political affiliation has been commonplace in Zimbabwe, but working for the independent press has been more daunting. Examples of state-sanctioned repression and intimidation of the private media can be seen in the 2007 incident involving veteran journalist Bill Saidi. A soldier, apparently unhappy with an article published in Saidi's *Standard* newspaper, left an envelope with a bullet and a handwritten note reading, "What is this? Watch your step" (Timberg, 2007).

Despite its fierce support for ZANU-PF, there have been several occasions when the newspaper attacked the party. *The Herald*, Chikuhwa (2004) reckons, bitterly criticized the government in the aftermath of the December 1997 national protest and the food riots a year later. Also, according to Mukasa (2003), police brutality, which rarely gets attention in *The Herald*, hogged the limelight after a teargas canister hit the newspaper's headquarters during the 1998 political disturbances, prompting editor Tommy Sithole to make a rare public attack on the police. However, this extraordinary criticism should not be taken as a sign of balanced journalism. Ideologically, the newspaper has always supported ZANU-PF. In the unlikely event of ZANU-PF becoming an opposition party, there is no evidence to suggest that the paper is prepared to switch its loyalty. Its roots are deeply enmeshed in the revolution against colonialism, and that identity is likely to remain its characteristic feature. President Mugabe's credibility as a freedom fighter, of which *The Herald* is keen to remind its readers, is there for everyone to see. At the World Summit on Sustainable Development in Johannesburg in September 2002, Mugabe was treated to elated applause for his "braveness" in telling Tony Blair to keep his Britain while he kept "his Zimbabwe" (*The Herald*, 2002). Mugabe's popularity, readers are told, is based on his desire to see colonial injustices corrected. This is, without a doubt, a non-negotiable stance shared by Mugabe, *The Herald*, and indeed their supporters.

Discussion: Representation and coverage

Endless repetition is a key technique used in propaganda. *The Herald* hopes that maintaining its sympathetic stance insofar as the government's land reform exercise is concerned helps convince the audiences of the need for agrarian reforms. Chief among its editorial lines is the continued endorsement of the land reforms. While critics argue that it is unjustified to hand over seized farms to black "war veterans" based on their war credentials and not their agricultural expertise, *The Herald* sees no problems with this. It views the land reform as enhancing economic expansion. Analyses of the reform exercise are always pro-Mugabe. It ignores the plight of white farmers losing the land or allegations from opposition parties that only those with close connections to ZANU-PF benefited from the land reform. While being repetitive is considered important in this case, consistency is also essential. These articles, for example, show the newspaper's unshaken and continuous loyalty and support for the land reform: "Zimbabwe: War against Land Reform Unwinnable" (Wafawarowa, 2009), "Zimbabwe: Land Reform a Success – Survey" (Farawo, 2011), "Zimbabwe: Farmer Reaps Fruits of Land Reform" (Guvamombe, 2009).

Through the *World Book Multimedia Encyclopedia*, the University of Leeds' Institute of Communication identifies three ways through which propaganda works:

(1) it calls for an action or opinion that it makes seem wise and reasonable;
(2) it suggests that the action or opinion is moral and right; and
(3) it provides a pleasant feeling, such as a sense of importance or of belonging. Stories in the newspaper normally remind readers of historical imbalances committed by Western imperialists.

This is a chorus position echoed by the newspaper, editorially taking a position that Mugabe is a liberator and in fact a victim of neo-colonialism. This argument appears convincing due to its ability to give Zimbabweans a sense of shared belonging. Name-calling the West as imperialists puts Zimbabweans in a victims' pot. Thus, the assumption could then be that they all have one enemy.

Race plays a major role in the newspaper's coverage of news. On a few occasions, President Mugabe has openly declared his dislike of white people (Associated Press, 2009). "The only white man you can trust is a dead white man", Mugabe said according to *The Telegraph* (2008). *The Herald* has followed his cue. That antipathy, however, is not extended to the country's white Olympic gold winner and former world record holder, Kirsty Coventry. While Mugabe has openly declared: "What we hate is not the color of their skins but the evil that emanates from them" (Radu, 2002), he calls Coventry a "golden girl", going as far as showing his gratitude to the sportswoman by offering her a diplomatic passport. Coventry's sporting heroics offers *The Herald* a chance to market Zimbabwe as a place where purported racial disharmony normally reported in the West press does not exist (*The Herald*, 2008c).

In contrast, Andy Flower, another white sportsman, was lacerated for teaming up with a black teammate and openly denouncing President Mugabe during a cricket match in Harare February 2003 (*The Herald*, 2013). Equally interesting is the way white ZANU-PF financial supporters John Bredenkamp and Billy Rautenbach are represented in the paper. The two businessmen are subject to unfriendly scrutiny and scornful attacks in the Western press. But a closer look at the way *The Herald* represents the two shows open bias. Stories such as "Zimbabwe: Bredenkamp Fights for Zim Citizenship" (*The Herald*, 2006b), "Zimbabwe: Court Grants Bredenkamp Reprieve" (*The Herald*, 2006c) and "Rautenbach Awarded Coal Mining Contract" (*The Herald*, 2007b), seek to portray the two as legitimate Zimbabwean businessmen with the country's interests at heart. Using these few examples of white Zimbabweans sympathetic to the regime, *The Herald* seeks to discount allegations of supposed anti-white antagonism by the party.

The Herald sees itself as a perfect answer to Africa's negative and contrived image often depicted in the Western and independent media. It accuses Western media outlets with correspondents based in the region and local independent newspapers of distorting and misrepresenting facts about Zimbabwe. Bashing the MDC for its alleged connections to the independent media, *The Herald* (2009) said on its opinion page: "The question is: Are the media in reality mouthpieces of political powers and governments for which they express sympathy?" While *The Herald* reproaches other newspapers for bias against ZANU-PF, it does not address charges that its own reporting is slanted towards meeting coverage expectations of the party. But can that be quantified? A sample of 25 political stories in February 2008 prior to national elections showed that ZANU-PF received overwhelmingly favourable coverage, with 17 stories profiling, reporting or openly professing a slanted opinion towards ZANU-PF candidates. There was minimal coverage of campaign rallies for the opposition parties during this period.

A close look at more headlines in *The Herald* also discloses an ideological bent towards ZANU-PF. "Annan Forced to Abort Visit" is a headline in a story suggesting the former UN secretary general would not visit Zimbabwe for a first-hand examination on the country's clean-up exercise to rid shanty houses. Annan, who had been accused by several pro-government commentators of siding with the USA and Britain on this issue, possibly handed the party a victory by calling off the trip, which Mugabe had previously called "politicized" (*The Herald*, 2005). Another headline, "Guarantee Safety of Scribes, MDC Leadership Told", appears to put blame on the opposition party after two journalists covering a rally were allegedly threatened (*The*

Herald, 2007a). A headline of this nature, intended for the ZANU-PF leadership, would not find space in *The Herald*, as it not only betrays the interests of the party but also potentially exposes it to readership scrutiny.

Conceptual framework

In his article on patriotic journalism, Ranger (2005) argues that hate journalism has flourished in the state-controlled media for many years. Die-hards in President Mugabe's government view the state monopoly of media as an effective tool to sell ZANU-PF's viewpoint while enforcing its patriotic agenda. After nearly 90 years of colonial and settler rule, it is understandable that nationalism and patriotism were paramount topics at independence in 1980. However, the two concepts remain on today's agenda thanks largely to *The Herald*, which is keen to promote values endorsed by ZANU-PF. In a weekly column that appears each Saturday in *The Herald*, a government official using the pseudo byline "Nathaniel Manheru" lashes out at President Mugabe's critics. The column, introduced by Moyo and fairly popular within Zimbabwe's political ranks, has never had kind words for anyone who disagrees with the ZANU-PF. Its approach is a deliberate division of the world into two racial pillars, namely "black" and "white". Anyone who disagrees with the Zimbabwean government is seen as siding with the white colonialists. Others are treated as patriots or nationalists.

Despite Western sanctions, Manheru portrays a picture of hope, arguing Zimbabwe does not need to make friends outside the developing world. His column leaves little room for any intermediate position other than "for us or against us". Here is what he had to say on Kofi Annan's departure from the UN's top office in 2006:

> In Shona, Annan means "who is he with"? One last word for the United Nations. Kofi Annan is an African, and may the good African Lord be with him in his last days in office. Zimbabwe's land question started in 2000, a good six years before the end of his term. He had lots of time to come, and indeed he came to the region countable times between then and now. Kofi Annan is an African who knows the West only too well. After all, the West is in his home, so to speak.
>
> (*The Herald*, 2006a)

According to Marxist media theory, the media is a "means of production" that is used by the ruling class to deny or defuse alternative ideas. *The Herald's* mission is evident on many of its pages. *The Herald* not only "tells the truth" but also ensures that alternative versions are discredited. The story headlined "Tsvangirai Begs for VP Post" not only attempts to tell the truth, but also denies other options being suggested in the rumour mill (*The Herald*, 2008a).

In Gramsci's (1971) hegemony concept, the intellectual community plays an important role in the success of hegemonic domination. Exerting government control over the people is impossible without intellectuals. In the case of Zimbabwe, academics regularly contribute to *The Herald*, trumpeting nationalist positions. Among them there are university professors and intellectuals, including Tafataona Mahoso, known to his opponents as "the Media Hangman", and Vimbai Chivaura, both educated in the USA. The majority of Mugabe's cabinet ministers and close associates hold degrees from Western universities, where they also send their children. Yet, ironically, their articles or comments in *The Herald* are decidedly anti-Western. The paper was scathing in response to Australia's decision to deport the children of ZANU-PF officials under the sanctions, denouncing it as a racist state (*The Herald*, 2007c). Former British prime minister Gordon Brown and his predecessor Tony Blair are portrayed as main culprits responsible for Zimbabwe's international isolation. *The Herald*, which makes no apologies for its support of ZANU-PF, has always maintained this view, arguing in its 22 September 2007 edition:

> Communicating with fellow Europeans through the British press [Brown] clearly indicated British diplomacy had come unstuck. Clearly British diplomacy has foundered in its backyard, with Brown adopting for the rest of Europe Blair's odious megaphone diplomacy against Zimbabwe.
>
> (*The Herald*, 2007c)

As noted by Frankfurt school stalwarts Adorno and Horkheimer, the media has the ability to transform enlightenment into barbarism (Neve, 2010). True to their view that economic prosperity breeds mass deception, *The Herald* has used Zimbabwe's once affluent economy to foster a formidable relationship with the country's ruling elite. As the only daily available in the country, it is certainly a widely read paper, powerfully delivering Mugabe's message of hope, political independence and economic prosperity, even when annual inflation was topping over 231 million per cent (Associated Press, 2008). *The Herald* still chose to defend the country's economic policies, dedicating pages of praise to central bank governor, Gideon Gono, the man criticized internationally for allegedly bringing down the country's economy. Additionally, the newspaper also ran articles in which Zimbabwe was allegedly commended by its southern African neighbours for pioneering "innovative economic policies" (*The Herald*, 2008b).

Perhaps indicative of the anger *The Herald* aroused among its critics, the paper's online version was brought down in May 2008 by an unknown hacker (Reuters, 2008). That happened after the vicious election campaign in which dozens of opposition supporters were beaten or killed, in a well-documented campaign of violence (*The Guardian*, 2008). Victims included Harare deputy mayor, Emmanuel Chiroto, whose wife Abigail was reportedly kidnapped and killed by suspected ruling party militias (*The Independent*, 2008). *The Herald* stood its ground, reporting pro-ZANU-PF stories while taking its usual line of attacking the opposition as a Western puppet, diverting attention from coverage over alleged killings.

Conclusions

This chapter has shown the mechanism employed by *The Herald* by showing its habitual siding with the ZANU-PF. The paper finds itself supporting the ZANU-PF in almost every scenario, perpetuated by the fact that the revolutionary party has deep-seated historical ties to the newspaper, hence pro-party editors have always been associated with the daily. The articles quoted reveal how *The Herald* uses propaganda to further extend its traditional relationship with Mugabe's party. Hence, the paper's ownership structure is pivotal in its quest to maintain the positive coverage. Understandably, the stories that are run by the newspaper tend to be openly biased towards ZANU-PF's political cadres. Without the paper's political steadfastness, it could be argued that Mugabe would not have managed to stay in power for over 30 years. Politically, *The Herald* has always been unapologetic of its pro-Mugabe stance. Faced with new Western-sponsored hostility, Mugabe has turned to the paper for much-needed support. The MDC has accused *The Herald* of turning a blind eye to its campaign materials, for example during the 2005 and 2008 elections. However, as long as Zimbabwe remains a country dominated by Mugabe's Marxist-centred party, *The Herald*'s disappearance from the Zimbabwean political arena cannot be foretold. It must be noted, however, that the same tactics employed by *The Herald* are also used by various newspapers seeking to discredit Mugabe.

In the eyes of *The Herald*, Mugabe has become a cult-like figure, incapable of error, but who has been victimized by a Western distortion of history. Blame is put on the West in *The Herald* while Mugabe's cadres are always presented as victims, regardless of the issue. Most importantly, Mugabe has redefined democracy thanks to *The Herald*. The newspaper convincingly applauds Zimbabwe's democratic credentials. These are questioned in the West, thereby creating confusion as to what the agreed definition and key characteristics of democracy are. But despite its evidently pro-Mugabe reporting, *The Herald* cannot be dismissed as irrelevant. It is used to sell the ZANU-PF brand. It is a weapon in the party's tactics to preserve power among all sectors of society, by reinforcing, for example, the party's relationship with war veterans and the educated elite. As the newspaper's majority shareholder, ZANU-PF may seek to justify its control of merely on the grounds of its overpowering investments in the company, which gives it absolute decision-making powers. *The Herald* therefore occupies a very important seat in Zimbabwean politics, one that should never be underestimated.

Author's note

The initial version of this chapter was presented at a conference in Riga in May 2013. A detailed version features in my unpublished PhD completed the same year at Leiden University.

References

Associated Press. (2008). Zimbabwe inflation hit 231 percent, 9 October. http://usatoday30.usatoday.com/news/world/2008-10-09-516966354_x.htm   Retrieved 31 July 2015

Associated Press. (2009). Robert Mugabe: White farmers must vacate their land. http://www.huffingtonpost.com/2009/02/28/robert-mugabe-white farme_n_170752.html, Retrieved 5 June 2010.

Bernays, E.L. (1928). *Propaganda*. New York: Liveright Publishing Corp.

Bhattacharyya, B. and Hodler, R. (2012). Media Freedom and Democracy: Complements or Substitutes in the Fight against Corruption? *CSAE Working Paper* WPS/2012–02.

Chikuhwa, J. (2004). *A Crisis of Governance: Zimbabwe*. New York: Algora Publishing.

Chitando, E. (2005). In the beginning was the land: The appropriation of religious themes in political discourses in Zimbabwe. *Africa* 75(2): 220–239.

Coombs, J.E. (1993). *The New Propaganda: The Dictatorship of Palaver in Contemporary Politics*. New York and London: Longman.

Cunningham, S.B. (2001). Responding to propaganda: An ethical enterprise. *Journal of Mass Media Ethics* 16(2–3): 138–147.

Ebo, B. (1992). "American Media and African Culture". In B.G. Hawk (Ed.), *Africa's Media Image*, B.G. Hawk (ed.), New York: Praeger, pp. 15–25.

Ellul, J. (1957). Information and propaganda. *Diogenes* 18: 61–77.

Fair, J.E. (1992). "Are We Really the World? Coverage of U.S. Food Aid in Africa, 1980–1989". In *Africa's Media Image*, B.G. Hawk (ed.), New York: Praeger, pp. 109–120.

Farawo, Tinashe. (2011). Zimbabwe: Land Reform a Success – Survey, *The Herald*, 5 February. http://allafrica.com/stories/201102140147.html, Retrieved 17 July 2010.

Fog, A. (2004). The Supposed and the Real Role of Media in a Modern Democracy. *Working Paper*, pp. 1–49.

Gramsci, A. (1971). *Selections from the Prison Notebooks of Antonio Gramsci*. In Q. Hoare and G. N. Smith (eds. and trs.), London: Lawrence & Wishart.

The Guardian (2008). Zimbabwe elections: Four activists found dead, says opposition, 19 June.

Guvamombe, Isdore. (2009). Zimbabwe: Farmer reaps fruits of land reform, *The Herald*, 15 September. http://www.politicsforum.org/forum/viewtopic.php?f=33&t=110293, Retrieved 17 July 2010.

The Herald. (2002). Keep your England, President tells Blair, 3 September 2002. http://allafrica.com/stories/200209030097.html Retrieved 31 July 2015

The Herald. (26 September 2005).

The Herald (2006a). Nathaniel Manheru no god from a machine. http://www.zwnews.com/issuefull.cfm?ArticleID=14451, Retrieved 16 July 2010.

The Herald. (2006b). Zimbabwe: Bredenkamp fights for Zim citizenship, 20 September.

The Herald. (2006c). Zimbabwe: Court grants Bredenkamp reprieve, 23 September.

The Herald. (2007a). Guarantee safety of scribes, MDC leadership told, 22 November.

The Herald. (2007b). Rautenbach awarded coal mining contract, 17 November.
The Herald. (2007c). Tsvangirai thanks paymasters for sanctions, 28 October.
The Herald. (2008a). Tsvangirai begs for VP post, 8 April.
The Herald. (2008b). Zimbabwe hailed over economic policies, 14 October.
The Herald. (2008c). Zimbabwe: Zim not for sale, 19 April.
The Herald. (14 December 2009).
Hobsbawm, E. (1992). *Nations and Nationalism since 1780: Programme, Myth, and Reality.* Cambridge: Cambridge University Press.
The Independent (2008). Harare mayor in hiding after Mugabe thugs kill wife, 19 June.
Jackall, R. (1995). *Propaganda: Main Trends of the Modern World.* New York: University Press.
Jowett, G.S. and O'Donnell, V. (1999). *Propaganda and Persuasion,* 3rd edition. Los Angeles: Sage Publications.
Jowett, G. and O'Donnell, V. (2006). *Readings in Propaganda and Persuasion New and Classic Essay.* London: Sage Publications.
Lal, R.M., Sharma, S.K., and Ahmed, N. (2007). Inherent barriers for mass media impact on Indian society. *International Journal of Business Research* 7(6): 47–63.
Lasswell, H.D. (1927). The theory of political propaganda. *American Political Science Review* 21(3): 627–631.
Lee, A.M. and Lee, E.B. (1972). *The Fine Art of Propaganda.* San Francisco, CA: International Society for General Semantics.
Levy, M. (2012). Mugabe close to death. *The Age,* 10 April. http://www.theage.com.au/world/mugabe-close-to-death-reports-20120410-1wls5.html?skin=text-only Retrieved 31 July 2015.
Maynard, R. (1974). *Africa on Film: Myth and Reality.* Rochelle Park, NJ: HaydenBook.
Moyo, D. (2005). The "independent press" and the fight for democracy in Zimbabwe: A critical analysis of the banned. *Daily News.* Westminster Paper in *Communication and Culture Special Issue,* pp. 109–128.
Mukasa, S. (2003). Press and politics in Zimbabwe. *Africa Studies Quarterly* 7(3): 171–183.
Munyuki, G. (2005). Media ownership in Zimbabwe. http://www.kubatana.net/docs/media/misaz_media_ownership_zim_051130.pdf, Retrieved 18 July 2011.
Neve, B. (2010). Theoretical approaches to mass media. http://people.bath.ac.uk/hssbpn/theories%20of%20media.htm, Retrieved 7 December 2010.
Ngoa, S. (2006). Agenda-setting: The neglected role of some agents of power. Unpublished PhD Thesis, University of the Witwatersrand, Johannesburg, RSA.
Nyahunzvi, T. (2001). The Zimbabwe Mass Media Trust: An experiment that failed. *Media Development* 48(2): 31–36.
Open Society Institute. (2009). Media programme publication. *Public Broadcasting in Africa Series.* http://www.africanminds.co.za/wpcontent/uploads/2012/08/13458152711090693332.pdf Retrieved 31 July 2015
Petty, R.E. and Cacioppo, J.T. (1986). *Communication and Persuasion: Central and Peripheral Routes to Attitude Change.* New York: Springer-Verlag.
Pratkanis, A. and Aronson, E. (1991). *The Age of Propaganda: Everyday Use and Abuse of Persuasion.* New York: W. H. Freeman and Co.
Pratkanis, A.R. and Turner, M.E. (1996). Persuasion and democracy: Strategies for increasing deliberative participation and enacting social change. *Journal of Social Issues* 52: 187–205.
Propaganda.   http://ics-www.leeds.ac.uk/papers/pmt/exhibits/727/propaganda.pdf, Retrieved 16 July 2010.

Radu, M. (2002). "State of Disaster". *National Review*. 27 May 2002.

Ranger, T. (2005). The rise of patriotic journalism in Zimbabwe and its possible implications. *Westminster Papers in Communication and Culture*. Special Issue, November 2005: 8–17.

Reuters, S. (2008). Zimbabwe official newspaper hacked, 12 May. http://in.reuters.com/article/2008/05/12/us-zimbabwe-election-hackers-idINL1271558720080512 Retrieved 31 July 2015.

"Role of Media in democracy". http://www.mona.uwi.edu/jct/documents/scott.pdf, Retrieved 16 July 2012.

Ross, S.T. (2002). Understanding propaganda: The epistemic merit model and its application to art. *Journal of Aesthetic Education* 36(1): 16–30.

Smith, T.J. (1989). *Propaganda: A Pluralistic Perspective*. Westport, CT: Praeger.

Sharuko, R. (2013). Black armband protest...Coltart's key advisory role in 2003 unmasked by Flower, *The Herald*. http://www.herald.co.zw/black-armband-protest-coltarts-key-advisory-role-in-2003-world-cup-demo-unmasked-by-flower/ Retrieved 31 August 2015.

Sproule, J.M. (1994). *Channels of Propaganda*. Bloomington, IN: EDINFO & ERIC.

The Telegraph (2008). Robert Mugabe's relations with Britain: In his own words, 5 June. http://www.telegraph.co.uk/news/2080893/Robert-Mugabes-relations-with-Britain-In-his-own-words.html Retrieved 17 July 2009.

Timberg, C. (2007). Zimbabwe paper hits "big nerve", *Washington Post*. http://www.washingtonpost.com/wp-dyn/content/article/2007/02/01/AR2007020101712.html, Retrieved 2 February 2007.

Wafawarowa, Reason. (2009). Zimbabwe: War against land reform unwinnable, *The Herald*, 17 April. http://allafrica.com/stories/200904170469.html, Retrieved 17 July 2010.

Wahl-Jorgensen, K. and Hanitzsch, T. (eds.) (2009). *Handbook of Journalism Studies*. New York and London: Routledge.

Willems, W. (2005). Remnants of empire? British media reporting on Zimbabwe. *Westminster Papers in Communication and Culture*. London: University of Westminster. Special Issue, pp. 91–108.

Windrich, E. (1981). *The Mass Media in the Struggle for Zimbabwe: Censorship and Propaganda under Rhodesian Front Rule*. Mambo Occasional Papers, Socio-Economic Series 15. Gweru: Mambo Press.

Zimbabwe Journalists. (2007). Charamba's Comments on Saidi Rile Journalists, 13 February. http://www.zimbabwejournalists.com/print.php?art_id=1749, Retrieved 14 September 2010.

11

Beyond Blind Optimism: The Case of Citizen Journalism in the Struggle for Democracy in Zimbabwe

Cleophas T. Muneri

Introduction

Internet usage has spread around the world and, in recent years, this expansion has been further accelerated by introduction of 3G mobile phone devices that make it possible for people to access the Internet in places that previously would have been difficult. Silverman aptly captures this when he says "the mobile is undoubtedly one of the most important cultural artefacts of our time, an indispensable social link and a vital business device" (Silverman, 2011, pp. 56–57). It is important to preface this chapter by highlighting the centrality of the Internet and mobile devices because the full realization of citizen journalism is predicated on Internet access and the media devices that enable it. These key aspects should be considered in relation to the political, economic and social environment under which different people across the globe seek to participate in the democratic process as citizens. This is important because, as Dahlgren points out, "there are mechanisms that can exclude individuals from networks – for example, class, gender, ethnicity, and sexual orientation can all impact on which networks we belong to" (Dahlgren, 2009, p. 159).

The phrase citizen journalism is very broad and has been defined differently by various scholars. Allan defines it as "a type of first-person reportage in which ordinary individuals temporarily adopt the role of a journalist in order to participate in newsmaking, often spontaneously during time of crisis, accident, tragedy or disaster when they happen to be on the scene" (Allan, 2013, p. 9). While the temptation is to view citizen journalism in relation to the explosion of new information technologies, what is at the core of citizen journalism is the extent to which media audiences, as citizens that have a stake in what ends up in the public domain, participate in the production of news and information.

This can be considered as an elevated view of audience not just as consumers but as citizens. And to describe audience members as citizens means that they are individuals or groups with rights and are stakeholders in the production and dissemination of news. The term citizens, as Dahlgren, borrowing from the work of T.H. Marshal (1950), highlights, includes "three by now familiar dimensions of citizenship – the civil, which aims to guarantee the basic legal integrity of society's members; the political, which serves to ensure the rights associated with democratic participation; and the social, which addresses the general life circumstances of individuals" (Dahlgren, 2009, p. 60).

At another level, this can also be considered as a broadening of the journalism field through involvement of citizens as participants, thereby enhancing the democratic process. The phrase citizen journalism can also be considered as an attempt to be inclusive and to acknowledge that professionally trained journalists do not always hold all the answers in making information available to the public. The practical needs and demands of fully fledged news organizations make it impossible for professional journalists to cover every nook and cranny of the news world. Involving citizens in the production of news can therefore enhance the role of journalism in society. The question then is whether the phenomenon of citizen journalism is new or it is something that has always been there? Allan argues that it is:

> [S]een by some as an outgrowth of earlier forms of public or civic journalism, the term citizen journalism gained currency in the immediate aftermath of the South Asian tsunami of December 2004 when news organizations found themselves in the awkward position of being largely dependent on "amateur" reportage to tell the story of what had transpired on the ground.
>
> (Allan, 2013, p. 9)

Theoretical background and positioning the debate

In addressing the role of the Internet and new media in the struggle for democracy in Zimbabwe it is important to highlight the fact that a number of media and journalism scholars have addressed this issue from various theoretical perspectives. These contributions range from the work of Last Moyo (2009a; 2009b; 2011), Dumisani Moyo (2009), Chuma (2014), Mano and Willems (2008) and Mabweazara (2011; 2014), to Chari (2014). In as much as there are a lot of interlocking issues in this debate, the mentioned scholars, focusing on Zimbabwe, have mapped out various strands of this debate. For example, Moyo (2009a) addresses the various theoretical moorings of new communication technologies in a manner that I think is very relevant to this chapter. First, and most importantly, is the issue of access to the requisite technologies that is needed for citizens to make meaningful contribution to citizen journalism. As Moyo (2009a) argues, access is undermined by issues of "scarcity, inequality, and conflict" (p. 122) aspects that have characterized the Zimbabwean economic and political landscape for close to two decades now. These issues cannot be ignored or downplayed in any discussion of citizen journalism as citizen journalism does not occur in a vacuum. Further to this important observation by Moyo (2009a) is the argument that "the disparities in the ownership and access to these media can potentially affect the access to information from the Internet by the disadvantaged communities and also create or reinforce the socio-economic inequalities based on the digital marginalization of the poorer classes and regions of the world" (p. 122).

Pointing out these issues is not an indictment of citizen journalism or a failure to acknowledge its potential or the fact that some aspects of it are already visible in Zimbabwe, but is meant to acknowledge the existing conditions, thereby tampering what I refer in the title of this chapter as "blind optimism". It is important to highlight this so that this optimism does not detract scholars from a balanced appraisal of the unfolding changes in journalism and their contribution to the democratization process in Zimbabwe. The context for citizen journalism is characterized by economic challenges, as Moyo (2009a) argues:

> the focus on such basic social needs invariably means that the telecommunications networks which are so indispensable for Internet connectivity are still relatively poor in most of the countries in the south compared to those in the north, mainly because access to information is one among an endless list of social needs. (p. 124)

This can create a divide in society, and when such a divide exists it can mean that people "cannot use the Internet's plethora of resources and facilities such as information and news in websites, blogs, podcasts and other interactive forums such as discussion forums, email and voiceovers for civic engagement" (Moyo, 2009a, p. 128).

The other key focus of this chapter is on how citizen journalism, which is premised on access to the Internet, can be harnessed for democratic ends. In a country such as Zimbabwe, where access to information is limited because of various reasons, the potential for its contribution remains high, as aptly captured by Moyo's (2009b) argument that:

> Although participation on the Internet is curtailed by factors like access, costs, censorship, lack of technological literacy and technophobia, it can be argued that generally the Internet is a relatively open and accessible public sphere where anyone who has access to a wired computer can freely express their views as long as they remain within the law and do not infringe on other people's rights. (p. 141)

The Internet has the potential to broaden citizens' participation as it provides communicative space that can largely be connected to Habermas' concept of the public sphere and theorization on civil society.

It is in this context of understanding the potential of the Internet as a public sphere that it can be connected with how mobile phone technology has become the means through which most people access the Internet. Research on mobile technology has focused on how this has opened up space for communication in a context where telephones have very limited reach in terms of access by the majority of people. Both Moyo (2009b) and Mabweazara (2011) have addressed this issue. As Moyo (2009b) points out:

> the mobile phone has also opened up a communication channel for citizens that were previously marginalized by other forms of telecommunications (especially in Africa where mobile phone growth is phenomenal), while also extending the interactive capacity of those that have always been in the mainstream of mass media and other forms of communications. (p. 147)

Mabweazara specifically focuses on how journalists use mobile phones in their everyday journalistic work. On the other hand, Chuma (2014) focuses on: "the extent to which the mobile phone has become deeply embedded in the everyday social practices among the youth. The multiple platforms and possibilities the device offers allow for the simultaneous affirmations of both individual and group identities" (p. 407).

The use of mobile phones, especially those with Internet capabilities for youths to enact their identities, can also be connected with Mano and Willem's (2008) research on how Zimbabweans, especially those in the diaspora, use news websites such as NewZimbabwe.com to "articulate, imagine and contest" (p. 102) their identities. Mano and Willem (2008) show how the Internet and mobile phone technology have opened up communicative space for various groups, and the hope is that this can be extended to the struggle for democratization through citizen journalism. In as much as the use of blogging by the majority of the population remains limited, it can be another front for citizen journalism. D. Moyo (2009) characterizes the bloggers as "institutional" because they are largely made up of members of non-governmental or civil society organizations. The reason why blogging is connected to these "institutional bloggers" is because of their access to resources which the majority of the population cannot access.

While there is evidence that some journalists and civil society groups are actively involved with some form of citizen journalism of one form or another, from blogging to social media, as Moyo (2011) and Mabweazara (2010b) have pointed out, there still remains room for this to be broadened, given the issues of access, and wider economic, political and economic context that underpin participation. This corroborates Mabweazara's (2014) observation that: "the increase in the use of social media as a source of news and story ideas by journalists in the newsroom studied appears to have impacted news access and sourcing patterns" (p. 79).

What this research and literature on the Internet and citizen journalism shows is, that for those with access to the Internet and attendant technologies, there is evidence of participation, but it is still limited to journalists and political activists in civil society, with the broader public yet to fully embrace and engage with citizen journalism, especially with regard to the struggle for democratization. Some of the participation by the general citizenry in Zimbabwe has largely been in the social and entertainment realm, with limited use of technologies for sustained political engagement. This is mainly because, as Kalathil and Boas (2003) note, "many citizens of authoritarian regimes use the Internet in much the same way as do citizens of democracies: they communicate with friends and family, consult easily accessible news sources, browse entertainment and sports sites, and look for information specifically relevant to their lives" (p. 143).

Assessing the situation in Zimbabwe

It is important to highlight the fact that citizens have always participated in the journalism arena, albeit in a limited form and on terms largely dictated by professional journalists or the dictates of media production that prevailed before the advent of the Internet and its attendant technologies. In commenting on American journalism, Junger argues that:

> The active participation of the public in collecting, reporting, analyzing, and disseminating news, and crowdsourcing, the outsourcing of documents, surveillance, news tips, or story assignments to volunteer groups, have been elements of American political and social culture much longer than Twitter, YouTube, or mobile phone cameras.
>
> (Junger, 2011, pp. 74–75)

Citizen journalism within the contemporary has gained increased academic scrutiny largely because of the convergence of various journalistic practices and new communication technologies that make it possible for members of the public, as active citizens, to be involved in news production and dissemination. These same technologies have resulted in massive changes to journalism practices, and thus have transformed traditional forms of media such as newspapers and radio. It is these transformations that are largely responsible for what is understood to be citizen journalism in the contemporary world. This type of journalism has the potential "to disrupt and change institutionalized journalism in particular ways in certain circumstances (although currently these instances are rare)" (Fenton, 2010, p. 14). It is therefore important to provide an outline of the attributes of citizen journalism and analyse how these measure up against recent experiences in Zimbabwe.

The major premise of citizen journalism is that news production is a partnership between news production organizations and citizens. As Fenton points out:

> [I]n the online environment, it is argued readers can have a greater impact on the news through an increase in the intensity of their exchanges with journalists and for example the presentation of their own views in online papers. News online is thus open to a higher degree of contestation than is typical of traditional news media.
>
> (Fenton, 2010, p. 10)

The question is "what are the different ways in which the public can participate in news production"?

The public participate by providing information to journalists as they cover various stories. This can entail members of the public submitting videos, photographs or eyewitness accounts as events unfolds. At times, it takes a while for reporters to arrive at the scene of a major breaking news story, and in most cases they are dependent on the accounts of eyewitnesses. As Allan points out, members of the public "may well strive to engage in a form of eyewitness reportage, perhaps using their mobile telephone to capture an image, generate a video, or craft a tweet in order to record and share their personal experience of what is happening in front of them" (Allan, 2013, p. 1). With citizen journalism, it is now possible for ordinary members of the public to take pictures and videos and then post them on websites of major news organizations, which now either provide platforms or links on which to do so.

In addition to photos and videos, the audiences can also participate through sending text messages and emails. As Allan points out: "other aspects of citizen journalism include – first person eye-witness accounts, audio recordings, video footage, mobile or cellphone and digital camera photographs typically shared online via email or through bulletin boards, blogs, wikis, personal webpages, and social networking sites" (Allan, 2013, p. 9). All allows journalists to provide a richer and broader coverage of news. At its most democratic, citizen journalism should allow members of the public to be an integral part of the news production process as active participants.

Citizen journalism can also result in the use of digital platforms that allow audience members to engage in debate with other audience members, something that has become the norm for most websites of major news organizations. This allows audiences members to participate in debates about major issues, and, at times, it has the potential of helping shape the debate and subsequent coverage of the initial reporting. As Dahlgren points out: "participatory journalism can take many forms, from the public's feedback on published stories to the initiation of news stories, and supplying materials such as visuals" (Dahlgren, 2009, p. 177). Whereas, prior to the development of these discussion boards, audience members had to take time to write a letter to the editor – whose chances of being published were limited given the constraints of space – in the digital age, the chances are maximized.

In addition to use of discussion boards, blogging is another platform that provides a good opportunity for the public to take part in citizen journalism. There are various ways in which citizens can perform this. Blogging can be done as a stand-alone activity where individuals can set up their own blogs online using already existing templates. Before the blossoming of the digital age, only a few could get space in traditional media to offer commentaries on issues of public importance. This, however, has been dramatically challenged by the countless online platforms that allow individuals to set up their own blogs without having to worry about editorial control and gatekeeping that are usually associated with traditional forms of media. Blogging can be considered as embodying some of the best tenets of citizen journalism but it also blurs the lines of who is a journalist. This is clearly captured in Fenton's evaluation that: "citizen journalism is said to bleed into mainstream journalism and vice versa. The blogosphere has been credited with taking on the major news corporations through instant feedback that is often lively, openly subjective and highly critical" (Fenton, 2010, p. 10).

Having outlined the key tenets of citizen journalism in broad strokes, it is imperative to provide some theoretical footing for the term citizen. To denote an individual as a citizen is to acknowledge that the person has certain immutable rights that cannot be taken away by either the actions of individuals or institutions with more political, economic, social, military, religious or cultural power. As a corollary to this, a discussion of citizenship presupposes the existence of a democratic political dispensation and fits in well with citizen journalism, which "inspires a language of democratization" (Allan, 2013, p. 94), for it is not possible for people to be regarded as citizens if they live in a political, economic and social environment where they cannot exercise freedoms and rights commensurate with a democratic political dispensation.

For citizen journalism to exist, this chapter will argue that there should be an enabling political and social environment that allows not only the media freedom to experiment with new technological changes, but it also requires the public to have freedom to know that they can contribute information of public interest without fear of negative repercussions. Unfortunately, the political landscape in Zimbabwe has been a minefield for journalists because of a range of issues. The breadth of these issues stretches from actual violence and threats of violence against journalists to a legal environment that makes it difficult for journalists to freely practise their trade without fear of being targeted as a result of their work. This is mainly because participation in the struggle for democratization for journalists and civil society organizations has been "affected by the strained political environment in Zimbabwe, where violence against opponents was also a commonly employed tool" (Muneri and Collier, 2014, p. 109).

In an environment where even journalists who have the protection of their news organizations are fearful to exercise their profession freely, it becomes even more challenging for members of the public to fully participate, even with the available tools of citizen journalism – whether it is in sending photographs or videos of news events taking place in their communities, especially when this involves political news stories. This is because of the limited protections that individuals or organizations which raise news stories that are critical of the ruling party have. Participating or engaging in citizen journalism can only take place when such journalism is not overly critical of the ruling party. Consequently, a lot of journalists and members of the public engage in a lot of self-censorship that makes it difficult for people to freely engage with public issues using the tools of citizen journalism. There are many incidents and examples of violence directed against media and journalists, with the most notable being the bombing of the *Daily News* printing press in 2001.

The use of both overt and covert threats against those that are considered to be threatening the status quo is just one of the myriad of challenges that journalists and members of the public face in Zimbabwe, making it difficult for them to engage in citizen journalism. In addition to the challenges mentioned, there are also legal problems, especially those connected to the regulation of journalism, through laws to which both the media as business institutions and journalists have to adhere.

While the trend in those countries with a more democratic media environment is for journalists to self-regulate, in Zimbabwe journalism is regulated by the government through the Zimbabwe Media Commission. This means that it is possible for journalists to lose their licence to practise. This adds to the difficulties that media have to contend with in order to contribute to robust debates consistent with citizen journalism. These legal issues are compounded by the government's persistence in using criminal defamation against both journalists and members of the public, especially when it comes to criticism of public officials such as the president. This remains a challenge despite rulings by the country's Supreme Court that criminal defamation is not consistent with country's constitution.

The restrictive political environment in Zimbabwe has spilled over to affect the economic fortunes of the country. These economic issues can be traced back to a number of events in the late 1990s that came to a head in 2000, when the government embarked on the controversial land redistribution programme that resulted in the government's repossession of white commercial farms. This spiralled into further economic problems as the country faced international isolation. This isolation was accompanied by economic sanctions imposed by mainly Western countries such as the

United States and the members of the European Union. With further political violence accompanying the 2000, 2002, 2005 and 2008 elections, this generated massive negative publicity for the country.

All these political developments had negative effects on the economic fortunes of the country, as evidenced in the unprecedented levels of migration that saw many highly skilled workers moving to other countries such as South Africa, Botswana, the United Kingdom, the United States and Australia. In addition to this massive haemorrhaging of skilled employees, a lot of companies closed, and those that operated performed at half or below half capacity. In short, since late 1990s, Zimbabwe has been experiencing a steady economic decline as some industries have completely collapsed, resulting in high levels of unemployment.

Under these economic conditions, it becomes easier for people to be concerned by economic survival, as both their resources and attention are turned to bread-and-butter issues. To be active participants in citizen journalism, members of the public should have the economic means to do so. The economic conditions described make it difficult if not impossible for a significant portion of the population to participate, thereby eliciting the need to be cautious in making broad generalizations or painting an overly optimistic picture about the impact and spread of citizen journalism in Zimbabwe. While it is very tempting to argue that in any environment there will always exist a significant part of the population that lacks access to means of communication on the one hand, and another that enthusiastically embraces and adopts technological changes and takes advantage of opportunities offered by citizen journalism, there is, however, a danger that scholarship will only focus on those that are actually participating in the communicative space that citizen journalism offers, thereby neglecting the rest of the populace.

This chapter seeks to make a broader case that an understanding and theorization of citizen journalism should be connected to wider issues of broadening democratic communicative space and participation. If citizen journalism is an extension of participation to citizens or members of the public that are already participating in the democratic process, then there is a strong possibility that the majority will be left out, thereby worsening the already unbalanced access to information, especially in the global South. The reason I am tying citizen journalism to participation in the democratic process is because of the ongoing struggles for democracy in Zimbabwe and in many other parts of the world, especially in Africa. The deficiencies in information access and quality of information is so glaring that it cannot be ignored, as the majority of the population still cannot participate because they do not have full rights consistent with citizenship because of the prevailing political and economic environment. The broader argument is that citizen journalism offers opportunities to achieve this, but there are so many challenges that make it impossible to attain this in the short and medium term because of reasons highlighted earlier in this chapter. The attention for scholars and policymakers should be on the best ways to leverage on the opportunities of citizen journalism.

There is need to move away from a one-size-fits-all approach when it comes to scholarship on citizen journalism, simply because of the way it has worked in developed countries, where economies are stronger compared to those in countries such as Zimbabwe. Having outlined the challenges that citizen journalism faces in making strong inroads in countries facing political and economic challenges, it is also important to highlight the fact that citizen journalism's success is also dependent on a technological infrastructure. This ranges from access to the Internet, to technologies that allow members of the public to engage meaningfully, such as computers, smartphones and cameras; in fact, my view is that knowledge of how to participate via the Internet should actually be considered as a civic duty. I think it is no accident that, in describing citizen journalism, the word "citizen" is part of the phrase, because to be a citizen entails having freedom and rights. For citizen journalism to be effective, it requires a higher level of civic engagement, where members of the public participate and are concerned with the public or common good. This is because "the process of 'becoming citizens', of socially and culturally developing civic identities, adds important analytic dimensions to the sociology of democracy" (Dahlgren, 2009, p. 69).

Just as voting, for example, is regarded as a civic duty, participating in citizen journalism can also be connected to wider public interests. Citizen journalism is therefore likely to be successful in social environments where higher levels of civic engagement and civic participation have deeper roots. In the case of Zimbabwe, levels of civic engagement are not particularly high if one considers how the public engages in public debate. It is therefore not enough to think that because people have access to the Internet and have all the technologies necessary to be involved in citizen journalism that they will end up participating. In Zimbabwe, this lack of participation has been worsened by the economic environment, which has resulted in people being more concerned with issues of survival. In short, the case for citizen journalism cannot be considered in isolation of the prevailing social and cultural context, as use of technology is also cultural. This is because "political activity is usually shaped by the circumstances, resources, and practices that characterize people's lives; to engage in democracy normally does not mean to step out of one's existing frames of realities, or one's dominant habitus" (Dahlgren, 2009, p. 149).

In as much as use of technology is cultural, it is also important to assess levels of access to various technologies that allow people to deploy it for citizen journalism purposes. In Zimbabwe, the level of mobile phone use has been very high, especially when compared to the history of limited connectivity to telephones. As Cameron has pointed out, "wireless telephony is increasingly being seen as a means of bridging the 'digital divide' in developing nations by skipping a stage in the development of the telecommunications infrastructure" (Cameron, 2011, p. 69). This has greatly improved personal communication, especially with respect to connecting people in rural and urban areas. Unfortunately, the increase in mobile phone access and communication in the country has not translated into its deployment in the service of citizen journalism. Some of this is connected to the economic downturn that the country is going through and has been experiencing since the year 2000. This has resulted in people focusing more on necessary communication only, mainly because of the high cost of airtime or mobile phone bills.

These economic conditions make it difficult to be involved with citizen journalism. In a thriving economy, these will not be issues that people worry about, but in Zimbabwe every little resource that people might have is considered essential, as the lack of airtime might make it impossible to convey an important message to a relative working outside the country. Access to mobile phones has not, therefore, directly translated into people having more opportunity to participate in citizen journalism.

The lack of participation also has a lot to do with access to the Internet, which largely remains an urban phenomenon, although access has started to trickle down to rural areas, especially with the arrival of 3G mobile technology that allows people to access the Internet through their mobile devices. Even with these changes, Internet access remains limited because of factors related to both costs and accessibility, as there remain areas in the country where access is impossible because the mobile phone companies and others tasked with making the Internet accessible have not installed the necessary technology. It therefore becomes difficult to have a vibrant form of citizen journalism if people do not have the requisite communication infrastructure to do so, as a lot of aspects related to citizen journalism are premised on Internet access.

For example, if participation entails either sending pictures or text messages, it still means members of the public have to still pay for this. At times, if accessing mobile phone network or the Internet is difficult or impossible, it becomes hard for people to be active participants of citizen journalism. At another level, participation in citizen journalism, especially when it means blogging or taking part in online newspaper discussion boards, requires access to a smartphone or computer that has access to the Internet. In most parts of the country, especially in rural areas where the majority of the population still reside, this is difficult to achieve, as the cost and availability of the Internet are still problematic, as has been highlighted. The argument being raised here is not that there is no participation but that this participation is very limited as it is confined to a small segment of the population, which is largely urban. Therefore citizen journalism has yet to make inroads to the majority of people in the country.

The potential for citizen journalism to take root is there, and I think this is what the citizen journalism debate should focus on, given the yawning gap between the euphoria about citizen journalism and the reality on the ground. To make the debate on citizen journalism only about a small but very visible segment of the population is to miss the focus, as this does not widen an understanding of citizen journalism and what needs to be done to broaden it in countries such as Zimbabwe. The debate on citizen journalism should not just be about the mechanics with regard to how it is done, nor should it, as in most cases, focus on practices emerging in developed countries. In noting these considerations, it should be acknowledged that the success of citizen journalism is also dependent on the media infrastructure in a particular country.

This is not only true with regard to newspapers but is similar in radio and television broadcasting. For television, this is exacerbated by an ownership structure that still makes television broadcasting a government monopoly. While a limited number of private radio broadcasters have been licensed, with more expected the granting of more licences at the beginning of 2015, there is still limited incorporation of citizen journalism. Most, if not all, the programming content is generated by paid employees of the radio stations and this applies to both privately and government-owned radio stations. As for the sole television broadcaster in the country, there is no attempt to even pretend to provide citizen journalism. This can be attributed to both the lack of technical capacity to do so and a heavy editorial control that has made the television broadcaster a ruling party mouthpiece. Under these conditions, even if members of the public want to participate in citizen journalism, it becomes difficult because of the heavy-handed nature in which journalism is practised in Zimbabwe. This is mainly because of the fear that characterizes the political environment, which has resulted in a great deal of self-censorship. If there is fear and self-censorship among journalists, it becomes even more difficult to expect members of the public to freely participate and contribute in any form of citizen journalism.

Despite all these challenges and limitations, there are isolated incidences and cases in Zimbabwe where some media organizations have tried to incorporate citizen journalism. The examples include online publications such as NewZimbabwe.com, Zimbabwe Situation website, and others that are not necessarily registered as news organizations, such as Radio Dialogue, which has been clamouring for a community-based radio licence since the year 2000.

While Zimbabwe's media laws are restrictive, especially when it comes to traditional forms of media such as radio, television and newspapers, it would appear they were enacted without much anticipation of the new platforms that have been made possible because of the Internet. For that reason, some of these websites have been very responsive to utilizing opportunities afforded by citizen journalism. This is mainly exemplified by NewZimbabwe.com and the Zimbabwe Situation website where citizens contribute both news stories about events in the country and political and social commentaries. In as much the Zimbabwe Situation website is no longer as active as it used to be, it relied a lot on contributions from various members of the public. It was most active at the height of the country's political problems, especially between 2000 and 2008, when political violence and repossession of commercial farms, largely from former white commercial farmers, were at their peak. Members of the public provided eyewitness accounts of violence, at times posting pictures of victims of violence. Some of the reports that the Zimbabwe Situation website covered were not covered by mainstream media or, when they were reported, they did not provide as much detail as one would find on these websites. These reports were carried out by either individuals who were members of civil society organizations, or communities that were on the receiving end of the political violence taking place in the country.

In conclusion, the foregoing analysis of the situation in Zimbabwe shows that the tale of citizen journalism has only just started, and that the various contours and trajectories it will take will continue to be compromised by the challenging political and economic environment. While most journalists in Zimbabwe (Mabweazara, 2014) now incorporate social media in their journalism practice, at an institutional level there are still gaps in as far as media organizations are able to provide platforms that allow citizen journalism to thrive. Citizen journalism has great potential to unlock citizens' participation in the democratic process by broadening communicative space and, for that reason, scholarship should focus on how to enhance participation by members of the public. It is too early to open the champagne or paint rosy pictures of citizen journalism in Zimbabwe, but there is also no reason to despair, given the fact that some inroads, albeit limited, have been made.

References

Allan, Stuart. (2013). *Citizen Witnessing: Key Concepts in Journalism*. Cambridge: Polity Press.

Cameron, David. (2011). "Mobile Journalism: A Snapshot of Current Research and Practice". In *The End of Journalism: News in the Twenty-First Century*, Stewart Gavin and Alec Charles (eds.), Oxford: Peter Lang, pp. 63–72.

Chari, Tendai. (2014). "Online News Media Consumption Cultures among Zimbabwean Citizens: 'Home and Away'". In *Online Journalism in Africa: Trends, Practices and Emerging Cultures*, Hayes M. Mabweazara, Okoth F. Mudhai and Jason Whittaker (eds.), New York and London: Routledge, pp. 191–206.

Chuma, Wallace. (2014). "The social meanings of mobile phones among South Africa's 'digital natives': A case study". *Media Culture & Society* 36: 398–408. Retrieved 1 May 2015. DOI: 10.1177/0163443713517482.

Dahlgren, Peter. (2009). *Media and Political Engagement: Citizens, Communication, and Democracy*. New York: Cambridge University Press.

Fenton, Natalie. (2010). *New Media, Old News: Journalism and Democracy in the Digital Age*. Los Angeles, CA: Sage.

Junger, Richard. (2011). "An Alternative to 'Fortress Journalism'? Historical and Legal Precedents for Citizen Journalism and Crowdsourcing in the United States". In *The End of Journalism: News in the Twenty-First Century*, Stewart Gavin and Alec Charles (eds.), Oxford: Peter Lang, pp. 73–86.

Kalathil, Shanthi, and Boas, Taylor C. (2003). *Open Networks – Closed Regimes: The Impact of the Internet on Authoritarian Rule*. Washington, DC: Carnegie Endowment for International Peace.

Mabweazara, Hayes M. (2010b). "'New' Technologies and Journalism Practice in Africa: Towards a Critical Sociological Approach". In *The Citizen in Communication: Revisiting Traditional, New and Community Media in South Africa*, Hyde-Clarke (ed.), Cape Town: Juta and Co, pp. 11–30.

Mabweazara, Hayes M. (2011). Between the newsroom and the pub: The mobile phone in the dynamics of everyday mainstream journalism practice in Zimbabwe. *Journalism* 12: 692–707. Retrieved 1 May 2015. DOI: 10.1177/1464884911405468.

Mabweazara, Hayes M. (2014). "Zimbabwe's Mainstream Press in the 'Social Media Age': Emerging Practices, Cultures and Normative Dilemmas". In *Online Journalism in Africa: Trends, Practices and Emerging Cultures*, Hayes M. Mabweazara, Okoth F. Mudhai and Jason Whittaker (eds.), New York and London: Routledge, pp. 65–85.

Mano, Winston, and Willems, Wendy. (2008). Emerging communities, emerging media: The case of a Zimbabwean nurse in the Big Brother show. *Critical Arts* 22: 101–128. Retrieved 1 May 2015. DOI: 10.1080/0256004080216630.

Marshall, Thomas H. (1950). *Citizenship and Social Class*. Vol. 11. Cambridge: Cambridge University Press

Moyo, Dumisani. (2009). Citizen journalism and the parallel market of information in Zimbabwe's 2008 election. *Journalism Studies* 10: 551–567. Retrieved 1 May 2015. DOI: 10.1080/14616700902797291.

Moyo, Last. (2009a). "The Digital Divide: Scarcity, Inequality and Conflict". In *Digital Cultures: Understanding New Media*, Glen Creeber and Royston Martin (eds.), Maidenhead: McGraw Hill Education, pp. 122–138.

Moyo, Last. (2009b). "Digital Democracy: Enhancing the Public Sphere". In *Digital Cultures: Understanding New Media*, Glen Creeber and Royston Martin (eds.), Maidenhead: McGraw Hill Education, pp. 139–156.

Moyo, Last. (2011). Blogging down dictatorship: Human rights, citizen journalists and the right to communicate in Zimbabwe. *Journalism* 12: 745–760. Retrieved 1 May 2015. DOI: 10.1177/1464884911405469.

Muneri, Cleophas T., and Collier, Mary J. (2014). "Dancing with Democratization: Civic Spaces of Struggle in Zimbabwe". In *Community Engagement and Intercultural Praxis: Dancing with Difference in Diverse Contexts*, Mary J. Collier (ed.), New York: Peter Lang, pp. 88–111.

Silverman, Jon. (2011). "YouTube If You Want To: New Media, Investigative Tele-Journalism and Social Control". In *The End of Journalism: News in the Twenty-First Century*, Gavin Stewart and Alec Charles (eds.), Oxford: Peter Lang, pp. 51–62.

Part III
Perceptions and Critiques

12
Political Participation, Alternative Media and Citizen Journalism in Lusophone Africa

Susana Salgado

Introduction

The overall objective of this chapter is to investigate grass-roots participation, alternative media and citizen journalism in four Portuguese-speaking African countries.[1] Angola, Cape Verde, Mozambique, and Sao Tome and Principe illustrate different processes of democratization, different media systems, but mainly these countries provide examples of very different levels of citizen democratic awareness and of diverse modes of political engagement.

These new democracies share the particular feature of having implemented a democratic system (although with different degrees of success) simultaneously with the worldwide expansion of the Internet. Through the Internet, novel tools and channels of information, communication and participation are available, thus making communication and participation easier and faster. The actors and goals of such online participation are still a matter for debate, as the new information and communication technologies (ICT) can also be used as tools to control and manipulate. Nonetheless, new online forms of communication have often been linked to improved access to political information and to higher levels of political awareness and participation. With easier access to different types of information, including information published abroad, citizens see other examples and consequently should expect more of their democracies: more possibilities to participate in political decisions, more transparency and less corruption, greater political accountability and so on.

Citizens have also the tools to be not only consumers, but also to become producers of information. Due to language and geographical barriers and to important financial constraints, the production of local and national information becomes especially relevant, and this includes not only occasional collaborations with the mainstream media outlets, but also alternative media: websites, online papers, weblogs and other user-generated content communication tools, which are fine examples of both the production of information more adjusted to context and of citizen participation in public debates.

The Lusophone African countries' experience clearly shows that citizen participation and alternative journalism practices, including different forms of user-generated content and citizen journalism, are socially and politically constructed. They are part of a much-needed process of political empowerment in countries experiencing democratization and recent democratic consolidation, but are deeply influenced by the constraints of these environments. The percentage of citizens with enough education to use appropriately the greater quantity of information available and the new media varies substantially in these four countries, as does the degree of tolerance to different opinions and overall freedom.

Lusophone African countries' democratic development

Angola, Mozambique, Cape Verde, and Sao Tome and Principe share a common language and several historical and cultural commonalities, but differ in other crucial aspects, including structural factors, such as the size of territory and population, and the levels of human and economic development. The degree of democratic development and the quality of democracy are also considerably different from one country to another.

Angola, Cape Verde, Mozambique, and Sao Tome and Principe gained independence in 1975, following the decolonization process initiated after the democratic revolution in Portugal in April 1974. These four countries are commonly considered African new democracies, included in what Samuel Huntington (1991) described as the "Third Wave of Democratization" that started in the beginning of the 1990s. In fact, after almost two decades of one-party rule, some democratic reforms were initiated in these four countries, namely the adoption of democratic constitutions, the introduction of a multiparty system, and the promise of holding regular and fair elections. Despite this, and although these four countries are usually categorized as new democracies, there is significant variation in their degree of democratic consolidation (regular elections, democratic rule of law, competitive political system, freedom of expression, press freedom, etc.) and, in cases like Angola, there are serious doubts as to whether using the term "democracy" is even appropriate (Chabal, 2002; Chabal and Vidal, 2007; Salgado, 2014).

It is possible to say that, in terms of democratic development, Angola and Cape Verde are on completely opposite sides, while Mozambique and Sao Tome and Principe are more or less in the middle. As to the competitiveness of their political systems, there are significant differences. Angola and Mozambique have had the same party in power since independence (MPLA – Popular Movement for the Liberation of Angola – and

FRELIMO – Mozambique Liberation Front), whereas in Cape Verde two parties have been alternating in power, and in Sao Tome and Principe several
different political forces have won elections and therefore have had the
opportunity to rule the country. The holding of elections has been regular
in Cape Verde, Sao Tome and Principe, and Mozambique, but not in Angola.

The political system has, in many different ways, a decisive weight in shaping both the structure and the functioning of the media system in these
countries. Examples of this influence are found not only in societies with
limited freedom (Angola), but also in societies experiencing more successful
democratization processes (Cape Verde).

The beginning of the democratization process also brought the promise of
free and independent media to these countries, which, for various reasons,
was never fully implemented and developed in most cases. Independent
media outlets face more difficulties in new democracies. Not only are journalists usually pressured, but they also have more problems in accessing
key political information (the governments prefer to use the news media
they control to convey their views and the information on their decisions).
Independent news media outlets experience other problems related to their
financial survival that result from very high prices of entry into the market
and almost unaffordable production costs, a very limited advertising market
and extremely reduced sales.

These factors, and the immature democratic development, explain why it
is so difficult to find independent media in the Lusophone African countries. Privately owned media is not necessarily equal to independent media,
and some of these countries, particularly Angola, are good examples of that.
In Angola, the ruling political elite has been buying most of the existing
private news media outlets and opening new ones in order to fully occupy
the market with media controlled by the MPLA (the party in power). So, in
addition to controlling the state media (the only news media with national
reach), the MPLA elite has been implementing a plan to control, directly or
indirectly, all the remaining news media outlets.

As noted, Cape Verde illustrates a very different situation in terms of
freedom and democratic development, as well as regarding the balance of
independence in its media system. In Cape Verde, the media system is
an accurate picture of the bipolarization of the political system: the two
main political parties, PAICV (African Party for the Independence of Cape
Verde) and MpD (Movement for Democracy), have been alternating in
government, and one at a time controlled the broadcasting sector, while
the weekly printed press publications are divided in their support between
these two political parties. The smaller political forces often complain about
the difficulties in conveying their messages through the mainstream news
media.

In Sao Tome and Principe, the high levels of poverty and the country's
incipient development in every meaning of the word make any discussion

about independence within the media system almost meaningless, were it not for a very few exceptions and for some noticeable effects of the Internet in the media scene. It is thanks to the Internet that the country now has a daily newspaper (*Téla Nón*) that is also one of the very few independent news media outlets. Other than this, some international assistance projects established in the country through several non-governmental organizations (NGOs) and religious groups have been fulfilling, in part, the role of the media in development and democratization, supporting the work of community radio stations and conveying all types of relevant information (about health, nutrition, elections, citizenship, etc.), particularly to those living in the most remote parts of the country.

Although Mozambique was already familiar with alternative media initiatives through community radio stations, but especially fax newspapers (periodic news publications usually run by journalists and sent by fax to circumvent some freedom limitations of the mainstream media and the very high printing costs), the Internet also gave an important boost to the development of independent media in Mozambique. Of the four, Mozambique is probably the country with more diversity and plurality of news sources and with more independent media initiatives, but the reach of such initiatives is still limited and the political authorities still control much of the media content that actually reaches the majority of the population. The Internet has allowed the further development of independent media through the emergence of more news outlets and the possibility of distributing some of the existing outlets in new formats (emails, websites, newsletters, blogs, other social media, etc.), and it has also motivated more people politically. It has increased the motivation of different actors to participate in debates not only through these new news media, but also through individuals' own means of expression, such as blogs. All in all, the Internet has given more national and international visibility to different points of view.

The positive effect of the Internet on democratization is therefore more perceptible in places where the authorities still hold some level of control over the media, but where there is also a degree of press freedom and freedom of expression. It is possible that more freedom is tolerated in the online news media simply because their reach is still rather low – given the low penetration of the Internet, especially outside the main urban centres – when compared to the other media, with larger audiences.

In varying degrees, according to the country, the Internet is facilitating access to information, multiplying plurality regarding both sources of information and producers of news content, and promoting freedom of expression. In the Lusophone African countries, many citizens publish their own blogs, and online newspapers have not only furthered the development of an independent and alternative press, but have also encouraged citizens to participate more through comments on news stories or even with their own news stories. These new types of news media are usually freer than the mainstream media, offer alternative views, including some that are critical of the authorities, and have an approach to issues closer to the citizens' perspective. They have also been crucial in increasing the amount of information available and in making it accessible in more places, including abroad. Furthermore, the online news media have, on many occasions, influenced the content of mainstream media outlets, and because they provide spaces for people to react to news stories and opinion articles, they are also stimulating habits of reading and participation in general.

There are, nonetheless, some problems. On the one hand, their reach is still limited. When compared to the rest of the world, the percentage of users in most Lusophone African countries is still very small, especially in Angola and Mozambique where Internet access is still very limited outside the main cities, a factor which ends up contributing to accentuating inequalities between regions and social classes. Mozambique is the country of the four with the least number of people connected to the Internet, only 4.3% in 2012. In Angola, the percentage of Internet users was 14.8%, and in Sao Tome and Principe it was 20.2% in the same year. Cape Verde is the country where most people have access: 32% of citizens were already using the Internet in 2012.

On the other hand, some online news media face credibility problems. They are often accused of unprofessionalism, amateurism, and of publishing rumours and information that has not been previously verified. The fact that some journalists in these media do not have the proper training explains some of the accusations; however, such critical positioning towards the authorities and the mainstream media controlled by the state also fuels the criticisms.

The need to improve journalistic quality and training remains a challenge in these four countries, including in the mainstream media outlets with wider audiences. Although the conditions for the exercise of the profession have been improving in recent years, there is still the need for more training and more resources in many newsrooms, even in Cape Verde, the country with the most favourable conditions, where approximately 150 professional journalists worked in 2012.

Self-censorship is frequent among journalists, and their working conditions and salaries are not good. This explains why most journalists want to work in the state-owned media, where salaries and working conditions are usually better, but to achieve that they have to please the ruling political elite. Sao Tome and Principe illustrates this situation well: politicians themselves choose the journalists they take with them on state visits; such journalists receive daily subsistence allowances, which are often higher than their monthly salary. On average, in Sao Tome and Principe, journalists are paid a salary of 2 million dobras (approximately 80 euros) per month and face job insecurity, which leaves them completely vulnerable to pressures, bribes and intimidation. Additionally, when the level of journalistic professionalization is not high (not every journalist has a university degree and specific training), journalists are also less prepared to recognize and deal with manipulation attempts. Finally, the lack of means is also reflected in the type of journalism produced in the Lusophone African countries in general: there is almost no investigative reporting and journalists mainly report on what is delivered to them.

In unfavourable contexts for mainstream journalism such as these, the development of alternative journalistic practices and alternative media gain particular relevance. Despite several constraints, the Internet has been transforming journalistic practices, including news-gathering, sourcing, writing, reporting and distributing in the Lusophone African countries, as in other African countries and in other parts of the world. The effects are strongly mediated by context, so the changes are more noticeable in some countries more than others. In addition to wide-ranging implications for the practice of journalism, the Internet has also encouraged alternative voices and alternative approaches to information and news.

The different journalistic styles and content formats and the openness to new voices have thus made the definitional boundaries between professionalism and amateurism in journalism even more fluid. Among the most important features of all journalistic practice is the goal of producing news stories connected to their audiences at reduced costs, which is particularly important in poorer newsrooms. The online has potential to enhance these objectives, while practices such as citizen and participatory journalism actively engage the audiences in the production of news, allowing for more diverse, varied and affordable news stories, from contributors with different professional and educational backgrounds and distinct experiences. So, the capacity to reach diverse audiences also has potential to improve.

Citizen journalism and mainstream media

The concept of citizen journalism has been debated for some time, but gained a new boost with the rapid development of the Internet and the new ICT, which have enabled the publication of online papers, blogs, posts in other social media and so on, because citizens now have accessible tools to become producers of information and are not just consumers of news and information. The depth of concept of citizen journalism is illustrated by its direct connection to important related debates such as, for instance, the normative nature of journalism (Banda, 2010), the role and power of alternative journalism, political participation and social movements, or even Chantal Mouffe's notion of radical democracy (Atton, 2009).

Simply put, citizen journalism means journalism that is produced not by professionals, but by amateurs outside mainstream media, citizens with little or no training and professional qualifications as journalists (Atton, 2009, p. 265). Moreover, citizen journalists are not "constrained by conventional journalistic processes or methodologies, and they usually function without editorial oversight" (Ross and Cormier, 2010, p. 66). Despite this, amateur journalists perform the same tasks as professional journalists; they also "gather, process, research, report, analyse and publish news", but mainly through and due to a "variety of technologies made possible by the Internet" (Ross and Cormier, 2010, p. 66).

The point of view may also differ from the professional journalists' approach: citizen journalists "write and report from their positions as citizens, members of communities, as activists" (Atton, 2009, p. 265). This helps to explain why citizen journalism has been closely linked to alternative media practices and effects. The benefits of the development of alternative media outlets and genres are – if aligned with democratic values – indisputable, especially in challenging democratization contexts where most of the mainstream media outlets are controlled by the state and by governments and powerful political and economic elites, as it often happens in African countries. According to Atton, alternative media are mainly characterized by their potential to "construct a reality that appears to oppose the conventions and representation of the mainstream media" (2009, p. 268).

The democratic and economic frailties of most African countries deeply influence the objectives and ways that alternative media are organized and operate in these societies, as well as the kind of citizen journalism that is actually practised. The motivation, ideology, attitude, literacy and education of citizen journalists and alternative media developers are not independent of the specificities of the context in which they operate. Persistent economic and social inequalities define who has access to education and technology, determining finally who is actually able to write and publish news and opinions online. In addition, the economic difficulties of many news media outlets have already caused some blurring of the boundaries of the profession, regarding not only the professionalization and training of journalists, but also the actual product of news coverage provided by newspapers, television and radio channels. As in other parts of the world, facts are often mixed with opinions, interpretations and analysis, which in turn are usually loaded with propaganda, biased information and misinformation, but also with gossip and unverified reports. Furthermore, as a result of poorly resourced newsrooms, some citizens are invited to provide reports and opinion articles on different occasions and through various news formats; however, their independence is not always assured; in fact, most of the time they are selected because of their political preferences.

The practice of citizen journalism in Africa has been often tied to democracy activists and to the use of participatory communication for social change. Citizen journalism adds new voices to the public sphere, often the people's voice, and also allows the reporting of complicated issues in more accessible ways to the general population. Community radio stations have long encouraged local citizens to collaborate with their information programmes. These radio stations are essential in Africa: they represent opportunities to move journalism away from party politics and urban sets, and are often the most important source of information for people living in rural regions. Although community radio stations are scattered throughout the territory, even in the most inaccessible areas for mainstream media outlets, they are unable to reach all areas to access news stories. So, as a result of human and economic resources constraints, reliance on citizen journalists is not completely unheard of in African countries such as Mozambique or Mali, for instance.

In moments of disruption, citizen journalism is seen as a major source of information, representing an alternative to mainstream media outlets or complementing the mainstream news coverage of events. As Khamis and Vaughn have noticed in the Tunisian and Egyptian revolutions, "citizen journalists can be the most reliable and credible source of news and information during significant political events" (2014, p. 165), simply because they know their country better than international news agencies and news networks.

There are, however, some issues related to the interpretation of these practices in the African context, which result in a lack of consensus regarding the role and the advantages and disadvantages of citizen journalism and alternative media, especially after their further development due to the Internet. While these types of media practices usually are heralded as enabling the voices of silenced actors to be heard and allowing different points of view to be included in debates, they can also be accused of spreading rumours and gossip, and of inciting disorders and even violent protests.

Mäkinen and Kuira (2008) explain how the social media enriched the process of democratization in the post-election crisis in Kenya: the social media enabled citizens to interact with news and share content, and functioned as an alternative medium for citizen communication or participatory journalism. Contrary to these assumptions, Moyo (2011) frames the use of blogs in a moment of crisis (violent election in Zimbabwe) as a form of alternative media and citizen journalism but with potentially different outcomes. To this author, the Web has occasioned new but radical counterhegemonic spaces and new forms of journalism that are deinstitutionalized and deprofessionalized. Moyo stresses that radicalism is reflected both in the form and the content of blogs.

Another issue that is worth noting is the growing interaction between mainstream media and citizen journalism. Atton (2009) sees alternative and citizen journalism as a sort of counterforce to the limitations of mainstream journalism, and Mare (2013) highlights the emergence of collaborative journalism practices and the convergence and symbiotic nature of the relationship between mainstream and social media during social protests in southern Africa: while social media are instrumental in breaking news, mainstream media weigh in with contextualization and amplification. However,

Atton (2009) and Paterson (2013) also question whether some cases presented as citizen journalism are actually participatory journalism and not simply an increasingly common form of subsidizing underresourced newsrooms. In fact, this modus operandi has become a regular routine in several African newsrooms. With the objective of expanding their sources of information and their capacity of news-gathering, many media outlets have, on different occasions, resorted to citizens to publish news stories. A good example is Mozambican newspaper *@Verdade* (means the truth).

This newspaper has always assumed a grass-roots positioning, addressing the low-income communities in particular, and is known for being critical of the government and for encouraging the participation of readers in suggesting and in writing news content themselves. *@Verdade* also launched an innovative experience during the 2009 presidential, legislative and provincial elections: it encouraged citizens to be reporters in their own neighbourhoods and to send their news stories to be published on a specific webpage of the newspaper's website (http://www.verdade.co.mz/eleicoes2009). This online resource included a directory list of the various inputs that were sent with the following information: report title, date, location and an indication of whether or not the report had been verified. The initiative allowed the newspaper to have different reporters in several locations during the campaign and as the voting occurred, making it possible, for instance, to know about incidents in different provinces and polling booths (Salgado, 2012; 2014).

To further the aims of monitoring the political decision-making processes, enhancing transparency, exposing corruption, as well as to helping to prevent electoral frauds, this initiative was reproduced in the following elections, first in the 2013 local elections and then in the 2014 general elections. Because *@Verdade* does not have the resources to cover all newsworthy events throughout the territory and, in the case of elections, cannot send journalists to every polling station in the country to monitor the voting process, it relied on its strong community of engaged readers and continued to enlist the help of thousands of its readers across Mozambique.

In the 2014 elections, *@Verdade* used Citizen Desk, a digital tool created to help aggregate, verify and publish news reports from citizen journalists. Its functioning is simple: the newspaper's readers send their comments, observations, photos and videos through social media, but mainly via SMS, given the low penetration rate of the Internet in many parts of the country and the high use of mobile phones; then, the *@Verdade* editors monitor those inputs, verify and publish the newsworthy reports, and in some cases even assign journalists to follow up the information.

@Verdade also used the Internet and the citizens' participation to report on the 2010 crisis. It uploaded and posted many articles and videos on its website and Facebook page, and integrated an Ushahidi crisis report tool on its website. Some journalists and citizens also disseminated news about the

crisis in English through Twitter, in an attempt to give international visibility to these events and to convey different perspectives from the government one about the popular protests (Salgado, 2014).

This practice of resorting to the Internet and to citizens to cover crisis situations has become rather common in the African continent. In Kenya, during the 2008 post-election crisis, the Internet was used to map violent incidents throughout the country. An Ushahidi (means testimony, witness) website was launched and used as a tool for information collection, visualization and interactive mapping by citizens, who had witnessed acts of violence in Kenya after the election, and reported them via emails and text messages. The website provided a map of the country with all the reported incidents, and some of these citizen reports were also incorporated into the mainstream media coverage of the crisis (Mäkinen and Kuira, 2008).

Paterson describes, giving the Malawi's *Nation* example, how newspapers in even some of Africa's poorest countries have been building networks of citizen journalists. He explains that George Kasakula, one of the newspaper's editors, told him that, in 2007, they asked citizen journalists from across the country to write their own news stories and send them to be published in the Saturday's edition of the paper: " 'The results were so overwhelming that the newspaper decided to allocate not only one page but two. Now we have a network of over 500 citizen journalists sending in stories using various ICT means' (Pers. Comm., 3 December 2012)" (2013, p. 3–4).

Blogging in Lusophone Africa

A different way of incorporating the voice of citizen journalists in mainstream media is through blogs. On the one hand, blogs have become an important communication tool for many citizens in Africa, including in the Portuguese-speaking African countries (Salgado, 2012; 2014), and, on the other hand, most mainstream media outlets have included blogs in their websites fed not only by journalists, but also from their audiences, from whom they also request ideas for news stories and programmes.

Citizens' blogs have often been credited with breaking news in advance of mainstream news media outlets. Schudson and Anderson (2009) acknowledge precisely this difficulty in conceptualizing blogging in relation to journalism. According to these authors, "boundary lines between 'insider and outsider', 'professional and non-professional', 'journalist and blogger' are blurred today and growing ever more fuzzy" (p. 98). Atton explains that blogging may be understood as a number of practices, which include the publishing of personal diaries by professionals (such as journalists and politicians), amateur investigative journalism, comment and opinion, and eyewitness reporting by observers and participants (2009, p. 271).

In routine periods, and especially during elections and in turbulent times, it has become common to see citizen bloggers sharing their versions of events on their blogs and on mainstream media websites. More than just sharing photos and videos, they share their experience and perspective with other citizens. Possibilities such as these illustrate the capacity of online alternative media to empower citizens and therefore assume particular relevance in democratization contexts. Blogs also have an important role in disseminating information. Some bloggers, rather than break news, review mainstream media news stories and express opinions about them. It is also common to find excerpts and summaries of news stories with links to the source, or simply the bloggers' selection of newsworthy stories and events. So, in some cases, news stories are simply reproduced in blogs, but in other cases, this reproduction is accompanied by contextualization, interpretation and commentary.

The increasing interaction between blogs, other online publications and the mainstream media is a noteworthy dimension of the influence of the Internet in politics and society. As noted, in some cases, bloggers and other online content producers can influence the mainstream media agenda-setting process. For instance, if blogs highlight an issue disregarded by the mainstream media, they can promote journalistic coverage and push that issue into public debate, or if someone gains visibility in the online social networks, he or she also usually gains mainstream media exposure. By selecting and highlighting some news stories to the detriment of others, bloggers act as gatekeepers and sometimes replace professional journalists in the mediatization process.

Blogs are also an important source of information for mainstream media journalists, either as a cited source or as an inspiration on how to frame issues. Given that many journalists are also bloggers it is not surprising that they read and cite each other's work, or are simply influenced by it. In Angola, where freedom is more limited, sometimes journalists cite blogs in order to express their opinions, but remain shielded by another person's comment.

In countries with limited freedom of expression, more than just intertwined with mainstream media, blogs can also constitute an actual alternative to state-controlled mainstream media, by providing information and opinion that is usually censored. Blogs are thus not just means of expression for citizens who feel they have something different to say, but also represent more sources of information and opinion, adding, therefore, to overall plurality and, in some cases, constituting an alternative news source for citizens.

Recently, blogs have lost some of their visibility with the rapid development of social network websites, but they are still important in many contexts, including in the Lusophone African countries. In Angola, Mozambique and Cape Verde, journalists, politicians, researchers, activists, artists and professors are active in the blogosphere. They present their work, comment on current affairs and on government decisions, promote active citizenship and give advice to fellow citizens. It is interesting to note that several bloggers state that their mission is to control the political authorities. Sao Tome and Principe did not develop this blogging culture to the same extent, due to low levels of engagement in general and to the low quality and excessively high prices of Internet access at the time blogging became more common.

Although there are blogs focusing on many different subjects, politics is a recurrent topic on several of them, and many times blogs help frame political issues differently. Blogs provide the citizen's perspective and contextualize issues and problems in ways that are closer to the citizen's personal experience. Bloggers also promote a closer and more informal relationship with their readers, with many allowing readers to leave comments, thus facilitating online discussions and encouraging others to share their opinions and other news. So, in addition to producing their own content, bloggers may also build connections with other bloggers and readers in general.

Due to the digital divide, low literacy levels and limited access to the Internet among the general population, many bloggers are from the middle and upper classes, have liberal professions and an academic level considered high when compared to the rest of the population. This is clearly reflected in the issues addressed and in the objectives of most blogs. However, the introduction of the Internet in schools, libraries, etc. in more recent years has been helping to increase the number of users and to democratize access. It is ever more possible to find more varied types of users, including those holding different political orientations. The coexistence of antagonistic points of view and a diversity of opinions are essential to deepen the process of democratization, and are even more important when the political authorities control the mainstream media.

The authorities do not control Internet access and content on a systematic basis, but there are reports of bloggers being ordered to cease their activities, especially in Angola and Mozambique. Because of this, and also due to the newness of freedom of expression, some bloggers prefer to remain anonymous and use nicknames instead of their given names. In Angola and Mozambique especially, many bloggers state that their mission is to control the political authorities and to promote debate and knowledge about issues. Dutton (2009) uses the term "fifth estate" to refer to the positive effect of the Internet in enabling networked citizens and a new source of accountability, which challenges the influence of other more established bases of institutional authority.

If the social network websites serve mainly the purpose of connecting people in the Lusophone African countries, blogs have assumed, at least up to now, a more complete role in furthering the countries' democratization processes: they complement functions usually attributed to mainstream news media, such as empowering citizens, enhancing pluralism, and promoting freedom of expression and information. It is difficult to separate alternative media and citizen journalism from political empowerment, participation and activism, they go hand in hand, but often they are also merged, as happens with these types of blogs.

Conclusions

The practice of journalism in Lusophone Africa has closely followed all of these countries' democratization complexities. Although there are many differences between them, the media system is a close reflection of the political system, the large majority of journalists still work in significantly underresourced newsrooms and face other constraints related to deficient professional training, low salaries, bribes and manipulation attempts and, in rarer cases, even persecution. Except in Angola, and at least in theory, the levels of freedom of expression and press freedom are, in general, good, but there are constraints related to the living conditions that ultimately have a determinant influence on the conditions to exert those freedoms.

As the development of democracy features also the development of media systems, journalistic practices are being shaped and redefined in various ways by the Internet and the new ICT, despite the pervasive connectivity issues. On the one hand, mainstream media now coexist with online alternative media, citizen journalists, bloggers and online activists, and, on the other hand, the Web has also revolutionized the way news is gathered, produced, reported, distributed and consumed. In a similar way to what has been happening more or less everywhere in the world, there is evidence that, in the Lusophone African countries, the Internet is being used, to varying degrees, by citizens to contribute to information exchange and news-making.

With the Internet – mainly through blogs, but also in collaboration with the mainstream media outlets on some occasions – citizens are playing an active role in the processes of collecting, reporting, analysing and disseminating information and news. The Mozambican newspaper *@Verdade* illustrates one of the most relevant initiatives of citizen journalism in the Portuguese-speaking African countries, but there are other initiatives. These practices help enhance freedom and increase the amount of information and variety of opinions available to the public. They also challenge some more repressive approaches to media coverage and to the dissemination of information. These changes have implications not only in politics, but also in the social and cultural aspects of the development of these countries. They impact, for instance, on the number of actors shaping reality and events; on the capacity of fringe political actors to communicate their messages; on the relationships between journalists and audiences; on the places where news is produced, disseminated and consumed; and on the variety of gatekeepers and drivers of readers to information and news.

Hopes have been high every time a new medium is introduced and its use developed in societies, but in the case of the Internet these hopes were even greater considering its attributes, which facilitate mobility and inter-connectivity, and its potential for citizen empowerment through new forms of participation and the greater exposure of user-generated content, including forms of citizen journalism. It is now relatively easy to produce and share all kinds of content. In countries that still experience some constraints to freedom and plurality, the Internet has promoted the development of alternative media, which, often more just a complement to mainstream media outlets, are in fact providing alternative interpretations of reality and diverse framings of issues.

This chapter has focused on four Lusophone African countries and looked into the grass-roots approaches to interpreting and reporting reality through the appropriation of new media technology, initiated both by citizens and by mainstream media. The active role of the citizen is at the core of any democratization process, especially when constraints are still experienced, and the Angolan, Cape Verdean, Mozambican and Sao Tomean cases illustrate not only different experiences of democracy-building processes, but also some of the ways through which citizens are appropriating technology to make their voices heard.

Note

1. Guinea-Bissau is not included in this study.

References

Atton, Chris. (2009). "Alternative and Citizen Journalism". In *Handbook of Journalism Studies*, Karin Wahl-Jorgensen and Thomas Hanitzsch (eds.), New York and London: Routledge, pp. 265–278.

Banda, Fackson. (2010). *Citizen Journalism and Democracy in Africa*. Grahamstown, South Africa: Highway Africa.

Chabal, Patrick. (2002). *A History of Postcolonial Lusophone Africa*. Bloomington, IN: Indiana University Press.

Chabal, Patrick, and Vidal, Nuno. (eds.) (2007). *Angola: The Weight of History*. London: Hurst Publishers.

Dutton, William H. (2009). The fifth estate emerging through the network of networks. *Prometheus: Critical Studies in Innovation* 27(1): 1–15.

Huntington, Samuel P. (1991). *The Third Wave: Democratization in the Late Twentieth Century*. Oklahoma: University of Oklahoma Press.

Khamis, Sahar, and Vaughn, Katherine. (2014). "Online Citizen Journalism and Political Transformations in the Tunisian and Egyptian Revolutions: A Critical Analysis". In *Online Journalism in Africa: Trends, Practices and Emerging Cultures*, Hayes M. Mabweazara, Mudhai Okoth F. and Jason Whittaker (eds.), New York: Routledge, pp. 156–171.

Mabweazara, Hayes M. (2011). "The Internet in the Print Newsroom: Trends, Practices and Emerging Cultures in Zimbabwe". In *Making Online News*, vol. 2: *Newsroom Ethnographies in the Second Decade of Internet Journalism*, David Domingo and Chris Paterson (eds.), New York: Peter Lang, pp. 57–69.

Mabweazara, Hayes M. (2015). African journalism in the "digital era": Charting a research agenda. *African Journalism Studies* 36(1): 11–17.

Mabweazara, Hayes M., Mudhai, Okoth F., and Whittaker, Jason. (eds.) (2014). *Online Journalism in Africa: Trends, Practices and Emerging Cultures*. New York: Routledge.

Mäkinen, Maarit, and Kuira, Mary W. (2008). Social media and postelection crisis in Kenya. *The International Journal of Press/Politics* 13(3): 328–335.

Mare, Admire. (2013). A complicated but symbiotic affair: The relationship between mainstream media and social media in the coverage of social protests in southern Africa. *Ecquid Novi: African Journalism Studies* 34(1): 83–98.

Moyo, Last. (2011). Blogging down a dictatorship: Human rights, citizen journalists and the right to communicate in Zimbabwe. *Journalism* 12(6): 745–760.

Paterson, Chris. (2013). Journalism and social media in the African context. *Ecquid Novi: African Journalism Studies* 34(1): 1–6.

Paterson, Chris, and Doctors, Simone. (2013). Participatory journalism in Mozambique. *Ecquid Novi: African Journalism Studies* 34(1): 107–114.

Ross, Ronald D., and Cormier, Susan C. (2010) *Handbook for Citizen Journalists*. Denver, CO: National Association of Citizen Journalists.

Salgado, Susana. (2012). The web in African countries: Exploring the possible influences of the Internet in the democratization processes. *Information, Communication & Society* 15(9): 1373–1389.

Salgado, Susana. (2014). *The Internet and Democracy Building in Lusophone African Countries*. Surrey: Ashgate.

Schudson, Michael, and Anderson, Chris. (2009). "Objectivity, Professionalism, and Truth Seeking in Journalism". In *Handbook of Journalism Studies*, Karin Wahl-Jorgensen and Thomas Hanitzsch (eds.), New York and London: Routledge, pp. 88–101.

13
Between "Bottom-Up" Journalism and Social Activism in Unequal Societies: The Case of GroundUp in South Africa

Wallace Chuma

It has been two decades since the dismantling of legislated racial segregation in South Africa, and the country's democratic transition has often been hailed across the world as nothing short of a miracle. Yet, despite the numerous gains freedom has brought, South Africa remains one of the most unequal societies on earth (Marais, 2011). The country remains largely divided across class and race, and these divisions impact on citizens' participation in the full spectrum of what democracy has to offer. The country's mainstream media are largely commercial institutions driven by commercial imperatives, and therefore generally privilege elite frames in reporting the South African story. Partly as a result of the mainstream media's neglect of poor and ordinary citizens' stories, and partly thanks to new information and communication technologies (ICTs), a new interesting trend of "bottom-up" storytelling has, over the past decade, emerged in the South African public sphere, to offer both competing and alternative narratives to the dominant stories. This chapter focuses on one such space of "bottom-up" storytelling, called GroundUp, a non-profit online news agency which generates news from both professional and "activist" journalists. The chapter explores the possibilities and opportunities this "weapon of the weak" (Couldry, 2002, p. 1) holds for increased participation and visibility of the marginalized outside of the "usual" dominant frames. It also debates the possible impact of this phenomenon on the quality of South Africa's democracy, and discusses the limits as well, from funding to issues around access.

Locating GroundUp on the South African media map

GroundUp (http://www.groundup.org.za) is an online community news agency founded by social activist Nathan Geffen in 2012. Based in Cape

Town, the portal reports on a variety of areas that affect the poor – namely health, education, housing, labour and immigration among others – and most of its stories are based in the Western Cape townships such as Khayelitsha and Gugulethu.[1] Several of its stories get taken up and republished by mainstream publications, both online and in hard copy. Funded by both local South African and international philanthropic organizations, the news portal is also strategically positioned as part of another non-profit group called the Community Media Trust (CMT) and the Centre for Social Science Research at the University of Cape Town (UCT). Before delving into a discussion of GroundUp proper, it is critical that we locate it within the South African media landscape.

The attainment of democracy in South Africa in 1994 created a fertile environment for substantial growth and diversification of the media in that country. With the *ancien régime* of communication policy gone, the new changes to local media structures were characterized by, among other things, transformation of media ownership, diversification of newsrooms (which were predominantly white pre-1994), transformation of the state broadcaster into a public service broadcaster, and the creation of conditions for diversity and pluralism of media content (see Olorunnisola, Tomaselli and Tomaselli, 2011). Transformation of media structures was considered a critical issue even in the multiparty negotiations that led to South Africa's first democratic elections. This was because of the historic role the media, especially mainstream media, had played in sustaining or helping sustain structures of domination during apartheid. As Horwitz (2001) notes:

> The institutions of communications – the press, broadcasting and telecommunications – were central to the evolution of the South African state and the apartheid system. The press gave voice to, and to some degree mediated the conflict between English and Afrikaans-speaking communities; broadcasting, a product of tense compromises between the white groups, embodied the terms of their hegemonic alliance and expressed the ideological content of racial domination; state-owned and operated telecommunications contributed importantly to the mechanisms that coordinated the apartheid economy. (p. 26)

The first decade of democracy witnessed a frenzied pace of change in the country's mediascape: the state-owned South African Broadcasting Corporation (SABC) was transformed into a public service broadcaster accountable to the public (through parliament) and broadcasting in all 11 official languages; a three-tier system of public service, commercial and community broadcasting was set in place and resulted in the licensing of over 100 radio stations across the tiers; and a privately owned, national free-to-air television, ETV, was licensed. Within the print sector, substantial changes also occurred during this period. Mining giants Anglo American and Johannesburg Consolidated Investments (JCI), which had been the predominant owners of the English language press in the country, divested themselves of their interests in the major media companies Argus and Times Media Limited; the former being sold to the Irish-based Independent News and Media, and the latter to a black-owned company, the National Economic Consortium (NEC), which marked the first major transfer of media ownership from white to black ownership in South Africa. Within the Afrikaans print sector, the giant company Naspers formed new firms and sold shares to black-owned companies (Tomaselli, 2011).

Besides changes in the structure and ownership of the mainstream press, there were also changes in the profile of journalists who reported for and edited the major South African media organizations.

In 1994, former president Nelson Mandela famously remarked that:

> With the exception of the Sowetan (newspaper), the senior editorial staffs of South Africa's daily newspapers are cast from the same racial mould. They are white, they are male, they are from a middle-class background, they tend to share a very similar life experience . . . while no-one can object in principle to editors with such a profile, what is disturbing is the threat of one-dimensionality this poses for the media of our country.
>
> (Quoted in Horwitz, 2001, p. 290)

However, by the end of the first decade of democracy, the tide had turned. Consistent with the country's employment equity legislation, the majority of South African newsrooms were now predominantly staffed by black journalists in occupying both junior and very senior positions. There were also different levels of editorial reorientation/realignment in some news media in the wake of new political realities. This was more so in mainstream Afrikaans newspapers, which had traditionally supported the apartheid establishment. Three elements of the post-apartheid media transformation are relevant for this chapter as they provide a context for GroundUp, and therefore need to be discussed, albeit briefly.

The decline of the alternative press

One of the ironies of the attainment of democracy in South Africa was the decline of what was termed the "alternative" press. This small body of mostly radical, anti-apartheid newspapers had been a consistent thorn in the flesh of the apartheid regime for decades, although it was often subject to harassment, closure, arrests and censorship from the state. Of the half-dozen or so regular "alternative" newspapers that published from time to time across the country prior to 1994, only the *Mail and Guardian* (formerly *Weekly Mail*) survived. The demise of most of this press had to do with the cut in donor funds, seeing that apartheid had been defeated.

And yet the dawn of democracy also brought to the fore new forms of social struggle around the material content of democracy itself; from issues around inclusion and exclusion in the economy, to access to basic social services, safety and security, health, education and other core essences of citizenship. The skewed access to all these – thanks in part to the inherited legacy of racially selective provision of essential services and in part to economic policies adopted after 1994 (see Marais, 1998; 2011) – opened a new post-apartheid frontier of struggles between the state and the citizen, especially the poor citizen. The profit-chasing mainstream media gave coverage to these new struggles, but generally gave prominence to issues of immediate relevance to elites, who were their target audiences. This was to be challenged in a way with the launch, in 2002, of the country's first national tabloid newspaper, the *Daily Sun*. The *Sun* targeted the ordinary poor citizens, and energized the media environment in the country. The "tabloid revolution" also saw the entry of other new players, namely the *Daily Voice* in the Cape and Afrikaans title *Die Son*. The tabloids became an instant hit among the "blue-collar" working-class communities, but attracted substantial criticism for, among other things, sensationalized reporting, mainstreaming make-believe stories in reporting and so on for a detailed discussion of the tabloids, see Herman Wasserman's monograph, *Tabloid Journalism in South Africa* (2010).

What is important to note is that while tabloids opened up interesting new spaces in terms of covering stories that affected poor and working-class communities, by their very nature they could not give sustained and in-depth coverage to these community issues. The traditional news values ensured that only the dramatic and the bloody, in many cases, made it to the prominent pages of the newspapers. The GroundUp initiative should arguably be seen as an attempt to fill the gap left by both the tabloids and the mainstream press, namely sustained, in-depth reporting of issues that affect poor communities, issues which do not lend themselves to screaming headlines, but are nevertheless important issues for citizenship.

The commercialization of the media

Another important development in the post-1994 era was the rapid commercialization of the media. While the mainstream media were commercial before 1994, the readmission of South Africa into the global economy increased the pace of commercialization and, in some cases, the internationalization of the media. Among the key developments here have been mergers and acquisitions, consolidation and conglomeration, substantial cuts in expenditure, synergies and so on. The media environment in the country is now such that only the big groups will survive the ravages of a hyper-competitive media industry. The irony is that, whereas in 1994, there were, the SABC aside, four major media groups in the country, twenty years later there are still four major groups controlling almost 90% of the newspapers in the country. The dominance of a few mega media companies (Naspers, Independent News and Media, Times Media Limited and Caxton) has had the ironic effect of limiting media diversity and pluralism, values which are provided for in the constitution.

Another aspect of the commercialization process has been the cost-cutting juggernaut across the country's newsrooms, especially in the wake of the 2008 global financial crisis. Most newsrooms in the country have witnessed substantial cuts, retrenchments and host of "cost-saving" initiatives, whose effects have been to reduce journalistic output, especially investigative journalism. In some cases, newsrooms have retired seasoned journalists and replaced them with juniors ("cheaper" to employ), whom they expect to perform the tasks of the departed seniors, and more. This is a process often referred to as the "juniorization" of the newsrooms.

Indeed, the South African newsrooms continue to experience not just cuts, but also moments of uncertainty owing to declining circulation (for print media) and uncertainty over the promise and potential of the Internet for revenue generation. Wits University Journalism Programme themed its 2013 annual "State of the South African Newsroom" report "Disruptions and Transitions" to highlight the turmoil in the country's newsrooms. The 2014 report was titled "Disruptions Accelerated". The case of GroundUp should also therefore be viewed against the backdrop of mainstream newsrooms undergoing profound and uncertain moments of change which impact rather negatively – at least for now – on their ability to report, on a sustained basis, stories that concern ordinary and poor South Africans.

The rise of the Internet and alternative forms of citizenship and participation

Another noteworthy development within the South Africa mediascape over the past decade has been the increase in the use of the Internet by South Africans, both via broadband connections and mobile phones. According to the 2013 report by Statistics South Africa, the country's official statistics agency, up to 40% of South African households had access to the Internet "anywhere", while 10% only had access to the Internet at home (http://beta2.statssa.gov.za/publications/P0318/P03182013.pdf). Although this pales into insignificance when compared with access to the Internet in the West, it represents a steady increase in the number of citizens accessing the Internet in South Africa. The Internet and other new ICTs have spawned a raft of changes and practices in journalism and the whole idea of "mediation". Phenomena such as "citizen journalism" have become possible thanks to new media, and in some countries have had substantial political effects (see Moyo, 2007; 2009). In South Africa, the rise and uptake of social media has had a significant impact on newsroom practices and routines (see Jordaan, 2013). That the new media "ecologies" hold the promise for enhanced citizen participation in democratic life is not in question. The challenges though, for South Africa and other parts of, especially the developing, world, range from access to new media (the "digital divide") to issues of costs, from issues of ICT "competences" to issues of language.

The case of the GroundUp online news portal should be viewed against the background of the promise of the Internet to facilitate in-depth and sustained reporting on issues of social justice, issues which would otherwise not receive substantial coverage in the mainstream commercial press.

Inequality in South Africa and the challenges of mediation

Despite making a successful transition from apartheid to democracy, and having a constitution considered one of the most liberal in the world, South Africa faces a raft of social problems that range from inequalities in the economy, to violence and crime, health and education problems and so forth. It is partly as a result of these problems that South Africa experiences several so-called "service delivery protests" – some peaceful, others extremely violent – every other day throughout the year (see Municipal IQ, http://www.municipaliq.co.za).

Hein Marais depicts the scope of inequality in SA thus:

> A wealthy country by continental standards, South Africa is also one of the most unequal societies on Earth. It has more luxury car dealers than any country outside the industrialised north, yet almost half of its population lives in poverty and more than a third cannot find waged work. An average assistant manager punching the clock in the service sector would need to work more than 102 years to earn the average annual salary of a corporate CEO...The country boasts shopping malls selling beds that cost up to USD 67 000, while the domestic workers who change the linen on those beds command a minimum wage of USD 44 a week.
>
> (2011, p. 7)

If this summation depicts a case of two "worlds" in one country, the mediation of South African life could also be characterized as such. As highlighted in "The commercialization of the media" section, the commercialization of the media has resulted in an increased journalistic focus on news concerning or about wealthier audiences, and a concomitant neglect of the rest, resulting in a phenomenon Robert McChesney has aptly characterized as "rich media, poor democracy", as the title of his book (1999). In cases where stories about the poor are covered in the mainstream press, there have been complaints that the predominant voices are those of officials and elites. For example, activist group Abahlali baseMjondolo (Shack Dwellers Association) issued the following press statement to complain about their coverage in the media in 2008:

We see many things planned for us, promised to us, and written about us in the newspapers but there is never our voice – always it is the words and empty promises and the visions of the politicians, the so called leaders, and the Municipality.

(Press statement from the shack dwellers social movement. Abahlali baseMjondolo baku Ash Road, 24 June, 2008)

There are obviously exceptions to this from time to time, but the trend both in South Africa and other capitalist democracies worldwide is the predominance of elite frames in mainstream news and a scant attention to issues of the 'other'. In the context of South Africa, GroundUp's strategy of telling stories of ordinary people in ordinary circumstances should therefore be viewed as an attempt to fill in the gap left by the mainstream media.

Alternative media in the era of new media ecologies

The phenomenon of 'alternative media' and what it entails or should entail has been the subject of contested debate over the past decade (see Atton, 2002; Couldry, 2002; Bailey *et al.*, 2008; Moyo, 2009). However, there seems to be consensus that at the very least, 'alternative media' must include three core elements which include serving the community, autonomy from the state and corporate influences, and ability to offer counter-hegemonic discourses to the mainstream (Bailey, et al 2008).

Couldry (2002) adds an interesting dimension to alternative media, which he characterizes as 'weapons of the weak'. He defines alternative media as consisting of "practices of symbolic production which contest (in some way) media power itself i.e. the concentration of symbolic power in media institutions themselves" (2002, p. 4). These varied practices, he argues, "operate across many sites and on many scales, with greater or lesser success and breadth of impact" (p. 6).

The conceptualization of alternative media as consisting of varied practices across several sites and at different scales is particularly useful in the analysis of GroundUp. This is because the news portal applies a fairly 'radical' 'bottom-up' approach to news production, and is unambiguous about its 'activist' stance about issues of social justice. And yet organizationally it is structured more or less like a traditional newsroom, with an editor/founder, a part time associate editor (who is a former editor of the Cape Town, one of two main dailies in the Western Cape Province of South Africa), reporters and freelancers. Elements of traditional journalism practice, such as writing to deadlines, the conventions of newswriting (such as the inverted pyramid and the 5 Ws and H) are also observed at GroundUp, while at the same time the fairly autonomous structure and flexibility (reporters are expected to file three stories a week although there is flexibility around this) allow room for sustained and in-depth coverage of community issues.

GroundUp: A Discussion

This discussion of GroundUp is based on a series of in-depth interviews with the news agency's editorial team, observations in the newsroom, and a close reading of some of GroundUp published stories. The focus on stories published is mostly on the themes, scope of the coverage and reporting styles. It is meant to be explorative in nature, ultimately with a view to establishing the extent to which a small, non-profit online news agency focusing on social justice issues can provide a useful platform for informed articulation of causes and issues of the marginalized in a democracy characterized by profound social inequalities.

GroundUp occupies a space somewhere in the continuum between mainstream and alternative media. It has elements of 'mainstream' because some of its stories get republished in the mainstream media, and also because it's news production process is somewhat centralized and 'professionalised'. And yet it also contains strong organic, if inherent, elements of the alternative media. It adopted a 'bottom up' strategy of making news, namely going into marginalized communities and giving the ordinary citizens a voice in their stories, and some of its journalists are social activists who have to negotiate the dual identities which, naturally, find their way into the stories they write. It is also alternative because it is not commercially driven, but driven by the desire for social justice, according to Geffen, the founder/editor. The intention, he said, was to give particular and sustained attention to social issues that affect the poor and yet rarely receive adequate coverage in the mainstream press because of a range of factors that include cuts in funding and financing of newsrooms, juniorisation, and a hyper-commercialisation logic which mainstreams news from and about elites. He said:

> While I was working at the TAC[2] I was always bothered by the fact that, while the media were supportive of the work we were doing, the quality and quantity of articles on HIV was poor. I thought it would be good idea to start a news agency or publisher that focused on publishing stories to do with social justice in more depth using working class reporters from the places where the stories took place. And then getting these stories republished in the mainstream media.
>
> (Geffen, Interview, 20 April, 2015)

The location of GroundUp outside of the state and outside corporate hierarchies is significant in that it allows the agency, in principle, to probe issues with relative autonomy. The five full-time reporters and a photographer working for GroundUp refer to themselves as "working-class" journalists-cum-activists who have to constantly negotiate their shifting identities as "professionals" and yet social activists, and whose own material conditions are, to a large extent, synonymous with, or nearer to, the subjects of their stories. Two of the journalists had some formal training, while the rest only received a two-week inductive programme at GroundUp when they were hired.

Profiling journalists-cum-activists

The problematic notion of journalistic "objectivity" notwithstanding, it is commonly accepted that factors such as the class, gender and, in some instances, even race of journalists influence how they report on issues. In a study on the interplay of class and journalistic reportage in Chile, which, like South Africa, is a very unequal society, Teresa Correa (2009), noted the following:

> Although work routines and organizational and extra-media pressures shape news content and explain, in part, this bias against the poor, it has been argued that individual reporters' prejudices also play a role. Most journalists are college-educated people who usually report about their known environment and who have been socialized in a profession and in organisations that tend to value more powerful sectors of society. (p. 654)

References to both President Mandela's observation in 1994 and a press statement by *Abahlali baseMjondolo* cited above, in a way also demonstrate the extent to which both the class and professional orientation of journalists impact on the media framing of the "other". In 2005, Guy Berger argued that "too much" of South African journalism was "dull, dry and predictable – and of interest only to a bunch of middle-class elites", and added: "Much else is trivial entertainment for dumbed-down masses, without any illuminating information" (2005, p. 19).

Against this background, one would perhaps ask whether the GroundUp experiment of engaging working-class journalists to write stories about poor communities is likely to make a difference. The journalists believe this is so. One of the reporters joined GroundUp two years ago, having worked for Equal Education, a non-profit activist organization that advocates equal access to education for especially poor communities. She grew up and still lives in the townships, and claims to understand all its dynamics. "When gangs are planning a fight," she said, "they first give me a call to come and witness" (interview, 21 April 2015). The GroundUp reporter covering immigration and issues to do with foreign nationals, including xenophobic violence, is a Zimbabwean-born activist. She said, of her identity and its impact on her stories:

> Being a Zimbabwean is an advantage because other foreigners have mistrust when it comes to dealing with South African journalists. When I do these stories I write or speak with conviction because it affects me directly. When I report about issues like xenophobia, I am talking from experience and understand how it feels to be attacked or to wake up with all your

furniture you have worked for taken away. I understand and feel the loss.
(Interview, 30 April 2015)

Moving the centre? Reflecting on the impact of GroundUp stories

In interviews, reporters recalled several instances where their published stories attracted action from concerned authorities, to the benefit of ordinary people. In one instance, journalists covered a story whereby several teenage schoolgirls in the townships had to miss school during their monthly period because they could not afford sanitary pads. In some cases, they resorted to using sacks or other such risky options. In the process of writing the story, they discovered that President Jacob Zuma had promised to provide sanitary pads to poor schoolchildren during one of his country tours, but nothing had materialized. When the story got published,[3] it forced a local graphic designer to mobilize funds to help buy and donate the sanitary pads. GroundUp also invited prospective donors to visit their offices and drop off pads. The government was also pushed to act on the president's promise.

The other story involved general workers employed by a company subcontracted by the City of Cape Town to manage the portable toilets in the informal townships. Part of their job was to empty the toilets and clean the containers. Journalists from GroundUp tracked down a group of workers on their daily routine and discovered that they did not have any facilities where they could sit up and have lunch (they actually sat on top of the poo containers to have their lunch), and also did not have changing rooms. Some workers were also forced to temporarily store the containers in their backyards overnight, something that was a community health hazard. GroundUp published a series of stories on this matter, starting with the one under the headline, "A house full of faeces in Khayelitsha".[4] The publication of the story pushed the City of Cape Town to act swiftly on the matter.

When robbers attacked a crèche in Khayelitsha on payday in March 2015, they made off with a substantial amount of money meant for wages for teachers and other staff. GroundUp ran the story, and within a month readers had made donations almost equal to the stolen wages.[5] In August 2014, GroundUp ran a story on a day care centre in Khayelitsha where kids were forced to relieve themselves in buckets because there were no toilets. The publication of the story attracted the attention of the City Council,[6] which donated half a dozen portable toilets to the centre.

GroundUp stories are not just about problems in the townships. They also highlight community success stories and seek to put them on the bigger map. One journalist remembers penning a feature on the first coffee shop to be opened in Khayelitsha Township, called the Department of Coffee.[7] The story made it an instant hit with the community and indirectly helped owners expand and open a second coffee shop in another part of the city. Stories highlighting local talent – sport, music, art and so forth – often find their way into the pages of GroundUp, and in some cases attract the attention of both government and corporates with a view to offering forms of support and assistance. While the topics or subjects vary, the overall thrust appears to be a foregrounding of the experiences of the "other". In a typical week, GroundUp readers will have a range of feature, op-ed and profile options to read; from an op-ed on the experience of being black at the (predominantly white) University of Cape Town (UCT)'s law faculty, to a profile of a Cape Town firefighter and mother who has to leave her township home at 4am to help fight a blaze that has raged in the city's southern peninsula for weeks; from a profile of a poor child who dared the odds and became a schoolteacher, to a harrowing account of an asylum seeker who has had to wait for a document from the department of Home Affairs for seven years and still waiting.

Funding and viability

Former *Cape Times* editor, Alide Dasnois, now associate editor of GroundUp, sees the online news agency as complementing, rather than competing with mainstream news media,[8] and sees its main strength as its ability to amplify the voice of the powerless in South Africa. Against the backdrop of a ruthless "stripping" of newsrooms across the board in the frenzy of cost-cutting, non-profit news production holds the potential to deepen the participation of the marginalized. But the existential question is one of long-term sustainability. From the experience of the alternative press after 1994, it is not inconceivable that GroundUp may be "grounded" in the future if donors pull out. Geffen admits that although they are certain to live through 2015 because of the nearly R2million (US$166,000) in grants they have received for the year, for the most part of its existence GroundUp has been living "from hand to mouth". It is important to note that GroundUp has to complete for funding with other small non-profit news production organizations such as Health e-news, which focuses on health news reporting, and Amabungane, the investigative journalism wing of the *Mail & Guardian*. Although the government set up the Media Development and Diversity Agency (MDDA) a decade ago to support media needs of marginalized communities too poor to be of interest to advertising-driven commercial media (see Pillay, 2003), the agency has been financially hamstrung for the most part and therefore is unlikely to support initiatives such as GroundUp in the long run. The reality therefore is that non-profit news production sector, of which GroundUp is an interesting case, will survive for as long as philanthropies are willing to keep them running, and nothing more, at least in the absence of viable alternative funding models.

Conclusion

This explorative study sought to understand an emerging phenomenon of bottom-up journalism within South Africa and reflect on its impact or possible impact on the South African public sphere. What emerges is the picture of a phenomenon which, while not dramatic and immediate in terms of its impact, is certainly and increasingly drawing public attention to issues of the country's poor, issues which often receive scant attention from the mainstream press. There are several examples of stories which actually resulted in some immediate or short-term changes, as highlighted throughout this chapter. It is not possible to say, with certainty, whether the impact of GroundUp will be substantial in the long term. But the fact that it is drawing attention is itself significant. That some mainstream newspapers and online publications are republishing GroundUp stories is a strong statement about its impact. It is possible that the GroundUp phenomenon could encourage other newspapers to invest in community journalism, a sector long ignored by the media in the wake of ruthless funding cuts in the industry.

GroundUp's role should be viewed as complementary to, rather than supplanting, the mainstream media. It is a critical addition to the citizen's reading list. However, issues of access to the Internet remain critical, given that the majority of the country's poor – the very people for whom and about whom these stories are written – do not have regular access to it. There are also issues relating to the predominant use of the English language, although some of the stories are translated into Xhosa, which is one of the dominant languages spoken in the Cape Town townships. Finally, in the absence of a long-term 'blueprint' for viability, GroundUp remains vulnerable to the vagaries of donor fatigue.

Notes

1. Townships or "locations" in South Africa are high-density residential places which are marginal and located several miles away from the main cities. They were designed by colonial and apartheid governments to house mainly blacks, who would provide cheap labour to cities, farms and mines. Townships are often heavily congested, with both formal houses and informal tin shacks. Khayelitsha and Gugulethu are among the biggest townships in Cape Town, with a combined population of nearly half a million people as of 2011.
2. TAC is the acronym for the Treatment Action Campaign, an HIV/AIDS advocacy group which is credited with, among many other things, successfully forcing the South African government, under President Thabo Mbeki, to provide free anti-retroviral drugs to HIV-positive South Africans, including pregnant mothers.
3. See link: http://groundup.org.za/article/i-use-sock-sanitary-pad-says-langa-learner_2418, accessed 7 May 2015.
4. See link: http://groundup.org.za/features/faeces/house_faeces_0005.html, accessed 7 May 2015.
5. See link: http://groundup.org.za/article/readers-help-khayelitsha-creche-recover-robbery_2894, accessed 7 May 2015.
6. See link: http://groundup.org.za/article/new-toilets-khayelitsha-creche_2131, accessed 7 May 2015.
7. See link: http://groundup.org.za/article/department-coffee-opens-new-branches_2097, accessed 7 May 2015.
8. Taken from Alide Dasnois's presentation on GroundUp to the Centre for Film and Media Studies, 7 April 2015.

References

Atton, C. (2002). *Alternative Media*. London: Sage.

Bailey, O.G., Cammaerts, B., and Carpentier, N. (2008). *Understanding Alternative Media*. Buckingham: Open University Press.

Berger, G. 2005. "Current Challenges." In *Changing the Fourth Estate: Essays on South African Journalism*, Adrian Hadland (ed.), Cape Town: HSRC Press, pp. 19–26.

Correa, T. 2009. Does class matter? The effect of social class on journalists' ethical decision-making. *Journalism and Mass Communication Quarterly* 88 (3): 654–672.

Couldry, N. (2002). Mediation and alternative media, or relocating the centre of media and communication studies. *Media International Australia* (103): 24–31.

Duncan, J. and Glenn, I.E. (2010). "Turning Points in South African Television Policy and Practice since 1990". In *Media Policy in a Changing Southern Africa: Critical Reflections on Media Reforms in the Global Age*, D. Moyo and W. Chuma (eds.), Pretoria: Unisa Press, pp. 39–72.

Horwitz, R.B. (2001). *Communication and Democratic Reform in South Africa*. Cambridge: Cambridge University Press.

Jordaan, M. (2013). Poke me, I'm a journalist: The impact of Facebook and Twitter on newsroom routines and cultures at two South African weeklies. *Ecquid Novi: African Journalism Studies* 34(1): 21–35.

Marais, H. (1998). *South Africa Limits to Change: The Political Economy of Transition*. Cape Town: University of Cape Town Press.

Marais, H. (2011). *South Africa Pushed to the Limit: The Political Economy of Change*. Cape Town: University of Cape Town Press.

McChesney, R. (1999). *Rich Media, Poor Democracy: Communication Politics in Dubious Times*. New York: The New Press.

Moyo, D. 2007. Alternative media, diasporas and the mediation of the Zimbabwe crisis. *Ecquid Novi: African Journalism Studies* 28(1–2): 81–105.

Moyo D. 2009. Citizen journalism and the parallel market of information in Zimbabwe's 2008 election. *Journalism Studies*, 10: 4, 551–567.

Olorunisola, A., Tomaselli, K., and Teer-Tomaselli, R. (2011). "Political Economy, Representation, and Transformation in South Africa". In *Political Economy of Media Transformation in South Africa*, A. Olorunisola and K. Tomaselli (eds.), Cresskill, NJ: Hampton Press, pp. 1–12.

Pillay, D. (2003). The challenge of partnerships between the state, capital and civil society: The case of the media development and diversity agency in South Africa. *Voluntas: International Journal of Voluntary and Nonprofit Organisations* 14(4): 401–420.

Tomaselli, K. (2011). "Political Economy of the Transformation and Globalization of the South African Media 1994–1997". In *Political Economy of Media Transformation in South Africa*, A. Olorunisola and K. Tomaselli (eds.), Cresskill, NJ: Hampton Press, pp. 167–180.

Wasserman, H. (2010). *Tabloid Journalism in South Africa*. Cape Town: University of Cape Town Press.

Wits University Journalism School. (2013). *State of the Newsroom South Africa 2013: Disruptions and Transitions*. Johannesburg. Wits University Journalism.

Wits University Journalism School. (2014). *State of the Newsroom South Africa 2013: Disruptions Accelerated*. Johannesburg. Wits University Journalism.

14

Citizen Journalism and National Politics in Zimbabwe: The Case of the 2008 and 2013 Elections

Joseph Mujere and Wesley Mwatwara

Introduction

In his analysis of the 2013 elections in Zimbabwe, Donald Moore stopped short of saying that Zimbabwean democracy had breathed its last. Moore noted that a combination of Zimbabwe African National Union – Patriotic Front (ZANU-PF)'s tricks, coercion, populism, regional peers' collusion and the opposition's lackadaisical campaign produced a ZANU-PF "victory" that even surprised the victors (Moore, 2014, p. 47). In this election, the incumbent, Robert Gabriel Mugabe, got a 61% share of the presidential vote against Morgan Tsvangirai's 34%. Given the various intrusions on individual freedoms in the run-up to and during the election, many scholars, like Moore, wondered whether the democratization process could be saved from this massive onslaught. Scholars have identified issues how ZANU-PF invested into its power-retention motive through a number of measures including the military-dominated registry and electoral commission, the marshalling of the military and militia to its cause (which organs in turn tortured, killed and raped perceived opponents especially in the 2008 presidential run-off elections), manipulating the inclusive government and hiring a foreign gang of election mercenaries (Moore, 2014, p. 147). Languages of catastrophe that emerged from academics seemed to give democracy no chance, and also took away the initiative from the ordinary person. Counter-narratives that emerged during, and in the immediate aftermath, of these elections have masked the various ways through which pro-democratic forces within the country had, against seemingly insurmountable odds, made their voices heard and perhaps even narrowed the avenues that had previously been shamelessly manipulated by the incumbent political party. In the process, these forces have created a database for most electoral-related issues – which might be exploited by those seeking a more nuanced understanding of what actually transpired during the 2008 and 2013 elections.

A broad range of activities by the populace – under the banner of citizen journalism – has also been deployed to counter the state meta-narrative and, of course, in some cases to affirm it. Thus, citizen journalism has played an important role in shaping political attitudes, altering the boundaries of political interaction, and bringing into existence new methods and channels for resistance since the build-up to the 2008 elections, and the 2013 elections. Although the ZANU-PF party, which was at the forefront of narrowing the media space, tried to counter unfriendly electoral messages by unleashing its own propaganda to bolster its waning support, this effort arguably failed to penetrate the political underground, as it was simply an extension of what the unpopular public media was spreading.

Although there are scholarly works on the Internet and radios as tools for alternative source of information during these elections, subterranean forms of activism mobilized by the ordinary people during this time are still to be examined trenchantly (Dombo, n.d.; Manganga, 2012). Munangi (2012) examines the proliferation of Internet humour in the economic and political crisis in Zimbabwe. Moyo (2012) explores the various ways in which the Mugabe regime used the mass media as a tool for constructing a version of reality that advanced its cause in the face of rising global and local criticism between 2000 and 2008. Unlike Munangi and Moyo, we attempt an analysis of the various ways citizen journalists made substantive commentary on the "ubiquitous" struggle of Zimbabweans. This chapter shows how Zimbabweans have reacted to the narrowing of the democratic space by resorting to subterranean methods. Thus, we argue that a narrow media in Zimbabwe incubated the rise of citizen journalism.

Indeed, as Goldstein and Rotich (2010) have observed, much of the digital technology that is being utilized in the struggle between democracy and dictatorship has not been around long enough in Africa for one to adequately assess its impact. Thus, we readily concede the complexity of the factors that shape the development of political attitudes in Zimbabwe, but we also posit that citizen journalism has played its role. As such, our effort should be seen as an attempt to contribute to unpacking the richness and complexity of the 2008 and 2013 Zimbabwean elections through the lens of citizen journalism. This chapter demonstrates that citizen journalism is a relatively easy way of passing information with little danger of detection by "media hangmen".[1] Globally, this new window of communications has given both voice and greater decision-making powers to disadvantaged and vulnerable groups, in addition to creating opportunities for participation in governance and the economy. This is because more people now have greater and speedier reach to information at much lower cost (Charles-Iyoha, 2010). We conclude that, despite countermeasures by the pro-Mugabe forces, such as hacking into people's emails, generating counter text messages and eavesdropping on telephone conversations, the cultivation of a culture of consent to state propaganda was made difficult by the state's failure to counter mobile republics.

Theoretical framework

This chapter deploys the concept of the public sphere popularized by Jürgen Habermas (1989), whose work focuses on the struggles for space between the powerful and the less powerful sections of the society. In his book, *The Structural Transformation of the Public Sphere* (1989), Habermas defines the public sphere as a discursive space in which individuals and groups congregate to discuss matters of mutual interest and, where possible, reach a common judgement by way of rational-critical debate. Following Habermas, Okolo (2009, p. 58) defines the public sphere as an area of social life that guarantees freedom of expression in identifying common problems which in turn influence political action. It is, however, important to note that the public sphere is not homogenous but heterogeneous. One of the shortcomings of Habermas' concept is that print media and electronic media in Africa have often expressed the interests and preoccupations of the urban elite. The emergence of alternative media, such as mobile phones, the Internet and social networking forums, have expanded the concept of the public sphere by creating horizontal networks. As observed by Allan (2007, p. 3), the new information communication technologies (ICT) have enabled many ordinary people to adopt the roles of journalists and to create horizontal networks. Following Habermas (1989), this chapter examines how alternative media such as mobile phones and social media have engendered the emergence of citizen journalism or what Castells (2007, p. 248) calls "mass self-communication".

Media: The Zimbabwean context

During the period under study, the mobile phone became the main vehicle for filling in information gaps, especially through the circulation of rumour and humour relating to the elections (Chiumbu and Nyamanhindi, 2012, p. 63). The collapse of state-owned Tel*One during this time inadvertently led to a major increase in the use of mobile telephones by the majority of Zimbabweans. Indeed, the country's three mobile telephone networks (Econet Wireless, Telecel and the state-owned Net*One) failed to cope with the market demand for their services in Zimbabwe's hyperinflationary environment (Chiumbu and Nyamanhindi, 2012, pp. 64–65). The popularity of mobile phones at a time when income was generally low and when there was low consumer appetite in other sectors is explained by peculiar conditions obtaining in the industry. One of the reasons for the prevalent use of the mobile phone during this time was the low tariffs. Chiumbu and

Nyamanhindi have shown that mobile service providers and affiliate service companies tried increasing tariffs to remain viable, but were persistently frustrated by the Postal and Telecommunications Regulatory Authority of Zimbabwe (POTRAZ) (Banks, 2008; Chiumbu and Nyamanhindi, 2012, pp. 64–65). For instance, between 2007 and 2008, Econet tried, more than 160 times, to have its tariffs approved by POTRAZ, without any luck (Chiumbu and Nyamanhindi, 2012, pp. 64–65). These sub-economic tariffs not only increased the subscriber base for the mobile phone companies but also made it cheaper for Zimbabweans to talk for hours on the phone. On average, Zimbabweans were spending 200 hours per month on the phone, against an international average of 40; hence, Zimbabweans were "literally sleeping on the network" (Chiumbu and Nyamanhindi, 2012, p. 65).

The Mugabe regime was aware of the danger of an uncontrolled public media as there had been examples of governments toppled by mobile activists. Notable ones include the deposition from power of Philippine president, Joseph Estrada, in early 2001, following text message-fuelled mass demonstrations in Manila (Banks, 2008), and the Arab Spring 2011. As such, a battery of laws had been passed to stifle dissent. However, the Zimbabwe government's enactment of legislation such as the Access to Information and Protection of Privacy Act (AIPPA) and the Interception of Communications Act and Public Order and Security Act (POSA) impacted negatively on accessibility of information. AIPPA restricted the activities of the opposition and civic forces in the public sphere and controlled the independent press (Raftopoulos, 2009, p. 215). Under its provisions: no one could operate a mass media service in Zimbabwe unless it had been registered (AIPPA: Section 66 [1]) and no mass media service or news agency could employ a journalist unless he or she was accredited (AIPPA: Sections 78 [4] and 79 [7]). Only Zimbabwean citizens were allowed to own mass media services, while non-citizens were not even allowed to hold shares in mass media services (AIPPA: Section 65). This provision made it difficult, if not impossible, for Zimbabwean mass media services to get foreign financing. Only citizens and permanent residents were allowed to be employed as journalists; aliens and non-residents could only be accredited for a maximum of 60 days (AIPPA: Section 79 [34]). Journalists and owners of mass media services who published false information could be imprisoned for up to two and three years respectively (AIPPA: Sections 80 and 64). News reporting became very difficult since journalists could not operate within the country unless vetted by a state-appointed commission. This effectively placed a ban on all foreign media. By 2009 it had resulted in the arrest of at least 40 journalists, even though few had been convicted (Media Monitoring Project Zimbabwe [hereafter MMPZ] Report, December 2008, p. 40). Newspapers that were viewed as critical of President Mugabe's controversial rule were closed for violating these laws. In November 2003, the *Daily News*, the country's remaining independent daily newspaper, was closed. By April 2010, the

Associated Newspapers of Zimbabwe (ANZ), publishers of the banned *Daily News* and the *Daily News on Sunday,* were still awaiting a licence despite meeting requirements since 2006 (MMPZ Report, December 2008, p. 40). Jonathan Moyo defended the law thus:

> With this law, it's not possible for any mischievous person to use the media for regime change. They [Western countries] are talking about removing the liberation regime and putting in the neo-liberalism regime, but we will change governments in democratic elections.
>
> (*The Herald,* 2 December 2004)

Though there were amendments to the laws (AIPPA, POSA and Broadcasting Services Act (BSA)) in 2007, there was no corresponding political will by the regulating authorities to abide by the reforms and enforce compliance. Individual journalists fell victim to these laws in the form of assault, arrest, detention, kidnappings, torture and even murder as in the case of one Edward Chikomba, a part-time Zimbabwe Broadcasting Corporation (ZBC) cameraman, who was murdered in March 2007 after suspected state agents abducted him at his Harare home (MMPZ Report, December 2008, p. 11). After the March 2008 harmonized elections, the opposition political parties were denied any form of direct access to the national broadcaster including paid advertising (MMPZ Report, December 2008, p. 11). Furthermore, despite a court ruling outlawing the government's monopoly of the electronic media in 2000, by 2008, ZBC, the state broadcaster, still had monopoly as no new players had been licensed. This is regardless of the fact that, throughout the period under study, Zimbabwe had the capacity to issue 56 district (community) radio stations; 31 commercial radio stations; three national television stations and two national commercial FM radio stations (Misa, 2011).

In addition to restrictions, the economic deterioration in the country further reduced people's access to alternative sources of information. The production of newsprint at Mutare Board & Paper Mills plunged to 30% of its capacity due to power cuts, coal and foreign currency shortages (*Financial Gazette,* 31 January 2008). In turn, these difficulties resulted in the thinning of newspapers and, in the process, undermined people's access to alternative sources of information. The rising cost of newspapers also meant that people's access even to "doctored" information was restricted severely. The cost of newspapers soared to levels beyond the reach of many Zimbabweans. For instance, just before the March 2008 elections, *The Herald* and *The Chronicle* cost Z$3 million and Z$2.5 million respectively, while the privately owned weeklies cost between Z$11 million and Z$15 million (MMPZ Report, December 2008, p. 42). At the time, there was an official exchange rate of Z$7.1 million per US$1 (http://news.bbc.co.uk/2/hi/business/7244769. stm). Just before the presidential run-off elections in June 2008, newspaper prices skyrocketed to $200 million for the dailies and $20 billion for the weeklies (MMPZ Report, December 2008, p. 42). All these developments made the mobile phone the cheapest source of information and therefore an alternative tool for spreading information not available in the public media.

Clearly, at the time of the 2008 election, mobile ownership was low by regional standards, but the locals showed remarkable adaptability through sharing information received via mobile phones. Regardless of low penetration percentage, text messaging influenced a lot of people, including those who did not personally possess the gadget. Generally, Zimbabweans are not individualistic when it comes to sharing information, especially that which spoke about the malpractices in government.[2] As such, mobile phones at times conveniently ceased to be personal gadgets as people shared information sent through texts. Kubatana, a non-governmental organization (NGO) promoting human rights and good governance in Zimbabwe, observed that:

> In the past, we have observed how many people share the same phone – for example, we can receive several different opinions on the same issue from the same number in a day. Or we receive multiple requests to send material to different names and addresses, all coming from the same mobile number. These addresses are typically from schools or growth points in rural Zimbabwe.
>
> (Atwood, 2010, p. 101)

"Breaking the barriers": The 2008 elections

Despite a strong system of disinformation and misinformation erected by the Mugabe regime by 2008, initiatives were developed by mobile phone users to circumvent this. Zimbabweans adapted the mobile phone to the social, political, cultural and economic realities of the country. The success of the pro-democratic elements in Zimbabwe against the regime was highlighted by the success of the opposition in a highly contested election in March 2008. Government crackdown on anti-government activists forced such people to resort to non-confrontational "asymmetric" methods of resistance. Since opposition was latent there was a false impression that the opposition had been crushed, and this partly explain the bravado with which the Mugabe regime went into the first round of the election. However, once they retreated into the "private sphere", anti-government elements activated their mobile phones to mobilize their friends, neighbours, associates and relatives. Regardless of its failure to stamp out this form of dissent, the state machinery managed to scare away some potential players in the texting game. When it became apparent that carrying or spreading "subversive" messages could earn someone time in the dungeons or even a premature death, some text messagers became very selective, resorting to sharing information only with people they trusted and thought would "never" report them to the police.[3]

Besides these uncoordinated activities by individuals, political parties and some NGOs made extensive use of text messages. Journalists from private media companies circumvented government censorship and cast an important spotlight on the violence in Zimbabwe through text messages (Banks, 2008). In some cases, the mobile phone was used in conjunction with the Internet and/or radio. Gerry Jackson's SW Radio Africa, founded in 2006, based in the UK and broadcasts to Zimbabwe on short wave, is an example of the relationship between the radio and text messages (Banks, 2008). In the face of jamming by government in 2007, SW Radio started sending text message-based news alerts to nearly 30,000 subscribers in Zimbabwe using FrontlineSMS.[4] Talking about the importance of text messaging during the 2008 March and June elections, Jackson revealed that, "the text messages definitely helped inform voters during the election period...It also kept hope alive during that terrible post-election time when Mugabe unleashed such appalling violence...and we named and shamed when we knew exactly who was perpetrating violence in particular areas" (Rhodes, 2009). SW Radio's texts were numerous, especially in the period leading to the March 2008 elections till the formation of the inclusive government in February 2009. By 2010, they had reduced mobile text releases from daily to twice-weekly, on Tuesdays and Fridays.[5]

In April 2010, the authors received several messages touching key issues in the country. One of the texts read, "WOZA [Women of Zimbabwe Arise] leaders arrested, Thursday at ZESA [Zimbabwe Electricity Supply Authority] demo. Cops use ZPF [ZANU-PF] cars to help to invade SA [South African] owned ranch near Beitbridge. Thursday was 10th anniversary of Chiminya, Mabika murder."[6] What this text message demonstrates is that SW Radio compressed messages and send them in a format that makes intelligible reading to those that are abreast of current affairs. As an instrument that was meant to "inform" people about certain events, its target group was a small section of society that accessed other sources of information such as the Internet and pirate radio broadcasts. Such messages assumed a prior knowledge which some did not possess. Using this example, it is clear some people may not have known what WOZA was, or who Chiminya and Mabika were or who killed them.[7] However, the case of one Tendai Tsapfura, a worker at the University of Zimbabwe, shows that some recipients of SW Radio texts shared information with colleagues who were not subscribed.[8] Tsapfura revealed that 20 university students congregated in his room "every night" to watch satellite news and to access SW Radio texts.[9] With some exaggeration, he emphatically stated that these university students duplicated and spread such information to their friends and relatives.[10] However, he mentioned something controversial but nonetheless worthy noting. From his personal experiences, he claimed that one of his regular visitors was one Adhala Maths, a neighbour who possessed a Net*One SIM card and therefore could not receive messages from SW Radio.[11] Despite the fact that SW

Radio text facility transcended boundaries created by the state's media policy, the extent to which the interpretations given to SW Radio texts were in sync with those of the original sender(s) remains unknown.

Another radio station, Voice of the People (VOP), set up by former ZBC staff with funding from the Soros Foundation, operates a radio station using a leased short-wave transmitter in Madagascar (Rhodes, 2009). Prior to these initiatives by VOP and SW Radio, in 2005 Kubatana started sending texts that gave the "latest" news to citizens. Kubatana also ran a "What would you like a free Zimbabwe to look like?" initiative. A combination of SMS and email was used in the initiative, with text messages such as "Kubatana! No senate results as at 5.20 pm. What changes do YOU want in a free Zim? Let's inspire each other. Want to know what others say? SMS us your email address" sent out to mobile subscriber lists (Rhodes, 2009). In May 2008, the AfricaNews website launched a project in which its staffers used phones enabled with GPRS (General Packet Radio Service) to send text, image and video files (Rhodes, 2009). The advantage of the method was that the journalists did not have to go to the heavily monitored cyber-cafés, and could film without drawing attention from state security details. Other mobile phone technology of which the opposition forces made use for campaigning purposes included e-cards, ringtones and mobile phone screensavers (*BBCNEWS/AFRICA*, 24 June 2008).

Text messages were politically important during the March and June 2008 elections. The Electoral Laws Amendment Act (2008) required that polling stations be in areas readily accessible to the electorate and for results to be displayed outside the polling stations. At the polling stations, polling agents representing different political parties sent the results to district command centres. From there, results were sent to the provincial command centres, and finally the National Command Centre for collation. Usually such results were texted.[12] Soon after the counting, agents from different political parties would SMS results before they were announced. Since each polling station was accounted for in this process, the mobile phone was used to keep the election "honest" and to narrow the possibility of vote rigging (Rheinhold, n.d.). This was similar to the Kenyan 2007 presidential elections. As votes in the Kenyan presidential election were being counted in precincts nationwide, reporters relayed the tallies by text message back to newsrooms in Nairobi (Rhodes, 2009). The count was updated regularly online and in other media. International election monitors later found fraud in the national vote counting using the early poll reports from journalists by mobile phone-based SMS (Rhodes, 2009). In Zimbabwe, the use of the mobile phone in the parallel collation of results, at the time made the election one of the most controversial ever held in Africa.

A brazen attempt by the Mugabe regime to stop the circulation of "subversive" mobile texts involved unleashing its militia on the general populace to "inspect" people's phones. Some interviewees alleged that, at some roadblocks, ZANU-PF militias demanded to see mobile texts. However, these methods were not effective in stemming the regime's unpopularity, as mobile text messages, in the words of one Spanish journalist, Eva Dominguez, "make news run like hell" (Rheingold, n.d. 227). Thus, despite a myriad of obstacles put in place by the Mugabe government, new ICTs, including the mobile phone, offered a vent through which people could continue to receive information which was not available on the public media.

By the time of the 2013 harmonized elections, numerous developments in ICTs had taken place, hence there was, in addition to mobile phone text messaging, a whole range of social media platforms, including Facebook, Twitter and YouTube, which had repercussions on information dissemination. These platforms were very important for politicians (on both sides of the political divide), civilians and civic society organizations. The case of Baba Jukwa, a faceless Facebook character, who emerged in March 2013 claiming to be a disaffected ZANU-PF insider with "top" secrets about the internal workings of that party, is very interesting in as far as it exposes how citizen journalism can cause despondency within the camp of those considered powerful. This shadowy character, who specialized in very controversial stories about top officials in government and ZANU-PF, as well as "exposing" cases of state violence, assassination plots, corruption and rigging of elections, epitomizes the efficacy of citizen journalism.

Baba Jukwa presented himself as a disgruntled top-ranking ZANU-PF official who was keen to expose the party's secrets and to assist "progressive forces" in toppling it. Judging by the number of people who followed Baba Jukwa on Facebook, by liking the page or just visiting it, it is evident that Baba Jukwa had risen to become a key source of information for many Zimbabweans. At times, he reported on ZANU-PF Politburo meetings in real time, and, to many Zimbabweans, his reports seemed to reveal the inner workings of ZANU-PF. Free from the fetter of restrictions imposed by the media laws such as AIPPA, and masked by the obvious use of a pseudonym, Baba Jukwa provided a platform that sought to counterbalance government propaganda. Although the popularity of Baba Jukwa among people sympathetic to the opposition political parties failed to translate into votes, the success of his Facebook page showed that citizen journalism was slowly transcending traditional journalism in the provision of information untainted by government propaganda. One reporter noted that "although the number of 'likes' is not transferable to the number of vote a party would get come election time, it does however reflect the number of audiences it is reaching with every message posted on the web page".[13] In a way, Baba Jukwa became the epitome of unfettered citizen journalism and, because of that, he gained both fame and infamy in equal measure.

With over 170,000 followers by June 2013, Baba Jukwa dominated discussions not only among affected ZANU-PF officials but also among many ordinary folks who could not go a day without clicking his page for the "latest" inside detail.[14] Baba Jukwa attracted such interest in the very heart of ZANU-PF that the party took the idea of silencing this character very seriously – offering a whooping USD$330,000 to anyone who could unmask Baba Jukwa. Indeed, when the Deputy Mines Minister and ZANU-PF member of parliament, Edward Chindori-Chininga was involved in a fatal accident, many believed that he had been silenced for being Baba Jukwa.[15] This, together with the arrest of other Facebook users for crimes such as insulting the president, put pressure on many users based in Zimbabwe to either tone down their messages or take down their pages. Consequently, the Baba Jukwa page was suddenly taken down in July 2014.[16] This was only after Edmund Kudzayi, the *Sunday Mail* editor, suspected of being Baba Jukwa, was arrested on 19 June 2014 and faced with a litany of charges including: attempting to commit acts of insurgency, banditry, sabotage or terrorism as defined under Section 189(1)(a) and (b) as read with Section 23(1)(a) of the Criminal Law (Codification and Reform) Act (ch. 9, p. 23); undermining the authority or insulting the president as defined in Section 33 (2)(a)(ii) of the same Act; and publishing or communicating false statements prejudicial to the state.[17] The ongoing search for Baba Jukwa in Zimbabwe following Kudzayi's acquittal presents a new stage in ZANU-PF's struggle to cultivate a culture of consent in Zimbabwe. Pinned as it is on the identity of a mobile phone owner in whose name an email account spreading "subversive" messages was opened, this phase presents a different case. This crusade provides a situation that is very different from that obtaining in 2008 when SIM card owners were not yet compelled by law to register their SIM cards, and when mobile phone activism was still a relatively safe mode of communication for pro-democracy voices.

Apart from Baba Jukwa, another Facebook character who also gained popularity among Zimbabweans, especially in 2013, was Mugrade Seven. At its height, his/her page had more than 200,000 followers. Mugrade Seven neither claimed to be a government insider nor stated his/her political agenda. However, Mugrade Seven gathered, synthesized and pasted articles from various newspapers. News items posted on the page ranged from sports to political news. However, just as in the case of Baba Jukwa, the government was not happy with a number of articles which Mugrade Seven posted, and the popularity which the page was gaining. In the end, as it began to be rumoured that Mugrade Seven was in fact a prominent journalist hiding behind a pseudonym, and as government efforts to unmask the administrator of the page increased, the page was suddenly pulled down, in May 2014, marking the demise of another popular Facebook platform challenging the hegemony of the state-controlled press. It was generally argued that the sudden pulling down of the Mugrade Seven page was prompted by the "unmasking" of journalists Mxolisi Ncube and Mkululi Chimoio by government agents as the people behind the Baba Jukwa Facebook page.[18]

It is evident that ZANU-PF had realized that, for its propaganda to work, it had to control the new media, especially mobile telecommunication and the Internet. Consequently, in the period leading to the July 2013 harmonized elections, ZANU-PF took its battle with the opposition to the mediascape. It targeted mobile telecommunication companies and social media, as well as "pirate" radio stations. It responded to the emergence of citizen journalism and use of social media by seeking to criminalize these activities. Freedom House reported that, in the week leading to the July 2013 harmonized elections, POTRAZ issued a "directive to mobile phone providers to block the dissemination of bulk SMS messages".[19] A number of people were also intimidated and arrested for posting "subversive" messages on Facebook or sending such messages via the WhatsApp platform.

Readers' comments on articles in online newspapers, as well as on posts on social networking platforms such as Facebook, can also be considered to constitute citizen journalism. One of the things that attracted viewers to the Baba Jukwa and Mugrade Seven Facebook pages were actually the myriad comments posted by people on various stories. Whilst some engaged in debate by posting comments, others just enjoyed the exchanges without commenting. According to Outing (2005): "Readers routinely use such comments to bring up some point that was missed by the writer, or add new information that the reporter didn't know about. Such readers can make the original story better." Thus, citizen journalism can take several forms. It is not just about reporting but can also involve reacting to stories which can trigger debate on the comments page. Although some people can use anonymous names to post objectionable comments, allowing readers to comment on stories opens up spaces for debate and allows the story to develop in various ways and directions.

One of the key weaknesses of citizen journalism in Zimbabwe ironically stems from its major strength, that is, its reliance on alternative media, especially mobile phones and social networking platforms such as WhatsApp, Facebook and Twitter. This alternative media arguably "remain in the hands of the 'media-literate' professionals" (Ford and Gil, 2001, p. 204). Furthermore, in Africa, Internet penetration is still quite low, which means that it can only be accessed by a small section of the populace. Moreover, information on the Internet "is often unreliable, transient, or biased" (Ford and Gil, 2001, p. 205). In spite of this, however, alternative media is often arguably the only option for people living under repressive regimes where communicative spaces are restricted.

Conclusion

This chapter contributes to the ongoing historical conversation on the Zimbabwean crisis by providing analyses of how citizen journalism contributed to the spread of anti-government messages in the 2008 and

2013 harmonized elections. It has revealed that, though conditions for the free circulation of ideas and information were absent in Zimbabwe before, during and after the 2008 harmonized elections, patterns of political behaviour have partly been shaped by the proliferation of alternative news offered by citizen journalists. The chapter has also demonstrated how citizen journalism altered the boundaries of human interaction, bringing into existence new methods of resistance. Social media platforms, including mobile phones, text messages, WhatsApp and Twitter, among others, offered an alternative source of information to the news-starved masses whose only sources of information in the previous elections had been the state-controlled media. Despite the not-so-promising result, especially for those who had expected a change of government in the 2008 and 2013 elections, it remains important to state that these ICTs continue to give people a platform on which to air their political messages without restrictions.

Notes

1. A term generally used in the media fraternity in Zimbabwe to refer to members of the Media and Information Commission, chaired by the pro-government media guru, Dr Tafataona Mahoso, who played a leading role in the incarceration of many journalists and the closure of privately owned newspapers.
2. Interview with Sylvester Dombo, 14 April 2010.
3. Interview with Chipo Nebu, 17 April 2010.
4. FrontlineSMS is a software that turns a laptop and a mobile phone into a central communications hub. Once installed, the program enables users to send and receive text messages with groups of people through mobile phones.
5. SW Radio sent a notifier in January 2010 that news items were not going to be sent daily as before but twice a week, on Tuesdays and Fridays.
6. Sender: SWRADIO, message centre: 61418070298, sent: 16/0/4/2010, 20:11:05.
7. Informal interaction with Kule Tempted, 19 April 2010.
8. Interview with Tendai Tsapfura, 14 April 2010.
9. Ibid.
10. Ibid.
11. Ibid.
12. Interview with Haddon Shava.
13. Zimbabwe: Political gladiators on social networks. *Financial Gazette* 11 April 2013. 14 April 2010.
14. Baba Jukwa warnings come true, *Daily News*. http://www.dailynews.co.zw/articles/2013/06/23/baba-jukwa-warnings-come-true, Retrieved19 April 2015.
15. Exactly how Chindori-Chininga died: Baba Jukwa, *ZimEye*. http://www.zimeye.com/exactly-how-chindori-chininga-died-baba-jukwa/, Retrieved 19 April 2015.
16. Mary Ann Jolly, Mugabe offers $300,000 for outing of anonymous whistleblower Baba Jukwa. *ABC News*, 17 July 2013. http://www.abc.net.au/news/2013-07-17/mugabe-offers-243002c000-for-outing-of-anonymous-whistleblower/4824498, Retriev 19 April 2015.
17. http://www.pindula.co.zw/Edmund_Kudzayi, Retrieved 19 April 2015.

18. Mugrade Seven quits Facebook, 2 June 2014. http://www.myzimbabwe.co.zw/news/196-mugrade-seven-quits-facebook, Retrieved 18 April 2015.
19. https://freeddomhouse.org/report/freedom-net/2014/zimbabwe, Retrieved 18 April 2015.

References

Allan, Stuart. (2007). Citizen journalism and the rise of "mass self-communication": Reporting the London bombings. *Global Media Journal* 1(1): 1–20.

Atwood, A. (2010). "Kubatana in Zimbabwe: Mobile Phones for Advocacy". In *SMS Uprising: Mobile Phone Activism in Africa*, S. Ekine (ed.), Cape Town: Pambazuka Press, 86–104.

"Baba Jukwa's brother arrested". http://www.myzimbabwe.co.zw/news/379-baba-jukwa-s-brother-arrested.html, Retrieved 3 July 2014.

Banks, K. (2008). Mobile phones play role in Zimbabwe. www.kiwanja.net/database/ . . . /article_PC_World_mobiles_activism.pd. Retrieved on 19 April 2015.

Castells, Manuel. (2007). Communication, power and counter-power in the network society. *International Journal of Communication* 1(1): 29.

Charles-Iyoha, C. (2010). "Mobile telephony: Closing the gap". In *SMS Uprising Mobile Phone Activism in Africa*, S. Ekine (ed.), Cape Town: Pambazuka Press, 116–123.

Chiumbu, S., and Musemwa, M. (eds.). (2012). *Crisis! What Crisis? The Multiple Dimensions of the Zimbabwean Crisis*. Cape Town: HSRC Press.

Dombo, Sylvester. (n.d.). Alternative or subversive? "Pirate radio stations" and the opening up of spaces of freedom and alternative politics in Zimbabwe, 2000–2010. Unpublished Manuscript, History Department, University of Zimbabwe.

Dzirutwe, M. (2006). Mobile phone boom eludes Zimbabwe. *Reuters*, 26 June 2006.

Ford, Tamara Villarreal, and Gil, Geneve. (2001). "Radical Internet Use". In *Radical Media: Rebellious Communication and Social Movements*, John Downing (ed.), London: Sage Publications, 201–234.

Goldstein, J., and Rotich, J. (2010). "Digitally Networked Technology in Kenya's 2007–08 Post-Election Crisis". In *SMS Uprising Mobile Phone Activism in Africa*, S. Ekine (ed.), Cape Town: Pambazuka Press, pp. 124–137.

Habermas, Jürgen. (1989). *The Structural Transformation of the Public Sphere: An Inquiry into a Category of Bourgeois Society*. Cambridge, MA: The MIT Press.

Hye won, K, Jong deok K. and Hae yun Lee (2009). *A Study of the Public Sphere of Mobile Media*. www.iasdr2009.or.kr/Papers/IASDR2009_Proceedings_abstract.pdf, retrieved 26 June 2014.

Laiton, C. (2014). Another Baba Jukwa arrest. *Newsday*, 26 June 2014.

"Madzibaba" in trouble for posing in police uniform on Facebook. *The Herald*, 6 June 2014.

Manganga, K. (2012). The Internet as public sphere: A Zimbabwean case study (19992008). *Africa Development* 37(1): 103–118.

Media Monitoring Project Zimbabwe. (2008). *The Propaganda War on Electoral Democracy: Report on the Media's Coverage of Zimbabwe's 2008 Elections*. Harare: Media Monitoring Project Zimbabwe.

Media Monitoring Project Zimbabwe. (2009). *The Language of Hate: Inflammatory, Intimidating and Abusive Comments of Zimbabwe's 2008 Elections*. Harare: Media Monitoring Project Zimbabwe.

MISA-Zimbabwe. (2011). *State of the media report*. www.misa.org/downloads/2011/All_STID2011.pdf, retrieved 4 June 2014.

Moore, D. (2014). Zimbabwe's democracy in the wake of the 2013 election: Contemporary and historical perspectives. *Strategic Review for Southern Africa* 36(1): 47–71.

Moyo, Dumisani. (2009). Citizen journalism and the parallel market of information in Zimbabwe's 2008 election. *Journalism Studies* 10(4): 1–17.

Moyo, Dumisani. (2012). "Mediating Crisis: Realigning Media Policy and Deployment of Propaganda in Zimbabwe, 2000–2008". In *Crisis! What Crisis? The Multiple Dimensions of the Zimbabwean Crisis*, S. Chiumbu and M. Musemwa (eds.), Cape Town: HSRC Press: pp. 176–198.

Moyo, Dumisani. (2013). Alternative media, diasporas and the mediation of the Zimbabwe crisis. *Ecquid Novi: African Journalism Studies* 28(1&2): 81–105.

Munangi, J. (2012). "'A Zimbabwean Joke Is No Laughing Matter': E-Humour and Versions of Subversion". In *Crisis! What Crisis? The Multiple Dimensions of the Zimbabwean Crisis*, S. Chiumbu and M. Musemwa (eds.), Cape Town: HSRC Press, pp. 161–175.

Musila, G.A., and Moyo, D. (2012). "Subterranean Faultlines: Representations of Robert Mugabe in South African Press Cartoons". In *Crisis! What Crisis? The Multiple Dimensions of the Zimbabwean Crisis*, S. Chiumbu and M. Musemwa (eds.), Cape Town: HSRC Press, pp. 199–224.

Okolo, M.S.C. (2009). Contesting the African Public Sphere: A Philosophical Re-imaging of Power and Resistance in Ngugi's "Wizard of the Crow". *Africa Development, 34*(2): 59–80.

Outing, S. (2005). The 11 Layers of Citizen Journalism. *Poynter online*.

Police claim Kudzayi is Baba Jukwa (See charge sheet copy). (2014) http://www.inews.co.zw/article/2231/Police%20claim%20Kudzayi%20is%20Baba%20Jukwa%20(See%20charge%20sheet%20copy), retrieved 07 August 2015.

Raftopoulos, Brian. (2009). "The Crisis in Zimbabwe, 1998–2008". In *Becoming Zimbabwe: A History from the Pre-Colonial Period to 2008*, B. Raftopoulos and A. Mlambo (eds.), Harare: Weaver Press, pp. 212–232.

Rheingold, H. (n.d.). *Mobile Media and Political Collective Action*. http://www.rheingold.com/texts/PoliticalSmartMobs.pdf. Retrieved on 19 April 2015.

Rhodes, T. (2009). In text-message reporting, opportunity and risk. *Committee to Protect Journalists*. http://cpj.org/2009/02/text-messaging-africa.php. Retrieved on 19 April 2015.

Zaba F. (2014). "Ministers face arrest over Baba Jukwa." http://www.theindependent.co.zw/2014/06/27/ministers-face-arrest-baba-jukwa-saga/, retrieved 7 August 2015.

Zhangazha, T. (2014). Madzibaba Chacha, social media and Zim's enthusiastic "Big Brother". *Nehanda Radio*. http://nehandaradio.com/2014/06/17/madzibaba-chacha-social-media-zims-enthusiastic-big-brother/#sthash.jvjWK5EI.dpuf. Retrieved on 19 April 2015.

"Zimbabwe inflation spirals again." http://news.bbc.co.uk/2/hi/business/7244769.stm, retrieved on 19 April 2015.

15

Citizen Journalism in Kenya as a Contested "Third Space"

George Ogola and Mike Owuor

Introduction

Outside the formal media structures, Kenya has always had a broad range of vibrant alternative sites for public expression and deliberation. As a reaction to successive post-independence governments' domination and control of mainstream media, Kenya's "cultural workers", through music, drama, comedy and "new journalism", have routinely developed a powerful oppositional narrative that constantly punctures the majesty of power, offering the "margins" not only a space but also a language with which to confront the excesses of the state. This was particularly so in the 1990s, during the clamour for political pluralism. Because the broader communication infrastructure was not radically changed despite political pluralism and media liberalisation in the 1990s (see Ogola, 2015), these spaces and expressive forms for alternative political narratives have remained profoundly relevant. Broadly conceived, citizen journalism, as one of these alternative expressive forms, has been instrumental for ensuring executive accountability and public participation in national debates.

There are a number of citizen journalism projects and experiments, which, though limited in scope, have attempted to reorient their journalism to privilege "outsider" voices in issues of national and community import. From small projects such as *Ghetto Mirror, The Kibera Journal* and *Kibera News Network* (Dugmore and Ligaga, 2014), to much better-resourced and organized examples such as Ushahidi, citizen journalism has made a powerful case for the problematization of mainstream media practices. That case has now been made even more strongly and unambiguously online: a platform now so fundamentally inalienable to contemporary national conversations. Yet, while broadly defined by its proclivity to harbour oppositional narratives, Kenya is also witnessing a gradual appropriation of citizen journalism by state actors. The realm of the "popular" is being fiercely contested, as both the state and the margins try to "own" the space – thus define the conversations therein – as well as its parameters.

This chapter seeks to explore two key issues alongside several secondary but no less important points in the wider conversation about citizen journalism in Kenya. First, drawing on specific examples used here for purposes of illustration, the chapter will examine citizen journalism more broadly, focusing on how it has sustained a discourse of accountability and public deliberation while speaking from the affective experiences of the "margins". We refer in part to its influence, however limited, on mainstream journalism, but also to its much more traditional "home" outside mainstream press, that is, individuals operating autonomously. Second, we will critically reflect on the emerging incursion into citizen journalism by state actors, and assess the impact of this on the character and orientation of this journalism.

Theorizing citizen journalism

Citizen journalism remains an untidy concept. Its definitions are notoriously muddied, largely due to the competing renderings of what it is, what it claims to be and what it ought to be. With new media technologies providing even more possibilities for communication and communication practices, the term has become ever more elastic. Mythen (2010, p. 45), for example, notes how citizen journalism has now been "facilitated by technological convergence and the development of an interactive media environment in which citizens are not simply sources of information and /or audiences, but also recorders and creators or news". Citing Bowman and Willis, he goes further, talking about technology enabling the emergence of various forms of citizen journalism, allowing the public to perform "an active role in the process of collecting, reporting, analysing and disseminating news and information" (Ibid.). Particularly noteworthy here is the significance given to the plurality of the form, a point we address when we look at specific examples. Moyo (2009, p. 553) similarly observes that new communication technologies are "heralding a new era where the power to define what is news has been recast and decentered". The role of new technology in dismantling gatekeeping hierarchies and creating more horizontal and non-linear relationships between news producers and consumers is an argument on which many scholars seem to agree. However, there is still little agreement on how best to define citizen journalism. Knight and Cook (2013, p. 95) observe that, although the term remains widely circulated, it is inconsistently defined. They cite several examples to reflect this lack of consensus, including, among other definitions, Jay Rosen's description of citizen journalists as "the people formerly known as the audience", but argue that this definition is too loose to be credible. They similarly have a problem with Mark Deuze's definition of citizen journalists as "news-producing" consumers. They seem to imply that, as with Rosen's attempt, Deuze's definition fails to provide a reliable understanding of what citizen journalism really is, focusing instead on those who produce it.

In an attempt to historicize its origins, and perhaps its evolutionary character and meanings over time, Knight and Cook (2013) argue that the term, or at least its contemporary meanings and renderings, can be attributed to three critical works: Dan Gillmor's book *We the Media* (2004), Bowman and Willis' (2003) *We Media* report and Jay Rosen's "Beyond Objectivity" (1993), all of which seemed to imply that citizen journalism was a corrective to a dysfunctional (American) press; one which was increasingly disengaged from its audience. Others, such as Dvorkin (2007) and Meyer (2007), however, claim that the "movement" can be traced to the 1988 US presidential elections when, as Mythen (2010, p. 47) observes, "sections of the American public expressed dissatisfaction about bland media reporting of the issues and disillusionment with mainstream politics". Collectively, these scholars seem to attribute the rise of citizen journalism to the growing quest for a journalism that is much more subjective, and is unrestrained by formal institutional journalistic norms and practices.

The criticism of mainstream journalistic practices in the United States and around the world is common among proponents of alternative forms of journalism. The mainstream press is said to necessarily construct and exclude marginal voices. In part, this is because mainstream journalism derives legitimacy from practices that, by default, privilege power, variously manifested in the nature of sources it uses, places covered and stories told (see Van Ginneken, 1998). The reliance, for example, on news values, discussed at length initially by Galtung and Ruge (1965) and later by others such as Van Ginneken (1998) and Harcup and O'Neill (2001), demonstrates how mainstream media exclusion of those on the margins and the privileging of the powerful are intrinsic to mainstream journalism. It is against this background that citizen journalism is seen by some as a corrective to institutionalized forms of exclusion.

The theorization of citizen journalism has, however, been described by some as an incomplete project. Campbell (2014), for example, argues that while scholarship on the subject has tended to focus on the "journalism" in citizen journalism, there is a remarkable silence on the nature of the "citizenship" in citizen journalism. To theorize citizen journalism, he argues, requires both a theorization of the citizenship as well as the journalism in citizen journalism. Writing on the "journalistic reporting of risk", he looks at citizen journalism as "a tool of citizenship and citizen journalism as constituting a form of citizenship in its own right" (2014, p. 2). Making a similar argument, Moyo (2009, p. 554) observes that: "new technologies of communication are seen by many as potentially restoring a critical element of citizenship, which is the ability to communicate or express oneself without political or formal institutional constraints". Analysing the coverage of the Zimbabwean elections of 2008, Moyo points out the legal and political barriers that inhibit the exercise of citizenship in the country. He argues that, since the year 2000, several laws have been introduced in Zimbabwe which limit the capacity of journalists and citizens to access freely and share information held by government officials (Ibid.). He then shows how citizen journalism in the country has helped circumvent some of these barriers through, for example, the creative use of SMS and web logs.

The denial of access to information and the right to free expression is, however, not unique to Zimbabwe. Elsewhere in Africa, a number of legal barriers continue to constrain mainstream media's ability to exercise these freedoms, which are entitlements of citizenship. Ogola and Gumede (2014) argue that, across the continent, a number of countries have established new legal regimes since the1990s, fundamentally aimed at frustrating African journalists. Even in countries with much more progressive constitutions, such as Kenya and South Africa, media laws remain punitive, denying journalists the right to enjoy some of their rights to citizenship. In Kenya, for example, the Information and Communications (Amendment) Act 2013 contains provisions which impose hefty fines for breaches and covertly allows the Minister of Information to censor the media in the interest of "good taste". In South Africa, the Protection of State Information Bill (Secrecy Bill) and the Media Appeals Tribunal, although ostensibly aimed at safeguarding media pluralism, were "widely seen as stealth attempts by the government to control the media" (Ogola, 2015, p. 95). Similar bills are to be found in many parts of the continent.

While there is no specific answer to these emerging regimes of censorship, it is arguable that the Internet now offers myriad communicative possibilities, enabling the exercise of the various freedoms legally and/or politically denied mainstream media. It is because of these communicative possibilities that, in recent times, citizen journalism has tended to be Internet-based. The online platform remains relatively unrestrained. For citizen journalists, this provides more freedom for self-expression and enables broader engagement with "disenfranchised" citizens, as well easy networking across spatial and temporal boundaries. It also dismantles or, at the very least, erodes certain "gatekeeping" hierarchies in news-making. Mythen (2010, p. 49) argues that: "at a rudimentary level, wider access to publishing technologies has increased the degree of citizen input, offered greater scope for public expression and allowed a plurality of views to be heard". He notably calls this possibility for citizen journalism "rudimentary", because such an argument can also flatten significant contradictions. For example, he suggests that "the ability to participate in these online conversations even outside institutional forms and formats remains uneven" (Ibid.) He observes that "material divides still exist between those that are able to express themselves-both economically and culturally – through news media technologies and those that remain excluded". He therefore concludes that "the extent to which citizen journalism presents a radical challenge to the hegemony of global multi-media corporations is critically dependent on access". Herein lays the fundamental problem, as "material restrictions on access intertwine with culture and class to impose barriers to participation". He rightly observes that "participation is not just about being able to gain technological access, it is also about being suitably equipped with the right economic, educative and cultural resources to learn how to travel along the information superhighway" (Ibid.). This is an argument particularly apposite in the cases of countries in the developing world, such as Kenya.

Additionally, some scholars have raised questions about distortion, reliability and quality of outputs (see Mythen, 2010, p. 51). For Mythen, there is also the problem of citizen journalism's inability to reshape the news agenda. He argues that "the exclusionary news values famously identified by Galtung and Ruge have become amplified rather than transformed by online journalism", and that "an alternate set of values is yet to emerge". He notes that "set against a cultural climate in which individualisation, personalisation and self-reflection are encouraged, mixes of pre-existent news values – such as unpredictability, frequency and threshold have ossified" (Mythen, 2010, p. 52, citing Meyer, 2007).

The triumphalism with which citizen journalism, and the communicative possibilities the online platform provides, is often discussed, must therefore be tempered with the realities of its unrealistic assumptions, which ignore pertinent issues such as access, participation and the reality of the conflicting agendas of a very diverse group of practitioners. It is against this background that we look at citizen journalism in Kenya.

Citizen journalism in Kenya and the making of a "third space"

Citizen journalism must be seen here as part of the country's broader expressive forms which seeks, in the main, to provide a corrective to mainstream journalism, even as it collaborates with it. The extent to which it succeeds in doing either or both, however, remains at best conjectural. While this chapter looks mainly at Internet-based citizen journalism practices, it locates these practices within broader cultural traditions which have historically defined various expressive forms in Kenya. This section is divided into three parts. The first looks at a group of citizen journalists we categorize as "non-state actors". We focus particularly on key bloggers through whom we explore the character, roles and context within which citizen journalism is practised in Kenya. The second proceeds to look at citizen journalism's incursion by "state actors", as a way of subverting and contesting alternative voices and narratives that populate what we call the "third space" – a space neither "owned" by the state nor mainstream media but potentially powerful enough to be contested. In the last part of this section, which also provides a summation of the chapter, we reflect on this duel between "non-state" and "state actors" in their various attempts to define the content and parameters of the "alternative". We further tease out the emerging contradictions within citizen journalism, as a space that enables but also constrains debate.

Some of the most popular bloggers in Kenya include Robert Alai, Cyprian Nyakundi, Abraham Mutai and Boniface Mwangi. Other Kenyan bloggers such as Ory Okolloh sometimes operate from outside Kenya but appear to be well informed about what is happening in the country

The impact they seem to have on national conversations, not only online but also offline, is significant. They have a large following on social media and between them they have millions of "followers" on Twitter, Facebook, Google+ and Instagram. Importantly, however, it is useful to state that because these bloggers wear many caps, they variously describe themselves as activists, social and political commentators, citizen journalists or simply as bloggers. Mythen (2010, p. 51) reminds us of the need to be "reflexive enough to recognise that the categories we create are not necessarily experienced or upheld by those whom we profess to talk for". He observes that "citizen journalists as a constructed category have, in reality, intricate, diverse and contradictory attitudes towards news journalism" (Ibid.). Still, within the context of this chapter, due to the fact that the bloggers we refer to above are engaged in: (a) practices that allow for either the performance of citizenship through the creation and dissemination of information, or that (b) those very acts constitute acts of citizenship, we will perceive of them as citizen journalists.

These bloggers are engaged in daily commentary on issues relating to, for example, corruption, abuse of state power and social justice, as well as more mundane issues such as discussions about sports, entertainment programmes and other everyday experiences in Kenya. Individually and collectively, however, they have created a significant "third space" from which have emerged alternative renderings of news and information, often relying on non-traditional sources and allowing for a much more inclusive conversation on issues of national importance. For example, in January 2015, when a school playground in Lang'ata, Nairobi, was allegedly grabbed by a private developer for the expansion of a hotel, mainstream media ignored the story when it emerged that a powerful politician, later alleged to have been the deputy president, was the owner of the hotel (Agutu, 2015). Boniface Mwangi, a citizen journalist and activist known for taking on authority, mainly through his ability to mobilize Kenyans to protest against issues relating to corruption and abuse of state power, began a campaign on social media condemning the alleged land grab. He created a Twitter hashtag "occupyplayground", noticeably inspired by the "Occupy" movement, to rally Kenyans to protest against the alleged grabbing of the school playground. The hashtag attracted huge local and international attention (Mwangi, 2015). People discussed not only the land in question but also corruption in Kenya more generally and the government's inability to address the problem. The story was widely and intensely debated, not just on social media but also in the mainstream press, which had previously ignored it. These hashtags allow for more horizontal participation in "news-making", which is not possible with mainstream media where hierarchies and careful gatekeeping processes inhibit popular participation in such controversial debates involving powerful individuals.

While the fear of prosecution is sometimes real despite the "anonymity" that Twitter, for example, gives those who tweet, that fear is often mitigated through the use of humour in Kenya. Kenyans have often taken to humour to "prosecute" and to deliver "judgements" on accused persons, almost as a brazen affront to the formal institutions of justice, which many see as deeply compromised. Using humour and jokes to express their "anger" at the controversial land case, various memes of the deputy president dressed as a Sikh and hashtags satirizing the Minister of Land were tweeted and circulated online. The minister, Charity Ngilu, had named four individuals, all with the surname 'Singh' as the owners of the disputed land, something Kenyan social media users considered a cover-up. Despite no evidence provided to prove the deputy president's involvement in the alleged land grabbing, they went on to create jokes and memes pointing to his guilt.

A cartoon depicting the deputy president as a Sikh wearing a turban was also published in a national newspaper. Some of the "jokes" under the hashtag "NgiluSinghJokes" included:

@mamangilu. Official handle for Hon. Charity Ngilu, Cabinet Secretary in The Ministry of Land, Hou singh and Urban Planning.

It's all fun and games till some of you start going miSingh for contributing to on this TT NgiluSinghJokes

Langata land was just the start the next one will be the i-singh on the cake NgiluSinghJokes.

> (http://jokes.groupkenya.com/2015/01/ngilusinghjokes-
> kenyan-trends-rock part_23.htm)

Humour has always been a form of political practice in Kenya. It is a tradition made especially popular by the late Kenyan writer Wahome Mutahi, who, through his then popular column, "Whispers", published at various times by the country's two leading newspapers, *The Nation* and *The Standard*, poked fun at the state and its excesses through a humorous self-deprecating style that to use the words of the Ugandan writer John Ruganda (1992) "told the truth laughingly". Mutahi's newspaper column was a site of transgressive social, cultural and political expression, at a time when freedom of such expression was highly constrained by the state. Through a fictional universe he created in his column, and which was inhabited by a "fictional" family modelled around his own, Mutahi echoed life in Kenya in all its banality but also in its distinctiveness, making legible the silent stories that mainstream media could not cover for fear of state repression and prosecution (see Ogola,

2015). We see this tradition now adopted by citizen journalists in the country and Kenyans on Twitter (KOT) more generally as a way of "disciplining" power.

Robert Alai, who, like Mwangi, variously describes himself as a blogger and social activist, is arguably one of the most popular citizen journalists in Kenya. Known for his controversial tweets and blog posts, which have often got him in trouble with powerful political functionaries, Alai has come to represent the new face of Kenya's citizen journalism – bold, brazen and controversial. In an interview with *The Standard*, Alai claimed that he has a specific interest in social justice and attempts to ensure the weak "are not trampled on in the stampede of survival in Kenya" (*The Standard*, 19 October 2013). He claims 90 million weekly impressions on his social media pages, including Facebook, Twitter and Google+. He has been involved in a number of social media campaigns, including one that he claims forced Kenya's deputy chief justice out of office. He has also become a focal point of reference for those seeking redress from powerful corporate organizations, or those in need of help with such things as school fees, those frustrated by government bureaucracy and inefficiency, or those demanding the provision of social amenities by town councils or county governments. Incidentally, corporate organizations also now use him to communicate with their customers and the public in general, almost as they do in mainstream newspapers. In early 2015, however, Alai came under criticism when he tried to force a journalist from a TV station (Nation Television) to drop an investigative story he was working on regarding an aviation college in Nairobi which was allegedly awarding bogus degrees for a fee. In a recording covertly taped by the journalist in his conversation with Alai, the blogger referred to the aviation college as "his client" and asked the journalist not to run the story (*Nairobi News*, 2 February 2015). This transactional relationship between bloggers and big business demonstrate how social capital, arising from the work citizen journalists do, is now also subject to abuse.

Alai's effectiveness as a citizen journalist, however, has been most visible during moments of crisis in the country. For example, he was among the first to break the "story" of the Westgate Mall terrorist attack in Nairobi in September 2013. He posted real-time updates about the attack, including information from some of the victims of the attack holed up in the Mall. As this was an unprecedented terrorist attack, local news media struggled to cover the incident. Some media organizations were also accused of pandering to state pressure and propaganda by covering the attack mainly through the lens of state house operatives. Live media coverage of the attack was also discouraged by the government, which claimed that such coverage aided the terrorists. Alai filled this information vacuum with his posts. His "updates" proved so popular that a number of international news organizations relied on them in their coverage of the attack (Genga, 2015).

Kenyans have also often turned to another famous blogger, Ory Okolloh, for information during moments of crisis. Okolloh is an alumnus of Harvard University where she studied law, and has been the Policy Manager, Africa, for Google. She has previously been named as one of Africa's most successful women by *Forbes Magazine* in 2012, and appeared in *Time Magazine* as one of the 100 most influential people in the world (Dyson, 2014). She became well known in Kenya – and beyond – following her work with Ushahidi, a crowd-sourcing platform that used citizen journalists to map incidence of violence in Kenya during the 2007–2008 post-election riots. Ordinary people around the country sent pictures and text messages using their mobile phones to report violent incidents. These were then mapped to show the trouble hotspots.

Okolloh is a regular commentator on everyday happenings in Kenya, from national stories focusing on governance, to the more mundane ones affecting ordinary individuals. As is the case with Alai, people tag her in their tweets, which she then either retweets, comments on or uses her considerable social capital to, for example, engage relevant authorities. In April 2015, when Al-Shabaab terrorists killed 147 students at the Garissa University College in Garissa Town, Okolloh rallied Kenyans against the government's poor response to the attack. A carefully managed PR exercise, intended to control the news narrative on the government response, was laid bare through "alternative" voices such as Okolloh's. These voices destabilized the state's narrative, showing instead the extent to which poor coordination by various security agencies, and their slow decision-making processes, contributed to the abject response to the attack. Alternative information was sourced from both disgruntled state officials and also from ordinary citizens.

In the aftermath of the attack, Okolloh helped sustain this debate through a Twitter hashtag "147isnotjustanumber". It was, she said later, a way of "memorializing" the students. This hashtag trended not just in Kenya but worldwide. It became a pivot around which discussions on terrorism, insecurity, failures of government, corruption and patriotism were discussed, with numerous contributions from KOT. The hashtag also triggered the organization of vigil nights in Kenya and around the world – from the USA to Pakistan – in memory of the departed 147. Okolloh demonstrated how citizen journalism and her considerable social capital could be mobilized, through the power of the Internet, to trigger important debates on issues of national importance.

Okolloh is also co-founder of Mzalendo Watch, a website that describes itself as "a non-partisan project" whose mission is to "keep an eye on the Kenyan parliament". Mzalendo "seeks to promote greater public voice and enhance public participation in politics by providing relevant information about the National Assembly and Senate's activities" (http://info.mzalendo .com). Mzalendo means "patriot" in Kiswahili and the team that is behind it also has a Twitter handle @MzalendoWatch. Unlike other bloggers who restrict their activities online, Mzalendo also tracks and accesses official parliamentary records to audit MPs' performance. It then uses this information to rank the best and the worst performers. The information is released in the form of a report that is widely circulated.

A similar "project", which uses Twitter as a tool for public deliberation, is MaskaniYaTaifa (@Maskani254), a Twitter handle which "holds" regular debates on the Twitter hashtag MaskaniConversations. These are often open conversations relating to politics, the economy or various social issues affecting the country. Participation is unhindered by hierarchies.

Other citizen journalists, such as Mutai and Nyakundi, have, for their part, mainly focused on exposing cases of corruption, such as controversial tendering processes, mismanagement of public funds and similar. They use their Twitter pages to serialize, for example, reports linking individuals to corrupt practices, often invoking the wrath of those accused or the state. Mutai, for instance, was arrested after making allegations of corruption involving members of the County government in Isiolo (BBC Trending, 2015).

Nyakundi, on the other hand, was sued in the Nairobi High Court by communications giant Safaricom, Kenya's most profitable company, in June 2015 for defamation after he published a series of articles on his blog that alleged the was involved in malpractices that included stealing from customers, and infringing on their privacy (Okuttah, 2015). Meanwhile, Kahawa Tungu, a blog associated with Alai, has since early 2015 been publishing stories alleging that national carrier Kenya Airways was in deeper financial crisis than the management was willing to admit. Alai and several other bloggers suggested the mainstream media was unwilling to investigate the story for fear of losing advertising. In July 31, 2015, Kenya Airways announced a loss of before tax $260 million, one of the biggest in Kenya's corporate history, prompting Kahawa Tungu to remind its audience of the previous posts.

"Invading" citizen journalism: The state as an emerging actor

On its ascension to power in April 2013, one of the key changes the Uhuru Kenyatta administration made was to restructure and rename the Presidential Press Service (PPS), which had existed since independence in 1963. The new entity, the Presidential Strategic Communication Unit (PSCU), was created with the mandate to ensure coherence, clarity and consistency in communication from the presidency and other government departments.

One notable inclusion in the new body was the position of Director, Digital, New Media and Diaspora Affairs. This was in response to the emerging importance of the digital platform in governance and in wider political practice and participation. The government notably increased its presence online, particularly on social media. This now includes directly providing information on upcoming state events, uploading pictures and speeches, the live tweeting of presidential events and generally engaging with citizens online. The president's speeches and the outcome of Cabinet meetings, for example, are usually uploaded on Scribd and are therefore accessible to the public.

President Uhuru and Deputy President William Ruto now have personal Facebook and Twitter accounts that are regularly updated, while the PSCU team has various social media accounts they use to communicate government policy. A PSCU official claimed that the social media accounts help them to gauge the public mood by directly getting feedback on policy (interview with the authors, 15 April 2015).

The significance of the government's growing presence in the online space can also be considered in light of the growing Internet penetration, boosted by access through mobile phones.

The government has actively adopted the use of the emerging new communication tools and platforms in its broader governance structures and political practices. It does this through creating platforms that provide space for popular participation in such debates, but simultaneously counters such participation by covertly undermining alternative voices attempting to destabilize state narratives. The president's official website, for instance, allows residents to directly complain about corruption. This, according to a PSCU official, is important in two ways: first, to show that the government is committed to fighting corruption and, second, to get direct feedback from the public. Meanwhile, PSCU officials are particularly active on popular social media sites such as Facebook and Twitter, populating these spaces with pro-state narratives. The digital director of PSCU, Dennis Itumbi, has been especially active in his attempts to (re)define news narratives online. This he does in a number of ways. For example, he routinely creates hashtags which seek to set the agenda for discussions online whenever the government comes under criticism. In one such case, in the aftermath of the Garissa attack, a section of disgruntled Kenyans who were unhappy with the government's performance created the hashtag #2YrsOfHopelessness on Twitter. This was on 9 April 2015 as the government marked its second year in office. PSCU immediately attempted to counter this with an alternative hashtag – #2YearsofSuccess – around which pro-Jubilee supporters "congregated" to contest accusations of government failure. Both hashtags enabled public participation on the failures and successes of the government. Interestingly, those who were unhappy with the PSCU's attempt to "hijack" the discussion resorted to using the PSCU-generated hashtag to express their opposition, effectively subverting the government's case.

Other hashtags created by PSCU have included #MyPresidentMyChoice and #KenyaIsMe in November 2014, after the president was criticized for purportedly suggesting that victims of terrorist attacks should do more to take care of their security. In 2013, after the Westgate Mall attack where 67 people were killed by Al-Shabaab terrorists, through the hashtag #WeAreOne, the government effectively managed to rally the country together, briefly managing to contain the emerging narrative about rampant insecurity and the bungling of a rescue operation at the Mall.

The dark side of the Internet has also seen PSCU adopt covert operations in its attempt to set the agenda on this alternative space. For example, it is now suspected that the government may be paying bloggers to tweet, comment on and retweet messages in support of government positions. Fake accounts are created, while the use of bots is also suspected, although this has been denied by PSCU. In an interview with the authors, a PSCU official described social media as "a jungle", and stated that sometimes they "need numbers" to counter an opposing narrative and reinforce the state's position. He described the use of some of these covert measures, such as paying some bloggers to write things that support the government's position as "normal.... because even corporates pay for their products to be promoted". This, he says, is part of their online strategy (interview with authors, 17 April 2015).

In December 2014, during the airing of *Press Pass*, a popular Kenyan television programme that focuses on the journalistic practices in local media, one of the topics of discussion was the coverage of insecurity plaguing Northern Kenya following an attack by Al-Shabaab. The government had reiterated the need for citizens to take more responsibility for their security and insisted that the Kenyan military, a part of the African Union forces that went to Somalia in 2011 to fight Al-Shabaab, would not be withdrawn from the country. Al-Shabaab had attributed their attacks to the presence of Kenyan forces in Somalia. In the programme, the opposition's stand that Kenyan forces should be withdrawn from Somalia was mentioned. The battle for the control of the narrative on how best to respond to the Al-Shabaab threat quickly ensued online. Curiously, several tweets bearing the same message were simultaneously posted to the programme's hashtag #presspass. The message read: "It is unacceptable that the opposition has the same stand as Alshababa. #presspass." All the tweets had the name of the terrorist group misspelt as "AlShababa". Other tweets in support of the government's argument, calling for citizens to take more responsibility of their own security, were also posted. These were sent from multiple accounts at exactly the same time with the same wording: "There is a role for citizens when it comes to security. #presspass." Such examples are indicative of the possible use of bots or fake accounts to counter oppositional narratives.

Meanwhile, more local administrators are also being trained and encouraged to use social media to communicate government policy in their engagement with citizens. One of the most prominent users of this form of engagement is Chief Francis Kariuki, a local administrator in Kenya's Rift Valley town of Nakuru, who encourages citizens to alert him about crime, lost livestock, flooding, poor services and other issues of concern to them. He also uses social media to pass on information about upcoming community meetings and events, and then tweets and blogs about them.

In his discussion of Chief Kariuki's use of social media, Omanga (2015, p. 10) argues that, through Twitter, the chief is able to constitute a public that is "apparently indeterminate, boundless and organic in growth, is severally constituted in apparent contrarieties as homogenous or heterogeneous or as either active or passive, or as either bounded or boundless". While he does this, in part, "for purposes of instant group action" (Ibid.), such action, in turn, gives government visibility but, more importantly, credibility. It is a "template of local administration" (Ibid.) now being actively encouraged elsewhere in the country.

Conclusion

It is arguable that citizen journalism has undoubtedly created a "third space" in Kenya where alternative news and information now reside. As access to the Internet, either through computers or through mobile phones, becomes more commonplace and affordable, social media, and particularly Twitter and blogs, are becoming the citizen journalists' platforms of choice. These platforms and tools for communication afford both citizen journalists and the public myriad communicative possibilities. Although there is increasing attempts by the Kenyan government to regulate the online platform, it remains much freer than mainstream journalism and is therefore exploited in multiple ways. Citizen journalists now find it easy to construct their publics around specific issues, particularly through the use of Twitter hashtags. These hashtags enable fairly substantive discussions, with participation largely unhindered as long as one has access to the Internet. The gatekeeping processes usually found in typical newsrooms is largely absent. The public is also developing creative ways through which to hold those in power accountable, by appropriating various popular cultural practices to critique the state and discuss various issues affecting the country. In "telling the truth laughingly", they are able to confront power with little fear of state intimidation.

Another important finding emerging from this discussion is the fact that social capital has become an important driver in citizen journalism. Some of the most influential citizen journalists in Kenya also seem to have considerable social capital, gained offline via their professional capacities or previous achievements, as is the case with Ory Okolloh, or "made" online, as has been the case with the likes of Alai and Mutai. This, no doubt, has implications on the character of Kenya's citizen journalism. It is also arguable that, by and large, although popular participation is enabled by new technologies, it is also the case that "professionals" now play a significant role in generating and amplifying particular issues and stories and not others. The platform and the tools are free to use but, increasingly, citizen journalism is also becoming ever more professionalized, agenda-driven and sometimes even amenable to co-option by the very holders of authority practitioners seek to hold accountable. The power to communicate or influence may be dispersed online but it is also asymmetrical in its own ways, an issue which may, in fact, inhibit its perceived openness to horizontal participation and inclusiveness.

The incursion by state actors also provides a new dimension to citizen journalism. Just as is the case with mainstream media, citizen journalism is amenable to manipulation. The Kenya government, through the PSCU, has managed to "invade" this space, which it now formally and informally inhabits through its own interventions but also through proxies who do the bidding on its behalf. This incursion by state actors, as we ponder in this chapter, now raises profound questions regarding the oppositional character of citizen journalism, or indeed its capacity to refuse capture by the state or its various apparatuses.

References

Agutu, Nancy. (2015). Police use teargas to disperse Langata pupils fighting for grabbed playground. *The Star*, 19 January 2015.

BBC Trending. (2015). FreeSpeechStories: Arrested for a tweet. http://www.bbc.co.uk/news/blogs-trending-30922600, Retrieved 20 April 2015.

Bowman, Shayne, and Chris, Willis. (2003). *We Media: How Audiences Are Shaping the Future of News and Information*. New York: Media Center.

Campbell, Vincent. (2014). Theorizing citizenship in citizen journalism. *Digital Journalism*. (ahead-of-print) DOI: 10.1080/21670811.2014.937150, 1–16

Dugmore, Harry, and Ligaga, Dina. (2014). "Citizen Journalism in South Africa and Kenya: The Quandary of Quality and the Prospects for Growth". In *The Future of Journalism in the Developed and Developing World: A Cross Continental Analysis*, Peter Anderson, George Ogola and Michael Williams (eds.), London and New York: Routledge, pp. 248–263.

Dvorkin, Jeffrey. (2007). Media matters: Can public radio be re-invented? *NPR*. http://www.npr.org/yourturn/ombudsman/2001/010705.html, Retrieved 20 April 2015.

Dyson, Esther. (2014). The activist who helps Africans exercise their power. *Time*. 27 April 2014.

Galtung, Johan, and Ruge, M. Holmboe. (1965). The structure of foreign news. *Journal of Peace Research* 2(1): 64–91.

Genga, Shirley. (2015). This man Alai. *The Standard*, 19 October 2015.

Gillmor, Dan. (2004). *We the Media: Grassroots Journalism by the People, for the People*, 1st edition. Sebastopol, CA: O'Reilly.

Harcup, Tony, and O'Neill, Deirdre. (2001). What is news? Galtung and RugeRevisited. *Journalism Studies* 2(2): 261–280.

Knight, Megan, and Cook, Clare. (2013). *Social Media for Journalists: Principles and Practice*. London: Sage.

Meyer, Philip. (2007). *Public Journalism and the Problem of Objectivity*. http://www.unc.edu/~pmeyer/ire95pj.htm, Retrieved 20 April 2015.

Moyo, Dumisani. (2009). Citizen journalism and the parallel market for information in Zimbabwe's 2008 election. *Journalism Studies* 10(4): 551–567.

Mwangi, Boniface. (2015).OccupyPlayGround: Police used teargas on our children, but for now we celebrate the win. *The Guardian*, 20 January 2015.

Mythen, Gabe. (2010). Reframing risk? Citizen journalism and the transformation of news. *Journal of Risk Research* 13(1): 45–58.

Ogola, George. (2015). African journalism: A journey of failures and triumphs. *African Journalism Studies* 36(1): 93–102.

Ogola, George, and Gumede, Ylva-Rodny. (2014). "The Future of Quality Journalism and Media Accountability in South Africa and Kenya". In *The Future of Journalism in the Developed and Developing World: A Cross Continental Analysis*, Peter Anderson, George Ogola and Michael Williams (eds.), London and New York: Routledge, pp. 227–263.

Okuttah, Mark. (2015). Safaricom sues blogger over posts. *Business Daily*, 24 June 2015.

Omanga, Duncan. (2015). "Chieftaincy" in the social media space: Community policing in a Twitter convened Baraza. *Stability: International Journal of Security & Development* 4(1): 1–16. DOI: http://dx.doi.org/10.5334/sta.eq.

Rosen, Jay. (1993). The people formerly known as the audience. *Pressthink 2016.* http://archive.pressthink.org/2006/06/27/ppl_frmr.html, Retrieved 20 April 2015.

Ruganda, John. (1992). *Telling the Truth Laughingly.* East Lansing: Michigan State University Press.

Van Ginneken, Jaap. (1998). *Understanding Global News: A Critical Introduction.* London: Sage.

16
Citizen Journalism and the Ebola Outbreak in Africa

Winston Mano and viola c. milton

This chapter analyses responses to news coverage of the 2014 Ebola virus by African media, a subject that has so far not been adequately discussed. It examines cases from "citizen media responses" in Zimbabwe and South Africa to determine the uniqueness of the African response to an African crisis. It investigates the attitudes and interpretations that were put forward by digital news media and responses from the news users. Our analysis of the news media responses highlights the importance of voice and agency, as it illustrates what happens when disenfranchised groups become the agents of their own stories. While there was, to some extent, significant overlaps between responses from within and outside of the continent, most interesting was perhaps the ways in which the stories revealed African citizen journalists as people with agency and power to define and shape the world around them.

Digital news and citizen responses

News media coverage of the 2014 Ebola crisis in Africa was notable because of how the audience responded. The audience's feedback, which is about how ordinary people play "an active role in the process of collecting, reporting, analysing and disseminating news and information" (Bowman and Willis, 2003, p. 9), is a key aspect of citizen journalism. The chapter is written at time (2015) when ordinary readers and users are increasingly commenting and sharing news stories. News, as Tuchman (1976) points out, is a constructed version of its source material and is a selective version of original realities. News is a deliberately constructed reality and a form of social knowledge (Allan, 1997). It is our argument here that responses to news stories on the 2014 outbreak of Ebola illustrated key elements of the emerging citizen-facing social media space in Africa. We are especially interested in how African readers/users responded to news on Ebola on online news sites. How was this form of citizen journalism responsive to the Ebola crisis, and what does it say about the media, users and their contexts? We analyse citizen responses to news coverage of the 2014 Ebola outbreak in Zimbabwe and South Africa. How did southern Africans respond to the 2014 Ebola virus outbreak in West Africa?

Citizen journalism, it could be argued, gives people that are generally excluded or misrepresented by the mainstream commercial news the chance of making themselves heard. For a continent where democracy is constantly wavering, where much is still being negotiated in terms of its identity as a continent and the countries' identities as individual (though connected) nations, a belief that Africans' participation and contributions are not only voiced and listened to, but can make a difference, is crucial to restoring dignity and worth to those continually excluded and or marginalized in the cut-throat world of global politics. In fact, as O'Donnell and colleagues (2009), Couldry (2009) and Couldry and Ruiz (2012) argue, Cultural Studies has long assumed that the voices of those most affected by contemporary forms of oppression and exclusion need to be heard, and that academics who feel an affinity with these perspectives should work to facilitate that hearing. This chapter is one attempt at facilitating such hearing.

The 2014 Ebola outbreak in Sierra Leone, Liberia and Guinea

The journalists covering the 2014 Ebola virus can argue that they did not create the virus but simply represented reality or facts as it emerged. However, the news was constructed and influenced by news values and journalists' work environments, including expectations of their audience and employers. Ebola was in places that were not readily reachable or deemed unsafe by the media. This point is especially significant when considered alongside the view that journalists' construct news. As is observed by Schudson (2005, p. 173), journalists shape news texts, "They shape them, but they do not shape them as they choose." Unlike with previous disease outbreaks in Africa, this time, news about how Ebola has affected communities in Sierra Leone, Liberia and Guinea, a specific region of Africa, was also captured and shared via phone technology, recorded telephone interviews, WhatsApp audio and photo functions, and SMS, both by professional and non-professional journalists. It is arguable that how the event was reported produced different forms of reality. It can be observed from the start that Africa has a population of 1.1 billion, 54 countries and is home to 15% of the world's population. Surprisingly, a crisis on the continent can result in the reduction of the continent to "one country" and the tarnishing of the image of all Africans across the world. The panic and sensational responses to the outbreak of the Ebola virus prompted one Hannah Giorgis (2014) to observe that: "The problem with the West's Ebola response is still fear of a black patient" – the heading of her story published by British newspaper, *The Guardian*. Her account captured the exaggerated fear and widespread racialized responses by the "West" or some developed countries to the outbreak of the Ebola virus, then largely restricted to Liberia, Sierra Leone and Guinea. Our analysis of digital news coverage and responses to the 2014 outbreak of the Ebola in Africa must be considered within the context of local and global transformations. It can also be argued that, to a large extent, Western media responses to the 2014 Ebola outbreak added to historical and contemporary accounts of "othering" Africa (Mano, 2015). This chapter is an attempt to unpack the debate arising from media articulations by Africans in African media spaces. We wanted to investigate the extent and character of local debates on the crisis.

The news of the Ebola virus was not new, as initial reports date back to the 1970s minor outbreaks in Zaire, Sudan and Reston among other places. It can be observed that the specific strain (EBOV) of the 2014 outbreak in West Africa was similar to the one in Zaire in 1976 (WHO, 2015). It was traced to the Ebola River region of the Democratic Republic of the Congo (DRC), from where the name is derived. The main symptoms varied from case to case but the most common indications are diarrhoea, abdominal pains and vomiting, which, over the course of several days, escalate to bleeding internally and externally through eyes, ears, nose and mouth. The virus is transmitted through contact with infected bodily fluids. Ebola has a fatality rate of 90% of all those diagnosed.

We should make it clear that the disease produced fear and stigma across Africa. It is our view that there was even more fear that Ebola would threaten Westerners, as had happened with HIV and AIDS. Flights to and from West Africa were cancelled. Western soldiers were deployed to West Africa to deal with the problem. In relation to this, Giorgis (2014) pointed out that:

> Ebola now functions in popular discourse as a not-so-subtle, almost completely rhetorical stand-in for any combination of "African-ness", "blackness", "foreign-ness" and "infestation" – a nebulous but powerful threat, poised to ruin the perceived purity of western borders and bodies. Dead African bodies are the nameless placeholders for (unwarranted, racist) "panic", a conversation topic too heavy for the dinner table yet light enough for supermarket aisles.

If, as stated in this quote, the Western response was racist and negative, one would expect African responses to be different and more appreciate of an African crisis. We wanted to know how citizens using African digital social media dealt with the problem. In the section "The emerging Internet space in Africa", we discuss the increasing role of the Internet and digital connectivity in Africa.

The emerging Internet space in Africa

The Internet reaches only a minute proportion of African urban dwellers and virtually none outside the elite of the larger cities (Njogu and Middleton,

2009). Regardless of this observation, it is increasingly accepted that the Internet is opening up new possibilities that have allowed both citizens and journalists in Africa to creatively engage with mainstream politics (Jensen, 2000; Nyamnjoh, 2005; Spitulnik, 2002). As with other parts of the world, despite the slow growth in the numbers of Internet users, "a rather small minority of these Internet users has the capability to use it in ways that are creative and that augment their ability to participate effectively in today's knowledge societies" (Mansell, 2004, p. 179). This is linked to the point that what is most essential to understanding the technical, organizational and cultural characteristics of the Internet is the way other communication networks have converged into the Internet (Castells, 1996, p. 351). Digital technology has enabled people to package multimedia messages, including sound, images and data "without using control centres" (Ibid.). In Africa, this has particularly been the case after 2000, when there has been a relative increase in Internet media. The new and diverse types of media are allowing new voices and are exerting pressure on political processes in Africa (Tettey, 2009). The establishment of more media from below has encouraged ordinary Africans to begin to theorize about both new and old media in new ways. For example, the notion of victimhood, which often presents Africans as powerless victims of officialdom, is now being reconsidered in the context that, however powerful and repressive some African governments or global conditions are, "there is always room – sometimes through radical or alternate media for initiative and agency to challenge domination, exploitation and the globalisation of poverty" (Nyamnjoh, 2005, p. 204). Moyo (2009) adds to this that on the Internet, "[t]he non-professional journalists are not accountable to anyone but themselves, and their 'journalism' is not guided or constrained by any ethical norms or principles but rather by gut feeling and commonsense. In a crisis situation . . . citizen journalism could worsen things by spreading untruths and half-truths which could lead to panic and disorder" (Moyo 2009: 12). We sought to consider the responses to digital news on the 2014 Ebola outbreak in Zimbabwe and South Africa as way of gauging the role and function of citizen journalism during a major African health crisis.

Methodology

The research adopted a qualitative design in the sense it mainly involved content illustration of the news stories on Ebola alongside textual analysis of key examples chosen. It preferred convenient sampling of evidence left by readers/users of African digital news sites. Unlike content analysis, which offers a systematic account of words within texts by quantifying and analysing them, content illustration is more concerned with providing examples of the character and tone of coverage, using headlines and other elements of the news stories. If done properly, content illustration can also enable one to make inferences about the attitudes and meanings from writers and audiences on news stories in relation to the issue of Ebola. The overall framework for the collection and analysis of data was according to the priorities set by us as the researchers. A robust research design allows one to deal with the core issues under investigation. The identity and behaviour of online audiences is complex and susceptible to manipulation to some extent; this should be considered when evaluating their feedback.

Ebola in the Zimbabwean media

In the wake of the Ebola crisis of 2014 the Zimbabwe government created a website on 30 October 2014. Paul Chimedza, the deputy minister in the Health Ministry, described it as a response to the lack of knowledge about the disease among locals that had resulted in public fear. Of interest here is how the website was also a response to discourses about in Ebola in social media:

> We were losing the fight in our quest to tell the people that there is no Ebola in the country on the social media.... A lot of false stories, some of which include that there was an Ebola patient in Murehwa circulated on whatsapp (sic) and we realised the need to set up this social media platform to dispel such stories officially.

In a way, the problem illustrated the impact of social media practices on the news agenda of the government. As discussed by Hirst (2011, p. 109): "digital media are creating the conditions for audience members to make the transition from 'passive receivers' to 'proactive consumers', who decide what they want, when they want it and how they want it". However, one can question the extent to which the Zimbabwe government's website managed to defeat the "rumours" on the Ebola situation within citizen journalists' platforms.

The emergence of new forms of media is dependent on existing media. In the case of Zimbabwe, the century-old and government-controlled *Herald* newspaper has adapted and evolved into the digital era. Apart from its daily print run of 100,000 and a big secondary market where one copy can be read by 5–10 people, *The Herald* has an online edition that is also read by an estimated 3 million people in the diaspora. Digital readers/users leave comments and, in the process, share news. As is noted by Jenkins (2006, pp. 18–19):

> Convergence requires media companies to rethink old assumptions about what it means to consume media, assumptions that shape both pro-gramming and marketing decisions. If old consumers were assumed to be passive, the new consumers are active. If old consumers were pre-dictable and stayed where you told them to stay, then new consumers are migratory, showing a declining loyalty to networks or media. If old

consumers were isolated individuals, the new consumers are more socially connected. If the work of media consumers was once silent and invisible, the new consumers are now noisy and public.

In the Zimbabwean case, the new consumer using new media tools is complementing and changing the news agenda, which has, so far, been dominated by news institutions such as *The Herald*.

Prior to the March 2014 outbreak of Ebola in West Africa, *The Herald* had last published a major story on the disease on 18 September 2012, entitled, "Ebola claims up to 32 lives in DRC: WHO". It routinely reported the deaths of ordinary people from DRC, including that of a woman who had just given birth. It can be observed that the number of Ebola news stories in *The Herald* in the aftermath of the March 2014 outbreak was low, but the stories later gathered pace and were in line with the pro-government character of the newspaper in assuring the public that Zimbabwe was able to deal with Ebola. While the online edition of *The Herald* reported on the suffering and deaths from Ebola abroad, it also hyped the Zimbabwe government's preparedness to tackle the disease. It sought to downplay perspectives that the Zimbabwe government was not in control of the Ebola problem as illustrated by the examples that follow (Table 16.1):

Table 16.1   Selected headlines of news stories in the digital edition of *The Herald* (2014)

Headline	Date	Overall tone
"Ebola claims 59 in Guinea"	24 March 2014	Disease out of control
"Fear grips Guinea"	27 March 2014	Disease out of control
"Zimbabwe on the lookout for the Ebola virus"	27 March 2014	State able to protect citizens
"Ghana responds to Ebola threat"	28 March 2014	State able to protect citizens
"Senegal closes border over Ebola"	31 March 2014	State able to protect citizens
"Liberia confirms first case of Ebola"	1 April 2014	Disease out of control
"April outbreak response scales up"	12 April 2014	Disease out of control
"Ebola outbreak: Ghana tests US man"	8 July 2014	State able to protect citizens
"Govt commences Ebola specialists training"	7 August 2014	State able to protect citizens
"Zim sets up Ebola monitoring at borders"	21 August 2014	State able to protect citizens
"Govt warns over Nigeria visits"	22 August 2014	State able to protect citizens
"21-day quarantine for Ebola suspects"	29 August 2014	State able to protect citizens

Table 16.1   (Continued)

Headline	Date	Overall tone
"SA turns truckers away over Ebola"	1 September 2014	State able to protect citizens
"Zim can handle Ebola outbreak says US expert"	28 October 2014	State able to protect citizens
"20 Zim experts to help fight Ebola"	8 November 2014	State able to protect citizens
"800 screened for Ebola virus"	24 November 2014	State able to protect citizens
"Screening for Ebola intensifies"	23 December 2014	State able to protect citizens
"Ebola affects Zim tourism"	30 December 2014	State able to protect citizens

Not all the digital news stories on Ebola in *The Herald* attracted comments from the readers. As the headlines in Table 16.1 show, the coverage emphasized the government's preparedness, training issues and the availability of expertise to handle the Ebola crisis should it enter Zimbabwe. The dominant tone was to assure citizens of state protection. In response to a story in *The Herald* entitled "Ebola: Sick American to be treated in the US" (2 August 2014), one reader responded as follows: "These guys are brave . . . if I see you laying (sic) there, blood coming out of your eyes and mouth, frothing and sh#t . . . you aint gonna make it." The comment illustrated the fear that the public had of Ebola and seemed to justify the reassurance that was evident in *The Herald*. The discourse in *The Herald* was in sharp contrast with critical coverage in privately owned media, which emphasized that Zimbabwe had no capacity to conduct tests to detect the deadly Ebola disease, as specimens from suspected cases were being referred to South African laboratories for verification. The Zimbabwe government was also worried about the negative stories on Ebola because of its effect on tourism, as was shown by the story from 30 December 2014. In response to that story, a more critical reader observed:

> Anon: This has little to do with Ebola but more to do with how we have priced ourselves out of competition. Visitors who have travelled to Zim recently says (sic) it is an expensive country to visit and word goes round quickly. There is a big world out there where you can get more bang for your bucks.

This is a clear case of citizen journalism challenging the official view that Ebola rumours were affecting tourism. To some extent, citizen journalism has provided the means to challenge and correct distorted official views. In response to a news feature entitled, "The most effective treatment against

Ebola 'might be having a white skin' " by Kwei Quartey, published in *The Herald*, one reader, Ian, stated:

> This should serve as a wake-up call to Africa to start making serious effort to stand on its own feet rather than continuing to depend on other people for all its needs. Being one of the richest continents, Africa can and should be able to easily find solutions to such problems as Ebola. Unfortunately, this is currently not being done due to corruption, etc.
>
> (*The Herald*, 1 December 2014)

The reader offers a critical interpretation, and focuses on corruption as the main issue in dealing with Ebola. As will be seen in the South African case, the disease was an opportunity for locals to attack maladministration and the self-centred approach by Zimbabwean leaders.

In response to the news story, "800 screened for Ebola virus", in *The Herald*, 24 November 2014, one reader stated that they would not be surprised if Ebola did come to Zimbabwe, which again was a criticism and vivid mockery of the preparedness of Zimbabwe in the face of the disease. More interesting in response to the same story, a reader, describing their role as that of a Command Centre, stated that: "Mortality rate according to your figures is (5,100/13,000) = 39.23%. Therefore survival rate is 61.77%.... I don't know if I am wrong. Interesting, Ebola has no cure, but more than 60% of affected people SURVIVE(D), Health experts, tell US!!!" The cynical comments from readers are even clearer in response to the story headlined "Zimbabwe can produce Ebola drug" published on 14 November 2014:

> *Guest: hahahahahahahahahahahaha* [a laugh, which represents an ability to see through and a refusal to be taken in]
>
> *Doufi: I can grow rubber trees, so I can produce vehicle tyres. I farm cocoa and can produce chocolate to compete with the Swiss. Really, our biotechnology graduates already that good? Clever nations work quietly and only announce after a breakthrough including clinical trials. I think we talk too much as a nation.*
>
> *Mazorodze: Doufi: Zimbabwe will host the next olympics!*
>
> *Changoti Bruuuuu: Muchitamba nezvimwe murikutadza kupa vanhu mvura yakachena makutaura zve Ebola*
>
> *GR8ZIMBO: We can dream of killing a lion .... yet we cant (sic) even dare to face a chihuahua (sic). Zimbo reasoning for you*
>
> *James Bond: Both the writer and his main source must grow some brains*

It is clear from this that the readers doubted the stance of the government and openly expressed their fears in comments on the stories. The citizen feedback illustrated mixed views on the origins and effects of the disease, and mocked official claims on preparedness.

Ebola stories on New Zimbabwe and feedback from the readers

A Google search of Ebola stories on www.newZimbabwe.com revealed 24,000 news stories, but not all of them were written by journalists on the site. Privately owned NewZimbabwe:

[A]dvertises itself through various slogans such as "the Zimbabwe news you trust", "the biggest name in Zimbabwe news" and "breaking news as it happens". The website features news items, both written in-house and compiled from other sources, as well as showbiz news, sports, columns and opinion articles.

(Mano and Willems, 2010)

The front page of NewZimbabwe is modelled along the lines of a British tabloid, with headlines in big capital letters and bold and provocative headlines. As stated by Mano and Willems (2010), apart from news articles and advertisements, visitors are also encouraged to join "the debate" on the discussion forum section of the website, which has proven very popular with the 8,152 members registered in May 2006. New members can join by simply choosing a username and password, which provides them with access to the forums. The forum section has been divided into debates on different categories of topics: general discussion, high school reunions, audience with a politician, talking sport, hot gossip, humour, relationships, technology, music and entertainment, religious corner, health and lifestyle and so on. Discussions are mostly held in English and Shona, or Shonglish, which refers to the mixture of Shona and English that is common among Zimbabweans, and sometimes Ndebele is also used. This shows that Zimbabwean news publications are read and used by citizens in and outside the country. Previous research has suggested that a significant number of participants in the NewZimbabwe forums are Zimbabweans based in the United Kingdom (Mano and Willems, 2010).

As can be seen in Table 16.2, headlines on the 2014 Ebola outbreak on the NewZimbabwe site were sensational and alarmist, exaggerating the impact.

The stories appearing on the NewZimbabwe site differed from those in *The Herald* in the sense that they projected the image of the Zimbabwean government as hiding Ebola information for fear of losing tourism. They highlighted possible cases of infection and provided information on "suspects", alongside allegations from Namibia. One of the stories to attract feedback from readers was "Ebola: Zimbabwe monitors suspects", which was written by a NewZimbabwe staff reporter (10 August 2014). It was shared on Facebook 103 times and tweeted 4 times. The NewZimbabwe readers challenged Zimbabwe's health authorities's ability to stop the deadly Ebola virus

Table 16.2 Selected headlines on the Ebola 2014 news stories on www. NewZimbabwe.com

Headline	Date	Overall tone
"Ebola costs Zimbabwe tourism $6m: ZTA"	29 September 2014	State hiding Ebola victims
"Ebola outbreak threat in Zim 'real': Minister"	31 July 2014	State hiding Ebola victims
"Ebola: Zimbabwe monitors suspects"	10 August 2014	State hiding Ebola victims
"Ebola: Namibians told to avoid Zimbabwe"	25 September 2014	State hiding Ebola victims
"There is no Ebola here Zim tells Namibia"	28 September 2014	State hiding Ebola victims
"Lockdown in Harare over Ebola scare"	9 October 2014	State hiding Ebola victims
"Wilkins still closed over Ebola scare"	13 October 2014	State hiding Ebola victims
"Ebola affects local tourism industry"	30 December 2014	State hiding Ebola victims

from entering the country, and mocked the 21-day health surveillance for Ebola symptoms as ineffectual. As stated by one James Bond: "I hope to high heavens Ebola doesn't spread to Zimbabwe, as I fear that will be the end of a nation given the socioeconomic malaise we are faced with." Similarly, another reader by the name Wilbert added: "In a country that cannot even guarantee clean running water in all its major cities and towns, Ebola outbreak will mean hell! The measures this Mugabe regime has put in place to stop the spread of the virus are laughable!" The readers used the story to debate the inhabitable conditions in the country. They expressed cynicism by using kkkkk – (symbols, signalling laughter among social media users in Zimbabweans). The overriding concern with governance in the responses to one of the major initiatives Zimbabwe government can be seen as follows:

> **ngozi yemakhosi:** *They can't even handle Cholera (sic) let alone Ebhola (sic). Nxa!*
> **Dr. Nikuv Riggington (PhD):** *Tazopera manje!* [We are finished]
> **Nkosinathi:** *But we have been having Ebola for a very long time in Zimbabwe. Zanu is a deadly Ebola disease that has no treatment and it has been spread by Mugabe since 1980*
> **Guest:** *Kikikikikiki nhasi ndaseka!!!* [I have laughed so much today!!!]

Using English, Ndebele and Shona languages, these online Zimbabweans take advantage of their anonymity to attack the Zimbabwean government response to the crisis. They base their arguments on how the Zimbabwean government has failed to deal with HIV, AIDS and cholera. Indeed, they perceive the government led by Mugabe as the problem. It is also true that online behaviour can be staged or manipulated by non-state interests. Reading through the responses on NewZimbabwe, one can discern activism for and against the state. The communities on the site seem to have rehearsed positions from which to comment on every issue. Nonetheless, the fact that the Ebola issue is read into local challenges is unmistakable.

Ebola in the South African Media

South Africa's top digital news platform, News24.com, comprises both a "professional" journalism space as well as a dedicated citizen journalism space, MyNews24 (located at http://my.news24.com). MyNews24 is touted as a citizen journalism website, albeit one that was launched, marketed and run within the mainstream, commercial news site News24. Coverage of Ebola in both these spaces started slow, with only 15 articles on News24 during March 2014 and none on MyNews24 at all for the same period. The slow uptake of the Ebola story on the citizen journalism website is not surprising, as a cursory glance of the headlines generated by the "ebola-tag" on its parent website, News24.com, reveals that news was slow on the topic until July 2014 – thus roughly the same time as the international community led by WHO – recognised Ebola as a crisis of epidemic proportions. By then, there were already thousands of deaths attributed to the virus. The first article in this regard, entitled "Ebola – the scary truth", was posted on 4 April 2014. Highlighting the fact that Ebola was starting to enter the consciousness of users and readers of MyNews24, is the fact that this article clearly generated readership interest – it was viewed 2599 times although it only attracted 9 comments. Table 16.3 below, provides an overview of the headlines of the Ebola news stories on MyNews24, with their corresponding thematic fit which is indicative of the overall tone of the stories. The stories are ranked in order of readership, that is, the story which generated the most views – regardless of when it appeared and how many comments it attracted – is considered the top story in terms of what users of the MyNews24 space considers newsworthy. As can be seen though, there is generally congruence between the most "newsworthy" stories in this respect and the most "comment-worthy" stories from a reader's perspective. As with the coverage of other deadly diseases – i.e. HIV/AIDS, SARS, etc. – the headlines assumes a war rhetoric in which the disease becomes the perpetrator and the regions and peoples affected become the victims. In this rhetoric, as evidenced below, it is inevitable that binary oppositions will function prominently in an effort to not only make sense of disease, but also to emerge victorious from its grip:

Table 16.3   Ebola news stories on MyNews24 ranked in order of "newsworthiness"

Headline	Number of views	Number of comments	Theme and overall tone of coverage
Reports of Ebola conspiracy are worrying	7,248	16	Conspiracy theories
Ebola outbreak – the scary truth	2,599	9	Ebola "winning" the "fight"
Ebola Haven	1,559	4	Healthcare
SA at risk from Ebola?	1,274	20	Impact on South Africa
EVD, Africa's leading fatality	835	13	Ebola "winning" the "fight"
Guttersnipe media and the Ebola crisis – what are they playing at?	778	7	The media and Ebola: analysis of media coverage and impact
Ebola insurance	557	1	Impact on South Africa; Healthcare
Ebola: How does it affect us?	365	4	Impact on South Africa
Ebola outbreak exposes lack of cooperation and solidarity among African nations	322	1	One Africa?; Africa's Ebola friends and foes
Ebola and you	300	11	Ebola "winning" the "fight"
Why I love West Africa – minus Ebola	226	2	One Africa?
Is God upset with Africa?	137	10	An African disease?

We hypothesized that coverage of Ebola by citizen journalists from southern Africa would differ in range and tone from the coverage of the disease by mainstream Western journalists and news outlets, and, for the South African case study under scrutiny here, we further assumed that citizens would shift the focus of the Ebola stories to better serve their socio-political interests and affiliations. The remainder of this section tests these assumptions through a qualitative analysis of the Ebola news stories on MyNews24. While it is tempting to discuss the stories in thematically outlined depth, the restrictions imposed on any individual chapter in a book does not allow for such an approach. Instead, we will treat the stories and their thematic foci in a generalized analytical discussion geared towards highlighting the ways in which "ordinary" citizens interact with the media, and the spaces that such interaction opens up, allowing a range of views on any singular topic.

It is perhaps not surprising that the first story penned by a citizen journalist on MyNews24 adds to the Ebola panic instigated by mainstream coverage of the disease at the start of the outbreak. The story, headlined

"Ebola Outbreak – The Scary Truth", at first glance appears to be one that would advance some or other conspiracy theory (i.e. the "scary truth"), but upon reading it, one soon realizes that the article is, rather, an attempt at scientific explanation of what Ebola is, how it evolves and what its impact is. Nonetheless, like countless Western accounts meant to scare and awe, this article opens with a dramatic account of the impact of the disease, noting in its opening sentence that: "Doctors work quickly to remove the infected body of one of the Ebola virus' victims." Here already, the binary "perpetrator" versus "victim" – so evident in war rhetoric – is set up. The author then devotes the entire first paragraph to illustrate just how "dreadful" the disease is via a death tally (83 dead), emphasizing the devastation of the disease (" . . . incurable, devastating, painful") and finally – tapping into another popular theme in mainstream news coverage of the disease – noting its impact on border crossing both within and outside the continent (Saudi Arabia stating that they will refuse entry to citizens of the affected countries, and Senegal having already closed its borders "completely"). The article had attracted 2,599 views at the time of writing this (2015) – second only to the article entitled "Reports of Ebola Conspiracy are Worrying", which attracted 7,248 views. The popularity of the "scary truth" article can perhaps be explained by the double entendre in its headline, which appears to suggest, like many articles espousing conspiracy theories, that there might be a hidden truth not yet shared with readers which will be revealed in this article. In spite of this not being the case here – as mentioned, the article presents a medical-scientific explication of Ebola – the article attracted nine comments – this is the sixth highest response rate for all articles about Ebola on MyNews24. In comparison, the story entitled "EVD, Africa's leading fatality", which similarly attempts to explicate Ebola from a medical-scientific point of view, generated only 835 views, but attracted 13 comments. This story touches on the same themes as the first one, including a focus on Ebola as a killer of "numerous" people, medical facts about the virus, the need for travel precautions, if not restrictions, and the virus's possible impact on South Africa (quoting the Health Minister, the article concludes that the risk is minimal, but that South Africa is prepared should a case/cases be detected). The story entitled "Ebola: How does it affect us", attempts to explicate Ebola in relation to other virus outbreaks from a medical-scientific point of view. Stating that it wishes to "THINK" about Ebola through a focus on some facts which would allow us (author and readers) to " . . . draw our own conclusions", the article weaves through a focus on, by now (4 November 2014 – nine months after the first reports of an epidemic), well-known facts about the disease, through a focus on historical information about the first recorded outbreak of a "filovirus", which the author traces to Germany in 1967. In this story, posted on the website by a medical doctor, at least five themes emerge. The first trace of a conspiracy theory about Ebola as an invention by the West emerges (the author implicates "bioterrorism" and specifically mentions the " . . . Nazi scientists who were working on a variety of biological weapons in their laboratories…"). The story also attempts to respond to media coverage of Ebola, noting and commenting on what it sees as the media's disregard for African life ("Fast-forward to 2014. For the first time in history a Filovirus has reached American soil and the headlines are global. Thousands died in West Africa but that didn't make as much noise in the media… I wonder why."). The author then expands on his conspiracy theory, now implicating neoliberal capitalism by noting that, after the first reported case of Ebola in the USA, "Out of the blue, a cluster of pharmaceutical companies who have been 'working on' the virus for years have discovered 'experimental' treatments to curb its spread." Bringing his conspiracy theory in line with his inference about the disregard for African lives, the author further notes that: "These treatments are available to the Liberian man in America. They are however not available to the Liberian victims in Liberia." Following this, the author then turns his attention to South Africa espousing what the author deems to be "some facts" about Ebola and the South African situation:

> As much as viruses need people to spread; people need transport systems to spread viruses. 1st world transport infrastructure is, well, 1st class! The roads are generally functional, the planes work well and the buses reach their destination. The capacity for rapid spread of a contagious virus like Ebola within a first world country is potentially more rapid that in Africa. Our roads are faulty and our bridges are collapsing. Our buses are breaking down and for Ebola to spread from its focal point in West Africa is surprisingly, difficult. Infrastructure problems in Africa are actually assisting its containment.
>
> (Tawenga, 2014, http://www.news24.com/MyNews24/
> Ebola-How-Does-It-Affect-Us-20141104)

Having delivered his assessment of the "African condition", the author then states emphatically that this is "… NOT a West African problem alone anymore. It is a virus that has world-changing potential." He concludes this section of his article by lamenting the fact that: "Unfortunately for all human beings everywhere; these things are first handled by the politicians before the people with actual skills get ahold of the matter." Surprisingly, given the popularity of conspiracy theories in terms of "newsworthiness" within the citizen journalism sphere, this article has a relatively low view count (365 views at the time of writing) and also attracted only four comments, one of which accuses the author of trying to "… cook up a conspiracy theory" through omission of facts, and one of which praises the author's "brilliance". The remaining two comments were nonsensical. In contrast, the other two stories explicating the virus attracting more comments, with all 13 comments attracted by "EVD, Africa's leading fatality" focusing on the misrepresentation of medical and "leading cause of death" facts by the author; four of the comments were authored by the same individual.

In terms of socio-political commentary, the first comment on this article is especially noteworthy, with the commentator calling out the author's poor choice of words:

Arthur Harding – August 13, 2014 at 10:13

"Two patients in South Africa, suspected of containing the virus were tested of EVD and have been cleared of all suspicion." You make it sound like catching a disease is a criminal offence.

This is an astute observation, for, as has been noted by Foucault and Crewe (1992), such "criminalization" of disease serves a psychologically reassuring role. Being able to blame others is psychologically reassuring: the fact that it is their fault divides us from them. We are innocent, at the mercy of fate; they are guilty, and have behaved in such a way as to put us all at risk (Crewe, 1992, p. 14). This, it is argued, functions to give concrete form to the desire to create boundaries between the diseased and the clean, which in turn structures public opinion of both disease and those living with disease.

Attempting to historicize this reaction, Crewe (1992, p. 17) writes that:

Throughout history, the dominant sector of society has held socially marginalized groups, ethnic minorities and the poor responsible for epidemic diseases. Jews were blamed for the Black Death in Europe, the Irish were blamed for cholera in New York and the Italians were accused of introducing polio into Brooklyn. Foreigners were blamed for syphilis – the French called it the Italian disease, while the Italians called it the Spanish disease.

Drawing heavily on Foucault, Crewe sees the resultant moves towards isolation and quarantine for the afflicted as ways of expressing public fears about outsiders or socially unacceptable groups. Evidence that this "fear about outsiders" still functions in the consciousness of even groups traditionally at the receiving end of such fear-mongering are ample in the Western and commercial media coverage of Ebola, as well as in some government responses to the disease. It functions in the decisions by governments to close their borders as well as in the calls by citizens for a closer monitoring of borders, including screening people coming into countries, as evidenced in some stories and comments in the citizen journalism space:

Steve Price – April 6, 2014 at 11:59

The SA authorities were so worried about Swine Flu and Bird Flu that they took steps at our international borders to monitor people entering the country.

I think the way this virus has the potential to spread through our some-what porous international borders with our neighbours is far more scary. (Commenting on the "Ebola Outbreak – The Scary Truth" story)

The article entitled "SA at risk from Ebola?" similarly notes that "South Africa could be declared an Ebola hotspot in the not too distant future…"; stating as support for the assertion (and amongst other assertions that: "With borders more porous than Swiss Cheese, it's only a matter of time before the killer virus migrates to this backend of Africa. It's almost as if there are no border controls in place with people coming and going as they please."

The majority of stories and comments in this space, however, advocate for tolerance, education and understanding about Ebola, while calling out stories and comments that are geared towards "fear-mongering", "conspiracy theories" and blaming people affected by the disease. The story headlined "Ebola Outbreak Exposes Lack of Cooperation and Solidarity among African Nations", for example, advocates for better understanding among African nations and doing away with "…artificially colonial-demarcated boundaries. Issues regarding Africa should not be seen as superiority contest or an avenue for grandstanding but a collective issue that demand collective action." Similarly, the article headlined "Why I Love West Africa – Minus Ebola" argues for doing away with misconceptions about (West) Africa and making an effort to understand our African brothers and sisters. Commentaries on stories also picked up on the theme of understanding the disease and African solidarity:

konfab – January 20, 2015 at 06:33

Typical middle class fear. You are more likely to die of TB or Malaria. Ebola is only spread through contact with bodily fluids. The only people who get Ebola are those who directly handle people with Ebola.
(Comment on a story about Ebola insurance coverage
for South Africans)

The vast majority of comments on the MyNews24 website were, however, reserved to (1) question African governance; and (2) question the maxim "African solutions for African problems". In this respect, the stories and the commentaries clearly illustrate – similar to the Zimbabwean case study – that while citizen journalists can and do respond to news stories of national and international importance, they do so on their own terms. Not surprisingly perhaps, what seems to be non-negotiable for southern African citizen journalists is a focus on issues that directly impact upon the everyday – that is, there is a clear focus on calling African governments to do better. This call is markedly different from Western media calls in this respect though, as it primarily discards and even mocks coverage that seems to suggest that African citizens cannot think for themselves, and while they may be attracted to so-called conspiracy theories – even indulging in espousing such theories from time to time – it is clear that such indulgence is rooted in a desire to reposition the African continent and its place in global socio-politics.

Conclusion

The critical responses to digital media coverage of the 2014 Ebola crisis should be considered in the context of democratization within the two transitional societies. Leslie (2007) reminds us that communication online tends to be driven by crisis, "but when circumstances are normal, exchanges of information with different objectives prevail" (p. 124). Responses from African citizen journalism to the 2014 Ebola crisis illustrates the behaviour of new-generation Africans who want to tackle challenges without hypocrisy, corruption, inefficiency, ineptitude, incompetence or buffoonery. The online users see through the double standards of their leaders (Ayittey, 2005). The responses to the 2014 Ebola crisis can ultimately be seen as a way in which African officialdom and blogspheres are in contest. This can only deepen democratization.

References

Ayittey George, B.N. (2005) *Africa Unchained: The Blue Print for Africa's Future.* New York: Macmillan/Palgrave

Bowman, S. and Willis, C. (2003), *We Media: How Audiences Are Shaping the Future of News and Information.* The Media Center at the American Press Institute, www.ndn.org (retrieved 11 May 2015).

Castells M. (1996) *The Rise of the Network Society.* Oxford: Blackwells.

Couldry, N. (2009). Rethinking the politics of voice. *Continuum: Journal of Media and Cultural Studies* 23(4): 579–582.

Crewe, M. (1992). *Aids in South Africa: The Myth and the Reality.* London: Penguin Books.

Hirst, M. (2011) *News 2.0: Can Journalism Survive the Internet?* Crows Nest NSW: Allen & Unwin.

Giorgis H. (2014) "The problem with the west's Ebola response is still fear of a black patient", 16 October, 2014, http://www.theguardian.com/ commentisfree/2014/oct/16/west-ebola-response-black-patient (accessed: 16 October 2014).

Jenkins, H. (2006) *Convergence Culture: Where Old and New Media Collide*, New York: New York University Press.

Jensen M. (2000) Making the Connection: Africa and the Internet. *Current History* 99(637): 215–220.

Leslie M. (2007) "The Internet and Democratisation". In *Media and Democracy in Africa*, G. Hyden, M. Leslie and F.O. Ogundimu (eds.), New Brunswick/London: Transaction Publishers

Leslie M. and F.O. Ogundimu (eds.) *Media and Democracy in Africa.* New Brunswick/London: Transaction Publishers.

Mano W. (ed.) (2015) *Racism, Ethnicity and the Media in Africa: Mediating Conflict in the Twenty-First Century*, London: I.B. Tauris

Mano, W. and Willems, W. (2010) "Debating 'Zimbabweanness' in Diasporic Internet Forums: Technologies of Freedom?" In *Zimbabwe's New Diaspora: Displacement and the Cultural Politics of Survival*, McGregor, J. and Primorac, R., (eds.). Forced migration (31). Berghahn, Oxford, UK, pp. 183–201.

Mansell, R. (2004). "The internet, capitalism, and policy". In *Internet Research Annual, Volume 1*, M. Consalvo-et-al. (ed.), New York: Peter Lang, pp. 175–184.

Nyamnjoh F.B. (2005) *Africa's Media, Democracy and the Politics of Belonging.* London/New York: UNISA Press.

Njogu K. and J. Middleton (eds.) (2009). *Media and Identity in Africa*. Edinburgh: Edinburgh University Press.

O'Donnell, P., Lloyd, J., and Dreher, T. (2009). Listening, pathbuilding and continuations: A research agenda for the analysis of listening. *Continuum: Journal of Media and Cultural Studies* 23 (4): 423–439.

Schudson, Michael (2005) *Why Democracies Need an Unlovable Press.* Cambridge/Malden: Polity Press.

Schudson, Michael (2001) "The objectivity norm in American journalism", *Journalism*, 2(2): 149–170.

Spitulnik, D. (2002). "Alternative Media and Communicative Spaces". In *Media and Democracy in Africa*, Hyden, G., Lesilie, M. and Ogundimu, F.F., (eds.). Transaction Publishers: New Brunswick, NJ, pp. 177–205.

Tettey W.J. (2006) "The Politics of Media Accountability in Africa: An Examination of Mechanism and Institutions", *The International Communication Gazette* 68(3): 229–248.

Tawenga, B. (2014). Ebola. How Does It Affect Us? *MyNews24.com.* http://www.news24.com/MyNews24/Ebola-How-Does-It-Affect-Us-20141104   Accessed 12 May 2015.

Tuchman, G. (1972) "Objectivity as Strategic Ritual: An Examination of Newsmen's Notions of Objectivity", *American Journal of Sociology*, 77(4) (Jan., 1972): 660–679.

Tuchman, G. (1978) *Making News: A Study in the Construction of Reality,* New York: Free Press 070.1 TUC.

17
From Citizen Journalism to Human Rights Journalism: Framing the Ebola Epidemic in Sierra Leone on Facebook

Ibrahim Seaga Shaw

Introduction

This chapter seeks to contribute to the growing scholarly debate about the widening democratic deficit of citizen journalism in serving as a counter-hegemonic model to mainstream journalism. Moreover, earlier scholarly criticisms of citizen journalism have tended to focus on its limits in fostering a liberal democratic political participation and professional journalism. What has received little scholarly attention is a critical look at the shortcomings of citizen journalism in the promotion of human rights and development. What is more, the few studies that exist on this, for example by Allan (2006; Allan *et al.*, 2007) looking at the potential and limits of citizen journalism in reporting Hurricane Katrina in 2005 and the Tsunami in 2004, and Madianou (2013) on the Kony 2012 humanitarian campaign video, only looked at the challenges of citizen journalism without necessarily identifying a journalism practice that would complement it (CJ) or serve as a kind of remedy. It is the aim of this chapter to offer a contribution to filling this gap in provision in the context of human rights journalism. Shaw (2012) talks about how human rights journalism can help address the shortcomings of citizen journalism in the promotion of human rights but only uses general examples. This chapter goes further, not only to throw more light on the latest developments in the debate, but to look at a specific case study of the framing of the Ebola epidemic in Sierra Leone by a Facebook discussion forum, to determine the extent of the potential or deficiency of citizen journalism in the promotion of human rights. What is even more unique about this chapter is that it is, so far, the first to offer a human rights journalism critic of the "democratic deficit" of citizen journalism in the social media framing of Ebola. The limited access to, and use of, the Internet by most members of the public means that there are still many people who do not necessarily participate in social media discussions, and are therefore not democratically empowered by the Internet and citizen journalism.

The following section of this chapter explores these shortcomings of citizen journalism in the lense of human rights journalism.

From citizen journalism to human rights journalism

The main aim of this section is to explore the model of citizen journalism and offer a critic of its shortcomings in serving as counterhegemonic journalism to mainstream journalism. Each of the deficits of citizen journalism discussed in this section will be juxtaposed with how human rights journalism can serve as a panacea. The concept of "citizen journalism" has recently expanded to include not only the process of creating content for formal online news outlets such as blogs or independent websites, but also citizens' follow-up participation in the news process, such as social media posting, reposting, linking, tagging, commenting and rating (Goode, 2009; Kim and Lowrey, 2015). While news websites and blogs run by citizen journalists attracted much earlier scholarly attention, "citizen journalism activity through social media such as Facebook and Twitter is becoming increasingly relevant and important" (Kim and Lowrey, 2015, p. 298), questions abound as to what makes citizen journalism different from mainstream professional journalism. Differences have mostly been seen in the sense of new forms and practices in the digital age (Lewis *et al.*, 2010). In the context of traditional news production, professional gatekeeping routines such as "selecting, writing, editing, positioning, scheduling, repeating and otherwise massaging of information" (Shoemaker and Vos, 2009, p. 73) are followed, whereas, in the new media production context, such traditional boundaries of gatekeeping are blurred, which means anyone with access to the Internet can participate in the production, distribution and consumption of news (Benkler, 2006; Bruns, 2008; Jenkins, 2006). This blurring of professional boundaries, thanks to the Internet, has posed a major threat to mainstream journalism practice and its role in society (Benkler, 2006; Bruns, 2008; Carpenter, 2010; Deuze, 2005; Goode, 2009; Jenkins, 2006; Joyce, 2007; Kaufhold *et al.*, 2010; Lewis *et al.*, 2010; Pease, 1990; Singer, 2003; Williams and Carpini, 2004). Citizen journalists have come under attack for lacking training in professional news production and gatekeeping, which, critics believe, may risk undermining accuracy. The fact that there are concerns over blurred boundaries between news production and consumption in the citizen journalism context means there are times when traditional news production conventions or routines such as objectivity, accuracy, fairness and balance may be compromised. It is therefore necessary to explore how citizen journalism production contexts differ from those of traditional journalism, and how they can potentially influence each other.

Moreover, one thing that has made mainstream professional journalists treat citizen journalists with contempt is their sweeping aside of professional journalism standards such as objectivity and balance, since most of those who participate in the news production processes by contributing texts, images or videos take stands or positions. Little wonder that the whole notion of citizen journalism has raised several questions such as: Who is a journalist? Can any blogger be a journalist? Can any citizen who posts a newsworthy video on YouTube be considered a journalist? Can you be a journalist if you have never worked for a traditional media outlet? Can anyone who performs a "random act of journalism" using the Internet be considered a journalist? These are questions that continue to provoke a rethink of the journalism of our time.

Yet another even more contentious issue of citizen journalism is its proclamation as the "radical" alternative journalism model to mainstream journalism. It is seen as an alternative plebeian public sphere (Atton, 2001; 2002; Habermas, 1989), in a historical context as "insurgent journalism" (Curran and Seaton, 2009, p. 16), and in a more contemporary context as a "counter-hegemonic journalism" (Harcup, 2005, p. 372). Salawu (2011, p. 185) sounded even more optimistic by describing citizen journalism as a "journalism of the people, by the people, and for the people".

Shaw (2012) sees CJ as different from mainstream journalism in that it is centred around people more than around elites; democratic more than profit-centred; less conceptually ambiguous; more partisan and empathic, more participatory, engaging and empowering; and more oriented towards problem-solving. CJ gives voice to the marginalized "them"; hence Atton's phrase "native reporting" (2002, pp. 112–117), a concept developed from Spurr's (1993) study of colonial journalism. This new journalism practice consists of activities that relate to political reporting; political weblogs (Matheson and Allan, 2003) and the open publishing strategies of an international, revolutionary online news agency such as Indymedia or Independent Media Channel (IMC), which rely on news and opinions contributed by participants involved in a diverse range of social and political activism. Citizen media narrative practices emphasize "the first-person eye witness accounts by participants, reworking of the populist approaches of tabloid newspapers to recover a 'radical popular style of reporting'; collective and anti-hierarchical forms of organisation [...] an inclusive, radical form of civic journalism" (Atton, 2003, p. 267).

However, as this chapter seeks to argue in the remaining part of this section and others to follow, the democratic potential of CJ has been found to be fraught with some serious shortcomings, which I will now examine in juxtaposition with what I have described as the radical alternative model of human rights journalism. Before going any further I would like to unpack the concept of human rights journalism and present the key features that make it a truly counterhegemonic model of journalism practice. Shaw (2012, p. 46), who proposed HRJ, defines it as the diagnostic style of reporting which gives a critical reflection of the experiences and needs of the victims and perpetrators of human rights violations (all types – physical as well as cultural and structural) to understand the reasons for these violations so as to prevent or solve them in ways that would not produce more human rights imbalances or violations in the future. Moreover, it is a journalism that challenges, not reinforces, the status quo of the powerful dominant voices of society against the weak and marginalized ones in the promotion and protection of human rights and peace. Shaw (2012) describes journalism that reinforces the status quo of the dominant voices of society against the weak and marginalized and that fails to monitor and ensure the realization of human rights for all as human wrongs journalism (HWJ).

In the discussion to follow I refer to the HRJ variables listed in Table 17.1 I also draw on the five principles of the rights-based approach to reporting, namely linkages to human rights standards, participation, accountability, non-discrimination and empowerment, some of which feature among the HRJ orientation variables.

The first democratic deficit of Citizen Journalism is its lack of clarity of definition, especially in its role in society. While some see it as merely expanding the participation of citizens in public discussions, others see it as a reform movement advocating change in society. The emergence of Citizen Journalism is grounded in the "civic and public journalism 'reform' movement in the late 1980s and grew with the proliferation of the internet" (Kim and Lowrey, 2014, p. 299; see also Flew and Wilson, 2010; Kperogi, 2011). Nip (2006) looks at how Citizen Journalism is different from mainstream journalism via a taxonomy of journalistic forms: traditional journalism, interactive journalism, public journalism and participatory journalism. Advocates of Citizen Journalism are yet to agree on a clear and widely accepted conceptual definition of the concept. On the contrary, HRJ has not only been historically rooted in human rights reporting since the days of James Creelman, William Howard Russell and so on, but it is conceptually defined as a pro-active journalism that knows no borders, no race, no age, no gender and no class – a journalism with a human face and for the human race. This definition is largely inspired by Article 1 of the UN Universal Declaration of Human Rights (1948): "All human beings are born free and equal in dignity and rights" (UN. Doc A/810).

The second criticism of CJ relates to its limited democratic participation, as most grass-root voices are still excluded. Advocates of CJ argue that, in its case, there is no danger of class exclusion from coverage or impact, since the structures and processes of news production are very much embedded in the normal life of the citizens who are in the driving seat (Rodriguez, 2001, cited in Atton, 2003, p. 267). For example, any member of the public with a smart phone can shoot pictures of some dramatic events as fire or shooting incidents, often just for the fun of it, and post them on the Internet to be accessed by other citizens free of cost. However, low funds and a poorly paid or voluntary staff of citizen media "might affect the ability to access a wide range of sources and make those experiments with news routines that have been so often associated with alternative media" (Atton and Wickenden, 2005, p. 351). Moreover, although Indymedia channels claim to be independent, "they are not independent in the strictest sense of the word as the code and content of the news are made and regulated by people" often affiliated with many different movements, which contribute their own content (Platon and Deuze, 2003, p. 338). While blogs and other sites owned by community interest groups can engage people on defined sets of issues, such as robust criticisms of mainstream media content, they do not necessarily stimulate sustained debate, deliberation and action on a range of issues, especially ones that do not affect people directly or personally (instead they affect "others"; Haas and Steiner, 2006, p. 252).

On the other side of the spectrum, there is no room for a democratic deficit in HRJ, because it is based on the idea of journalism without borders, be they physical or structural. This resonates with its third, human face-oriented variable, which focuses on care and empowerment for all. Humanitarianism and empowerment are among the four clear values of human rights journalism, the other two being truth and holism. The human rights journalist would find it difficult to exclude the weak and poor people of society because they tend to strictly follow the human rights principles of non-discrimination, equal participation and empowerment. If they demonstrate any bias at all, this will favour the weak and vulnerable by way of positive action; not be against them (see Table 17.1) (see also Shaw, 2012). The human rights journalist therefore has the moral responsibility to challenge, and not to reinforce, the existing individual, local and global imbalances (Beman and Calderbank, 2008).

Table 17.1 Basic binary features of HRJ and HWJ

Human Rights Journalism (HRJ)	Human Wrongs Journalism (HWJ)
Non-violence/structural/cultural violence oriented: proactive/preventing direct violence/Triple win; everybody comes out happy and smiling	Competition orientated: Violence/drama/evocative: solution after damage/business profit or loss; some people come out happy and smiling while others come out sad and crying
Expose all human wrongs	Expose "some" or "their" human wrongs
People/human face-orientated/care for and empower all but biased in favour of vulnerable people	Demonization-orientated: Focus on the human rights violations by "them", "others" or "our enemies", and on "our" or "our friends'" victims
Holistic problem-solving: now/tomorrow and surface/hidden problems	Partial solution-orientated: Focus on immediate physical needs only at the expense of long-term structural solutions

The third deficit of CJ is its firm location in corporate capitalism-driven media conglomerates such as Google, Microsoft, Facebook, Twitter, LinkedIn, YouTube and so on. Critics of CJ, especially critical political economists, say that this problem makes it difficult for it to operate outside the influence and manipulation of such organizations. They argue that the focus of these conglomerates is to increase their profit margins by selling their audiences (citizens) to the highest bidding advertisers. Posts that do not promote their bottom line are, all too often, simply deleted. Take, for example, the Kony 2012 video that went viral on YouTube appealing for support to capture Ugandan war lord Joseph Kony, and raising awareness on the plight of children as victims of his atrocious war in Northern Uganda. The maker of the video, which apparently idealizes the ethos of social media activism, and co-founder of the Invisible Children charity, Jason Russell, explained in the opening seconds of the video:

> Right now there are more people on Facebook than there were on the planet 200 years ago. Humanity's greatest desire is to belong and connect. We hear each other. We share what we love. And this connection is changing the way the world works.

But journalist Jonathan Albright (2012), despite describing this as "a resonating" and powerful statement, appears less impressed, as he said "only there's one problem; we can't actually hear each other. At least not on the Kony YouTube video", because, as he puts it, all comments have been removed, 500,000 of them, and that with the comment feature now disabled, all feedbacks, including many criticisms of the video itself. This example shows that CJ may sometimes parallel mainstream journalism in terms of being susceptible to the propaganda of the elite and corporate market classes. On the contrary, the human rights journalist goes in search of the honest truth and is overly sensitive to propaganda that will prevent him or her from exposing all the hidden agendas and causes of human rights violations. As HRJ is honesty-oriented (see Table 17.1), it is bound to be free from any economic or political manipulation; this freedom gives it the strength to expose all human wrongs.

The fourth deficit of CJ is its top-down rather than bottom-up orientation, mainly due to its reliance on mainstream news values and sources. Citizen reporters or community correspondents occasionally use mainstream media as sources (Atton and Wickenden, 2005). Additionally, the personal and activist groups' websites sometimes have a close affinity with the often elitist political philosophy of their owners. For instance, during the 1998 protests at the World Trade Organization in Seattle, the online IMC (Indymedia) relied heavily on liberal activists and development non-governmental organizations (NGOs) for news and views about what was going on. This means that citizen journalists are not completely free from the elitist spin: "The extent to which its journalists are deemed to be unproblematic allies 'in solidarity' with their sources and the extent to which sources are deployed for ideological ends raise further questions about the critical practices of alternative journalism" (Atton and Wickenden, 2005, p. 358).

HRJ, on the other hand, creates a conversation that is basically oriented towards humanity, whereby everybody is cared for and empowered with the knowledge and opportunity of becoming active participants in the kind of life they would like to lead. It is a form of journalism rooted in what Berlin (1969) and Ignatieff (1998) described as "pluralism", which recognizes that "human goals are many [...] and in perpetual rivalry with one another" (Berlin, 1969, p. 171), and where "the only moral political system was that which maximised liberty to allow individuals to make their own compromises among conflicting values" (Plaissance, 2002, p. 216). Placing Berlin's claim in the context of the modern world, which is replete with ethnic or class conflicts, Ignatieff calls for a "precarious equilibrium", and sees pluralism as the answer to all difficult conflict situations (1998, p. 217). Pluralism provides an atmosphere of what Carey calls "democratic mediation", in which people need to transcend the "narcissism of minor differences" and return to a common ground language, symbolic of our shared humanity (Plaissance, 2002, p. 217). Carey's notion of "democratic mediation" (2009) and Berlin's and Ignatieff's idea of "pluralism" and "shared humanity" resonate with Chourliariki's (2013) idea of "cosmopolitan logic", which is the opposite of "communitarian logic.

The final deficit of CJ is its limited interventionist and problem-solving orientation. Just like mainstream journalism, the reach of citizen journalism is, to a very large extent, limited to the notion of a (particular) political community, whereas HRJ has a much wider global reach owing to the fact that it covers "universal" moral communities with a diverse history and culture – in short, cosmopolitan society as a whole. While political realists believe in the idea of "particular" political communities, cosmopolitans believe in the idea of a "universal" (moral) political community. Thus, while citizen journalism is based on selective problem-solving, being limited more or less to the "particular" political community – just like mainstream journalism – human rights journalism is based on distributive problem-solving; open to the global human community as a whole. Such a community is inspired by the stoic idea of a human society where every human being – every life – is important, and hence worth protecting in the cosmopolitan context of global justice.

Chouliaraki (2006) refers to the concepts of cosmopolitanism and communitarianism as two broad ethical norms that have traditionally informed the representations of distant suffering and humanitarian communication. She sees the cosmopolitan version of global connectivity as premised on the idea that, by rendering visible the suffering of others, the media develop a process of critical reflexivity and in this way contribute to a "democratisation of responsibility", based on the idea that concern for others becomes an increasing part of the daily lives of more individuals (Thompson, 1995, p. 263). The main difference between this cosmopolitan perspective and the communitarian one is that, in the latter, the focus on critical reflexivity and responsibility for a global humanity is absent. While it is true that a communitarian perspective, like the cosmopolitan one, emphasizes "a feeling in common" among spectators who are brought together through the simultaneity of broadcasting and the capacity of electronic media to transcend national boundaries, what is actually missing is "an orientation to the distant other" (Chouliaraki, 2008, p. 378). Thus, while communitarian humanitarian communication orientates towards values and interests shared by a particular community of communicators and spectators or audiences, the cosmopolitan humanitarian communication orientates towards values and interests shared by a global human community of communicators and spectators or audiences.

Framing Ebola in Sierra Leone on a Facebook discussion forum

In this section, I draw on content and framing analyses to critically investigate how the Ebola epidemic in Sierra Leone was framed by posts on a Facebook Sierra Leone Ebola discussion forum (FBSLDECF). It investigates the extent of the democratic potential or deficit of posts on this forum by citizen journalists, mostly from the Sierra Leone diaspora, and the extent to which the framing was influenced by political, business and media elites, or grass-root citizens. As I noted in section two in this chapter, the Curran and colleagues (2013) study debunks the widely held claim that the Internet has empowered the otherwise voiceless members of civil society, as the study found the news websites studied from nine countries used more elite state, business and expert sources than even the mainstream presses in those countries, and far above those of civil society. It is therefore the aim of this chapter to contribute to the research by Curran and colleagues (2013) to test the validity of the "empowering" role of the Internet by looking at the framing of Ebola on Facebook.

I first draw on de Bonville's model of quantitative content analysis (2000), on the basis of quantitative measurement of the aggregate data of posts on the FBSLDECF between February and April 2015. This discussion forum was chosen because it was the most popular forum on Facebook focusing on Ebola, with 8,731 members, mostly from the Sierra Leone diaspora. The reason for the choice of the period of study is because two highly controversial issues, the release of the audit report exposing alleged corruption and the sacking of the country's vice president, which generated a lot of heated debate on the forum, happened during this time. I gained access to the discussion by joining the group, and announced my intention to use the forum as my case study for this chapter. All posts and user-generated content (UGC) posted on the forum during these three months were coded to constitute the unit of analysis. All posts posted repeatedly on the forum were excluded from the coding. In all, 438 posts were retrieved and coded from the forum; the posts included articles, comments and press releases shared from other media, state or NGO sources or bloggers, UGC comments, ads, public notices and so on. For the framing analysis I use Entman's model, which is based on the idea that the more an issue is framed in the media, the more it is likely to remain on the news agenda – which has the knock-on effect of setting the agenda for the public as well (Entman, 1993). The content and frame analyses will explore the following research questions:

RQ1) Were posts by elite sources more frequent and dominant than those by grass-root sources?

RQ2) Were posts based on facts more frequent and dominant than those based on comments?

RQ3) Were posts about political party politics (communitarianism) more frequent and dominant than those about Ebola and its victims (cosmopolitanism)?

Research question 1 (RQ1) will investigate the validity of the criticism indicated in the introduction and developed in the first section of this chapter, "From citizen journalism to human rights journalism": that citizen journalists focus on using mainstream media sources, or politically or commercially deploy elite sources of information (Atton and Wickenden, 2005) instead of grass-root sources. Research question 2 (RQ2) will investigate the validity of the criticism of citizen journalism in favouring journalism of detachment (objectivity) as opposed to journalism of attachment (advocacy) also made in the introduction and developed in the first section of this chapter, "From citizen journalism to human rights journalism". Finally, research question 3 (RQ3) will investigate the validity of the criticism of citizen journalism for favouring the empowering of small communities (communitarianism) instead of global humanity or society (cosmopolitanism) also made in the introduction and developed in the first section of this chapter, "From citizen journalism to human rights journalism".

Dominant and less dominant posts

I will start by answering RQ1: Were posts by elite sources more frequent and dominant than those of grass-root sources. Elite sources include mainstream media, state/ruling party, opposition party(ies), NGOs and development/relief agencies, while grass-root sources include citizen media, grass-root individuals, communities, and civil society groups or activists. It is important to investigate the validity or not of the criticism of CJ as over-focusing on using information from elite as opposed to grass-root sources,

Table 17.2 Fact- and comment-based posts, and total posts

PBOFs	291
PBOCs	83
Total posts	374

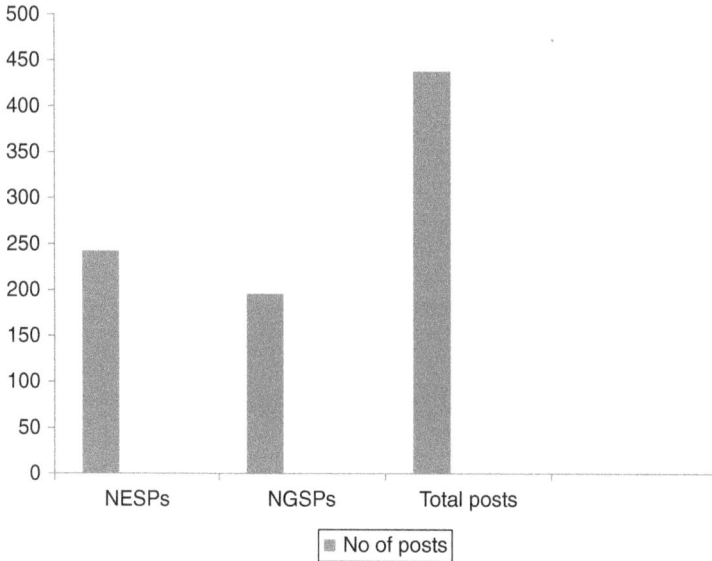

Figure 17.1 Elite and grass-root sources' posts

and thus failing to address the democratic deficit of mainstream journalism. All 438 posts coded were content analysed to determine which were contributed by elite and which by grass-root sources. The analysis is represented in Table 17.2 and Figure 17.1, under the two categories: number of elite sources posts (NESPs) and number of grass-root sources posts (NGSPs), followed by a discussion of the results.

Discussion of results

As we can see from the data represented in Table 17.2 and Figure 17.1, the volume of posts by elite sources is larger than that by grass-root sources. While the margin might seem slightly lower in the case of social media discussion fora, as the one in this study, compared to we normally see in the case of the mainstream media, it is important to note that these results show that citizen journalism, which is actually supposed to give voices to the voiceless and empower them to take active part in democratic discussions and interventions, is failing to address the democratic deficit of mainstream journalism. From these results, we can see that the majority of the posts on the FBSLDECF was by elite sources, especially from mainstream media, state and commercial institutions, and not by grass-root sources such as ordinary citizens and otherwise marginalized community interest groups whose voices are barely heard in the mainstream media. Although there are a significant number of grass-root sources posts (196 out of total posts of 438 during the period studied), this number is still surpassed by a significant margin of about 50 by elite sources posts (242). These results confirm criticism of CJ relating to its tendency to exclude some grass-root voices in favour of elite ones, which makes it more top-down than bottom-up, and which makes it more like mainstream media, as discussed in the first section of this chapter, "From citizen journalism to human rights journalism", and confirmed by earlier research by Curran and colleagues (2013). Moreover, since the results of the analysis in Tables 17.1 and 17.2 also show that some of the posts from elite sources, such as the mainstream media or the state, were actually shared on the Facebook discussion forum by regular users and members, this confirms criticisms by Platon and Deuze (2003), also discussed in section two earlier in this chapter, that some so-called independent citizen journalists are not independent after all, as they help share content that is often produced and regulated by people affiliated to elite establishments and movements.

Facts vs comments in framing the discussion on the Facebook forum

Using content and frame analyses I now look at RQ2: Were posts based on facts more frequent and dominant than those based on comments? It is interesting to discover whether facts featured more than comments or vice versa, as one of the criticisms, as discussed in section two in this chapter, has been that citizen journalism is increasingly losing its radical adversarial flare of advocating for social justice via critical comments asking right questions, and is now adopting a more mainstream journalism style of objectivity. The posts based on facts include mostly news reports from local and international mainstream media, press releases, Ebola updates, information and so on, shared by users on the Facebook discussion forum, while comments include mostly comments and opinions by users or shared by users but authored by others outside the forum, and UGC comments. However, UGC comments that were made up no more than ten words were excluded from the coding, while posts such as public notices and ads were also excluded from the coding. All coded posts, here totalling 374, were analysed to determine the frequency of posts based on facts, represented in Table 17.3 and Figure 17.2 as PBOC.

Table 17.3 Elite and grass-root sources' posts on FBSLDECF between February and April 2015

NESPs	242
NGSPs	196
Total posts	438

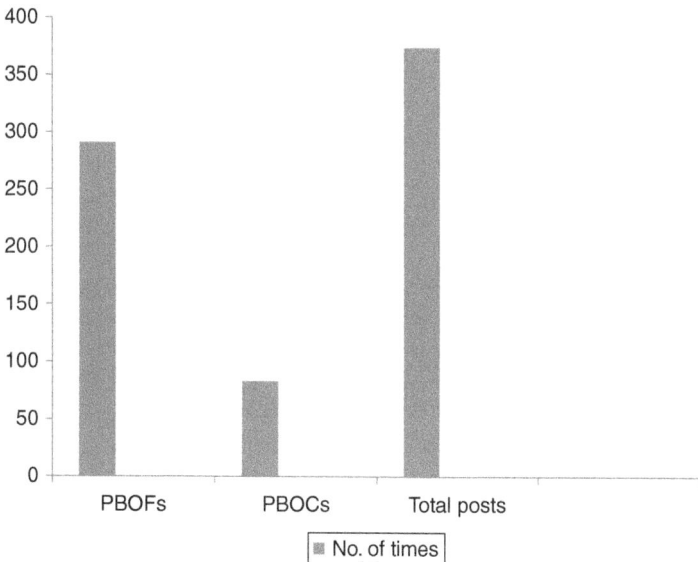

Figure 17.2 Fact- vs comment-based posts

Discussion of results

As seen in the data represented in Table 17.2 and Figure 17.2, the posts based on facts are more frequent and dominant than those based on comments. The fact that the margin is so wide makes the result even more interesting, as it goes to confirm the stated criticism of CJ as now fast moving away from being an "insurgency" or "challenger" form of journalism –which it was celebrated for in its early days – to a much more mainstream form of objective journalism where the emphasis is on facts. It is quite interesting to see that most of the facts-based posts either came from state or business elite sources, or were authored by Sierra Leone journalists such as Kabs Kanu, Josephine Kamara or Yusuf Keketuma Sandi, writing for mainstream Sierra Leone newspapers which are also available online, as well as by journalists writing for the mainstream international media. Indeed, some of these fact-based posts were shared by citizen media such as Mamba TV and Sherix

Webradio, run by Sierra Leoneans in the USA. The fact that there are very limited comment-based posts, as low as 83 out of a total coded posts of 374, speaks volumes about how citizen journalists are now less concerned with asking very difficult questions with regard to existing power relations, and are instead more interested in mimicking the objective journalism ethos of mainstream journalism. What is more, some posts contributed or shared by grass-root users were fact-based, often about breaking news, and not necessarily comments voicing their opinions on important issues of the day. One such post (19 March 2015), by Ayodele Manley, was about the breaking news of the appointment of Victor Foh as vice president of Sierra Leone, following the sacking of Samuel Sam-Sumana. Posts based on facts instead of opinions were regularly sent on the Facebook forum which means the citizen journalists were more interested in the drama and entertainment of soft news rather than the more interrogative and largely opinion-oriented hard news.

Discussion forums, such as the one studied here, were, in the early days of the Internet, especially before the emergence of big social media conglomerates such as Facebook, celebrated as providing space for otherwise marginalized voices to come forward, speak out and challenge mainstream media discourses. Sadly, however, this now seems to be a thing of the past, as the results of this analysis show. Yet, if objectivity means balance and fairness, then we can safely say that the increasing dominance of fact-based posts that more or less spin the line of elite mainstream media, and the dominant political and economic class of society in citizen journalism, means that so-called citizen journalists, just like their mainstream counterparts, are more subjective or biased than objective. Where human rights journalists are different is that, while trying to be as fair as possible in empowering all voices, they make sure that, if it comes to tipping the balance, or taking a position which is, in most cases, inevitable, they do so on the side of the victims of human rights violations and not in favour of those contributing to their suffering.

Political party politics vs Ebola and victim frames

In this final subsection I examine RQ3: Were posts about political party politics (communitarianism) more frequent and dominant than those about Ebola and its victims (cosmopolitanism)? This question is quite important, as it would help us understand the extent to which the discussions of the forum were framed in favour of issues that touched on basic human right issues, such as health and well-being, which should be enjoyed by all human beings (cosmopolitanism), or on issues of political party or community interests (communitarianism). All 438 posts initially coded during the three-month period were analysed to determine which particularly framed political party issues, especially those involving claims and counter claims between the ruling All People's Congress (APC) Party and the main opposition, the Sierra Leone People's Party (SLPP). The following three frames are

Table 17.4 PPPF, EAVF, OF and total posts

PPPF	208
EAVF	189
OF	41
Total posts	438

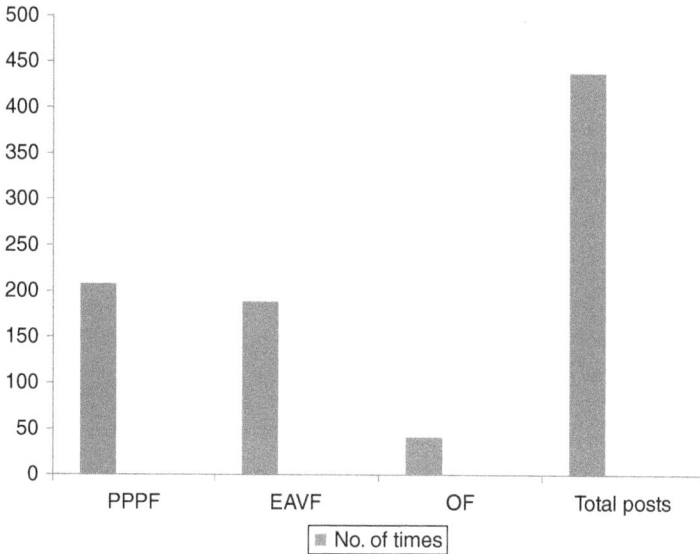

Figure 17.3 PPPF, EAVF and OF

investigated: political party politics frame (PPPF); Ebola and victims' frame (EAVF); and others' frame (OF). The first two will include posts involving party politics issues and Ebola and victims' issues, respectively, while the last one will include all posts not related to the first two frames. Posts included in OF are ones about bereavement, ads, public notices and personal issues. The analysed data will be represented in Table 17.4 and Figure 17.3.

Discussion of results

As we can see in the analysis in Table 17.4 and Figure 17.3, the number of posts on political party politics issues and events is greater than those on issues and events about Ebola and its victims in Sierra Leone, even if the margin is not so huge as it is just 19 posts separating the two. These results are interesting but disappointing, especially given the fact that it is largely assumed the main idea of the FBSLDECF, when it was set up, was to encourage discussions that would provide a voice and support to efforts at combating the deadly disease. The results show that, at the very least, the forum was quickly hijacked by users who were more interested in using it to score political points in discussions that are largely polarized along ruling (APC) party and opposition (SLPP) lines. The results also confirm criticism earlier in this chapter (second section: From Citizen Journalism to Human Rights Journalism) about the increasing focus of citizen journalists on partisan communitarian issues instead of on cosmopolitan issues of global humanity and justice. The opportunity was lost by the local Sierra Leone media, as well as the citizen media in the diaspora – that are largely polarized along ruling and opposition party lines – to provide an independent critical evaluation of the many allegations of corruption and mismanagement of funds raised to combat Ebola, and the controversy surrounding the alleged unconstitutional sacking of the country's vice president. In fact, the attention of the Sierra Leone media quickly shifted from evaluating and following up on the audit report on the alleged misuse of Ebola funds to the controversy over the sacking of the vice president, thereby letting alleged corrupt officials off the hook.

One other interesting finding of the analysis is that most of the posts shared by users but authored by journalists from the mainstream media, such as Reuters, Agence France-Press (AFP), *Time Magazine*, the BBC, CNN and so on, framed issues and events of Ebola and its victims far more than "issues of local politics, even if their reporting was more on the side of the dramatic and evocative than the contextual and diagnostic type typical of mainstream reporting of humanitarian crises."

Conclusion

To conclude, my theoretical framework on the increasing democratic deficit of citizen journalism in the opening and following two sections of this chapter, "From citizen journalism to human rights journalism" and "Framing Ebola in Sierra Leone on a Facebook discussion forum", coupled with my empirical testing of this framework by my content and frame analyses of the FBSLDECF discussion on Ebola, has confirmed this failure is largely due to the increasing focus on elite instead of grass-root sources (Atton and Wickenden, 2005); focus on the churning out of more fact-based comments largely framed by these same elite sources instead of the provision of more critical comments challenging status quo facts, which are often distorted; and, finally, focus on the empowering of small partisan voices and interests – what Choulliariki (2008) called "communitarian" logic – instead of empowering the voices and interests of all humans in a global society – what Choulliariki (2008) called "cosmopolitan" logic. Shaw (2012) proposed human rights journalism as the counterhegemonic journalism model to mainstream journalism to address this democratic deficit of citizen journalism, because it is more proactive in exposing and addressing all human wrongs, and has a more holistic problem-solving approach to the problems of global society.

Despite the limited scope of this research in terms of using just one case study of a Facebook discussion forum involving a campaign by the Sierra Leone diaspora in the fight against the deadly Ebola disease – which makes it difficult to use its findings to reach a general conclusion regarding the criticisms of citizen journalism for failing to address the democratic deficit of mainstream journalism – it provides a useful starting point for much broader future research, which would provide a more nuanced and convincing conclusion.

References

Albright, J. (26 March 2012) Kony 2012 and the case of the invisible media. Blog. http://theconversation.com/kony-2012-and-the-case-of-the-invisible-media-5954 (Accessed 27th April 2012).

Allan, S. (2006). *Online News*. Maidenhead, UK: Open University Press.

Allan, S (2006) *Journalism: Critical Issues*. London: Open University Press.

Allan, S, Sonwalker, P and Carter, C (2007) Bearing witness: Citizen journalism and human rights issues. *Globalisation, Societies, and Education*, 5(3): Special Issue: Globalisation, Humans Rights and Education.

Atton, C. (2001). *Alternative Media*. London, UK: Sage.

Atton, C. (2002). *Alternative Media*. London, UK: Sage.

Atton, C. (2003). What is "alternative" journalism? *Journalism* 4(3): 267–272.

Atton, C., and Wickenden, E. (2005). Sourcing routines and representation in alternative journalism: A case study approach. *Journalism Studies* 6(3): 347–359.

Beman, G. and Calderbank, D. (eds.) (2008). *The Human Rights-Based Approach to Journalism: Training Manuel Vietnam*. Bangkok. UNESCO (Accessed online 12/07/09).

Benkler, Y. (2006). *The Wealth of Networks: How Social Production Transforms Markets and Freedom*. New Haven, CT: Yale University Press.

Berlin, I. (1969). *Four Essays on Liberty*. London: Oxford University Press.

Bruns, A. (2008). *Blogs, Wikipedia, Second Life, and Beyond: From Production to Produsage*. New York: Peter Lang Pub. Incorporated.

Carey, J (1989) *Communication as Culture. Essays on Media and Society*. Boston: MA Unwin Hyman.

Carpenter, S. (2010). A study of content diversity in online citizen journalism and online newspaper articles. *New Media & Society* 12(7): 1064–1084.

Chouliaraki, L. (2006). *The Spectatorship of Suffering*. London, Thousand Oaks, New Delhi: SAGE Publications.

Chouliaraki L. (2013). *The Ironic Spectator – Solidarity in the Age of Post-Humanitarianism*. Cambridge: Polity Press.

Curran, J., Coen, S., Aalberg, T., Hayashi, K., Jones, P.K., Splendore, S.,Papathanassopoulos, S., Rowe, D. and Tiffen, R. (2013) Internet revolution revisited:a comparative study of online news. *Media, Culture and Society* 35(7): 880–897.

Curran, J., and Seaton, J. (2009). *Power without Responsibility*. London: Routledge.

De Bonville, J. (2000). *L'analyse de Contenu Des Médias: De la problématique au traitement statistique*. Universite de Quebec, Quebec, Canada.

Deuze, M. (2005). What is journalism? Professional identity and ideology of journalists reconsidered. *Journalism* 6(4): 442–464.

Entman, R. (1993). Framing: Towards clarification of a fractured paradigm. *Journal of Communication* 43(4): 51–58.

Flew, T., and Wilson, J. (2010). Journalism as social networking: The Australian Youdecide project and the 2007 federal election. *Journalism* 11(2): 131–147.

Goode, L. (2009). Social news, citizen journalism and democracy. *New Media & Society* 11(8): 1287–1305.

Haas, T. and Steiner, L. (2006). Public Journalism: A reply to critics. *Journalism* 7(2): 238–254.

Habermas, J. (1989). *The Structural Transformation of the Public Sphere.* Cambridge: Polity.

Ignatieff, M. (1998). *Isaiah Berlin: A Life.* New York: Henry Holt and Company.

Jenkins, H. (2006). *Convergence Culture: Where Old and New Media Collide.* New York: NYU Press.

Joyce, M. (2007). The citizen journalism website "Ohm news" and the 2002 South Korean presidential election. *Berkman Center Research Publication* (15): 1–40.

Kaufhold, K., Sebastian, V., and Homero, G.D. (2010). Citizen journalism and democracy: How user-generated news use relates to political knowledge and participation. *Journalism & Mass Communication Quarterly* 87(3–4): 515–529.

Kim, Y., and Lowrey, W. (2015). Social media environment? Personal and social determinants of citizen journalism activities. *Digital Journalism* 3(2): 298–314.

Kperogi, F.A. (2011). Cooperation with the corporation? CNN and the hegemonic co-optation of citizen journalism through IiReport.com. *New Media & Society* 13(2): 314–329.

Lewis, S.C., Kaufhold, K., and Lasorsa, D.L. (2010). Thinking about citizen journalism. *Journalism Practice* 4(2): 163–179.

Madianou, M. (2013). Humanitarian campaigns in social media. *Journalism Studies* 14 (2): 249–266

Matheson, D. and Allan, S. (2003). Weblogs and the War in Iraq: journalism for the network society? paper presented to the Digital Dynamics conference Loughborough, UK.

Nip, J.Y.M. (2006). Exploring the second phase of public journalism. *Journalism Studies* 7(2): 212–236.

Pease, E.C. (1990). Ducking the diversity issue: Newspapers' real failure is performance. *Newspaper Research Journal* 11(3): 24–37.

Plaissance, P.L. (2002). The journalist as moral witness: Michael Ignatieff's pluralistic philosophy for a global media culture. *Journalism* 3(2): 205–222.

Platon, S. and Deuze, M. (2003). Indymedia journalism: A radical way of making, selecting and sharing news? *Journalism* 4(3): 336–355.

Salawu, A. (2011). Citizen journalism off-line: The (Nigerian) punch's model. *Journal of Communication* 9: 185–196.

Shaw, I.S. (2012). *Human Rights Journalism: Advances in Reporting Humanitarian Interventions.* Basingstoke: Palgrave Macmillan.

Shoemaker, P.J., and Vos, T.P. (2009). *Gatekeeping Theory.* New York: Routledge.

Singer, J.B. (2003). Who are these guys? The online challenge to the notion of journalistic professionalism. *Journalism* 4(2): 139–163.

Spurr, D. (1993) *The Rhetoric of Empire: Colonial Discourse in Journalism. Travel Writing and Imperial Administration.* Durham, NC and London: Duke University Press

Thompson, John B. (1995). *The Media and Modernity,* Cambridge: Polity.

Williams, B.A., and Carpini, M.D. (2004). Monica and Bill all the time and everywhere: The collapse of gatekeeping and agenda setting in the new media environment. *American Behavioral Scientist* 47(9): 1208–1230.

Index

Note: The letter 'n' following locators refers to notes.

Printed and bound by CPI Group (UK) Ltd, Croydon, CR0 4YY

.